The Saga Kings

Carsten R Jorgensen

Copyright © 2015 Carsten R Jorgensen

All rights reserved.

No part of this book may be reproduced, stored in a database or other retrieval system, or transmitted in any form, by any means now existing or later discovered, including without limitation mechanical, electronic, photographic or otherwise, without the express prior written permission of the publisher.

Written and published in Canada.

ISBN-10: 0-9949338-0-0
ISBN-13: 978-0-9949338-0-5

The Saga Kings

CONTENTS

	Acknowledgment	i
1	Introduction	1
2	Krakatoa	3
3	The Story Teller	9
4	Odin	11
5	The Jotuns	23
6	Thor	25
7	Dan	26
8	The Ynglings	27
9	Frey	29
10	Yngve	30
11	Freya	31
12	Lothar	32
13	Skjold	33
14	Gram	37
15	Hadding	41
16	Peace Frode	51
17	Swanwhite	54
18	Fjolne	57
19	Sveide	58
20	Attack on the North	59

21	Herman	60
22	Scandinavians	61
23	Germanicus	62
24	Peace Frode in Germany	63
25	Frode in Britain	64
26	Ulfhild	65
27	Dan Mikellati	65
28	Vanlande	66
29	Boadicea	67
30	Visbur	68
31	Domald	69
32	Domar	69
33	Dygve	69
34	Dag	70
35	Agne	71
36	Alrik and Erik	72
37	Yngve and Alf	73
38	Hugleik	74
39	The Siklings	75
40	Ottar	76
41	Alf and Alfhild	78
42	Starkad	81
43	Hake	84
44	Hagbard and Signe	85

45	Jorund and Eric	88
46	Jorund	90
47	Frode the Vigorous	91
48	Halfdan	93
49	Starkad and Helga	94
50	Starkad and Ingjald	98
51	Starkad and Ole	100
52	Fridleif the Swift	102
53	Swanhild	103
54	Heimdal (Rig)	105
55	Tyrfing	106
56	Angantyr	108
57	Hervor	111
58	Heidrek	114
59	Angantyr	118
60	Frode the Bold	120
61	Frode's War	138
62	Frode and Balamir	142
63	Ond the Cruel	148
64	Egil	149
65	The Jutes	151
66	Ottar Vendel Crow	152
67	Onela	154

68	Halfdan and Ingjald	155
69	Roar and Helge	156
70	Helge	159
71	Roar	164
72	Beowulf	165
73	Rolf	166
74	Rolf Krake	168
75	Hott	169
76	Bjarke and Hjalte	171
77	Bjarke and Rut	174
78	Rolf and Adils	175
79	Rolf Krake's Last Battle	180
80	Attila and Bleda	187
81	Uffe (Offa)	188
82	England	191
83	Attila the Hun	192
84	King Arthur	193
85	Hugleik	195
86	Frode and Harald	197
87	Frode	199
88	Ragnarok	201
89	Starvation	205
90	The Battle of	210

The Saga Kings

	Camlan	
91	Vidar	212
92	Solve	215
93	Halfdan	216
94	Yngvar	220
95	Onund Yngvarson	222
96	Ingjald	225
97	Hjorvard and Grandmar	227
98	Rorik Fling-Bracelet	230
99	Ivar Vidfadme	232
100	Hamlet	235
101	Rorik and Helge	245
102	Audrey and King Radbard	250
103	Harald Wartooth	252
104	Olaf Tree Feller	255
105	Skjold of Varna	257
106	Halfdan White Legs	258
107	Islam	259
108	Charles Martel	260
109	The Battle Slaughter	261
110	Sigurd Ring	268
111	Ragnar	269

112	Ragnar Lodbrok	271
113	The Viking Age	274
114	The Saga of Ragnar Lodbrok	276
115	The Lodbrok Sons	279
116	Ragnar Lodbrok and Eystein	280
117	Charlemagne	284
118	Godfred	286
119	Hemming	291
120	Harald Klak and Reginfred	292
121	Harald Klak	293
122	Horik	294
123	Viking Raids	296
124	Ireland	297
125	The Kings of Dublin	298
126	Britain	299
127	Western Europe	300
128	Ragnar Lodbrok Sagas	301
129	Horik The Younger	305
130	Bjorn Ironsides	306
131	Russia	307

132	Lodbrok Sons Sagas	308
133	The Great Army	309
134	The Lodbrok Sons in England	310
135	Guthorm and Alfred	312
136	Sigurd Snake-Eye	314
137	Helge	316
138	Gudrod The Hunter	317
139	Halfdan the Black	319
140	Sigurd Hart	322
141	Halfdan the Black's Yule Feast	323
142	Harald	324
143	The Battle of Hafers Fjord	333
144	Turf Einar	337
145	The Kings of York	340
146	Rolf Ganger	341
147	Erik Blood Axe	344
148	Harald Fairhair and Aethelstan	347
149	Haakon the Good	349
150	Olaf, Gnupa, and Gurd	350
151	Gorm the Old	351

152	Erik Blood Axe in England	355
153	Harald Bluetooth	356
154	The Sons of Erik Blood Axe	366
155	Haakon Jarl	369
156	The Fugitives	371
157	Harald Grey Cloak	373
158	Harald Blooetooth and Haakon Jarl	375
159	Erik Haakonson	381
160	Otto II's Attack on Denmark	382
161	Palnatoke	386
162	Styrbjorn Staerke	387
163	Harald Bluetooth's Memorial Stone	386
164	Svend Forkbeard	390
165	The Joms Vikings	393
166	Olaf Tryggveson	400
167	The Battle of Maldon	403
168	Haakon Jarl and Olaf Tryggveson	408
169	Erik the Red	412

170	Leif the Lucky	413
171	Thorfin Karlsefni	416
172	Freydis	418
173	Harald Grenske	422
174	King Olaf Tryggveson	422
175	King Aethelred	429
176	Svend Forkbeard in England	430
177	Knud	433
178	King Olaf	436
179	Knud the Great	444
180	The Kings of Dublin	457
181	Brian Boru	458
182	Sigtryg Silkenbeard	460
183	Saint Olaf	461
184	Tryggve Olafson	467
185	Magnus the Good	468
186	Svend Estridsen	474
187	Harald Hardruler	477
188	The Kingdom of England	490
189	William the Conqueror	495
190	Svend Estridsen and Olaf Kyrre	498

191	Appendix	501
192	The Vikings in the New World	501
193	Travel in Scandinavia	503
194	Viking Ships	504
195	Status of Women	508
196	Geneology	510
197	Skjoldungs (Scyldings)	510
198	Angles (Mercians)	512
199	Ragnar Lodbrok	513
200	Bjorn Ironsides	514
201	Ivar the Boneless	515
202	Sigurd Snake-Eye	516
203	The Jarls of Lade	517
204	The Jutes	518
205	The Ynglings	519
206	The Knytlings	522
207	The Normans	523
208	The Siklings	524
209	The West Saxons	525
210	The Chronological Lines of the Kings	527
211	Kings of Norway	527
212	Kings of	529

Denmark

213	Kings of Sweden	532
214	Svinfylking Battle Formation	536
215	References	539

ACKNOWLEDGMENTS

My thanks go to my daughter Anika Jorgensen for doing the illustrations. Robert DeLint and my daughter Dana Woodard were a great help in editing and making suggestions.

My history teacher in Denmark , principal Marborg and my grandmother Signe Dam and her sister Katrine Bundtmager provided me with inspiration and encouragement.

1 INTRODUCTION

In 1950, I was eight years old and attended Herstedvester public school in Denmark. The Danish saga history fascinated me in my grade 2 history class. The fascination stayed with me. After retiring in 1996, I began to write about the saga history of Denmark so my children would become familiar with their historical culture. After I had written a lengthy manuscript, my daughter, Dana said, "Dad, you have written so much. Why don't you make it a book?"

Later I watched the TV program PBS Program — "SECRETS OF THE DEAD: Catastrophe!" (5–15–2000, 8:00 p.m.) The program explained that the volcano Krakatoa exploded in the year 535 causing a three year nuclear winter which resulted in drought, famine, and war. I thought to myself that this sounded very much like Ragnarok from Norse mythology. To me this was very intriguing because that would mean that Ragnarok was not just mythology but an actual historical event. Thus I proceeded to search for Ragnarok in the historical sagas. This led to investigating the sagas not only of Denmark but of all of Scandinavia.

The influence of environmental perturbations has received very little attention from historians. History was written about great men, politics and wars. Eventually this was linked to trade and commerce. Climate and the environment have for the most part been considered to be relatively stable in history, but this is not reality. Environment and climate is constantly changing. Life; plants, animals, and people have to adapt to these changes. More recently, some historians and environmentalists have started to look at how the environment has affected history (Worstad, D. ed. 1988). Even today there are climate concerns about global warming trends.

There is still some reluctance on the part of historians to take climate into account and some historians have denied that the catastrophe of Krakatoa in the year 535 ever happened, but the archeological evidence is overwhelming.

Studies of tree ring growths have been used to extrapolate temperatures and growing conditions in the past. Scientists, working independently, were able to build their own chronologies based on oaks. Tree ring records were replicated among multiple trees at one site. Then there were replications between sites. Fossil trees enabled a study into the far past. With replication constructed by different workers, the margin of error is zero years. This redundancy in the tree records is so complete and the record is so accurate that it has become the standard against which radiocarbon dates are calibrated.

2 KRAKATOA

In the BBC television documentary, Mike Baillie, professor of paleoecology at Queen's University in Belfast, U.K. said, "When you look at the overall picture there seems to be about a decade of really bad conditions starting 536 and running on into the mid 540's at least. The implication from lots of bits of information is that it was extremely cold and that this reduced sunlight and cold caused crop failure. So basically, people in an area like this would be forced back onto non-agricultural produce. They would be forced to fish, they would be forced to hunt and that would put a lot of strain on a population which was used to having agricultural produce to see them through the winters for example. So I think things would have been bleak here."

The non-agricultural produce which people would seek by hunting and fishing would be in an ever decreasing supply because the ecological carrying capacity would be decreasing over time. With the exception of anaerobic forms, all life depends on chlorophyll on both the land and in the sea. The herbivores such as deer and rabbits would be unable to find green growing things and would have to subsist on twigs and bark. According to the dendrological studies, the earth did not fully recover until about the year 800, approximately the start of the Viking age.

In such a situation, people would raid their neighbours for food. Wars would be fought over food supplies. These wars would escalate and intensify as revenge would be sought over the atrocities of the original raids and wars. It has been estimated that 85% to 90% of the world's population died in this period.

Mike Baillie also stated that mythical stories seemed to point to a catastrophe striking the earth at about the right time and that King Arthur died in this period. He said, "Mythology tells you and history doesn't and that raises some very interesting questions because the implication is that you could suppress the written word but you couldn't suppress oral tradition."

The event of the volcanic eruption in the year 535 and the extensive exploration of America by the Scandinavians have both been suppressed by our modern historians and archaeologists.

In Scandinavia, the event known as "The war of the gods" was described in skaldic format and survives in Voluspaa. It describes three years of no summer, the Fimbul Winter (The Terrible Winter), followed by the world war called Ragnarok (a very graphic description of the events after the explosion of Krakatoa in the year 535).

Gradually a few written records were gathered:

Praetorian Prefect Magnus Aurelius Cassiodorus Senator (485-585) wrote a letter documenting the conditions, "All of us are observing, as it were, a blue coloured sun; we marvel at bodies which cast no mid-day shadow, and at that strength of intensest heat reaching extreme and dull tepidity So we have had a winter without storms, spring without mildness, and summer without heat. The seasons have changed by failing to change; and what used to be achieved by mingled rains cannot be gained by dryness only."

A Byzantine, Procopius of Caesarea, (500-565) wrote, "And it came about during this year that a most dread portent took place. For the sun gave forth its light without brightness, like the moon, during the whole year, and it seemed exceedingly like the sun in eclipse, for the beams it shed were not clear nor such as it is accustomed to shed."

John of Ephesus (507-596), a cleric and one of the earliest and most important of historians wrote, "The sun was dark and the darkness lasted for eighteen months, each day it shone for about four hours, and still this light was only a feeble shadow ... the fruits did not ripen and the wine tasted like sour grapes."

The recording of the conditions of this time was also found in the Gaelic Irish Annals:

"A failure of bread in the year 536 AD" – The Annals of Ulster.

"A failure of bread from the years 536 – 539 AD" – The Annals of Innisfallen.

"An extraordinary plague throughout the world, which swept away the noblest third of the human race; 543 AD" – The Annals of the Four Masters.

There was a hypothesis that a volcano in the tropics could have thrown up dust and ashes and caused the effect. Sulfate deposits in Greenland and Antarctic ice cores do support the volcano hypothesis. The sulfate spike for 535 was even more intense than that which accompanied the climatic aberration in 1816, which is known as "the year without summer" which was connected to the explosion of the volcano Mount Tambora in Sumbawa, Indonesia.

The Greenland sulfate ice core evidence is consistent with tree ring data from around the Northern Hemisphere that show reduced growth rates lasting more than a decade starting in 536 A.D. The tree ring and sulfate ice core data show that the sixth century eruption was much bigger than Indonesia's Mount Tambora eruption of 1816.

> The presence of sulfuric acid in both Arctic and Antarctic ice cores verified that dust, ash, and huge amounts of water vapour had been in the

atmosphere worldwide. Ice cores from Greenland and Antarctica show sulfuric acid spikes during this time interval, and for the Byrd core (Antarctica), it is the largest in the last 2000 years. (Wohletz, 2000).

Ken Wohletz, a volcanologist at Los Alamos, New Mexico, worked with David Keys to try to identify a volcano that could produce such a climate change. The eruption had to be four or five times bigger than the 1816 eruption of Tambora.

Ken Wohletz said that ocean depth measurements between Sumatra and Java where Krakatoa exploded in the well-known 1883 eruption indicate the presence of a caldera up to 50 kilometers in diameter and a recent survey uncovered evidence of ash and pumice layers formed in the area during the appropriate time frame.

When Krakatoa erupted in 1883, ash from the explosion fell on Singapore, 840 kilometers to the north, the Cocos islands, 1155 kilometers to the southwest; and ships as far as 6076 kilometers west northwest. Darkness covered the Sumatra Strait from 11 am until the next day. Giant waves were produced measuring 40 meters above sea level. The giant waves devastated everything in their path and hurled choral blocks ashore weighing as much as 600 tons. 36,417 people were killed, mostly by the giant waves and 165 coastal villages were destroyed. The passages of the tidal waves were recorded at sea. They reached Aden in 12 hours, a distance of 3,800 nautical miles, usually traversed by a good steam ship in 12 days.

The sun was seen as blue in some places and green in other places as fine ash and aerosol were blown more than 50 kilometers into the stratosphere and circled the equator in 13 days. This dust veil lowered the global temperatures by as much as 1.2 degrees Celsius and temperatures did not return to normal until 1888.

When Krakatoa erupted in 1883, the explosion was heard 4653 kilometers away on Rodriguez Island. If the explosion had occurred in Toronto, it would have been heard simultaneously in Vancouver, British Columbia and in London, England.

The shock wave from the much more powerful 535 eruption was heard in the far northern parts of China and when the shock wave was heard in Scandinavia as a low rumbling bass sound (very much like a thunder roll rumbling on for hours), the people said it was the god Heimdal blowing his horn calling the Aesir to war.

As the deafening roar of the volcanic detonation went on for hours, 200 cubic kilometers of material (equivalent to the whole of Prince Edward Island) was hurled into the air with the force of 2,000 million (2 billion) Hiroshima sized nuclear bombs. The column of debris obscured the sun. The tsunami spawned by the eruption killed hundreds of thousands and many more died slower, more horrible deaths asphyxiated by ash and/or burned by cinders. A layer of dust, containing microscopic particles of ash and sulfur dioxide, 150 meters thick filled the stratosphere (Wohletz, 2000).

The sky became an endless grey. Temperatures dropped all around the globe. Because most of the sun's rays failed to penetrate the atmosphere, there was little evaporation and therefore less rainfall and droughts throughout the globe. Krakatoa in 535 had produced a nuclear winter.

Ranggawarsita (1802-1878) wrote about the event of 535 as follows (Winchester, 2003):

"In the year Saka, a thundering noise was heard from the mountain Batuwara, which was answered by a similar noise coming from the mountain Kapi (today called Krakatoa), lying westward of the modern Bantam. A great glaring fire reached out of the last named mountain. The whole world was greatly shaken and violent thundering accompanied by heavy rains and storms took place.

Not only did this heavy rain not extinguish the eruption of fire of the mountain Kapi, but it augmented the fire. The noise was fearful. At last the mountain Kapi burst into two pieces with a tremendous roar and sank into the deepest of the earth. The water of the sea rose and inundated the land. The country to the east of the mountain called Batuwara, to the mountain Kamala, and westward to the mountain Raja Basa, was inundated by the sea.

The inhabitants of the northern part of the Sunda country to the mountain Raja Basa were drowned and swept away with all their property.

After the water subsided the mountain Kapi which had burst into pieces and the surrounding land became sea and the single island [of Java-Sumatra] divided into two parts. The city of Samas Kuta, which was situated in the interior of Sumatra, became sea, the waters of which was very clear, and which was afterwards called the lake Sinkara. This event was the origin of the separation of Sumatra and Java."

Illustration 1

BEFORE 535 A.D.

Illustration 2

AFTER 535 A.D.

3 THE STORY TELLER

In Scandinavia, the oral tradition involved a story teller who would tell the stories wherever he went. This often took the form of poetry and sometimes as songs. The people familiar with the stories would not let the story teller change his recitals so consistency was maintained.

The hall rang with the sounds of children. "The story teller is coming! The story teller is coming!" yelled eight year old Inga from the door. The children all rushed to the door to see. Up the path came an old man dressed in a long grey cloak and a wide brimmed grey hat. His hair and beard were white and had a silvery appearance. His right hand grasped a long, stout, oak walking stick. Thorvald whispered to Erik, "I think the old story teller looks like a wizard".

Grete met the old man at the door and led him to a seat by the fireplace. Khalle stood up and said, "Welcome skald and I speak for us all and say that we really appreciate you coming here to tell us these sagas".

Grete handed the skald a mug of beer. The old skald set the mug on the oak table and removed his hat and cloak. His shirt and pants were grey. He laid his hat and cloak on the bench, sipped the beer and made himself comfortable. "I am indeed a skald. I am the very last skald" he said.

"I would like to tell you about your history", continued the story teller. "Because I am the very last story teller, it is important that you know of all the kings in the sagas. I will tell you the stories of all the saga kings in Scandinavia so that they will not fade from memory".

Khalle called for drinks. Serving girls appeared through the door to the kitchen and handed bowls of mead to all the adult guests. Another group of serving girls handed bowls of milk to the children.

"What was it like before the Fimbul winter?" asked eleven year old Inga.

"Before the Fimbul Winter", replied the story teller, "There was a golden age. Arthur was High King in England and Rolf Krake was King in Denmark. It was a time of prosperity and wonderful crops on the farms."

"Oh", said ten year old Erik disappointedly, "I was hoping you would tell us some Viking stories".

"Oh, but Rolf Krake was considered the greatest King in Scandinavia and is still toasted as the example for all Kings to live by", said the story teller, "And in England, King Arthur is still held in the highest regard. In fact, during their reigns there truly was a golden age. Rolf Krake was a Skjoldung. The Skjoldungs traced their ancestors all the way back to Odin."

"They traced their ancestors all the way back to a god?" asked Erik.

"Odin was not a god." said the story teller "He was a man".

The story teller raised his bowl to his host and said, "To the memory of Odin."

Then he drained his bowl.

4 ODIN

Grete handed the skald another bowl of mead. The old skald took a drink and set the bowl on the oak table. "Where did Odin come from?" he asked.

Erik jumped up in his excitement and exclaimed, "Odin was descended from King Priam of Troy".

"The evil Hector had been killed and the Greeks had conquered Troy by hiding in a wooden horse", continued Erik.

"Indeed", replied the story teller, "but why do you say that Hector was evil?"

"Well", said Erik, "He helped Paris who stole Helen from Menelaus".

"My young svend, Hector was defending his city from invaders", said the story teller, "We should not label people as either good or evil. In fact Hector was a great and honourable hero. In those days it was a common practice to obtain a wife by stealing or capturing her."

At this Thorvald exclaimed, "But his name is Erik not Svend. Please continue the story".

The story teller chuckled and said, "An apprentice is called a svend. Young Erik here seems to me an apprentice story teller and thus I might refer to him as svend from time to time".

"Before the Greeks left Troy, they divided the spoils among themselves", began the story teller, "The wife of King Priam, Hecuba, became the slave of Ulysses".

"When did all this happen?" asked Inga.

The story teller chuckled and took a sip of beer. Then he replied, "In those days, time was recorded differently than it is now. How do we measure years now?"

"We measure the years from the birth of our Savior, Jesus the Christ", replied Inga.

"In those days, time was measured by years since the last great battle. But by our way of measuring time, the Trojans were defeated about 2500 years ago. At that time the surviving Trojans, about 30,000 people, left Troy and followed their great leader to the islands of Thrace. There they took up fishing and piracy and became known as the people of the sea.

Thirty years after their arrival in Thrace most of the Trojans left and sailed to northern Italy where they became known as Etruscans. The remaining Trojans, about 12,000 warriors and chiefs, eventually left Thrace and sailed north into the Black Sea. They beached their ships on the east coast of the sea and began to build houses and till the land close to where the river Tanis empties into the Black Sea.

The people who lived there were fierce nomadic warriors called Scythians and they attacked the newcomers who, in their view, had taken a part of their land. The Scythians used bronze weapons and rode in war chariots. The Trojans, now known as Thracians, did not use chariots but rode upon horse back and their weapons were made of iron. The Trojans easily defeated the Scythians. The Scythians called their conquerors the 'Iron People' ('Aes') and the Trojans became known as the Aesir in those lands. The sea to the south then became known as the Sea of Aes or the Aezov Sea (The Iron Sea) or the Aegean Sea. After a few years, the Scythians left the region and migrated west where they joined the Celts.

Before I tell you about Odin, it is important that you know the politics of the world at that time. The Romans from a small beginning became a mighty empire by conquering their neighbours one by one. Their army was extremely disciplined. They built mighty cities and considered themselves civilized. They called their conquered people barbarians. In fact, they called all other people savages and barbarians. They considered themselves the police of the world. They said that they conquered countries to free them from the tyranny of their rulers. But their real purpose was to take the resources of these countries: metal, lumber, fur and slaves. The captured countries also supplied mercenaries for the Roman armies.

There was a second civilization, the northern people. Some of the people of the north decided to migrate south and eventually made contact with the people of the south. There was hate at first sight.

The wild Cimbri and Teuton warriors, naked from the waist up, slid down the mountainsides of Austria on their shields and attacked the Roman legions at Noreia. The sight of these wild half naked blonde giants so terrified the Roman soldiers that most of them fled. They did not stand a chance against these berserkers. The Cimbri (formerly called Cimmerians) came from Vendsyssel, the northern most part of the peninsula of Denmark known as Jutland (the land of the Jutes) and together, with the Saxon tribes and Herules, they defeated the Roman army in 113 b.c.e. in the battle at Noreia. From Austria, the Cimbri and Teutons went into Helvetia (Switzerland) where they were joined by the warrior tribe called the Ambrons.

By 110 b.c.e., the Cimbri, Teutons, and Ambrons were in Gaul moving down the Rhone valley. The Roman Consul of Gaul, Silanus met with the tribal chiefs to negotiate. The tribes wanted land so they could take up farming but Silanus told them, "No way!!"

The tribes prepared to move further down the valley but Silanus had his 200,000 Roman mercenary troops bar their way. Instead of turning away though, the Cimbri, Teutons, and Ambrons all wielding battle axes, charged the Romans and most of the Roman troops were killed.

Then Consul Mallius Maximus with 80,000 trained Roman legionnaires went after the tribes and intercepted them at Arausio (Orange) on the Rhone River. When the wild Northern warriors attacked, the Romans broke ranks and tried to flee across the Rhone. All the legionnaires were killed.

The Northern tribes pitched a winter camp along the Rhone near Avignon. During the winter an inter-tribal quarrel came about which made the Cimbri leave the other tribes in the spring. The Cimbri went south to go looting in Spain, but they were stopped in the Pyrenee mountain passes by the Celts.

By 102 b.c.e., the Cimbri, Teutons, and Ambrons had already defeated five Roman armies in Gaul and another Roman army in Arausio. This caused a panic in Rome and so the Roman army was strengthened and reorganized. The Roman soldiers under Marius were re-organized into phalanxes and cohorts. The Cimbri succeeded in passing the Alps and went into Italy driving the army of the consul Q. Lutatius Catulus across the Adige River. In 101 b.c.e., General Marius battled against them on the Raudine Plain near Vercellae. The King of the Cimbri, Boiorix fell in that battle and the whole Cimbri army was destroyed.

At this time Odin was Chief of all Asgaard. Odin was a great King and a conqueror. He would often put his brothers Vile and Ve in charge of Asaheim and go on long trips sometimes up to half a year at a time. On one of these trips Odin had headed north on the Tanis River and was gone longer than expected. Odin had been away from Asaheim for over half a year and his wife Frija (Frigg) was worried about him. Vile came out of court and surveyed the town. His brother Ve was waiting for him. "Frigg is down at the docks again", said Ve.

"Let's go and calm her down", said Vile.

Frigg saw them as they strode towards her. "Boats!" she yelled and pointed up river, "boats are coming from the north!"

Vile and Ve ran down to stand beside her and people from the town began to go down to the docks.

Twenty-four boats made from hides stretched over wooden frames were seen gliding towards the docks. In the lead boat was Odin. When the boat had docked Odin jumped out and embraced Frigg and they held each other for several minutes.

Odin looked at Vile and Ve and said, "Come to my house. We need to talk."

Odin, Vile, Ve and Frigg went to Odin's house. Frigg called her servants to lay out food and drinks. Odin sent someone to get the priests. "Were there any problems while I was away?" asked Odin.

"None that we could not handle" answered Ve.

The priests arrived. Njord entered first followed by the twins Frey and Freya. They were Druids. Njord and Frey were priests and Freya was a priestess.

"Any news of the Romans?" asked Odin, I have been away for a while".

Vile answered, "Our scouts report that The Roman General Pompeii has invaded Asia-Minor.

He could be at our border soon."

"Our warriors are great fighters", said Odin "but we will be unable to withstand the might of Rome in a prolonged war."

"Is there an alternative?" asked Ve.

"Let me tell you of my trip", said Odin. "We rowed up the Tanis River. On the way north we encountered some waterfalls which we portaged around. When we reached the source of the river we went west overland. We came to a great sea and launched our boats, still heading west. We reached a beautiful land and beached our boats. There were people on the beach who watched us but did not come near and a few of them ran off. The ones who had run off soon returned with a group of warriors. They all stood at a distance while one of them put aside his weapons and approached closer. I put down my weapons and went to talk with this man.

The man said that he was bringing word from his King whose name was Gylfe. The King had sent an invitation inviting us to a feast and we accepted the invitation.

At the feast we learned that these people were called Svears. Their country was called Sweden. We spent several weeks enjoying the Swedish hospitality. King Gylfe told us that often raiders came from the south and that he was hard pressed to defend his people. One day while we were there, raiders came in ships and we Aesir helped Gylfe against them. We easily defeated the raiders and their few survivors fled. Gylfe was very grateful for our help. He was so grateful that he invited us all to come and live with him and to help defend his country.

Now we must decide what to do."

Vile was in favour of staying and defeating Pompeii. Ve thought that staying was hopeless and they should all go to Sweden. Njord, Frey and Freya said that they should sacrifice to the Great Goddess and wait for a sign from her.

After listening to the assembly argue for a while, Odin said, "We are deadlocked. I will confer with my wise friend and we will all abide by his decision".

Odin got a big jar from a cupboard, stuck his hands in the jar and pulled out an embalmed severed head. He put the head on the table and requested that everyone wait outside. Njord, Frey, Freya, Frigg and Vile went out the door. Ve was the last one out and he closed the door behind him.

The five people stood quietly waiting and watching the door. They heard loud voices talking inside the house. They could not make out the words or how many voices were talking but the discussion was quite animated.

Erik said, "Njord, Frey and Freya were not Aesir".

"You are quite right young svend" said the Story Teller, "After the Scythians had left Asgaard and the Aesir had settled into their new home east of the Tanis River where it empties into the Black Sea, another tribe arrived. These were the Vanier".

"I have heard of this!" interrupted Erik excitedly.

"Indeed", said the story teller and looked at Erik with a twinkle in his clear blue eyes, "then perhaps you would continue".

"Well", said Erik, "The Vanier were also known as the Elves. They had a witch called Gullveig. One day Gullveig went walking to Asgaard. When the gods saw her approach, they were afraid of her powers. So they captured her and raised her on spears and set a fire under her so that she died on the spears and was consumed by the flames. But the next day, she was reborn and came again walking to Asgaard. The gods caught her and again raised her on spears and burned her again. Three times this happened.

When the Vanier heard what had happened they raised an army and came to Asgaard. The gods went outside Asgaard and arrayed themselves in battle order. When the two armies were facing each other, Odin took his spear and hurled it into the masses of the Vanier army and thus started the first war in the world".

The story teller chuckled and took another sip of mead. "That is a myth my young svend, the Aesier were not gods but men. But the first battle between the Elves and the Aesier did start with Odin hurling his spear into the Elven army. The Aesir battled for years against the Vanier, and in one of the battles Odin lost an eye. The loss of an eye did not daunt Odin. He remained vigorous and strong.

One day the Aesir and Vanier decided that they were tired of bloodshed and grief of war, and sent ambassadors back and forth between the two kingdoms. They had battled long enough and finally they made peace.

As a part of the peace treaty, hostages were exchanged, and the Vanier sent their prince Njord, along with his son and daughter Frey and Freya. In return, the Aesir sent their wisest man Mimer and his brother Hoenir to Vanaheim. The Vanier made Hoenir a chief and a judge, but to their dismay they found that Hoenir was stupid. The Vanier felt cheated! In retaliation, the Vanier beheaded the wise Mimer and sent his head back to Odin. The grief stricken Odin embalmed Mimer's head and kept it with him always. For really important decisions, Odin would consult with Mimer's head.

After consulting with Mimer, Odin decided they should accept Gylfe's invitation. Vile, Ve, Njord, Frey, and Freya all agreed. Frigg said, "I think that is the right decision."

The long journey up the Tanis River began. The boats of the Aesir were made from hides stretched over wooden frames and could be portaged easily around rapids and waterfalls on the rivers. When they reached Gardarike in 88 b.c.e., they turned west and rowed into the Baltic Sea. When they reached Sweden, King Gylfe was joyful to see them and came out to meet Odin's people and bade them welcome.

Odin was a guest in Gylfe's hall. At the feast a young serving girl brought Odin's son Dan a drinking horn of mead. Dan thought this was the most beautiful girl he had ever seen. After the feast, the girl followed Dan wherever he went. Dan did not mind. He was hopelessly in love with her.

The girl took Dan by the hand and said, "Let me show you around".

After showing Dan all the building and sheds she led him into an Oak grove. There she looked him in the eyes and finally kissed him tenderly. "What is your name", he asked.

She answered, "My name is Gefion and I am Gylfe's daughter".

Dan and Gylfe kept seeing each other on a daily basis and finally decided to get married. Gylfe was very pleased because his daughter would be happy and Gylfe's family and Odin's family would be even closer.

Odin had twelve priests with him called Druids and they set up a place of worship in Uppsala. After Njord and Frey became priests in Sweden and Freya a priestess, they set up altars for making blood sacrifices for good weather and good harvests.

Gefion and Dan were married. Dan received Zealand (Sjaelland) as a dowry and became King of Zealand. Dan's people became known as Danes and the country became known as Danmark, which means Dan's field".

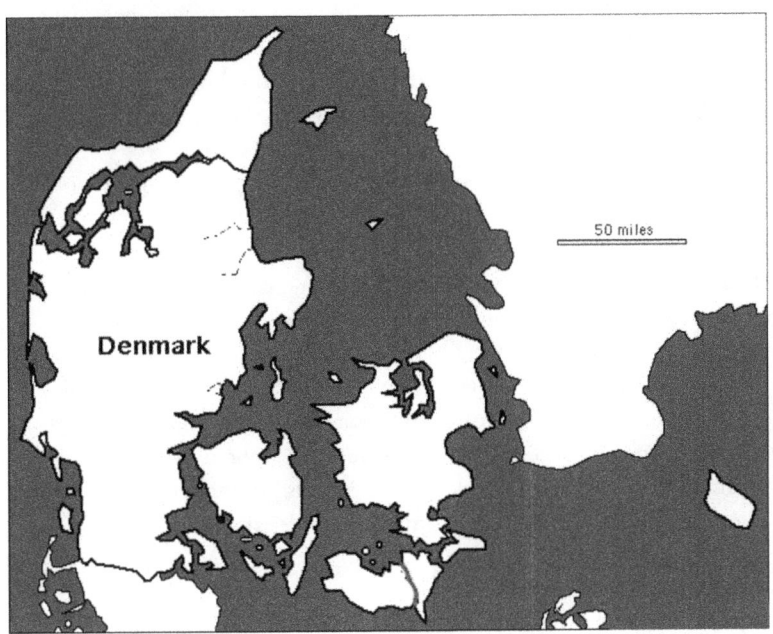

Erik said. "My Mother told me about it. She said that Gefion, using four oxen, ploughed the island of Zealand out of Sweden and the hole that was left became Lake Malaren".

"Gefion from Gylfe drove away,

To add new land to Denmark's sway"

(Brage the Old)

The story teller chuckled. Then he drained his bowl and placed it on the table. Grete brought the skald another bowl of mead. The young boy, Erik said, "Who was Brage the Old?"

The story teller smiled and said, "It is uncertain who he was. Some say that he was a skald (bard), others say that he was a farmer, but it is also said that Brage the Old was Odin himself.

Now, Odin chose to make his home on the island of Fyn and built his stronghold, which was called Odin's Ve (Odin's sacred place, which was later pronounced Odense). So victorious was he, that his men believed victory were wholly inseparable from him. If he laid his blessing hand on anybody's head, success was sure to attend him. Even if he was absent, if called upon in distress or danger, his very name seemed to give comfort.

Odin's warriors were masters of martial arts and were capable of extraordinary feats of strength and endurance. There were three clans: the wolf, the bear, and the wild boar. The wolf cult warriors wore wolf skins over their chain mail, and they fought singly as guerillas, ambushing their enemies. They were assassins and gave rise to the were-wolf legends.

The bear cult warriors were called berserkers. They went without mail-coats, were frantic as dogs or wolves, bit their shields and were as strong as bears or boars, and legends say that neither fire nor iron could hurt them. In battle they often hurled their shields at the enemy. The berserkers were used to change the tide of battle, if a battle line was faltering.

The third warrior cult, the wild boar, was experts at team fighting. They set up shield walls and led charges. In battles, they used the formation known as svinfylking, (the boar's head), which was a formation modelled on the shape of a boar's head. It was a wedge shaped squad, led by two champions known as the rani (snout). Behind the champions were three warriors. Behind the three warriors were four warriors. And so on. If the army was large enough there would be several wedges set up. They were also masters of disguise and escape.

Odin invaded Jutland and conquered the various tribes by having his army use the svinfylking formation. Odin placed himself right in front, just behind his two rani champions. His fighters beat on their shields with their swords and battleaxes while yelling "Odin" in unison. Odin would hold up his spear and his fighters would become completely silent. Then Odin would hurl his spear at the opposing army's leader. If there was no apparent leader, he hurled it as far as he could over the opposing army. As the spear flew, Odin's army started a running charge and the wedge behind the rani severed the enemy line and split their army in two. This was usually very devastating to the enemy forces.

Odin set his son Heimdal up as King of northern Jutland. Heimdal made his stronghold in Himmer rige.

Then Odin went into the land of the Saxons and conquered Saxony without losing a single battle. He set one of his sons, Angul, to rule southern Jutland. Angul's people became known as Angles. Over the southern Saxons, Odin placed another of his sons, Baeldag.

Odin established a free, self-regulated society. Law and order was based upon the Thing system. The Thing was a meeting, which had legislative and judicial powers. Men, women and handicapped people attended the Thing and brought their grievances and disputes for judgment. All the people were equal in the society. Since the laws were not written down, the Thing was opened by a man called 'Law Sayer Man', reciting all the laws, which he had memorized by heart. This was done to insure that no one changed the laws. One of Odin's most important laws was that the dead must be either burned or buried. There were no jails, so the man who did criminal activities or dishonourable acts which did not warrant a death sentence was declared an outlaw. An outlaw was outside the law and it was unlawful for his family to protect him, and there was no punishment for killing him. The people elected their King at the Thing. However, only the Aesir, the ruling class and their descendants were elected as Kings. The Thing was an occasion for a large market place and festival which usually lasted several days.

Odin loved animals. He took in two orphaned ravens and taught them to talk. When the ravens were old enough, they flew away. But they returned off and on and sat on Odin's shoulders, one on his left shoulder and one on his right shoulder. Odin called them Hugin and Munin.

Odin also took in two orphaned wolf cubs that would lie at his feet when he held court. Odin named the two wolves Gere and Freke and they were quite a sight when they were full grown lying at Odin's feet in his court. Sometimes while holding court the two ravens, Hugin and Munin would fly in and sit on his shoulders. Hugin would say, "Hello."

Munin would say, "Good morning."

The people began to believe that Hugin and Munin brought news of the world to Odin and he did make quite a sight holding court with two wolves lying at his feet and a raven perched on each shoulder.

Most Scandinavians of the Viking and pre-Viking period lived peaceful lives. They concentrated on earning a livelihood mainly from farming but also from fishing and trading. The trade routes were traveled in the summer and went down the Russian rivers to Mikkelgaard in Asgaard. Mikkelgaard was also known as Byzantium or Constantinople.

5 THE JOTUNS

After Odin had established his realm, he sailed to Norway where he met some people who called themselves Jotuns. The Aesir called them Frost Giants. Odin sailed all the way up to Halogaland or Loke's Land where he met the Jotun chieftain called Loke. The two took a liking to each other and became blood brothers and Loke went to live with Odin.
"What were the Jotuns?" asked Erik.

"The Jotuns were ugly trolls!" yelled Thorvald.

Helga shivered and said, "The Jotuns were ogres".

The story teller chuckled. He said, "No. The Jotuns were humans. They were a race of humans which have existed much longer than our race. Many people did considered them ogres or trolls and tried to exterminate them.

However, it was considered that a race which was very ancient must also be very wise. Odin found it very difficult to match wits with the Jotun Vafthrudner in a game of riddles.

Some of the Jotun women were considered very beautiful. These women were beautiful enough to marry. Njord married the Jotun Skade. Frey married the Jotun Gerda and Volsung married the Jotun Hljod. There were other intermarriages as well".

"I thought that the Jotuns lived in Jotunheim", exclaimed Erik.

Inga glared at Erik, but the story teller chuckled again and said, "Yes, that area called Jotunheim is a frozen mountainous area in Halogaland and at that time was known as Udgaard. The chief of the Jotuns who fought Thor was called Udgaard Loke, and was not the same Loke who became Odin's blood brother".

Odin established a kingdom for his son Thor in Trudheim, where Thor lived in constant war with the Jotuns".

"Why is Thor always at war with the Jotuns?" asked Jens. "When Odin could live peacefully with them, why could Thor not do so too?"

The story teller gave a little smile and said, "Odin lived at Gylfe's town in Sweden where he was no threat to the territories of the Jotuns. Thor in the far north in Norway was considered by the Jotuns as an invader and land grabber. Therefore they waged war against him."

6 THOR
"What did Thor look like?" asked Erik.

"Erik!" exclaimed Inga, "stop interrupting!"

The story teller laughed softly and said, "It is all right Inga. Thor was tall and had a powerful build. He was easily recognized by his red hair and beard. In battles Thor would throw his hammer. He was so accurate at throwing war hammers that they usually hit his opponent in the forehead. His special hammer was named Mjolnir and had a short handle making it easier to throw. It is said that after Mjolnir had hit its mark, it would fly back to Thor's hand."

"Where was Trudheim?" asked Erik.

The story teller smiled and said, "Trudheim is today called Trondheim.

In northern Norway, Thor had many successful battles against the Jotuns. He gained a reputation of invincibility. When Thor died, his remains were taken to Sweden where his body was burned and his ashes were buried under a huge mound. The farmers began to worship Thor as a god. When a thunderstorm was over the land, people said that the rolling thunder was the sound of Thor's chariot being pulled by two goats. Lightning was thought to be caused by the horns of the goats ramming against each other in their headlong gallop. The common man called on Thor during battles while the upper class called on Odin who was the god of the warriors and the skalds."

Helga announced, "The meal is ready. Let's take a brief pause while we serve dinner."

Inga brought the story teller a mug of cold beer which he sipped while watching the serving ladies put out the meal. The guests made the sign of the cross and Thorvald said, "The bishop is not here to say grace. Bless the food Lord. Amen."

The people then began to eat. The story teller ate some peas and a chicken thigh. Then he took a swig of his beer and continued his story.

7 DAN

Odin the Old Chief of the North retired by giving Fyn to Dan and moving to Uppsala in Sweden to be with Njord, Frey and Freya. A few years later, Odin lay on his sick bed in Uppsala. When he felt death approach, he let himself be stabbed with a spear and said that all men who died by weapons should belong to him. He said that he would travel to Godheim and welcome friends there. The Swedes thought he meant the old Asgaard and that he would live forever there. They started to believe he was a god and thereafter prayed to him. Odin's body was burned along with many possessions and a huge mound was erected over his ashes. After Odin's death, warriors often thought that he showed himself just before a battle.

When Gylfe died of old age, the Swedes declared that they wished for Njord to rule them."

The storyteller paused to take a small sip of beer. Then he said, "Dan had a long reign in Denmark and was loved by his people. Dan had two sons, Humble and Lothar. When Dan died the farmers called a Thing to choose a new King and Humble was elected. But Lothar was jealous and waged war on his brother. Humble lost a battle and was taken captive. Lothar offered Humble his life if he would give up his crown and swear allegiance. Humble accepted the offer and was very happy about his loss of title because he preferred to be a farmer.

8 THE YNGLINGS

Erik then asked, "So all the kings of Scandinavia descended from the Aesir?"

"No" said the story teller, "Odin's descendants became the kings of Denmark, not Sweden. After Gylfe died, Njord became ruler in Sweden. The descendants of Njord became rulers in Sweden. As you already know, Odin's son Thor ruled in Trudheim in the northern part of Norway. At that time Norway was divided into many small kingdoms and many of his descendants became kings.

After Thor killed one Jotun king in particular, King Tjasse, in battle, his daughter Skade wanted revenge. She was wise enough to know that she had no chance in an open battle against Thor. Instead, she planned to go to Uppsala and kill all the Aesir there. With a great army of Jotuns she spent two months travelling over land and finally reached Uppsala.

While scouting to see the defences of Uppsala, Skade saw Njord walking by the sea shore. She was attracted by his good looks. After spying on the Aesir for a few weeks, Skade became aware of Njord's daily habits. She had her warriors hide in the forest, as she went to the sea shore and waited on a rock. There Njord saw her and fell in love with her. Skade was already deeply in love with Njord.

Njord began walking the sea shore every day hoping to see Skade. He did see her every day because she every day she kept her warriors hidden in the forest and went to the sea shore to meet Njord. After some time had passed, Njord became worried that the Aesir might see him with Skade and maybe kill her. He thought that the Aesir would not find a lone female Jotun dangerous and decided to bring Skade to meet the Aesir. The two went to Uppsala together but found that the Aesir were very upset to see a Jotun amongst them. Njord somehow managed to convince them that Skade was very friendly and not an enemy at all. When Njord told the Aesir that he wanted to marry Skade, they accepted Skade and congratulated Njord. A wedding feast took place and Njord and Skade were married. During the wedding, Frey spent a lot of time with one of the wedding guests, an extremely beautiful Jotun named Gerda. The two fell hopelessly in love and a short time later, Frey married Gerda.

Njord ruled in Sweden and the Swedes attributed good health and good crops to him. Years later, when Njord lay dying of old age, just before he passed away, he had himself stabbed with a spear so that he could, in death, go to be with Odin. Njord's body was burned along with many of his possessions.

After Njord died, people began to worship him as a god just like Odin and Thor. When the Jotun Chief, Loke died, people began to worship him as a god also because he was Odin's blood brother. Loke was called the god of luck and was not to be trusted in all things.

9 FREY

Njord's son Frey succeeded him as ruler of the Swedes. He built a stronghold in Uppsala, where he ruled with Gerda and the land was peaceful and the harvests were good. As they had done with Njord, the Swedes also attributed good health and good crops to Frey. They started to worship him as a god while he was still alive. Frey enjoyed a good life in Sweden. He held feasts, orgies and ruled over sacrifices.

When Frey died of old age in Sweden, his courtiers kept it a secret because people considered him a god and attributed good crops and good fortunes to him. They kept collecting tax in his name, and drove his corpse on tours in the country in a chariot. The corpse was tied in an upright position to make the farmers think that Frey was still alive.

Eventually Frey's corpse deteriorated so much that it could no longer be driven around in a chariot, and his remains were buried in a mound with many treasures. However his courtiers had a hole made in the mound so that worshippers of Frey could deposit gold and silver into the mound. What was unknown to the worshippers was that the courtiers had fixed the mound with a secret door so they could come and remove the treasures.

10 YNGVE

When Frey's body had completely disintegrated, Yngve, Frey's son was a grown man who resembled his father. Frey's courtiers toured the country with Yngve, telling people that Yngve was really Frey. When Yngve stopped at villages to feast with the people, Frey's former courtiers mingled with the people and convinced them that Yngve was really Frey. In most places they were very successful and therefore in many myths and legends, Yngve is synonymous with Frey. It was because of this masquerade that the god Frey was later called Frey-Yngve. Yngve spent much of his time travelling to other lands and he also became known as a god in Frisia where he was called Ing. One of his sons settled in Frisia and from him came the family called Ingvaeone (Baeksted, 1965). The kings of Sweden were descendants of Yngve and were called the Ynglings.

11 FREYA

At this time, Freya was still alive, and was the last of the people to come to Scandinavia with Odin. Freya was now greatly revered by all Scandinavians, and women all took her name as their own. Married women began to be called Freya. It was eventually shortened to Fru, and to this day married women are still called Fru. Years later, after Freya died, she was worshipped as the goddess of love, beauty and fruitfulness.

12 LOTHAR

In Denmark Lothar was a greedy hard ruler who taxed his people with huge taxes, and he placed himself above the law. Therefore the people soon became fed up with King Lothar. A farmer sent round the war-arrow among all the farmers of Zealand. The farmers armed themselves, marched against King Lothar and killed him. Humble refused to be King and Lothar had no heirs. Therefore Denmark (Zealand or Sjaelland) was unprotected for some years and endured many Viking raids. The Danes, without a ruler, were defenseless against the raiders and pirates who came and went unchecked in Denmark. The most feared of those raiders were the Herules.

"What is this war-arrow?" asked Erik.

The story teller smiled at Erik, and said, "The war arrow is a special stick with runes carved into it. Whenever the farmers saw the war arrow being passed around they knew it was a call for all the farmers to unite together to fight a war to protect their lands."

13 SKJOLD

A ship drifted by the shore of Zealand. There were no oars in the water and there was no one at the tiller. It was a snekke under full sail. Some Danes saw it drift onto the beach. They found that the ship was full of gold and weapons, but the only person on board was a baby boy sound asleep on bundled oat sheaves.

The Danes brought the baby to a Thing, placed him on a holy stone and chose him as their King. The people chose him as their King because they believed that he was the son of Odin.

The Danes were known in the north as the Shield people because all the warriors bore round wooden shields made of oak and reinforced with iron. Since the baby's identity was unknown they named their new king Skjold which is the Danish word for shield. All Danish royalty that came after King Skjold were called Skjoldungs (Shield Cubs). Just as Danish royalty were called Skjoldungs, Saxons were known as the Dagger people and were named after the old word Sax which means dagger.

The new young King Skjold was taken to a large farm to be raised by the chief of the farmers in the area who became his foster father. The farmer's family worked hard and life was peaceful. They loved food, growing things, and malt beer.

When Skjold was seven years old, the chief called a Thing and announced that Skjold was old enough to start to rule as King, but not on his own. Twelve regents were chosen to bring him up and to rule for him until he became of age, which was the age of twelve. Unlike the royalty in other places, the only noble title the Danes had was jarl and it was the King who appointed the office. The appointment of the jarls was done by having the King hold a sword by the blade and the jarl by the hilt while the jarl swore his allegiance. It was the duty of a King's jarl to avenge him if the King fell.

When he was 12 years old, Skjold, while on a hunting trip, left his guardians and ran into a bear of extraordinary size. He had no spear with him, but with the belt that he commonly wore he managed to tie the bear up, and gave it to his escort to kill.

At the age of 15, Skjold had participated in many holmgangs (duels fought on an island or peninsula). Skjold became a feared warrior and kept raiders away from his shores. Even the fierce Herules stopped raiding in Denmark. The people loved King Skjold for many reasons. He did away with unrighteous laws and made good laws, he paid off all men's debts from his own treasury, fostered the sick and provided medicine to those who were sick. He also enriched his jarls with home taxes, and in war he gave the plunder to his warriors, and the glory to the jarls.

Skjold established a stronghold at Lejre and made it his home. He courted the beautiful Alfhild, daughter of the King of the Saxons. Alfhild, had another suitor however, a famous warrior named Skat who was the King of Allemania. In order to make sure he was the one who would marry Alfhild, Skjold challenged the King of Allemania to a duel and ended up slaying him. Shortly thereafter, Skjold married Alfhild. The Allemanians were upset at the loss of their king and declared war on the Danes, but Skjold conquered them as well and forced them to pay taxes from then on".

"Where was Lejre?" asked Erik.

Inga stood up in exasperation, put her hands on her hips, and glared at Erik. This made the story teller roar with laughter. When he had recovered he said, "Lejre was located on the coast of the big fjord in North Zealand where Roskilde stands today. It was well chosen because numerous ships could be sheltered there.

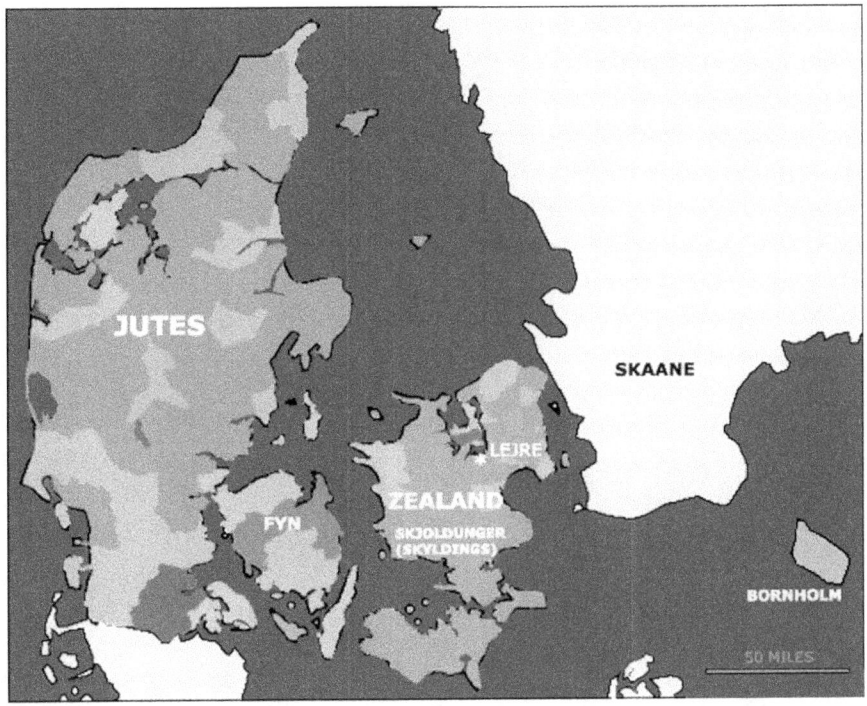

Skjold ruled for many years until he was an old man. When Skjold died, his body was put on the ship in which he arrived. The people piled gold and weapons around him on all sides. Then the ship was pushed out to sea and the people watched as the current and wind took the ship out of sight. Skjold's ship was never seen again".

Erik exclaimed, "Skjold sailed to his Father, Odin!"

The story teller smiled. Then he said, "It is thought that Skjold's father may actually have been Humble and not Odin as they once believed.

The Danes were once again without a king. So they held a Thing and proclaimed that Gram, the son of Skjold was to be their new King.

14 GRAM

Gram was brought up by his foster father, Roar Jarl. When Gram became King of Denmark, he showed his gratitude to his foster father by marrying his daughter. But his advisors told him that he should marry someone of royal lineage. Therefore he divorced Roar's daughter and gave her in marriage to his champion fighter Bess.

Gram considered courting Groa who was the beautiful daughter of King Sigtryg of Gothland, but a wandering skald came to Gram's court with the news that Groa was betrothed to a Jotun. Gram was shocked that Sigtryg would give his daughter to someone who was not of the Aesir royal lineage. The thought of a beautiful princess marrying a Jotun, a troll, made him so furious that he sent a message to Sigtryg telling him to call off the wedding. When Sigtryg refused, Gram declared war on Gothland. He took a fleet of ships and sailed to Gothland where he drew his ships up on the beach. After disguising himself as a Jotun, he left his men at the ships and walked inland with Bess.

In Sigtryg's stronghold, Groa tried to drive the thought of her coming marriage out of her mind. Her fear of Jotuns and the thought of having to be the mate of such an ogre sent shivers through her whole body. It was so depressing. She considered running away but could not imagine how to go about it. This day she decided to take a walk in the woods to escape her depression. Her serving maidens followed her out of the gates. The sky was clear and the breezes brought scents of wild flowers. The serving maidens chattered and giggled as they walked along behind her. Groa reached the oak forest and entered along a narrow path. Her serving maidens followed in single file.

Rounding a bend in the path, Groa saw two figures striding towards her. One was a man and the other was a Jotun. It must be the Jotun to whom she was betrothed! He must have just arrived. Groa, terrified, stopped and watched the two figures approach. As she stared at the approaching Jotun, she began to tremble with fright. The Jotun was wearing goatskin clothes and a hood of goatskin and carried a huge wooden club. When the two strode up to her, Groa was so frightened that she was shaking. The serving maidens fell silent.

Gathering her courage Groa greeted the two travelers. Looking at the Jotun she asked, "Giant, why have you come to this forest?"

The Jotun stared at her in silence but the man said, "Maiden what is your name and lineage?"

Groa, suddenly aware that she was staring at the Jotun turned her attention to the man. She replied, "My name is Groa and my father is the King. Tell me who you are".

The man replied, "I am Bess, the warrior".

"And whom do you serve?"

Bess answered, "I serve King Gram of Denmark and he is here to make war".

"Turn back and go home before my father King Sigtryg catches you and hangs you".

Then the Jotun took off his goat skin disguise and said, "I am Gram, King of Denmark".

Groa suddenly speechless with surprise stared at this King. He was tall, over six feet. His eyes were sharp and dreamily blue and his hair was a copper toned red. His clothes protruding from under his mail coat were regally blue. He told her that he wished to woo her and thought it a shame that she was betrothed to a Jotun. Groa was so relieved that Gram was not a Jotun. She thought this might be the chance for her to get out of the marriage arrangement and so she went with Gram and Bess to their ships.

Groa's entourages of maidens were very alarmed that Groa would go off with two strangers. They ran back to the King's hall and announced to the King that Gram had carried off Groa. When Sigtryg heard that Groa had been carried off, he called his warriors together in pursuit. Gram brought his warriors up from his ships and attacked Sigtryg's army. Sigtryg's warriors fled but Gram and his men pressed forward and attacked Sigtryg's stronghold. In the battle, Sigtryg fell and that was how Gram added Gothland to his Kingdom. Gram sailed his fleet back to Lejre with Groa where he married her.

Not long after, a messenger arrived at Gram's court with the news that in Gothland Swarin Jarl wanted the people to make him King. Gram was not going to stand for this so he sailed back to Gothland and challenged

Swarin to a duel. The duel was fierce and Swarin was killed. As a result, Swarin's 16 brothers demanded revenge and challenged Gram to meet them in duels on an island. Gram met them one at a time and all 16 brothers were killed.

While Gram was in Gothland, Ring, who was of royal birth, rallied many Zealanders to support him as King. Gram sailed back to Zealand and in the battle, which followed, Ring fell.

In the summer, Gram and his champion Bess often went raiding in other lands. They also attacked and looted merchant vessels".

Erik exclaimed, "Vikings!" with a big grin on his face.

The story teller smiled and said, "No Erik. They were not called Vikings. In those days many people went raiding like the Vikings. But they were called Grams after King Gram, the great raider. Anyone who took up piracy or raiding in those days was called a Gram. The Grams found that raiding was very profitable.

One summer Gram gathered a great army and went raiding in Finland, and attacked King Sumble's stronghold. When Gram caught sight of King Sumble's daughter Signe, he called a halt to the battle. He promised peace with Sumble in return for his betrothal to Signe and vowed to divorce his wife Groa and marry Signe.

While Gram was away on raids, King Svipdag from a Kingdom in Norway visited Zealand. He took Gram's sister without Gram's permission, and sailed back to his home.

Gram was furious over the actions of Svipdag, and sailed his fleet to King Svipdag's Kingdom in Norway and waged war. During this time, a messenger arrived at Gram's war camp in Norway. He brought the news that Signe had been promised in marriage to Henry, King of Saxony. Gram was very upset about the news. He left his army fighting in Norway under the command of Bess, and took a ship to Finland.

When he reached King Sumble's hall the wedding had already begun. Gram put on a tattered brown shirt and baggy brown pants. To hide his sword he put on a hooded grey cloak which had patches cut from brown cloth. He looked just like a beggar. He walked into Sumble's hall unchallenged. He found a seat near the door where the commoners sat.

Two of Sumble's men strode over to him. "Who are you?" said the man at the left, "I have never seen you before".

"I am a wanderer. I have never been here before."

"What do you do?" said the one on the right.

"I am skilled in leech craft".

Late at night when all were drunk and many had fallen asleep, Gram leaped up, cut Henry down, felled most of the guests, and carried the bride off with him in his ship.

Meanwhile in Norway, Gram's army was defeated and Bess fell in battle. Svipdag sailed his fleet to Saxony where he obtained many warriors who wanted to avenge Henry. Then with a combined army of Norwegians and Saxons, he sailed to Zealand and attacked King Gram in Lejre. In the fierce battle Gram fell and many warriors with him. Svipdag then married Gram's daughter and became the King of Denmark".

The storyteller smiled, sipped his beer and continued speaking.

15 HADDING

"Gram's two sons were Guthorm by his wife Groa and Hadding by his wife Signe. They lived with their foster father Brage. One day when Hadding was about seven years old, Brage came up to him while he was playing outside and told him that he was afraid Svipdag would kill Hadding and his older brother. He said that he was taking them to a safe place in his ship.

Hadding went to his room, packed his clothes, and ran down to the docks where Guthorm and Brage were waiting for him. They boarded the ship and Brage's warriors rowed out of the bay. When they were out of the bay, the sail was hoisted and the wind took hold of it.

The ship landed in Sweden. Brage and his warriors walked many days into the woods with the two boys until they reached a little settlement with a few log houses. As they approached the hamlet, Hadding noticed that the people looked different. He became alarmed and stopped because he suspected that these people were Jotuns whom he knew from stories to be grim trolls. Brage assured him that these people would keep him safe. Hadding asked why the people looked so different. Brage replied that the people were Jotuns and were his friends. After thinking about it, Hadding concluded that grim trolls that were friendly would certainly keep him safe.

Brage's party walked to the center of the hamlet where two huge Jotuns were engaged in conversation. The two Jotuns stopped their conversation and looked at the approaching party. Brage introduced Hadding and Guthorm to the two Jotuns who were called Wagnhofde and Hafle. They were tall and muscular and wore clothes made from goat skins. Wagnhofde had long black hair and a short black beard. Hafle wore a hood made of goat skin and his beard was brown.

Wagnhofde greeted them warmly and invited everyone to a feast in the hall. During the feast Hadding was informed that Wagnhofde and Hafle would now be his guardians and that Wagnhofde's fourteen year old daughter, Hardgrep would be attending to him. Hadding shouted indignantly, "I do not need a baby sitter!" and in his embarrassment he ran from the hall.

Hardgrep got up and ran after him. When she reached Hadding, he was standing at the edge of the forest. He looked at her and thought that she was very pretty. She wore a blue short sleeved dress and goat skin boots. Her hair was red and she had freckles. Hardgrep smiled at him and her big blue eyes seemed to twinkle. Finally she broke the silence by saying, "I was hoping we could be friends".

Hadding looked down at his shoes in embarrassment and said, "I would like that very much" and he didn't really mind it when Hardgrep hugged him.

The following year Brage returned to the hamlet. When they heard he was coming, Hadding was excited and went to the edge of the hamlet to wait for him. As Brage and his warriors appeared out of the woods and into Hadding's line of sight, he noticed that a regal lady was with them. As the party drew closer, Hadding saw that it was his half-sister. He ran to her and gave her a big hug.

Wagnhofde put on a feast for the visitors. During the feast, Hadding's sister told them that she had married Svipdag. Hadding was shocked that his sister had married her father's killer. Brage told him that she really would have had no choice in the matter.

Hadding's sister said that she had pleaded with Svipdag to bring back her brother Guthorm and make him ruler of the Danes and Svipdag had finally agreed to her wishes provided that Guthorm promised to pay tribute. Guthorm agreed to pay tribute and to be the King of Denmark. The next day, Brage and Gram's daughter escorted Guthorm back to Denmark to be King.

Hadding was determined to someday retake Denmark and avenge his father. He spent most of his time practising his fighting and battle strategies. Hardgrep was his sparring partner. At first they used wooden sticks. She taught him the proper stances and maneuvers with the shield, the sword, the axe and the spear. Then she taught him archery and javelin throwing. His play with Hardgrep had turned into weapon practice.

Hardgrep began to really enjoy her time with Hadding and she soon fell in love with him. Hardgrep took to kissing and hugging Hadding when no one was watching. She also tried to seduce him into her bed. Hadding enjoyed the attention but refrained from going to bed with her.

When Hadding became of age, he announced that he was going back to Zealand and set out to walk through Skaane. Hardgrep did not want to lose him so she dressed like a man and went with him.

Erik asked, "How old do you have to be to become of age?"

The story teller raised his eyebrows and looked at Erik. Then he said, "A little older than you. At that time it was twelve years".

The story teller sipped his beer and continued, "Hadding and Hardgrep walked over the Fyris plains and entered the great oak forest of Skaane. One evening in the forest Hardgrep and Hadding made camp and built a shelter of poles and twigs. At night while they lay in the shelter, a band of Jotuns attacked. Hardgrep leaped up, drew her sword and fought back. She yelled for Hadding to stay behind her. Hadding drew his sword and stayed behind Hardgrep. He hacked at Jotuns who tried to go around Hardgrep and surround them. After a few Jotuns were killed the rest realized that they would not win the fight and so they fled. The fight had taken it's toll though. Hardgrep was very weak and bleeding and she sank to the ground. Hadding was unable to stop the flow of blood and by morning Hardgrep was dead. She had lost her life defending Hadding. Hadding wept.

After burying the body of Hardgrep, Hadding continued walking through the forest and met an old one-eyed man wearing a grey cloak and a wide brimmed grey hat. The old man took a liking to Hadding and guided him to the beach where a fleet of long ships had been drawn up in the sand. The beach was dotted with many warriors. The chief of the warriors was a rover named Lysir and the old man in the grey cloak introduced him to Hadding. When Lysir saw that the old man had taken a liking to Hadding, he not only took Hadding into his service but also made him his blood brother".

"How can that be?" said Erik, "Blood kin are from the same parents".

The story teller replied, "Becoming blood brothers means that you are now as if you were born of the same parents. Therefore if one is killed the other must avenge his death. To become blood brothers they would each cut their wrist and hold the two wounds one against the other so that their flowing blood is mingled. The first blood brothers were Odin and Loke, Chief of one of the Jotun tribes in Halogaland (Loke's Land).

Lysir took Hadding with him. They were on their way north to attack the King of the Jotuns, Loke."

Erik's eyes widened in surprise as he exclaimed, "Odin's blood brother?"

The story teller laughed. "No Erik" he said, "That Loke died long before Hadding was born. This Loke was King of Halogaland (Loke's Land) and was a descendant of the Loke called Udgaard Loke. Halogaland was often called Udgaard. Lysir was on his way north to make war on Loke who had been making raids against the Kurlanders and Lysir was going to retaliate. Unfortunately, in the battle that followed Lysir's army was defeated. Lysir fell, and Hadding was wounded. The old man took the wounded Hadding and fled with him on horseback. Hadding was delirious with his wounds and had the impression that they were galloping over water and that the horse had eight legs. Eventually they reached the old man's house where he attended Hadding's wounds.

After the old man had healed Hadding's wounds, Hadding gathered Lysir's warriors and obtained some ships. He sailed to Gothland and laid Gothland under him. With his army strengthened by Goths, he sailed to Gardarike and conquered it. On his way back from Gardarike, Swipdag came against him with a big fleet off the coast of Skaane. Swipdag's fleet was also destroyed and Swipdag fell in battle. Hadding then sailed to Zealand, where the Danes held a Thing, and proclaimed him King of Denmark.

When King Asmund of Skaane, was given the news that Hadding had killed his father, Svipdag, he declared war on Hadding to avenge him. He did not have to wait long. Hadding brought his army to Skaane and attacked Asmund. In the ferocious battle that ensued, one of Asmund's sons was killed. This was too much for Asmund, and upon seeing his son fall, he went berserk. He put his shield on his back, gripped his sword hilt with both hands, and went furiously forward slaying any warriors who were near him. Hadding and his warriors had to retreat.

After the darkness of night made it impossible to fight, Hadding sent runners to his allies asking for help. The battle immediately resumed at first light of day. At mid-morning Wagnhofde rode up with an army of Jotuns and joined Hadding's warriors, causing renewed effort by the Danes. But Asmund's warriors defended with fury until finally Hadding threw a spear, which penetrated Asmund, and he fell to the ground. The battle stopped as everyone turned to watch Hadding as he went over to Asmund. But Asmund was not quite dead and struck a final unexpected blow at Hadding with his sword. Hadding deflected the blow with his shield but the sword penetrated Hadding's foot and the wound caused

Hadding to walk with a limp for the rest of his life.

Hadding brought the dead body of Asmund to Uppsala to be buried. When Gunhild, Asmund's wife, saw that Asmund was dead, she was filled with grief and killed herself with a sword. Gunhild's body was placed beside Asmund's and a burial mound was erected over them.

After the burial of Asmund and Gunhild, Hadding went into Skaane where he looted and laid waste the land. Since the Skaanians had been defeated, Asmund's son Uffe knew he could not beat Hadding in a pitched battle, so he took a fleet to Hadding's homeland of Zealand and attacked the farmers there instead. When Hadding heard about the invasion in Zealand, he took his army home to attack Uffe. But as soon as Uffe heard Hadding had come to Zealand, he sailed off and escaped back to Skaane.

When Hadding returned to Lejre, he discovered that his treasure room had been robbed. He immediately had its keeper Glumer hung. Then he announced that if any of the robbers brought back the treasure they would receive the same post of honour as Glumer had filled. One of the robbers brought back his share of the treasure. The other robbers seeing that their partner was in favour with the King also brought back their share of the loot. Hadding gave the robbers promotions and favours. Then a short while later, he had them all hung.

Both Uffe and Hadding spent the winter raising their armies. In the spring Hadding took his army to Skaane and spent the next five years battling against Uffe. In the fifth year the war started to go bad for Hadding and he was forced to retreat into the woods. His army ran out of provisions and there was no place to get more food. At first his warriors lived off the land, but eating mushrooms and wild berries was not enough and Hadding's warriors became emancipated. Eventually they devoured their horses and later they ate carcasses of dogs and human limbs. One night as the Danes lay down to sleep, a witch approached them and cursed Hadding. She foretold the doom of the Danes. The doom came early in the morning when Uffe's warriors attacked and slaughtered many Danes. Hadding fled with the remnants of his army to Helsingland.

After some time recovering in Helsingland, Hadding prepared his fleet to sail home, but he could not shake the feeling that he was still under the witch's curse of bad luck. During the voyage, Hadding was standing beside his helmsman and noted that the sky had turned very dark and the breeze had turned into a stiff wind. The wind became stronger as the white capped waves grew to be giants. Water swelled over the bow. A cold driving rain pelted down. The waves kept growing. Hadding ordered the sails to be taken down and for the rowers to head into the wind. This maneuver worked well until a huge wave broke over the bow. The water from the wave uprooted the rowers and swept them towards the stern. Without forward momentum the ship turned sideways into the waves. Water poured over the railings and Hadding yelled, "Abandon ship!"

The ship shuddered and quaked. As Hadding leaped overboard, the ship's bow nosed into the sea. Hadding swam to the surface, grabbed a floating chest and clung to it. All the ships were sinking. Clinging to the chest, Hadding swam with the waves towards land. A wave took him high into the air and swooshed him back down and under the water. When he rose to the surface, another wave took him back up towards the sky. In this fashion, Hadding reached the shore where a wave deposited him far up on the beach. Not wanting to be dragged back to sea by a wave and despite feeling extremely heavy from his wet clothes and exhaustion, Hadding staggered up the beach towards a path. Hadding realized that he was the only survivor. He followed the path as the rain pelted down on him until he finally saw a house in the distance. Hadding made his way to the house. He knocked on the door and yelled, but no one answered so he entered and shut the door. The house was empty. He rummaged through the closet where he found some dry clothes that he thought would fit him. So he removed his wet clothes, dried himself on a towel, and put on the dry clothes. With the sound of the rushing storm outside he searched the cupboard for food. He found vegetables and some beer. After eating, he collapsed on a bed and fell asleep.

Sometime later in the night, a loud roar woke Hadding completely. The storm had taken the roof off the house and rain was whipping him. Hadding sat bolt upright and saw the walls shaking. He ran outside and proceeded inland. A loud crash made him stop and look back. The house was gone. The walls had collapsed under the pressure from the wind. After the storm had passed Hadding hailed a passing ship which took him to Lejre. There he sacrificed to the gods so that they would lift the curse which had been placed on him.

A wandering skald came to Hadding's hall in Lejre with the news that a Jotun wanted to force King Haakon of Throndheim to give him his daughter Ragnhild as wife. Hadding became furious".

A voice sounded from one of the dark corners in the hall, "Why?"

The story teller peered into the corner. A tall man dressed in a blue tunic slowly stood up and took a step forward. His blonde hair and beard was well combed. It was Ejvind Evaldsen.

"Why would Hadding become furious?" asked Ejvind, "He had Jotun friends".

"He believed that Scandinavian royalty should not marry Jotuns. Hadding went to Throndheim and invited himself as guest of Haakon without giving his name. When the day came for the Jotun to come and get Ragnhild, Hadding sneaked out of the King's hall and went up the road to meet the Jotun. When he met the Jotun, Hadding immediately attacked him with a sword and in the fight he slew the Jotun but was himself badly wounded. Ragnhild had taken a liking to Hadding and followed him up the road and saw the fight. When the fight was over she had Hadding carried to a secure shack in the woods where she bound his wounds. While Ragnhild used stitches to close some of his cuts, she sewed a ring into one of his legs.

Meanwhile King Haakon's men found the dead Jotun lying on the road and brought the news to the King but no one knew the name of the slayer. When Ragnhild told her father what had happened, Haakon was so happy that he gave her permission to choose her own suitor to wed. Ragnhild asked her father to put on a feast for all her suitors so that she could choose one of them there. King Haakon did as his daughter asked and young men came from far and wide hoping to be chosen by Ragnhild. By this time Hadding had recovered from his wounds and went to the feast. During the feast, Ragnhild walked around and looked at all the guests, and when she saw the ring in Hadding's leg she took him by the hand and led him up to her father sitting in his high seat. She gave a speech in which she described the fight between the nameless warrior and the Jotun. She then announced that this was the nameless warrior and that she had chosen him to be her husband.

Haakon was not happy about his daughter marrying a nameless warrior even though he considered it better than marrying a Jotun. Then Hadding gave a speech and announced that he was King Hadding of Denmark whereupon King Haakon immediately performed the wedding ceremony. The feast lasted long into the night.

Uffe had a very beautiful daughter and decreed that the man who slew Hadding should have her as is wife. Thuning of Perm wanted Uffe's daughter so he gathered warriors to go against Hadding. When Hadding heard that Thuning was gathering an army to go against him, he took his fleet and sailed towards Perm to meet him. As he sailed along the coast of Norway, an old man wearing a wide brimmed grey hat waved for him to land. Hadding's men were opposed to landing, but Hadding recognized the old man and beached his ships. Over the next few days, the old man taught Hadding how to fylke his warriors (arrange his warriors in the svinfylking formation) and use archers to fire at the enemy from behind the front lines of sword and axe men. Then he gave Hadding a strong bow as a present. Hadding thanked the old man and continued north until he reached Perm. As Hadding beached his ships, Thuning's warriors came out to meet him. Hadding and Thuning with their armies met on a large field. Thuning set up his battle standard and arrayed his warriors. Hadding also set up his battle standard and arrayed his warriors, however, he arranged them in the svinfylking formation. Behind his battle formation, Hadding placed many archers. In no time, Thuning and many Perms fell in battle. Hadding defeated the men of Perm quickly and easily by battling as the old man had taught him.

After he had returned from the land of the Perms, Hadding received an invitation from Uffe to attend a feast to negotiate peace. Hadding took a fleet to Skaane to attend the feast. The feast went into the night and secure in the knowledge that peace was at hand, most of the Danes became drunk. Sleeping quarters had been arranged in another house and late into the night the Danes eventually got up to leave for bed. However, peace was not what Uffe's plan was at all. Instead, he had set a warrior with a big sword just outside the door so that as each Dane went out he mowed off their head. Uffe had expected that Hadding would be the first out the door, but instead Hadding had lingered behind. He what was happening and managed to escape through a window with his remaining warriors, and they ran to the ships and sailed away.

Hadding did not let this betrayal go unrewarded. He gathered up more men and he returned to Skaane with a big army and took on Uffe in a large battle. This time, Hadding killed Uffe and defeated his army. After erecting a big mound over the body of Uffe, Hadding appointed Hunding, the brother of Uffe, to rule in Skaane.

After this, Hadding spent several years at peace with his neighbours. He tended his farm, raised crops, and had Hunding over for a feast each fall. Hunding and Hadding became great friends.

A few years later, in Jutland, a chief called Toste collected warriors, and attacked the farmers of Jutland. After burning and looting, he took his army into Northern Saxony and attacked the farmers there too. Toste's activities of attacking his own countrymen earned him the name "Toste the Wicked" from the farmers. King Syfrid of the Northern Saxons, in an effort to stop him, brought his army against Toste. Syfrid however did not fare well in the battle that ensued. After losing the battle, he sent messengers to Toste to seek peace. Toste promised to be Syfrid's friend if Syfrid would help him conquer Denmark. Syfrid did not want to fight his good friend Hadding but he agreed to help Toste so that Toste would stop attacking the Saxon farmers.

So Toste and Syfrid took a fleet of ships to Zealand. When they heard that Toste was coming, the Danish farmers fled. King Hadding brought his army against Toste and Syfrid, but being outnumbered, Hadding lost the battle and his army scattered and fled in all directions. Hadding, himself, fled to the shore where Toste and Syfrid had beached their ships. There was no one guarding the ships because they were all elsewhere involved in the battle. So Hadding bored holes in as many of the ships as he could. Then he took a small skiff and with one of his warriors rowed out to sea.

Toste thought Hadding had died in the battle and for a long time he searched for Hadding's body. When he did not find it he went back to his ships and saw a skiff far out in the sea. Toste launched some ships and sailed towards the skiff, but of course his ships began to sink which forced Toste to return to shore. He searched all the ships and finally found one that did not have holes in it. Then he launched it and sailed towards the skiff. When Hadding saw the long ship coming closer and closer, he asked his warrior whether he could swim. When the warrior said that he could not, Hadding upset the skiff so that it floated upside down, and he and the warrior held on to a seat inside the hollow of the overturned boat. When Toste saw that the boat was upside down he assumed that Hadding was dead and took his ship back to the beach.

After dark, Hadding returned to Zealand and gathered the farmers and asked them to fight for him. At daybreak he attacked Toste the Wicked. Hadding's men who were arranged in the svinfylking wedge broke through Toste's army. Toste's warriors were cut down and Toste fled to Britain where he disguised himself as an ambassador. But Toste just could not stay away and the next year he returned to Vendsyssel in Jutland. When Hadding heard that Toste had returned, he brought his army to Vendsyssel and there he finally slew Toste the Wicked.

Hadding's daughter, Ulfhild was married to Guthorm. Ulfhild wanted very badly to be Queen of Denmark. She nagged and nagged her husband until finally he agreed to assassinate Hadding. She invited her father to a feast and Hadding accepted the invitation. That same night, Hadding dreamed he was at his daughter's feast. In his dream he was sitting beside Ulfhild eating a pork chop when Guthorm walked up to him and killed him with a dagger. The disturbing thoughts of this dream stayed with him every day leading up to the feast. When the day of the feast arrived, Hadding told his bodyguards to stay alert and keep an eye on Guthorm. Sure enough, Guthorm made his move and the body guards were ready. When Guthorm drew his dagger from under his robes, the bodyguards drove their swords into Guthorm, killing him.

Even though the assassination attempt against Hadding had failed, rumours went around that Hadding had been killed. The news of Hadding's assassination reached King Hunding of Skaane. In great sorrow, Hunding called his Jarls together and had a funeral feast in honour of his good friend, Hadding. A great vat was set in the middle of the hall filled with ale, and Hunding himself went about pouring ale for his guests. As he was passing through the hall, he stumbled and fell headlong into the huge vat of ale and drowned. When Hadding heard of his friend Hunding's death, he was so distraught that he went outside and hung himself.

16 PEACE FRODE

The story teller paused and stroked his grey beard. Then he took a sip of beer, and said, "After Hadding's death, Frode, Hadding's son, became King of Denmark, and Ulfhild married Ubbe Jarl. There was peace throughout the world. Most people claimed it was because the Romans had declared 'Pax Romana', Roman peace."

Grete interrupted the story teller and said, "No! There was not peace because of the Romans. The bishop said that the peace took place because the Virgin Mary gave birth to Jesus the Christ Child in Bethlehem, and close to Bethlehem angels appeared to shepherds keeping their flock by night saying,

"Glory to God in the highest

And on earth peace among men

With whom he is pleased."

(Gospel of Luke 2:14)

The bishop said that because of that, there was peace in the whole wide world".

The story teller smiled at Grete took another sip of beer and said, "There was indeed peace in the whole world. In Denmark there were no thefts, and when a gold ring was left in the market place, no one took it. Nobody fought duels, and there was neither raiding nor piracy. The Danes attributed the peace to their King and called him Peace Frode.

King Frode took a fleet of warships to Kurland."

"Frode was called Peace Frode when he was going to war? Did that change his nick name?" asked Jens, a red headed man who had been sitting in the middle of the hall listening with keen interest.

"No. There was a definite peace in his own country", the story teller replied with a grin.

"Nobody opposed Frode at the beach of Kurland. When he marched his warriors inland, smoke was billowing from all the farm fields. As far as the eye could see, all the fields were on fire. When King Dorn of Kurland heard that Frode had arrived with an army, he had burned all the crops on the farms and lay waste to his own land. Having destroyed anything that could be used by invaders, he retreated all his people to a fortified town. This did not sway Frode though and he made an encampment in front of the town, but did not attack it. At night his soldiers dug several very deep trenches within his encampment. As they dug with shovels they filled baskets with dirt, carried the baskets down to the river, and quietly poured the dirt into the river. After many nights had passed, the Danish campsite was full of trenches and pits several meters deep, and it was very difficult to walk about because of them. The trenches were covered with branches, and a mass of turf was placed over the branches to hide the traps.

The day after the trap was ready, Frode pretended to panic and when his soldiers fled in disarray, the town gates opened and the Kurlanders poured out in pursuit. When the Kurlanders ran through the Danish encampment, the weight of several soldiers over the traps snapped the branches under the turf. The ground was soggy so when the Kurlanders fell into the trenches, the ground collapsed causing the Kurlanders behind the front pursuers to slide with the subsiding earth into the trenches. The Danes came back and sent showers of spears into the trenches easily killing the Kurlanders.

While still in Kurland, Frode received word that the Ruthenians were raiding in Denmark so Frode decided to retaliate by attacking them in their own land. When King Trannon of Ruthenia heard that Frode was coming, he took his fleet out to meet him, but Frode was cunning and hid his ships behind an island. While he waited for the Ruthenians, Frode made a number of pegs from sticks, and loaded a skiff with them. As the Ruthenians sailed by one evening, Frode kept his fleet hidden which was made easier under the cover of darkness. Using the darkness to his advantage, Frode approached the enemy's ships in the skiff, and bored holes under the water line in the hulls of each of the vessels with an auger and plugged the holes with the wooden pegs he had made. When he thought there were enough holes to sink the whole fleet, he pulled out all the plugs. He quickly surrounded the sinking enemy fleet with his ships that he brought out of hiding. The air was filled with arrows and casting spears and the Ruthenians fought well, but none of that mattered since their ships were sinking. Frode was victorious and as a result, began to levy tribute from King Trannon.

Not long after this, the envoys, who normally levied the tribute from Frode's territories in Russia, were horribly murdered. Frode gathered a fleet, sailed to Russia, and laid siege to the town of Rotel. Before Frode arrived, the people of Rotel felt very safe because a wide river separated the town from Frode's army preventing any assault. But Frode was a wise man and he built a dam on the river, making the riverbed dry so that his warriors could cross it on foot. The soldiers of Rotel immediately surrendered knowing that they were no match for the Danes. The King of Rotel swore allegiance to Frode and began to pay tribute to him.

Next, Frode took his army inland to the city of Paltisca where Vespasins was King, and lived in a castle, which was known to be unassailable. Frode laid siege to the city for a few days and then went into hiding, telling no one about it except a few of his berserkers. These berserkers reported that Frode was dead. Since Frode's men did not know that Frode was in hiding, they were filled with grief, held a wake, and erected a huge burial mound. Frode's soldiers all went into mourning and the castle relaxed its defenses and life went on as usual. Frode took this opportunity to suddenly come back and he attacked the castle while the gates were open. Many Paltiscans fell in the battle and Vespasins also swore allegiance to Frode and began to pay tribute.

17 SWANWHITE

Thorhild, the widow of Hunding, hated her stepsons, Regnar and Thorwald and while Frode was away campaigning in the east, she made them thralls (slaves) and put them to work as shepherds. Swanwhite, Frode's sister, was angry with Thorhild for her treatment of Regnar and Thorwald and was determined to set things right. She took her sisters as retinue and traveled with some warriors to Skaane where she found that Thorhild was not only treating Regnar and Thorwald as thralls, but would also send men to the fields to mock and jeer Regnar and Thorwald as they worked.

One night Thorhild's men went out and stole all the sheep while Regnar slept. As the light was beginning in the east, Regnar awoke because he missed the sound of the sheep. He was quickly aware that the whole flock had disappeared. He spent most of the day looking for the sheep while dreading what Ulfhild might do as punishment. When he realized that he could not find them, he crept into a small thicket to hide from Thorhild and her warriors.

Swanwhite, who was aware of what Thorhild's men had done, went out with her warriors and searched for Regnar and found him in the small thicket. He was ashamed of being dressed in the rags of a thrall but even more ashamed that he had lost the sheep. He explained that he was hiding to avoid punishment for their loss. Swanwhite said, "The sheep are not lost. They were stolen by Thorhild's men".

She gave Regnar a sword and fitting garments. After talking with Regnar for a while, she was so impressed with him that she quickly fell in love with him.

That night, an army of men attacked Swanwhite and Regnar. Swanwhite's warriors who were camped nearby came to her assistance and they spent all night in battle. At dawn, Swanwhite and Regnar had won the battle and among the fallen they found Thorhild herself. Swanwhite had the bodies piled in a heap and burned. Regnar Hundingson was very impressed with Swanwhite and so he married her. Thus he became King of Skaane.

Meanwhile, Frode reached the city of King Handwan and laid siege upon it. The city had been burned by Hadding a while back, so Handwan had improved his fortifications so that the fortress was impenetrable. Frode decided to enter the town to see if he could find a weakness in its defenses. He dressed himself as a serving maid and he made one of his attendants also dress as a serving maid. The two went to the town in disguise and easily entered it. They casually wandered into Handwan's hall to spy. It wasn't long before Handwan's daughter entered the hall. When Frode saw her he thought that she was absolutely beautiful and he fell in love with her. The next day, Frode sent his attendant out to his army to tell his men to come up to the city walls at night and he would make sure that the gates were opened.

That night Frode opened the city gates and Frode's warriors rushed in and looted the place. Handwan, seeing that his city was lost, put all his royal wealth onto a ship and sank it in the sea. He wasn't about to let his enemies get their hands on his wealth. After the city was taken, Frode sent an ambassador to Handwan to ask for his daughter's hand in marriage. Handwan was surprised that Frode would ask for his daughter since he could have taken her without asking. He thought that there must be some honour in Frode and sent back the reply that if Frode wished to marry his daughter in an honourable fashion, he should spare the city and form an alliance with Handwan. Frode was so impressed with Handwan that he gave him back his realm. He married Handwan's daughter soon after and in that way he gained Handwan as an ally.

Meanwhile at Lejre in Zealand, Ubbe, at the advice and pleadings of his wife Ulfhild, seized the Danish throne and had himself declared King of all Denmark. When Frode heard that his whole kingdom in Denmark had been taken over, he immediately began his journey home.

Frode brought his fleet to Skaane where he landed and fought a great battle against his sister, Swanwhite, in which he was beaten and fled with his ships. He had lost many men but Frode was not one to give up that easily. That night Frode boarded a skiff and rowed out to Swanwhite's ships intending to bore holes in their hulls. He selected a ship and started to boar a hole. Suddenly from the darkness he heard "Why were you rowing so silently in diverse meandering courses?"

The startled Frode recognized his sister's voice. Slowly he turned to look at her and said, "Why were you rowing so silently in diverse meandering courses?"

She was in a skiff and had rowed silently out to Frode's skiff to take him off guard. She ignored his question and instead said "Before the eastern wars, you gave me permission to marry whomever I chose."

Frode remembered that he had indeed said that and realized it was only the honourable thing to do to live up to his word. In light of this he forgave Regnar and made peace with them. Regnar and Swanwhite gave Frode the number of soldiers for his army, which he had lost in his battle against them. They all went to Swanwhite's hall and feasted. At the feast Frode had the opportunity to get to know Regnar better and he became very pleased with both Swanwhite and with Regnar.

While Frode stayed and rested in Skaane visiting his sister Swanwhite, Regnar entered Denmark and captured Ubbe and brought him back with him to Skaane. Frode had Ubbe brought before him and despite having stolen the Danish throne out from under him, he gave Ubbe a full pardon. However, he took Ulfhild away from Ubbe and forced her to marry his friend Scot instead. The wedding between Ulfhild and Scot took place with much feasting and drinking. Regnar treated Ulfhild as he would any one of royalty and escorted the bride and groom to Scot's ships in the royal chariot. Scot sailed with his bride back to his land, which was named after him and called Scotland. Although Ulfhild remained a queen and was forgiven by her family, she was not satisfied, and she kept on plotting to kill Frode and become the master of Denmark.

18 FJOLNE

When Yngve, the ruler of Sweden died his son, Fjolne, succeeded him. The Swedes did not have Kings. The gods Njord and Frey-Yngve had ruled them. Fjolne's title was Drottnar and his wife's title was Drottningar. His court was called the Drott.

During the Frode peace, Drottnar Fjolne of Sweden and King Frode of Denmark were great friends. They took turns hosting large feasts for each other. One year Frode prepared one of these feasts for Fjolne at Lejre, and invitations to it were sent all over the country. The feast lasted far into the night and all the guests had a very good time and became very drunk. Frode had a large house, and in it there was a great vessel many meters high, and made of large pieces of timber. Directly above the vessel was a loft with an opening in the floor through which strong liquor called mead was poured into this vessel to keep it full for the guests down below. In the evening the drunken Fjolne, with his attendants, was taken into the adjoining loft to sleep for the night. In the night Fjolne, who was very sleepy and still exceedingly drunk, went out to seek a place to relieve his bladder. As he came back to his room he went along the gallery and took the wrong door. His foot slipped and he tumbled into the vessel of mead and was drowned.

19 SVEIDE

After the death Fjolne, his five-year-old son Sveide became Drottnar of the Swedes. Sveide wanted to see the land where his ancestors came from so his twelve guardians went with him on a journey to Vanaheim east of the Black Sea.

When he was older, Sveide decided that his wife should be an Elf from Vanaheim so he journeyed back again to Vanaheim. A few years later he returned with a wife.

One day Sveigde and his wife Vana journeyed back to Vanaheim once more for a visit. They never returned. Thiodolf of Kvine sang of it:

"By Diurnir's elfin race,

Who haunt the cliffs and shun day's face,

The valiant Sveigde was deceived,

The elf's false words the king believed.

The dauntless hero rushing on,

Passed through the yawning mouth of stone:

It yawned -- it shut -- the hero fell,

In Saekmime's hall, where giants dwell."

When the Swedes knew that Sveigde would not return, they took his son Vanlande as their Drottnar.

20 THE ATTACK ON THE NORTH BY THE ROMANS

During the reign of Peace Frode, the Roman Emperor Caesar Augustus, the adopted son of Julius Caesar, decided to bring the Germanic tribes under Roman rule. Therefore, in the year 5 AD the Roman General Tiberius advanced with his army against the Saxons holding the frontier at the Rhine River forcing them to retreat to the Elbe River. Some Roman ships came up to the coast of Jutland and fought the Jutes. The Romans had only limited success though because the east coast of Jutland is treacherous due to the westerly winds washing the North Sea waves that crash against Jutland's shoreline. At the northern tip of Jutland, the strait called Skagerrak is dangerous because of cross winds and some of the Roman ships floundered and sank there. General Tiberius decided to conquer the north countries by going overland instead. In 8 AD he took the Roman army into Germany and waged war against the north. The Saxons stopped him at the Elbe River. Tiberius built a fortress there called the Teutoberger fortress. The purpose of the fortress was to collect soldiers for an invasion across the Elbe River.

21 HERMAN

In 9 AD Herman, a Saxon mercenary in the Roman army, left the Romans and returned to Saxony. He went from tribe to tribe and collected Saxon warriors and trained them to fight as teams in battle formations just like he had learned while in the Roman army.

Caesar Augustus commissioned General Varus to take an army beyond the Elbe River and take the northern Germany and Scandinavian territories and bring those people under the Roman Empire. Varus marched three legions north of the Elbe River across Germany towards Jutland, the Danish peninsula. His guide, Herman, showed him a route through the Teutoberger forest. At a lonely place in the forest, Herman's Saxon warriors attacked the legions with guerilla style actions all along the Roman columns. The Roman legionnaires were used to fighting in formation in open fields but in the forest, the Roman tactics were useless. All three Roman legions, 10,000 to 12,000 highly trained and battle-hardened legionnaires were wiped out in four days of fighting on the narrow forest paths. When General Varus saw that all hope was lost, he killed himself.

After the battle in the forest, Herman and his Saxons scaled the Teutoberger Wall and in the ferocious battle many Roman soldiers were slain and the remnants of the Roman army fled. Herman drove the Romans back across the Rhine River. The Saxons again held the frontier at the Rhine.

22 SCANDINAVIANS

In 13 AD Tiberius brought a fleet of Roman ships up the coast of Jutland. The poor ships of the Saxons and the Picts did not impress the Romans, but when the Roman fleet rounded the Skag (Skagen) in Skagerrak and went into the Kattegat Strait, the Romans were amazed at the ships they saw there. The ships in the Kattegat Strait had a prow at each end and were so maneuverable and swift that they could easily out maneuver the Roman ships. The Romans talked to some of the people in the long ships. The people told the Romans they were Scaanians from Scaane or Scanie. After that the Romans called the people north of Germany Scandinavians.

23 GERMANICUS

In 14 AD the Roman Emperor Caesar Augustus died. Meanwhile the Roman northern army had internal problems and the Roman soldiers along the Rhine revolted. Germanicus came from Rome and put down the revolt. Then he crossed the Rhine and began a military campaign against the Germanic tribes beginning with the Frisians. But in 16 AD Rome discontinued its war against the Germans because it was too expensive and Germanicus, who had been sacking German villages north of the Rhine, was recalled to Rome.

24 PEACE FRODE IN GERMANY

Frode collected warriors and outfitted ships to raid in the west. He put out to the ocean and sailed his fleet around the Skag, then south along the east Jutland coast, and continued south to Frisia, where he ran into a fleet of Frisian ships under the command of the rover Witthe. The Frisians immediately sounded their war horns and rowed towards the Danes. Frode ordered his men not to fire or throw any missiles at the Frisians, so when the Frisians were close enough to hurl spears, the Danes defended by using their shields only. As the two fleets drew closer and closer, more and more spears flew from the Frisian ships towards the Danes. Because no missile was fired back, Witthe was encouraged. The Frisian horns blew and more Frisian spears flew at the Danes. At last when the opposing ships were very close to each other, the Frisians had not a single spear left. Then the Danes put away their shields and showered the Frisians with spears. Overwhelmed by the missiles of the Danes, the Frisians fled and were cut to pieces along the shoreline.

When Germanicus had returned to Rome, mercenary scouts reported that after Germanicus had left Germany, the Germans fought among themselves. This was not true. The Germans were fighting Peace Frode who had sailed up the Rhine River attacking village after village. He spent a year exploring the country along the Rhine and attacking villages. Frode sailed back down the Rhine to the ocean where he found a fleet of Frisian ships waiting for him. There was a ferocious battle, but the Danish ships were better and more maneuverable which gave them a winning edge. The Frisian ships got stuck on shoals during the fight and the Frisians became shipwrecked.

25 FRODE IN BRITAIN

Frode proceeded south along the coast, crossed the English Channel, and landed in northern Britain. After defeating the chief in the district, Frode prepared to go against the Scottish chief, Melbrik to the north. He marched his warriors north through fields and had just reached a forest separating the land of the Britons from Scotland when a scout came running from the south and said that the King of the Bretons was closing on them with a great army. Frode then told his men to throw away all the gold and silver they had collected as booty so that they could fight without being weighed down with extra weight and burdens. Thorkill, a distinguished warrior, opposed this order and made a long speech about it. But the men followed the wishes of Frode and unloaded the packhorses and emptied their belt pouches of the gold and silver coins and jewelry. They scattered gold and silver all over the field. Then they proceeded north into the forest.

The Bretons came up to the field sparkling with gold and silver and the soldiers broke pursuit to gather up the treasures. When the King of the Bretons told them to leave it alone and pursue the Danes, all of his men ignored him with the exception of some of his knights who, instead of ignoring him, instead argued with him over his order.

After marching through the great forest separating Britain from Scotland, Frode and his warriors met Melbrik and his men. The Scots were armed with only spears and no armour, while the Danes were in full chain mail armour, wore shields, and wielded battleaxes and swords. The Scots fled to avoid a fight. The Danes pursued only a little ways because Frode did not want to be attacked from the rear by the Bretons.

When Scot heard Frode had landed in Britain, he collected a great army and marched south to help him. Scot's army met Frode just after Melbrik's men had fled, and Scot persuaded Frode to abandon the pursuit of the Scottish army and turn back into Britain. After Scot and Frode were victorious over the King of the Bretons, Frode took his army south to London, but the strength of its walls gave them no chance of victory. So Frode devised a plan. He pretended to be dead and the Danes feigned surrender. Daleman, the governor of the town accepted the surrender of the Danes and opened the gates. Once the Danes were in town they began their attack. It wasn't long before Daleman was cut down in battle and the city was taken.

26 ULFHILD

After Frode had returned to Lejre, Skat Jarl threw a feast for Frode, and in the middle of the feast, a warrior named Hunding challenged Frode to a fight. Frode took up the challenge and although he won, he received a dangerous wound. Thinking that Frode would back down from him because of the wound, the berserker Haakon taunted him. But the wound did not stop Frode from challenging Haakon and in the duel that ensued, Haakon was killed.

Ulfhild had never abandoned her desire to rule the Danish kingdom and she kept coming up with plots to kill Frode. She had bribed two of Frode's chamber servants to kill him, but the plot was discovered and Frode had the two chamber servants taken aboard a ship. Out at sea they were tied to huge boulders and thrown overboard.

Ulfhild finally succeeded in her plan by spreading rumors that Regnar had committed treason and then formally accused Regnar in Frode's court. Frode could not ignore the accusation and so entered into battle with Regnar. It was in Skaane, fighting Regnar, that he died.

An old man with a white beard had been listening to the story teller intently. He spoke up and said, "I am Lauritz Johansen from the Island of Mors. I am visiting Bjorn here. I think it is such a shame that Frode's sister Ulfhild should gain the Kingdom in such a fashion."

The story teller smiled and said, "I believe that the people at the time felt the same way.

27 DAN MIKELLATI

After the death of Peace Frode, the Danes chose his son, Dan as their King. Dan did not wage war and preferred to stay at home. He was considered a mighty king because he maintained the peace. He became known as Dan Mikellati (Dan the Peaceful).

28 VANLANDE

Vanlande, Drottnar of Sweden, went often on raids. One year, Vanlande over wintered with King Snow of Finland and married Snow's daughter, Driva. Vanlande and Driva had a son called Visbur. In the fall, Vanlande went back to Sweden without Driva but promised to return in three years' time. Visbur stayed with Driva who waited for Vanlande's return, but ten years went by and Driva was still waiting. Then she sent their son Visbur to Vanlande, and paid the witch, Huld, to either make Vanlande return to Finland or to kill him.

When Visbur arrived in Sweden, Vanlande was struck with a great inexplicable desire to go to Finland, but his friends and counselors advised him against it. He then began having nightmares, and cried out in his sleep that Mara was threading on him".

"Was Mara the name of the witch?" asked Bjarne.

The story teller raised an eyebrow and said, "Driva paid the witch named Huld. To either make Vanlande return to Finland or to kill Vanlande. Who or what Mara was, we do not know. Mara was in Vanlande's dreams. We do know that nightMaras or nightMares are named after Mara from Vanlande's dreams.

One night in a nightmare, Vanlande cried so loud that Mara was stepping on him that his men hastened to help him. But they could not wake him and Vanlande died screaming in his sleep. The Swedes said that Vanlande was killed by the nightmare, Mara.

The Swedes took Vanlande's body and burned it at the Skytaa River, buried his ashes, and raised a rune stone over the spot.

Thjodolf sang of Vanlande's death:

"And Vanlande, in a fatal hour,

Was dragged by Grimhild's daughter's power,

The witch-wife, to the dwelling-place

Where men meet Odin face to face.

Trampled to death, to Skytaa's shore

The corpse his faithful followers bore;

And there they burnt, with heavy hearts,

The good chief killed by witchcraft's arts."

29 BOADICEA

During the reign of Vanlande, in 61 AD, Prasutagus, King of the Iceni Celts in Britain died and in his will had left half his estate to the Roman government in Britain. The Roman Procurator, Catus Decianus wanted not half, but all the estate. He took an army to the Iceni and when Boadicea, the widow of Prasutagus, refused to give him the estate, he had her publicly beaten and had her two daughters raped by slaves. This made the Iceni furious.

Boadicea led the Iceni in a revolt against the Romans that lasted almost three years and she almost defeated them. In 63 AD, General Suetonius Paulinus defeated the Iceni, and captured Boadicea. He had planned to execute her but she killed herself before he had a chance.

30 VISBUR

After Visbur succeeded his father Vanlande, he married the daughter of Aud, the Rich, and gave to her, as a wedding gift, three large farms and a gold ornament. They had two sons. Their first son was called Gisle and their second son was called Ond. They seemed happy enough at first but it was only a few years later Visbur left his wife and took another wife. Visbur's first wife went home to her father and took their two sons with her. Visbur had another son with his second wife and they called him Domald.

When Ond and Gisle were ages 12 and 13, they visited their father in Sweden and told him that they wanted their mother's dower. When they knew Visbur would give them nothing, the two boys went to the sorceress Huld and asked her to destroy their father. Huld told them that she could bring it about that in the Yngling race an Yngling would murder a family member in each generation, and the brothers paid her to bring it about. Then Ond and Gisle collected warriors, and during the night Killed Visbur by burning him in his house.

Khalle said, "Would Ond and Gisle not worry about their own lives and that of their families in the future?"

The story teller smiled and said, "They could have killed their own father without the curse from the sorceress but Ond and Gisle were ages 12 and 13. At those ages the future seems so far away that it is non-existent. They needed to hear words of empowerment and they gave no thought at all to the curse. They asked the witch Huld to destroy their father and what they heard was that he would be destroyed.

31 DOMALD

After the Swedes chose Domald, the third son of Visbur, as the new Drottnar, there was a great famine and distress in the land. In the autumn, the Swedes made great sacrifices at Uppsala for good crops for the following year. But the following year was no better than the previous one and people were starving. So when autumn came again the Swedes sacrificed oxen. Again, the next growing season did not improve by the sacrifice of the oxen. So in desperation, the following autumn the Swedes sacrificed men. Still the next growing season had not improved by the sacrifice of men. So as a last resort, when the next autumn came, the Swedes sacrificed Domald. They offered Domald up in exchange for good growing seasons and sprinkled his blood on the altars of the gods.

32 DOMAR

Left without a Drottnar, the people chose Domar, Domald's son, to succeed him. Domar told them that he would accept only on the condition that he would not be considered responsible for neither the weather nor the crops, and the Swedes accepted his condition. The growing season was always good, and there was abundant harvest during Domar's reign.

Domar went to King Danp Rigson of Denmark and asked for the hand of Danp's daughter, Drott. Domar and Drott were married and lived at Uppsala for many good long years.

33 DYGVE

When Domar died of old age on his bed in Uppsala, he had reigned a great many years full of good seasons and peace. Domar's body was transported to the Fyris plains where it was burned, and his ashes were laid on Yngve's burial mound. A rune stone was erected over his ashes. The Swedes held a Thing and chose Dygve, the son of Domar and Drott to be their King. Dygve was the first of the Ynglings to have the title 'King'.

34 DAG

When King Dygve died in his bed in Sweden, Dygve's son Dag became King. Dag was considered to be very wise. He was considered to be so very wise because he talked to birds. After all, Odin talked to ravens. Dag however was so wise that he talked to all birds, and he had a sparrow that came to him every day. Dag considered this sparrow proof of his wisdom. One year, the sparrow failed to return to Dag and he was extremely upset about it because he feared that people would consider him less wise. A wanderer came to Dag's court and heard of the plight of King Dag. The wanderer decided to come up with a story of why this bird had not returned to the King. "I saw your sparrow", said the wanderer.

Dag grew excited and said "where did you see my sparrow?"

"Well" said the wanderer, "I have just come from the land of the Geats, Reidgotaland. There I stayed with a farmer on a farm called Varva. I remember it clear as day your Majesty. The sparrow arrived at the farm and perched on a window ledge. The farmer and I watched it for a few minutes. Then the sparrow flew into the farmer's grain field and ate a few pieces of grain. The farmer became very upset. He yelled at the sparrow,' get out of my field!'

The farmer suddenly dashed into the grain field and threw a stone at the sparrow and hit it. The sparrow died instantly. It did not suffer."

King Dag was angry and assembled a great army to avenge the sparrow. He sailed to Reidgotaland, landed his army and went to Varva where his men plundered and the people fled. After having killed many people and taken many prisoners, King Dag was returning in the evening to his ships. As they were going across a river at a place called Skjotan's ford, a labouring thrall ran to the riverside and threw a hayfork at the troops. It struck the king on his head so that he fell instantly from his horse and died.

35 AGNE

Agne was the name of Dag's son who became King after him. King Agne was a powerful and celebrated man who was an athlete and expert in all feats and was a mighty warrior. One summer, king Agne of Sweden landed his army in Finland and marauded there. In response, the Fins gathered a large army under a chief called Froste and went against Agne. There was a great battle in which Froste and many of his warriors fell. The victorious King Agne proceeded with his army through Finland and subdued it and took much booty. He also took Froste's daughter, Skjalv and her brother Loge with him.

When king Agne was sailing towards home, he landed at Stocksund and camped for the night.. He put up his tent on the flat of a river bank where there was drift wood for bonfires. The tent was under a huge tree to protect it from the heat of the sun in the daytime. There he married Skjalv. Agne's new bride begged him to hold a funeral feast to honour her father. Agne agreed, invited a great many guests, and held a feast right there by the riverside. Agne had become very famous by his expedition and many people came to the feast. For entertainment, a great drinking match was held, and King Agne along with most of his guests got very drunk. Now, King Agne had a gold necklace which had been in his family for generations. It was the one given to Visbur by Aud the Rich when he married Aud's daughter. Skjalv looked Agne in the eyes and said, "Agne your gold ornament has been in your family for generations. Take care of your gold ornament and make sure that you do not lose it in the night." So Agne tied the necklace securely about his neck with a cord before he went to sleep.

When King Agne was asleep, Skjalv took a noose and fastened it under the ornament. Then her men took down the tent poles and threw the loop of the noose over a stout tree branch. The men of Skjalv hauled on the noose so that King Agne was pulled up off his feet and hung under the branches. They then tied the rope secure and Agne died hanging there. Skjalv and her men ran down to the ships, took one and rowed away. In the morning, the Swedes found the body of their King hanging in the tree. Agne was buried on the spot, which was afterwards called Agnefet. It lies on the east side of the Tauren River and west of Stocksund. Skjalv had just been married to the Yngling, Agne, so this death counted as one of the murders in the Yngling family curse that was placed by the witch, Huld.

36 ALRIK AND ERIK

The sons of Agne were called Alrik and Erik. They became Kings together. They were powerful men, great warriors, and expert at all weapons. Alrik and Erik, quarreled over the inheritance left to them by their father. This quarrel caused Erik to leave Uppsala and Alrik hoped that by doing so they would find peace with each other. Erik travelled to the Goths where he received a welcome by their King. Leaving however, did not stop the quarrelling. Even before the brothers had ever started quarrelling there had been many border skirmishes between the Goths and the Swedes. During one of those battles, some time after Erik had left, Alrik's son, Gunnthjof, lost his life. When the news of his son's death reached Alrik, he swore revenge and journeyed with a large army towards the Goths. When the Goths heard Alrik was coming they gathered warriors together to go against him. On the battlefield the armies on both sides arrayed their warriors and that was when Alrik saw Erik among the Goths. Alrik yelled to Erik that family members should not be on opposite sides. Erik yelled back that the King of the Goths was his friend and that he would not desert him. Alrik yelled back that he did not wish to fight a family member and therefore would fight the King of the Goths in a duel to settle his business. Erik answered, "Our King is too old to fight duels so I will fight in his place".

Alrik did not want that at all. So with reluctance Alrik had the war horns sound and he led the charge on the Goths. In this battle, both of the brothers fell.

37 YNGVE AND ALF

Alrik's sons, Yngve and Alf succeeded to the throne in Sweden. Alf's mother was Dageird, a daughter of Dag the Great, and his wife was Bera, who was the most agreeable of women. She was very brisk and happy. Yngve was handsome, a great warrior, strong, sharp, and very popular, while Alf was silent, harsh, unfriendly, and unpopular. Yngve would go on war expeditions, while Alf would sit at home.

In the autumn, King Yngve Alrikson arrived at Uppsala from a Viking expedition. The Swedes celebrated Yngve's victories and exploits and there was much drinking. King Alf went to bed early as usual while Bera stayed up very late and talked with Yngve. After a while Alf came up and told Bera to come to bed. But Bera would not. She told Alf that she would be happier if she was married to Yngve instead of him. Alf became very angry but went back to bed.

Many nights passed with Bera staying up late talking with Yngve. The more Bera mentioned Yngve's name, the angrier Alf became. One night Bera and Yngve were up late, as usual, sitting on the thrones talking. There were guests around the tables but they were so drunk that they did not notice Alf enter the hall. King Alf strode directly to the high seat, drew a sword from under his cloak, and pierced his brother through and through. Before he died, however, Yngve leaped up, drew his sword, and gave Alf his death wound. Yngve and Alf were buried under mounds on the Fyris plains.

38 HUGLEIK

Hugleik was the name of Alf's son who succeeded the two brothers as King of Sweden. Just like his father, he was no warrior and sat quietly at home. He was very rich and had a reputation of being greedy. At his court he had all sorts of players who played harps, fiddles, and viols. He also had magicians and all sorts of witches. At this time, Yngve's sons Jorund and Eric, who were naturally more like their father, were constantly out on raiding expeditions.

There were many sea kings in those days. Homod and Hogrim were two brother sea kings who discovered that Hugleik was no warrior. This made it quite easy to raid Sweden and they took to pillaging and plundering in Sweden each summer.

"What is a sea king?" asked Erik.

The story teller smiled and said, "A sea king is a king with no land. He has an army, ships, people, and everything that makes him a king, but he has no land. Whenever an opportunity to claim land arose he wouldn't hesitate to take it. There were many sea kings in those days.

The sea Kings, Homod and Hogrim attacked Uppsala and Hugleik fled. Homod and Hogrim settled themselves in to rule their newly gained land of Sweden. Although Hugleik had fled he was not about to give up his land without a fight. He travelled through Sweden and raised a large fleet and brought it towards Uppsala.

Homod and Hogrim heard that Hugleik was coming with a big fleet. Knowing that Hugleik was no warrior, they confidently brought their own fleet out of the harbor and went against Hugleik's fleet. In the great sea battle which took place Homod and Hogrim were both killed. Hugleik, with new found confidence, went back and reclaimed his throne in Uppsala as King of Sweden. He had now earned a reputation as a warrior.

39 THE SIKLINGS

The story teller paused as Grete refilled his mug. The story teller sipped his beer and said, "Now I will tell you about the Siklings".

Yngwin was ruler of Sivord, a small kingdom on the island of Fyn. Regnald, a Danish sea king, of the family lineage called Siklings, wanted to rule Sivord. He made war on Yngwin and won the kingdom.

When King Regnald became old and died, his son Sigvald was chosen as King. Sigrid was Sigvald's daughter. She was beautiful and so modest that she would not even look at her suitors, of which there were many. The most persistent suitor was Ottar, son of Ebb. He tried very hard to get Sigrid to look at him but did not succeed, until finally he gave up and sailed away.

40 OTTAR

Sometime after Ottar had sailed away, a Jotun tricked Sigrid into going outside the village. Once outside the village where no one was to help her, he kidnapped her and took her to a cave. When Ottar heard that she was missing he went searching for her. It took some time but eventually he found the cave, slew the Jotun and carried off Sigrid. They stopped to rest in the forest where Ottar tried to untangle Sigrid's long hair, which the Jotun had bound back behind her head in a weird tangled knot. Ottar had to cut her hair with his knife because he just could not untangle it.

Ottar may have rescued Sigrid from the Jotun but she was uncomfortable with the companionship of Ottar and so she ran away from him too. After eluding him, she wandered in the forest and found a hut belonging to a witch. The witch kept Sigrid as a servant and set her the task of pasturing her goats. Ottar searched far and wide through the forest for Sigrid until he finally found the witch's hut. He offered Sigrid to set her free, but Sigrid declined the offer and would still not look at him. Ottar, tired and dejected, walked back to his fleet.

Sigrid escaped the witch of the woods on her own one day and wandered through the forest, and then over open fields. Finally she reached a farm, which belonged to Ebb. She was ashamed of her near nakedness and so she pretended to be the daughter of a pauper. Ebb's wife, who was the mother of Ottar, was not fooled and could easily see that the young woman was not born a pauper. She gave Sigrid nice clothes and kept her by her side. One day when Ottar came to visit his mother, he recognized Sigrid right away. Perhaps it was due to the bond she now had with his mother that Sigrid allowed Ottar to court her and even agreed to marry him. But Sigrid still did not look at Ottar. One night, Ottar gave Sigrid a torch to hold. When the flame had almost burned down it scorched Sigrid's hand, but she did not react. Ottar snatched the light away and told her to look at her hand. Sigrid instead looked Ottar in his eyes. She kissed him tenderly and the two went to bed together.

Meanwhile, Sigvald had heard news of the whereabouts of his daughter and arrived a few days later. At once he had Ottar seized, intending to hang him for defiling his daughter. But Sigrid told Sigvald all that had happened, and that she was pleased to marry Ottar. After hearing his daughter's story, Sigvald came to admire Ottar and gave permission for the two to marry.

It was during his stay at Ebb's farm that Sigvald met Ottar's sister and had fallen in love with her. A short time after, there was a double wedding, Ottar and Sigrid were married and King Sigvald married Ottar's sister.

News came that Ragnald of Sweden was marauding in Zealand. The festivities were cut short as Sigvald sailed his fleet to Zealand, taking Ottar with him, where they attacked Ragnald. For three days their men slaughtered one another, and it was difficult to tell how the outcome would be. Then Ottar, in true warrior style, hurled his shield at the Swedes, went berserk, and waded into the thickest of the foes felling each and every warrior he came upon. He broke through the Swedish shield wall and cut down Ragnald among the bravest of his soldiers. Witnessing this, the rest of the Swedes panicked and fled.

41 ALF AND ALFHILD

Siward, King of the Goths had two sons, Wemund and Osten. He also had a daughter, Alfhild. Siward was very protective of his daughter. He gave her a viper and a python to raise as pets and kept her locked in a room. Siward had also made a decree that if any man entered the room and failed to get past the snakes then that man would be beheaded. Whether it was the fear of the snakes as body guards or the fear of beheading, Alfhild was not bothered by anyone and was kept safe.

When King Sigvald of Sivord died his son Sigar succeeded him. Sigar had three sons, Sigvald, Alf, and Alger, and a daughter Signe. Alf heard about Siward and his daughter Alfhild. He liked a challenge, and sailed to Gothland with the intentions of wooing Alfhild. Alf covered his body with a bloodstained hide to make it harder for the viper to pierce him. He took a piece of red hot metal with a set of tongs and when the viper went to lunge at him he put it into the mouth of the viper so that the viper perished. Then Alf killed the python with a spear.

Alf thought he had won the maiden, Alfhild. But Siward told him that Alfhild would marry only the man she chose of her own free will. Alfhild wanted to marry Alf, but her mother was against it. She kept saying bad things about Alf until Alfhild felt enough pressure from her that she told him to leave. Without the prospect of marrying, Alfhild decided to do something else with her life. She was not content to sit around in her room waiting for potential suitors for the rest of her life. So she dressed as a man, ran away from home, and began the life of a Viking rover.

"Women Vikings!" exclaimed Erik, "I don't believe it".

The old skald laughed. Then he said, "There were women Vikings in those days Erik. Don't forget that in the battle of Troy there were women warriors called Amazons who came to fight for the Trojans. Under the laws of Odin women were not restricted as they are now under Christianity".

The skald sipped his beer and continued his story, "In her travels, Alfhild recruited young women who felt as she did. They got their own ship and went roving as a ship full of female Vikings. Such women were called shield maidens. As time went by, the shield maidens with a great reputation became transformed in legends to Valkyrie. When Alf heard what Alfhild had done, he set sail in search of her.

Meanwhile, Alfhild came across a band of rovers who had lost their chief in a raid. They were all fierce fighters and able sea men, but they all felt uncomfortable leading. They decided instead to make Alfhild their leader and they joined her and her fleet of shield maidens. Thus Alfhild had become a sea queen with a large fleet of ships and she continued to recruit women to join her band of Vikings".

Alf, following the rumors of female Viking raiders came upon some Black Men. After a fight, the Black Men surrendered and Alf took them prisoner. With some questioning Alf was able to determine from them that they had seen Alfhild's fleet sail towards Finland. Without hesitation, Alf set the prisoners free and turned his ships towards Finland.

"Black Men?" said a voice on the left side of the hall. It was Toke Bjornson, a large man with a wide red beard and dressed in a dark green tunic.

"I have never heard of that tribe. What country were they from?"

The story teller smiled and said, "They were traders from North Africa."

He wiped away some of the froth from his beer off his beard and continued the story, "When Alf's fleet reached Finland, they entered a narrow gulf. Alfhild had gone before Alf and had entered the same narrow channel. She saw Alf's ships approach from far off in the distance and she decided to attack with her fleet instead of waiting to be attacked. As they came closer to each other Alf's men had second thoughts and thought it was best not to attack such a large fleet with their few ships. But Alf, not suspecting that the fleet actually belonged to Alfhild, told his men that it would be a shame if someone had to report to Alfhild that he abandoned the search because of these ships.

So the sea battle began. Alf's ship made contact with the lead ship of their enemies. Alf leaped onto the ships prow and his berserker, Borgar followed him close behind. Alf and Borgar advanced towards the stern of the ship slaughtering all who withstood them. Borgar reached Alfhild first and took a swing at her. Alfhild was quick on her feet and jumped back fast enough that the blow only just struck off Alfhild's helmet. Seeing this the astonished Alf immediately called a halt to the fighting. He was overjoyed because he had found whom he sought.

Alf married Alfhild and Borgar married Alfhild's attendant, Groa. Alfhild gave birth to a girl and called her Gurid. Groa gave birth to a son and called him Harald.

At this time, the Frisians had fleets of trading ships and they made an alliance with the Danes and established trading centers at Aalborg, Viborg, and Hedeby.

42 STARKAD

A Jotun called Starkad kidnapped Alfhild. Alf's warriors hunted down and killed Starkad, and rescued Alfhild. But Alfhild was pregnant, and after a while she gave birth to a son and called him Storverk.

When Storverk grew up, he was bigger and stronger than most men. He was very handsome and had black hair. When he left home to make his way in the world, he went to king Harald in Norway and was taken into his service as a warrior. During this time Storverk ran off with Unn, the daughter of King Freke in Halogaland, and they had a son and called him Starkad. During the same year, King Harald also had a son and called him Vikar. The sons of Freke were not happy that Storverk had run off with their sister so they hunted him down and surrounded his house and set it on fire. Everyone inside the house was burned to death including Unn and Storverk. The only survivor was the baby Starkad who was taken to King Harald where he was raised with Harald's own son Vikar as his brother.

A few years later, King Hertjov from Hordaland attacked King Harald and killed him and laid his kingdom under himself. Among Hertjov's warriors was a man called Grane who took Starkad, who was three years old at the time, to his farm and raised him there.

Nine years later, Vikar came to the island where Grane had his farm, and found his foster brother Starkad. They were both twelve years old, and Vikar was astonished at the size and strength of Starkad. The two boys knew that the kingdom was rightfully theirs and they had every intention of getting it back, so they obtained a ship and sailed off. After they had collected warriors and formed an army, they sailed a fleet to Hordaland and attacked King Hertjov who fell in the battle. After they beat Hertjov's army, Vikar became King in both Agder and Hordaland. Vikar and Starkad now went on Viking raids in the summers and enjoyed the King's halls in the winter. All was again as it should be.

One summer Vikar and Starkad were sailing north with a large fleet. The weather turned against them and they had head winds, which prevented their passage north. After being forced to put ashore they all agreed that a sacrifice must be made to Odin before they could proceed. They then cast lots to see who should be hung as sacrifice. Everyone became quiet and downfallen when the casts were made it became clear that the lot fell on King Vikar. They all decided to hold a meeting about it in the morning.

At the meeting the next morning, the men decided that they should not really sacrifice their King but only an effigy of him. A rope had been thrown over a branch with a noose. Vikar put his neck in the noose as a symbolic gesture. Starkad then said, "I sacrifice you to Odin", and before anyone could stop him he yanked on the rope. The rope flew up and Vikar was hung in the tree. Starkad believed that an effigy would not be enough to pacify the gods and so as added measure he ran him through with a spear to make absolute sure that Vikar was dead. Thus died Vikar, King of Agder and Hordaland. For this deed, Starkad was hated in all Norway.

From then on Starkad raided with the Danish sea King, Bemune. When they went into Russia, they had to tie wooden planks to their feet because the inhabitants had planted sharp spikes in the ground when they heard that the Vikings were coming. Bemune and Starkad campaigned successfully in Russia all summer and in the fall Starkad went to Sweden and stayed with King Hugleik.

43 HAKE

After spending seven years in Sweden, Starkad became tired of the Swedish life style of feasts and sacrificial ceremonies. He left Sweden and took up with the Danish Sea King, Hake. In those days Kings would keep berserkers to act as bodyguards and to be their champion fighters. If things went bad in a battle, the berserkers would form a circle with the King in the middle and protect him at all costs. Many a King's life was saved in this fashion. Starkad was now one of Hake's twelve berserkers.

Hake sailed with his fleet to Ireland to raid there. The raids were successful and much gold was taken. Starkad had received grave wounds during these raids but recovered during the winter.

In 256 A.D. Hake raided into Russia. The Osterled army wanted to settle things with a duel and put forth their champion fighter, Visin. Hake accepted and chose Starkad as his champion. Visin was killed and the Osterledians paid tribute to Hake.

Hake proceeded south on the rivers to Byzantium. There again, the kingdom of Byzantium wished to resolve matters with a duel and put forth their champion Tunne. Starkad representing the Danes slew Tunne in the duel and tribute was paid to Hake by Byzantium.

The next year, King Hake came with his troops to Sweden against King Hugleik. Hugleik collected a great army to oppose Hake. Two brothers Svipdag and Geigad, both famous berserkers, came to Hugleik's assistance. King Hake himself was a feared berserker and he had about him twelve berserkers, among them was Starkad.

The two armies met on the Fyris plains, and there was a great battle, in which King Hugleik's army was soon defeated. Then the berserkers, Svipdag and Geigad, pressed forward. But Hake's berserkers were twelve against two and Svipdag and Geigad were both taken prisoners. After that it was simple for King Hake to penetrate within the shield circle around Hugleik, where he killed him and two of his sons. Seeing that their king was dead, the Swedes fled.

King Hake subdued the country and became King of Sweden. He now sat home as the ruling King while his men went on Viking raids each summer.

44 HAGBARD AND SIGNE

Hake had three brothers Helvin, Hagbard, and Haamund. They were the sons of King Haamund of Havbor in Zealand. Sometimes the brothers cruised the seas together and sometimes by they travelled by themselves. While on one particular expedition together, Hake's brothers ran into another Viking fleet. The leaders of the other fleet were the Siklings; Sigvald, Alf and Alger, the sons of Sigar, King of Sivord. Alf was the husband of Alfhild, the shield maiden.

The leaders of the expeditions decided to fight each other on land and so landed their ships on a nearby island. These land duals on islands were known as holmgangs. The holmgang began but it wasn't long before both side realized that the combatants could not get anywhere in the fight. The fighters were equal in strength and skill. It was because of this that a respect for each other quickly developed and they decided to be friends.

Haamund and Helvin continued on their Viking expedition. But Hagbard went home with his new friends, Sigvald, Alf, and Alger. At King Sigar's hall Hagbard met Signe, the sister of his new friends. Signe and Hagbard fell hopelessly in love with each other. Hagbard went to King Sigar and asked for Signe's hand in marriage. King Sigar already had an offer from Hildegisl, a Saxon. Therefore his answer to Hagbard was uncertain."

Ejvind interrupted the storyteller, "In Denmark, women chose their own husbands."

The story teller nodded in agreement, "yes, however it was a matter of courtesy to get the father's permission as well. If the father gave permission and the lady declined the offer, there was no marriage. Marriage was still a family matter.

Hagbard and Signe spent a lot of time together and got to know each other very well. Many weeks passed before Hagbard sailed home to Havbor.

Hildegisl knew that Signe favoured Hagbard over himself and knew he would lose his courtship. Therefore he paid King Sigar's man Bolvis to say bad things to the King about Hagbard and his brothers in an attempt to ruin their reputation and muddy their name. Hagbard and his brothers remained unaware of the vicious rumours being spread areound. Alf and Alger believed the lies and a hatred towards Hagbard and his brothers grew inside them. The hatred was so great that when Haamund and Helvin came for a visit Alf and Alger killed Haamund and Helvin .

Later Hagbard went to visit Signe. Hildegisl continued to make sure that the relationship between the two families was strained. When Hagbard discovered that his brothers had been killed a huge fight broke out and Hagbard killed Alf and Alger but not before it was discovered that Hildegisl was the source of the rumours and lies. Hildegisl was present when this realization was made and he immediately turned and ran. Hagbard grabbed a nearby spear and threw it at Hildegisl which hit him in the buttock. He lived, but with a great wound. Ever after, Hildegisl walked with a limp. After this event Hagbard immediately sailed home.

Later Hagbard became so lonely for Signe that he returned alone to King Sigar's hall disguised as a serving maiden. He went to Signe's house and was taken in by Signe. One of Signe's serving maidens was suspicious of the large new serving maiden. That night, Hagbard went to Signe's bedchamber and the two of them swore undying love to each other.

The suspicious serving maiden sneaked into Signe's bed chamber that night and recognized Hagbard as he and Signe lay sleeping. She carried off Hagbard's sword and ring mail and took it to king Sigar. She told him that Hagbard was in his daughter's sleeping chamber. King Sigar called some armed men and went with them to Signe's bed chamber and, ignoring the pleading of his daughter, hauled Hagbard away.

In the morning Hagbard was taken to the gallows outside the village. He asked that before they hang him that his cloak be hung up so that he could see how he would look hanging. Sigar granted his wish and Hagbard's cloak was hung on the gallows. Signe was watching from her window and when she saw the cloak hanging, she thought it was Hagbard. She broke down and told her serving maidens that she intended to burn her house down and herself with it. She told them they were free to leave if they wished. No one left. They all chose to stay with Signe. Then Signe set fire to her house burning both herself and her serving maidens.

When the people saw the smoke and the fire from the house they shouted that Signe was burning in her house. King Sigar could not see which house was burning from the place where the gallows was located. He heard the shouts and became alarmed and rushed to see if it was true. This did not stop the execution. Hagbard was given a drink of mead and shortly after was hung. When Sigar reached Signe's house, he ordered that the execution be stopped. But the messenger was too late because Hagbard was already dead. Sigar tried to rescue his daughter but could not. The house burned down and Signe and her servants perished.

News of the death of his brothers reached Hake, King of Sweden. Hake wanted revenge for the death his brothers, so he gathered a fleet to go against King Sigar. Starkad and Haakon Wigarson, the Zealander, deserted Hake because they did not want to fight against Danes. Starkad had been a guest of King Sigar many times and the two were friends. Starkad and Haakon left Sweden, while Hake left Uppsala with a great fleet and sailed for Sivord.

Hake landed at Sigersted in Sivord and killed whomever he came across. When his father, King Sigar, fell Sigvald took the leadership of the army of Sigersted. The people of Sigersted rushed to help Sigvald. The women took up arms and helped fight against Hake's army. With the added help of the local citizens, Hake's men began to be cut down. Hake escaped with only three ships.

A village near Ringsted is today called Havbyrd after Hagbard. Sigersted is also nearby which was where king Sigar had his hall.

45 JORUND AND ERIC

Jorund and Eric, the sons of Yngve, were marauding in Denmark. One summer, Jorund and Eric ran into King Gudlog from Halogaland. The sea battle that ensued ended with them clearing King Gudlog's ship and taking him prisoner. They carried him to the land of the Stromones and hung him there. Afterwards, Gudlog's men raised a burial mound over him.

Eyvind Skadaspiller sang of it:

> **"By the fierce East-kings' cruel pride,**
>
> **Gudlog must on the wild horse ride --**
>
> **The wildest horse you ever did see:**
>
> **'Tis Sigur's steed -- the gallows tree.**
>
> **At Stromones the tree did grow,**
>
> **Where Gudlog's corpse waves on the bough.**
>
> **A high stone stands on Stromone's heath,**
>
> **To tell of the gallant hero's death."**

At about this time Jorund and Eric heard that Hake's army had been thinned out. They steered towards Sweden, and gathered a strong force as they went. As soon as the Swedes heard that the Yngling brothers had come, they flocked to them in multitudes to join them. The brothers proceeded up the rivers to Malaren Lake, and then went over land towards Uppsala. King Hake went with his army out towards them and met them on the Fyris plains with far fewer warriors.

In the battle King Hake went forward in berserk and killed all who were nearest to him. At last he killed King Eric and cut down the banner of the two brothers. Jorund, who had been so sure that his great army would conquer King Hake, fled with all his men to their ships on Malaren Lake.

The victory did not come without a price for King Hake though. He was so grievously wounded that he could not live long. His warriors carried him to Uppsala on a shield. Hake ordered that a warship be put out to sea with all his dead warriors in it, that the tiller be shipped and the sail hoisted. He ordered tar-wood to be piled in the ship over his dead warriors. Then he had himself laid on top of the pile of tar-wood. Hake was almost but not quite dead when the tar-wood was lit. The wind was blowing off the coast. The ship flew east over the waves, burning in clear flame, out between the islands and into the Baltic Sea. The fame of this deed increased as time passed.

46 JORUND

Jorund, the King of Sweden took up residence in Uppsala. In the summer, he was often out on war expeditions. One summer, Jorund took his force to Denmark and plundered there. By the fall, Jorund had marauded all around Jutland. Then he went into the Lim Fjord and marauded there too. While Jorund's fleet was thus lying in Oddesund, King Gylog of Halogaland, a son of King Gudlog, whom Jorund had hung some years ago, sailed up with a great force. He entered the Lim Fjord and entered into battle with Jorund in Oddesund.

When the people of the country saw this, they swarmed towards the battle in great ships and small ships to help King Gylog. Jorund was overpowered by the multitude and his ships were cleared of their men. Jorund sprang overboard, but was caught and carried to land. Gylog ordered a gallows to be erected where he led Jorund to it and hung him there.

Jorund's ten year old son, Ond was then chosen as king of Sweden. He grew to be a wise man, who made sacrifices to the gods, and lived quietly at home.

47 FRODE THE VIGOROUS

Dan Mikellati (the Peaceful), King of all Denmark died of old age in his bed. When his son Frode was chosen King, many of the districts in southern Norway refused to acknowledge Frode as their King.

Frode sailed a large fleet north and defeated ten Kings in Norway. Then he sailed to Froger's kingdom. Froger was a mighty warrior and rich from Viking raiding. Froger was infamous throughout the lands because not only could Froger's lineage be traced back to Odin, but a witch had foretold that no man could defeat him except someone who could catch up in his hand the dust lying at Froger's feet.

This reputation did not stop Frode. He landed with his fleet and challenged Froger to a duel and Froger accepted. Before they began Frode asked Froger for lessons in fighting. Froger figured that Frode had heard stories about how great he was and he was flattered and readily accepted saying that Frode was wise in asking an experienced fighter for lessons.

So, Froger marked off two squares opposite one another on the ground and began by telling Frode the use of these squares. Each then took the side assigned to him. They were just getting ready when Frode asked to exchange arms as well as sides with Froger. Frode wore a gold hilted sword and breastplate and gold trimmed helmet that Froger was very impressed with. So Froger readily agreed to the exchange. After changing sides, Frode scooped up some dust from where Froger had been standing. Both Froger and Frode realized that Frode had fulfilled the omen of Froger's defeat. True to the prophecy, Froger was killed in the duel and it earned Frode the nickname 'the Vigorous'.

Meanwhile, Starkad, returning from a Viking expedition, was shipwrecked and was the only survivor. He made his way to Lejre and went to the King's hall. Frode knew Starkad's reputation and immediately took him into his service. Frode gave Starkad a ship and warriors so that Starkad could keep foreign marauders out of Danish waters and also go on Viking raids.

In 277 the Romans were battling the Saxons at the Rhine frontier and Frode lay at war with the Saxons on their northern border. Frode broke through the Saxon-Jutland border and the Saxons surrendered so they could concentrate on fighting the Romans on the Rhine. The Saxon King

Sverting pledged allegiance to Frode and began to pay him tribute.

In 282 the Rhine frontier between Rome and Saxony was secured and King Sverting began to plot on how to get rid of Frode. When the Saxons heard that Starkad was away on a Viking expedition, they sent a challenge to Frode to meet their champion Hame in a duel. Hame was a famous Saxon warrior who had won a reputation fighting the Romans on the Rhine. He was so famous in Saxony that the town Hamburg was named after him. There was no chance that Frode could beat him so Frode stalled and took a few days to think it over.

Unexpectedly Starkad returned home. When he heard about the challenge from Sverting, Starkad said, "A King should not fight underlings. That is unseemly and also ridiculous. Frode you should accept the challenge but have your champion, me, fight the Saxon champion. The Saxons were not expecting this change of plan but now they could not refuse. Starkad and Hame met on a field. Hame began by insulting Starkad and suddenly went after Starkad with his fists. The first blow made Starkad stagger and fall to his knees. Hame drew his sword expecting an easy kill. He underestimated the situation though. Starkad got up, drew his sword and with one blow cut Hame's body into two pieces. The Saxons now had to pay twice their tribute to Frode. Hanef, a Saxon Chief, was enraged over the double tribute and prepared to go to war.

Frode heard about the preparations Hanef was making so he took his army across the Elbe and attacked Hanef's army. In the battle, Hanef fell.

Sverting sent messengers to Frode inviting the Danish King to come to a feast. Frode accepted unsuspecting of the trap that lay in wait for him. During the feast, armed Saxons rushed into the hall and killed Frode. However, during the fight Sverting was also killed.

Frode had three sons, Halfdan, Ingjald, and Fridlief, and two daughters, Helga and Aasa. Halfdan was the oldest and was usually out on Viking raids. Fridlief and Aasa were only children and much younger than Helga, Ingjald and Halfdan. At a Thing, Halfdan was chosen King of all Denmark. Halfdan, who preferred to be out raiding, set Ingjald to run the country and continued his roving activities.

48 HALFDAN

Halfdan put his brother Ingjald in charge of Denmark while he went with his army against King Ond in Uppsala. There were several battles in which Halfdan was always victorious. At last King Ond fled into exile in Gotland. Halfdan was now King of Sweden. He set up his royal court in Uppsala and ruled there for 25 years.

Starkad left Lejre and went to Halfdan in Sweden. Halfdan immediately took him on as his berserker and the two of them were often out on Viking expeditions.

49 STARKAD AND HELGA

A rumor reached Halfdan that his sister Helga had taken a commoner for a lover. He sent Starkad to Lejre to investigate. Starkad found that the rumour was true and that Helga was with a gold smith. When Starkad came upon the two of them together he drew his sword. When he saw Starkad, the smith panicked but he was so terrified that he could not move. Starkad wounded the gold smith and escorted him outside the gates of Lejre. He told the smith to leave and to never come back. The smith did exactly that and ran away as fast as he could. Then Starkad went back to Helga and hit her with his hand. Helga let out a little cry and fell to the floor. Starkad put his hands on his hips, glared at her and snarled, "If you take a lover do not take one beneath your class."

There was a bruise on Helga's cheek where Starkad had hit her. Starkad was satisfied that he had interfered enough in Helga's love affair and sailed back to Sweden."

"Starkad did not kill the smith" said Erik, "Why not?"

"It would not be honourable for Starkad to kill the smith" answered the story teller. "The smith was not a warrior and was not totally to blame. Starkad always acted under rules he had made for himself. His rules set him so high in the admiration of other berserkers that he became the role model for them to follow."

With the blacksmith gone, Helge from Norway began to court Helga. Helge won Helga and received Ingjald's blessing. However, Angantyr, son of a Zealand jarl had also been wooing Helga and was upset to find that he had lost out to Helge. Angantyr challenged Helge to a holmgang with himself and his eight brothers. The holmgang was to take place the morning after the wedding. Helge was very nervous about fighting nine warriors on the day after his own wedding. Helga told him to ask Starkad for help."

With a few men, Helge took a ship and sailed to Uppsala. He invited Starkad to come to the wedding but Starkad refused to come. Then Helge told Starkad about the holmgang to take place the next morning after the wedding. Starkad asked about the date and place for the holmgang and promised to come.

True to his word, Starkad arrived at Lejre on the day of the wedding.

After the wedding feast, Starkad stood guard outside the bridal suite.

Early in the morning, Starkad entered the bridal suite expecting to escort a battle ready Helge to the holmgang. Instead he found Helge and Helga asleep in each other's arms. Starkad did not wake Helge because he felt that Helge was being cowardly and was purposely hiding in his new wife's arms. Besides, Starkad had made it a rule for himself to never ask for help and he did not want to be branded a coward himself. Softly, Starkad departed and went alone to the peninsula where the fight was to take place. He went to the top of a hill, removed his clothes and began to catch fleas as he waited. A light snow was softly falling.

Angantyr arrived at the other side of the hill with his eight brothers. They lit a bon fire to keep warm while they waited for Helge. The brothers waited some time, and finally one of them went to the top of the hill to look around. Just over the rise, the brother saw an old man sitting half naked covered in snow.

Angantyr asked Starkad whether he wanted to fight them one at a time or all together. Starkad replied that fighting them all together was no harder than killing a pack of dogs. Thus they all fought Starkad at once. Soon there were nine corpses lying in the snow and a naked Starkad alive but wounded. He had received such bad wounds that his guts were hanging outside his body. Tired and thirsty after the fight, he crept down to the brook for a drink but found the brook flowing with the blood of the nine brothers and would not drink. Instead, he crept over to the road and leaned against a huge boulder. Starkad's strength was almost gone. He had the rule that he would never ask for help so all he could do was to lean against the boulder.

A man came by in a wagon. He stopped and asked, "How much would you pay for my help?"

Starkad said "what is your lineage and status in life?"

The man answered "I am a servant in the village."

Starkad growled, "You are nothing but a mercenary dog. You scum. Leave now and get out of my sight!"

Another man came by in a wagon. The man said, "You need help. Let me help you into the wagon and take you to get help for your wounds".

Starkad said, "What is your lineage and status in life?"

The man said, "I am a free man and my wife used to be a thrall."

Starkad exclaimed, "You married a thrall! That is so shameful! No I will not take help from such a shameful fellow! Go away right now!"

The man looked bewildered. Then he drove off in his wagon shaking his head.

Next a woman came by. She looked at Starkad and said, "Oh you poor dear. Here let me tend your wounds."

Starkad glared at her and exclaimed, "What! Me take help from a woman? No way! Be on your way lass!"

The woman looked alarmed and walked quickly away.

A poor farmer came by in his wagon and offered to help Starkad. Starkad said "what is your lineage and status in life?"

This farmer said, "I have no royal lineage and I have never fought in battles, nor gained great riches. I am just a poor hard working farmer looking after my family."

Starkad said "I find that you are of high honour and I accept your help. The farmer put Starkad's guts back into his body and bound his wounds. He helped Starkad into his wagon. Starkad stayed with the farmer until he had recovered. As he was leaving the farmer, Starkad gave him a present, a red cloak, which had been given to him by Helga.

Helge now feared for his life because he knew that Starkad would seek revenge for deserting him when he should have been helping to fight Angantyr. Helga, who knew Starkad very well, gave Helge advice on how to deal with the situation. She told him to attack Starkad with his sword the moment he appeared.

When Starkad was well enough he journeyed back to Lejre. As soon as he entered the suite of Helga and Helge, Helge jumped up and hit Starkad in the head with his sword, completely taking him by surprise. Helge lifted his sword to hit him again and would have killed him if it wasn't for Helga's quick reactions. She grabbed a shield and threw it in the way and stopped the killing blow. Starkad now saw that it was not cowardice, which had kept Helge from fighting Angantyr. Therefore he forgave Helge and went back to Halfdan in Uppsala.

50 STARKAD AND INGJALD

The sons of Sverting, afraid that the Danes would make them pay for the death of Frode, offered their sister to Ingjald as a bride. Ingjald accepted and married the daughter of Sverting. From then on Ingjald partied and feasted with the sons of Sverting every night.

Starkad heard that Ingjald had married Sverting's daughter and was living in great friendship with Sverting's sons. This bothered him so much that he went back to Lejre. He carried with him a large sack. When people asked him what the sack contained, he answered that it was coal and that he would use it to harden King Ingjald's soft soul.

When Starkad reached Lejre, he entered the King's Hall and sat at his usual seat, next to the King's throne. The Queen entered the hall and spotted Starkad sitting in his seat. She did not know who Starkad was and she went over to him and told him to find a seat for a lower class. Starkad said nothing to the Queen but slowly got up and made his way to a seat that was the farthest from the throne. When he sat down, it was with a loud noise, which echoed through the hall.

Ingjald soon came home from a hunt. When he saw the angry old man sitting next to the door, he knew right away that it was Starkad. Ingjald tried at once to make it up to Starkad. He brought him to his former seat and had the Queen bring him the best food and drink. Starkard accepted this but he remained angry. He grew angrier still when the sons of Sverting entered the hall and he saw what good friends they were with Ingjald.

Starkad, being the honourable man that he was, did not show the anger that was brewing inside. Instead, he stood up and began to sing a ballad. He sang of the Skjoldungs Kings and he sang of King Frode. Ingjald was having such fun with Sverting's sons that he hardly listened. Starkad continued to sing. His song now told the story of Frode's death by the hands of Sverting and his sons. It was at this point that Starkad's song caught his attention and Ingjald began to listen. Finally, Starkad sang of how Frode's death went un-revenged and that Sverting's sons would rule over Denmark.

Now Ingjald turned and looked upon Sverting's sons, not as his brothers in law, but as the murderers of his father. With a cry of anger, Ingjald drew his sword and attacked the sons of Sverting and at his side fought

Starkad. When Sverting's sons and their Saxon followers lay dead in the hall of Lejre, Starkad saluted Ingjald as the son of Frode. Then he wished Ingjald luck and returned to Halfdan in Sweden. At this time, Fridlief Frodeson began to make Viking raids.

When Ingjald died, Fridlief took over the steering of Denmark. This was in the year 306, and Constantius, Emperor of Rome, went to Britain to face incursions by Picts. Constantius fell in battle, and his son Constantine became Emperor of the West. Constantine married a British princess and went to live in York. Then Constantine defeated Maxentius at the battle of Milvian Bridge, making Constantine the ruler of the Roman West in 312 AD. Twelve years later, in 324, Constantine defeated Licinius, Emperor of the Roman East to become the sole Emperor of Rome.

51 STARKAD AND OLE

When Fridlief's son, Ole, began to make Viking raids, Starkad the Old accompanied him.

Ole began to undermine his father, Fridlief's authority by demanding taxes from Jutland and Fyn and having the people swear allegiance to him. Ole became bolder and bolder and even demanded tribute from the Zealanders. The Danish Jarls took notice of the undermining of their King and began to plot against Ole.

The Danish Jarls paid Starkad the Old a huge sum of money to take the life of Ole. Starkad was now so old and feeble that he used a walking staff to support himself. He traveled to Uppsala to pay Ole a visit. Starkad waited for the right moment to take Ole's life. He knew that in a fight Ole would be no match for him but Ole's stare put everyone off. He knew that if Ole looked him in the eyes, he would be unable to take his life. One day when Ole was taking a bath, Starkad entered the room. When Ole asked what Starkad wanted, he could not look Ole in the eyes so he looked away. Ole knew that his own stare could be very overpowering so, out of courtesy to Starkad, he looked away and asked again what Starkad wanted. At that moment Starkad seized the opportunity and sprang forward and ran a sword through Ole.

Having been an honourable man his whole life, Starkad's conscience bothered him over having murdered his friend Ole. Whenever he heard the tale of the death of Ole, he could not hold back his tears. Eventually, his conscience bothered him so much that he went around killing the Jarls who had paid him to kill Ole.

Starkad's conscience was worse than ever because the Jarls he had killed were also his friends, one of which was named Lenne. By now Starkad was now so feeble that he was using two walking sticks to totter around.

While wandering in a forest, Starkad came across Lenne's son Hader who was out hunting. From a distance Hader recognized Starkad the Old as the man who killed his father. Hader tried to have two of his men ride Starkad down with their horses but Starkad hit them both at once with his two walking sticks and both men fell dead.

When his two men failed to kill Starkad, Hader decided to approach Starkad himself. Starkad, who did not know who Hader was, began to complain about his old age, his sins from his old days, and his present condition. Hader suggested that he trade in his sword and armaments for a horse and wagon so he could get around better. As they were talking, it eventually dawned on Starkad whom Hader was. He told Hader that he no longer wanted to live and offered Hader the money he had been paid to kill Ole to kill him. Hader declined, but then Starkad told Hader that he had to kill him to avenge his father, Lenne. Starkad handed Hader his own sword and eagerly stretched his neck forward. He told Hader that if he could leap between the head and the body before the body fell, he would for the rest of his days be unharmed by weapons. Finally Hader took the sword and in a single stroke, Hader severed Starkad's head from his body. But Hader did not try the leap, because he was afraid the falling body would crush him to death.

At this time the Goths established mighty kingdoms in Europe, the Ostrogoths in east and the Visigoths in the west.

52 FRIDLIEF THE SWIFT

The story teller paused, took a sip of mead and continued, "When Halfdan died on a sick bed in Uppsala, Fridlief became King of all Denmark.

Hurywill, the King of Oland, made a league with the Danes. He then soon after made an alliance in Norway with the sons of Finn; Brodd, Bild, Bug, Fanning, and Gunholm. With his new alliance, Hurywill broke the treaty that he had made with the Danes by attacking the southern side of Zealand. Fridlief responded by attacking Hurywill in the harbor. The fighting was so ferocious that both armies were destroyed and only a few were able to flee.

With dwindling numbers, the remnants of Hurywill's army lashed their ships together in the night in an effort to stay united. Just before dawn however, Bild and Brodd cut the cables holding their ships with the others and they were able to sneak out of the harbor and sail off leaving the others behind.

The next morning, Fridlief proposed that to save the lives of the remaining warriors on both sides, he would fight Hurywill, Gunholm, Bug, and Fanning in single combat one at a time. Hurywill and his companions agreed. In the duels that followed Fridlief killed off Gunholm, Bug, Fanning, and Hurywill one at a time, thus winning the battle.

Some time after the battle in the harbor and after he had time to gather more men, Fridlief took a fleet and made a successful raid in Ireland. After raiding Ireland, he crossed to Britain and went inland. It was there that the Roman soldiers converged on him and wiped out most of his army. Fridlief would have been finished off but he came up with a plan. When night fell Fridlief tied the dead corpses of his men to stakes so that they were upright. The next morning, the Romans hesitated to pursue Fridlief because it looked as if there was still an army to oppose them. It would have been too late anyway because Fridlief had taken the remnants of his army back to his fleet under the cover of darkness and had sailed off.

53 SWANHILD

Ermanarik was King of the Ostrogoths in southeastern Europe. He wanted to marry Swanhild because she was famous for her great beauty and she was also from his ancestral homeland in Gothland. Ermanarik sent his son Randver and his advisor, Bikke to King Jonaker of Gothland, to ask for her hand in marriage. Jonaker readily agreed to the proposal because he would gain the powerful Ostrogoths as allies.

"Wait!" said Erik, "Swanhild was the daughter of Sigurd Dragon Slayer."

The story teller beamed a big smile and said, "Erik, Swanhild was indeed the daughter of Sigurd and Gudrun. After Sigurd's death Gudrun attempted to commit suicide but it failed. Then she moved to Gothland with her daughter Swanhild where Gudrun married Jonaker. Thus Jonaker became Swanhild's step-father.

Swanhild agreed to marry Ermanarik, King of the Ostrogoths and Jonaker gave his blessing. Bikke and Randver took Swanhild with them in their ship and sailed down the Russian rivers. On the way back, Bikke kept telling Randver that Swanhild would make a better wife for Randver than for his old father, Ermanarik.

When they reached the hall of King Ermanarik, Bikke went to Ermanarik and told him that Randver and Swanhild were lovers and that they had slept together each night on the voyage. Ermanarik flew into a rage and decreed that Randver be hanged and Swanhild be trampled to death by wild horses.

While Randver waited to be hanged, he plucked all the feathers off his falcon. Then he sent an attendant with the falcon to his father. When Ermanarik saw the falcon he understood his son's meaning that Ermanarik was as plucked for hate as the bird was plucked for feathers. He ordered that the hanging be stopped. But it was too late. Randver was hanging dead.

Meanwhile, Swanhild was lying bound on the ground and Ermanarik's men were trying to drive wild horses over her. But the horses refused to step on her. Finally Bike covered Swanhild with a blanket. Since the horses could no longer see Swanhild they trampled her to death.

When Swanhild's half-brothers, Hamder, Sorle and Erp heard the news of

Swanhild's death, they were enraged and went after Ermanarik with an army. On the way there they got into a fierce argument with each other and Erp was killed. Despite this, the remaining two brothers continued with their army to Ermanarik's hall where they fought their way into the hall. In the savage fight, the brothers lost all their warriors. Being the only ones left, Hamder and Sorle went berserk causing the weapons of Ermanarik's soldiers to be almost useless. Hamder and Sorle fought their way towards Ermanarik himself and talked as they fought. They regretted that Erp was not with them. Hamder said, "If Erp was alive, Ermanarik would be missing his head by now".

An advisor to Ermanarik, an old man wearing a grey cloak and a wide brimmed grey hat, had told him that the only way to stop the two brothers was to throw stones at them.

"Odin." whispered Erik.

The story teller heard Erik and nodded. Then he continued, "So it was that Hamder and Sorle died under a shower of stones.

That same year, the Huns crossed the River Tanis (Don) and invaded the Ostrogoth Empire. The Huns were considered a people of mystery. They were nomadic horsemen and fierce warriors. The Huns' strength was in their mounted archers. They did not use fire, and they ate roots and raw meat. In battle they gave no regard to their own safety. They would attack in seemingly random groups, then retreat and regroup and attack again. When fighting in close quarters with swords, they threw nets over their opponents to entangle them.

In 375, the Hun invaders had split into smaller sub-groups and tribal units. Ermanarik's warriors were fighting the Huns all over the Ostrogoth Kingdom.

54 HEIMDAL (RIG)

Odin made his son Heimdal as King of all Jutland. Heimdal chose to have his court in the township of Himmerige in Vendsyssel. He decreed that each farmer have a horn. If any farm or home was attacked, the farmer was to blow his horn and anyone within earshot was then also to blow his horn and then rush to the aid of his neighbour. Whenever this happened and the defending farmers heard Heimdal's horn, which was called Gjallerhorn, they redoubled their efforts because they knew that the king and his army were coming to their aid. This was the beginning of how Heimdal fostered a family like unity within his community.

Heimdal liked to walk about in Jutland all by himself, visiting the various farmsteads. When he wandered he wore the clothes of a farmer ; a grey cloak and a wide brimmed hat and he called himself "Rig". He gave people advice on their crops, and imparted knowledge of how to grow things and of nature which greatly aided the farmers in his country. Rig also gave advice on many of his people's problems, and used the sayings of "Havamaal" to solve some of the problems he encountered. He could often be found sitting with a family he was visiting admiring the rainbow after a thunderstorm. Sometimes in the evening, while visiting a farmer, Heimdal would quietly sit outside after supper. If the farmer asked 'Rig' what he was doing, Heimdal would say that he was listening to the grass grow. For these endearing activities, his people loved Heimdal, and he called the people his children. It was from Heimdal's wanderings among his people, that the Jutes became closer to nature and appreciated the land. The farms were improved, and the farmers became prosperous. In times of need, the blowing of Gjallerhorn brought the army of Heimdal to defend Jutland. After Heimdal (Rig) died in Denmark, the Danes worshiped him as a god. Heimdal's son Danp Rigson was chosen King of Denmark".

Erik spoke up,"Heimdal is the God who guards the Rainbow bridge between Asgaard and Midgaard. Whenever the Aesier are attacked he will blow the Gjallerhorn calling the Aesier to war. His hearing is so good that he can hear the grass grow".

The story teller chuckled and said, "Yes Erik that is what the people tell about Heimdal after they started to worship him as a god".

The story teller sipped his beer and said, "Let's continue with the stories.

55 TYRFING

There was a King named Svafrlami who was a descendant of Odin. Once when Svafrlami was out hunting, he became separated from his men. At sundown he came by a cliff where two dwarves were sitting in front it. Before the dwarves became aware of him, the King held a rune sword over them so that they could not run back into the cliff. The King asked the dwarves what their names were. One was called Dvalin and the other's name was Durin. Both the dwarves begged pitifully for their lives. Svafrlami agreed to let them both live if they would smith him a sword which was better than any other sword. Dvalin and Durin agreed to craft Svafrlami the best sword they were capable of making. Svafrlami demanded that the sword be able to cut through iron as easily as through cloth, and that it never rust. The dwarves gave their word that they would make such a sword. Then they arranged for a date on which Svafrlami should come back to obtain the sword.

When Svafrlami returned on the predetermined date, the dwarves were outside the cliff waiting for him. When the King arrived Durin handed him the sword. Dvalin said, "The name of the sword is Tyrfing. This sword has been made to your specification but because of how you have dealt with us we have placed a curse on it. Every single time it is drawn it will cause a death, but it will also three times cause a shameful deed. Furthermore, Tyrfing will also cause your death."

Then Durin and Dvalin ran into the cliff where Svafrlami could not reach them.

Now in Bolm, there lived a person named Arngrim who was half human and half Jotun and who was often out on raids. One day he raided in Svafrlami's Kingdom. Arngrim went against Svafrlami in a duel. During the duel the sword, Tyrfing, cut Arngrim's shield a glancing blow and went into the ground. Svafrlami could not pull it out. Arngrim cut off Svafrlami's hand, yanked out Tyrfing from the ground and killed Svafrlami on the spot. Then Arngrim took Tyrfing, as much booty as he could carry, and he made off with Eyfura, Svafrlami's daughter.

56 ANGANTYR

Arngrim and Eyfura had twelve sons. The oldest was Angantyr, the second oldest Hjorvard, and the ten other sons were Brand, Biarbe, Brodd, Hiarrande, Tand, Tyrfing, Hadding, Hiortuar, Hiartuar, and Rhane. The Arngrim sons were berserkers and went often on Viking trips together. They were unbeatable. While celebrating their mid-winter feast in December, Hjorvard made a vow to wed Ingeborg, Yngve Alrikson's daughter in Uppsala. Ingeborg was famous for her beauty.

One spring, the Arngrim brothers sailed to Uppsala. Hjorvard went before Ingeborg's father, Yngve Alricson and asked for her hand in marriage. Yngve hesitated with his answer. Then one of Yngve's own berserkers, Hjalmar burst out with anger saying that Ingeborg was already promised to himself. Hjorvard then challenged Hjalmar to a holmgang. Hjalmar stipulated that Hjorvard would be without honour if he wed Ingeborg before the holmgang took place. There was a time set and the place was to be the island called Samso.

The day before the holmgang, Angantyr married Svava, daughter of Bjartmar Jarl, a good friend of Arngrim. After the wedding feast, the twelve brothers left for Samso. Angantyr took the sword Tyrfing with him.

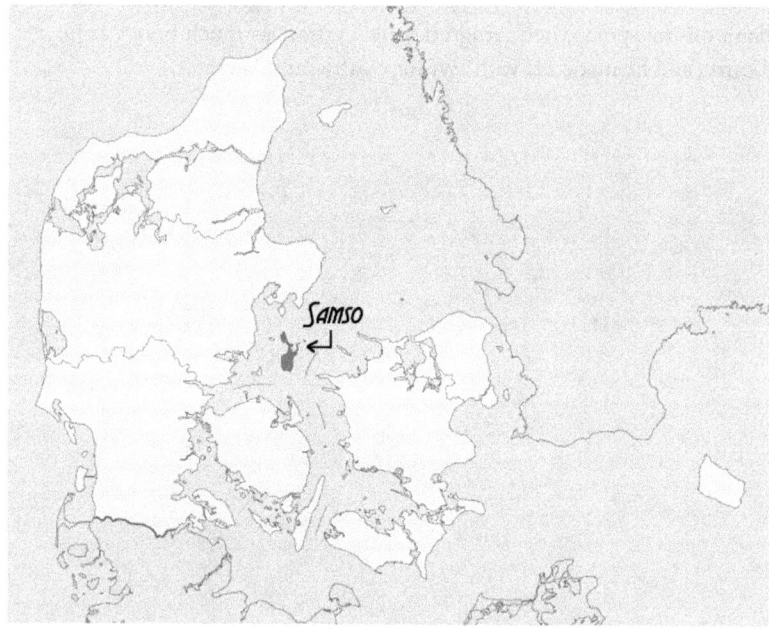

The Arngrim sons arrived on Samso at the same time as Hjalmar. Hjalmar had brought two ships. He was on one and his friend, Orvar-Odd was on the other. They landed on the opposite side of the island as the Arngrim sons so Hjalmar and Odd left their men at the ships and went inland looking for the Arngrim sons.

Meanwhile, while Hjalmar and Odd were making their way inland, the Arngrim sons came upon Hjalmar's two ships and immediately attacked the men at the ships. The Swedes were all killed and the Arngrim sons were unhurt but greatly exhausted from the battle. All the Arngrim sons thought that Hjalmar and Odd were dead, except Angantyr, who insisted that they search the island.

Hjalmar and Odd saw the brothers come up from the beach. They could see from the sunlight reflected from Angantyr's sword, that he was wielding Tyrfing. Odd was wearing a chain mail shirt on which no iron sword could bite; therefore he insisted, at first, that he fight Angantyr. But Hjalmar disagreed and insisted that he fight Angantyr himself while Odd was to fight the rest of the Arngrim sons.

When Hjalmar and Angantyr came together they agreed that the winner of their fight would erect a mound over the fallen and bury him with everything except his weapon, which the winner would take as a trophy. Hjalmar then engaged Angantyr while Odd conferred with the rest of the brothers. It was decided amongst them that Odd was to fight the brothers one at a time.

The first to engage Odd was Hjorvard, but it was not long before he fell. Although Odd's fight was uneven, it ended with him being the only one left alive. He was extremely exhausted but unwounded.

When his battle was over, Odd walked to where Angantyr and Hjalmar had fought. There was Angantyr lying dead, but Hjalmar sat leaning against a small mound looking like a corpse and was close to dying. He said, "Odd take my gold ring from my finger and bring it to Ingeborg, and tell her that I love her."

Then Hjalmar died. Odd stayed with Hjalmar's corpse all night long.

Odd spent a day erecting a mound over the sons of Arngrim and the sword Tyrfing was burried there with them. The next day he took Hjalmar's body back to Uppsala. Ingeborg's heart was so broken with sorrow that she died too. Hjalmar and Ingeborg were buried together in the same mound.

Bjartmar Jarl mourned long over the death of Arngrim's sons and his daughter Svava, Angantyr's wife, was heartbroken.

Early the next year Svava gave birth to Angantyr's child. The child was a girl and many gave the advice to Bjartmar to have her adopted out. But Bjartmar felt that she could continue the line of Arngrim and produce great warriors. She was given the name Hervor.

57 HERVOR

Hervor took a great interest in bows, swords, battle-axes and shields. She was uncommonly strong for a girl. She practiced weaponry and fighting. Bjartmar, who was trying to persuade her from these activities, now forbade her to carry on like that anymore. But Hervor ran off into the woods, where she built a little house. Then she went through the countryside fighting duels to make a living."

"She robbed people in the countryside!" declared Axel.

"Well, yes" said the story teller "you could put it that way.

Bjartmar Jarl, who had been searching for Hervor, finally captured her and lost some men in the process. She stayed with him for a while but she did not get along with the thralls and often fought with them. One day, one of thralls teased her saying, "You are the daughter of a pig herder! You are not as good as I am!"

Hervor was shocked and went crying to Bjartmar. After Bjartmar calmed Hervor so that she stopped sobbing, he told her that Angantyr was her father and related her family's whole history. Hervor wanted immediately to go to her father's burial mound.

Hervor secretly dressed like a man and ran away. She called herself Hervard and joined a group of roving Vikings.

Hervard persuaded her group of Vikings to sail to Samso. When she went ashore, the Vikings would not go with her, saying that Samso was haunted. Hervard went looking for the grave mound. She yelled long and loud the names of the Arngrim brothers who had died there. At last she found the mound and...."

Erik grew excited and said, "When she found the mound she yelled her father's name over and over very loudly. Then the mound opened. Inside was fire and Angantyr full of fire strode forward and handed her the sword, Tyrfing."

At that the story teller laughed out loud. This caused the listeners to laugh with him. "No Erik" continued the story teller, "You have come up with an excellent ghost story. Hervor dug up the sword Tyrfing, which she took with her.

When she got back to the shore, the ship was gone. She hailed the next passing ship. The ship was bound for Glaesisvellir, a small kingdom in Norway. Hervor continued to call herself Hervard and everyone thought she was a man. In Glaesiveillir, she entered the service of old King Gudmond.

One day in the hall of King Gudmond, the King was in troubles in a game of chess. Hervard left her seat and went to the King's side and helped him win. On her seat she had left her sword, Tyrfing. When she turned to go back to her seat, she saw that one of the King's men had taken Tyrfing from its scabbard and was examining it. She rushed over to the man, snatched Tyrfing, cut the man down, and ran from the hall. The man's friends were enraged. They jumped up, drew their swords and rushed for her. But King Gudmond had realized that Hervard was a girl and stopped his men from the pursuit.

Hervor ran down to the docks, joined a group of Vikings and went raiding again. After roving with Vikings for a while, Hervor went home to her grandfather, Bjartmar Jarl. There she put aside her sword and armour. She took up sewing and cooking, and went about keeping house for her grandfather.

A few months later, Hofund, son of King Gudmond of Glaesisveillir, arrived at the hall of Bjartmar Jarl to court Hervor. He asked Bjartmar for her hand in marriage and they were wed. When a son was born to Hervor and Hofund, they called him Angantyr. Their second son was named Heidrek.

58 HEIDREK

THE TYRFING SAGAS

While Hofund thought much of Angantyr, who was mild and good-natured, Hervor loved the broody and at times cruel Heidrek the best. Heidrek was fostered out to the wise Gissur. One day Hofund held a feast but did not invite Heidrek. Heidrek decided to go to the feast any ways. Hofund did not bid him welcome when he arrived unannounced, but his mother and brother made sure that he got seated. Hofund, who was unhappy with Heidrek's presence, went to bed early while Heidrek sat and drank and caused all the guests to fight. The next morning Hofund declared Heidrek an outlaw. Hervor and Angantyr sought to change Hofund's mind but it was to no avail. However Hofund gave Heidrek good advice before he sent him away.

Hervor took the sword Tyrfing and gave it to Heidrek as a going away present. Angantyr went with Heidrek intending to go back after seeing his brother off. On the way Heidrek wanted to look at the sword and drew Tyrfing from its scabbard. The curse of Tyrfing came into effect and Heidrek killed Angantyr.

Hofund mourned Angantyr and sent men after Heidrek. But Heidrek evaded capture and joined a band of Vikings.

Heidrek, chief of his band of Vikings offered his service to the old King Harald of Reidgotaland, an area in present day Jutland. Two of Harald's jarls were trying to take his kingdom. Heidrek defeated the two rebellious jarls and won thereby half Harald's kingdom and Harald's daughter Helga as wife.

When Heidrek and Helga's son was born, they called him Angantyr. In the same year, Harald had a son and called him Halfdan.

Heidrek took an army south and went against the Huns. He was victorious over the Hun Chief Humle. When Humle fled, Heidrek took a great deal of loot. He also captured Humle's daughter Sifka. Heidrek kept Sifka with him and took her back to Reidgotaland. After a few months, Heidrek sent Sifka back to her father. There she gave birth to Heidrek's son and called him Hlod. He grew up with his grandfather Humle among the Huns.

Next, Heidrek wooed Olof, daughter of the Saxon King Aage. He asked Aage for Olof's hand in marriage. Aage said yes and so Heidrek and Olof were married.

Olof, who was now Heidrek's wife, went back to Saxony often to visit her friends. She always took Angantyr with her. One day, Heidrek came unexpected to Aage's hall. He found Olof asleep in bed with another man. Angantyr was asleep in the same room. Heidrek took Angantyr and went back to his ships with the boy.

In the morning when Olof could not find Angantyr, she became scared. She found a dead dog and put clothes on it and buried it. She told people that Angantyr had died. Shortly after, Heidrek came to the King's hall and inquired about Angantyr. Olof showed him the fresh grave. Heidrek had the grave opened and saw the dead dog. Then he brought Angantyr forth from his ships and told the King how he had found Olof asleep with another man. They searched everywhere for the man and at last they found him in the kitchen. He was a kitchen thrall. The thrall was set out to wander in the forest and Heidrek divorced Olof. But Aage and Heidrek were still good friends. Heidrek went back home with Angantyr to Reidgotaland.

When Heidrek was raiding Finland, he took a girl back home to Reidgotaland with him. Her name was Sifka, like that of his ex-wife.

King Rollo of Gardarike was a mightier and more distinguished than Heidrek. He had a son and a daughter, Herlaug and Hergerd. The boy was two years old, and the daughter was seven.

Heidrek went to a feast hosted by Rollo, King of Gardarike. There he saw Rollo's children. Heidrek asked Rollo to be the foster father of Herlaug. Rollo was not very willing to let Heidrek foster his son. But in the end Heidrek had the boy with him when he sailed home. Now when Heidrek went on Viking raids, he had Sifka and Herlaug with him.

Heidrek went to visit Rollo in Gardarike who was happy to see him and looked forward to seeing Herlaug so he put on a feast for him. Heidrek took only a third of his men with him while the rest he hid in the woods and left a few by his ships. Heidrek wanted to test Sifka's loyalty so he had Herlaug hide in the woods with his men. Then he told Sifka that he had been hunting with Herlaug, and that when he had drawn his sword, Tyrfing had accidentally killed the boy because of the curse. He swore Sifka to silence on the matter.

Sifka had promised to keep the secret but she went straight to the Queen and told her everything. The Queen, in turn, told King Rollo who became furious. He attacked Heidrek, killed his men and took Heidrek prisoner.

Rollo was about to burn Heidrek when Heidrek's men appeared from the forest and the ships and freed Heidrek. They ran down to the beach and sailed for Reidgotaland. Shortly after, Herlaug wandered out of the forest and into the King's hall and was reunited with his father Rollo.

Once in Reidgotaland, Heidrek gathered a huge army and went back to oppose King Rollo. Rollo, now that he knew Herlaug was alive, did not wish to fight Heidrek, so he sued for peace. Peace was negotiated and, as a result, Heidrek married Rollo's daughter Hergerd.

Heidrek stopped going on Viking expeditions. He now devoted his time to peace work. He did away with unjust laws, made new laws, and set up twelve judges, wise and honest men, to judge in difficult cases and disputes.

After Heidrek's mother Hervor died, Heidrek and Hergerd had a daughter. They called her Hervor after Heidrek's mother, and fostered her out to Ormar Jarl.

One day King Heidrek of Reidgotaland went for a journey in his kingdom. The first night they were to make camp on the Havar fields. Heidrek was riding a fast horse and came to the fields first, followed shortly after by a few guards and nine thralls. It was getting dark so tents were put up and they made camp.

During the night, while the King slept, the nine thralls quietly killed the guards. Then they stole into the King's tent and killed him with his own sword Tyrfing.

The next morning, the King's warriors arrived to find the King and his guards dead and the nine thralls gone. Angantyr had a huge mound erected over Heidrek and the men who died with him. Then Angantyr was chosen King of Reidgotaland, but he could not put away the thoughts about the murder of his father and it was never far from his mind.

Angantyr went away alone to search out and find his father's murderers. He sought in the kingdom far and wide. One day he came to a river where he saw some men fishing in a boat. One of the men caught a fish and hauled it in. The man cut the head off the fish with a sword. Right away Angantyr recognized Tyrfing and so he hid himself in the woods awaiting the right moment to make his move. When night fell, the men went to bed in a tent. Angantyr came out of the woods. He knocked the tent over and killed all nine men in it. He then returned home to hold a funeral feast for his father in the town called Danpstad, taking Tyrfing with him.

59 ANGANTYR

Angantyr's half-brother Hlod still lived with his grandfather, the Hun Chief Humle. When news reached Hlod that his father was dead, he rode with a large force to Angantyr in Reidgotaland. There he demanded his inheritance of half the kingdom. Angantyr was unwilling to give him half and instead said Hlod could have one third. Naturally, Hlod insisted on half so Angantyr said he would battle against Hlod before Hlod could get half.

The old man Gissur, who had been Heidrek's foster father, said that a third was rich for a thrall woman's son. Upon hearing this insult, Hlod became very angry and rode back to his grandfather Humle. When Humle heard from Hlod what Gissur had said, he too became very angry.

During the winter, Humle and Hlod sat in their camp planning to go against Angantyr. When winter was over, Humle and Hlod rode to different Hun tribes, gathering a huge army. Ormar's castle, where Hlod's sister Hervor still lived after being fostered, had to be passed by Hlod and Humle on their way to Angantyr.

One morning Hervor stood and saw the dust cloud of the massive army of Huns emerging from the forest. She sent Ormar to the Huns to invite them to battle on the plains south of the castle.

The battle was hard, and Hervor saw her warriors fall in droves against the superior numbers so she challenged Hlod to a duel. He refused because he did not want to fight his sister. He wanted to capture her. But Hervor fought on until she fell dead from her horse, blood coming from her mouth.

When Ormar saw Hervor fall he ran from the battle. He arrived at Angantyr's hall sorely wounded and related to Angantyr what had happened. Angantyr took his army south to meet Hlod.

Hlod had a mound built over his sister. Then he went on and met Angantyr at Dunhede. Hlod's warriors numbered seven times those of Angantyr.

The next morning, the battle began. Right from the start it looked as if Hlod would win. The battle went bad for Angantyr until the evening. Then warriors started to arrive to help Angantyr, because Angantyr had sent word far and wide as to what was happening. Night and day warriors kept arriving to help Angantyr. But by the fifth day, the Geats were still becoming discouraged. They fought only because Angantyr was unwilling to quit. Angantyr charged forward in berserk frenzy wielding Tyrfing and the Geats followed. That evening, Herlaug, Angantyr's foster brother arrived with a huge army. Little by little, the battle began to turn in favour of the Geats.

On the tenth day King Humle came face to face with Ormar Jarl. They exchanged great blows and Ormar Jarl fell. At the same time the old Gissur cut Humle down from his horse. Then Hlod and Angantyr met. They fought a long time until Hlod fell. Once Hlod fell, Angantyr called to the Huns for peace and the Huns accepted. Of the huge army of Huns that they began with, only three hundred remained and they were all wounded and exhausted.

Angantyr found Hlod in the field and set his corpse up on a throne. Then he went back to steer his kingdom in Reidgotaland and to mourn his sister and brother.

60 FRODE THE BOLD

After the death of Fridleif, the Danes held a Thing and unanimously acclaimed his son Frode as King. Because the King was only seven years old, guardians were assigned to him until he would reach the age of twelve. The brothers, Westmar and Koll along with Isulf, Agg, and eight other men were charged with bringing up the King and administering the realm.

Gotwar, Koll's wife, was a very strong willed woman experienced in bargaining and was determined to profit from the guardianship over the King. "So", said Khalle, "she wanted the power in Denmark."

"Yes", said the story teller, "she was the real power at that time. She was very good at making and breaking agreements.

Westmar had twelve sons, three of whom had the same name, which was Grep. These three were triplets. The sons were all excellent swordsmen and fist fighters. Frode gave the responsibility of guarding the seas to Odd, a son of Frode's brother Ole. King Frode's sister Gunwar was nicknamed 'the Fair' because of her great beauty.

The sons of Westmar and Koll were very courageous but also very reckless and wicked. They enjoyed holding orgies. They enjoyed ravishing other men's brides and daughters. They got away with everything they did because the common people were afraid of them and the King was powerless. One of the triplets, Grep, was stalking the King's sister, Gunwar. The princess was afraid of Grep. To get away from him, she went into a fortified building to live because Frode had 30 armed warriors guarding the building at all times.

In 376, the powerful Ostrogoth kingdom was destroyed by the Huns and the Ostrogoth King Ermanarik committed suicide just before the decisive battle. The Huns then drove the Visigoths across the Danube, into the Roman Empire. The Visigoths received permission from the Roman Emperor, Valens, to settle in Thrace, on the condition that they give up their weapons and their male children.

The Visigoths gave up their male children but kept their weapons. After they had settled in Thrace they began to wander into Roman territory. Conflicts with the Romans led to open fighting.

Since their invasion of Europe the Huns had not lost a single battle. King Frode's advisors had a meeting about the Huns. Gotwar presented a plan to make an alliance with the Huns so that they would not come north and destroy Denmark. The advisors all thought that this would be best achieved by having Frode marry the daughter of Balamir, King of all the Huns.

Frode did not want to marry any one. He said to Gotwar, "My father told me that it is not expedient to seek alliances far afield. He also said that love should be reserved for neighbours".

However, Gotwar proceeded to educate Frode on marriages and alliances until finally Frode realized that he had to marry to make a political alliance. Frode gave in to Gotwar's persistence and when he did, he asked Gotwar to go to the Huns on the mission of arranging the marriage. Gotwar said, "Me? No. I am too old to go."

Frode brought out a beautiful solid gold necklace and said, "If you will go to Balamir and ask for his daughter for me, I will give you this gold necklace."

Gotwar smiled and said, "I will accept this task."

Frode ordered Westmar, Koll, and all their sons to go with Gotwar as envoys to Balamir.

Gotwar and her entourage went east in ships. On the eastern shore of the Baltic Sea they beached the ships and headed south on horseback. After many days they reached the land of the Ostrogoths and searched for Balamir. They found a guide who took them to Balamir's hall. The hall was magnificent with carvings of dragons on its roof beams. Westmar said to Koll, "I know that the Huns are nomadic warriors. How could they have built such a grand hall?"

Koll replied, "They do not normally have great halls. This one was built by the Ostrogoths. It used to be Ermanarik's hall."

King Balamir greeted his visitors in a very friendly fashion and provided a delicious banquet for the ambassadors. Gotwar, Westmar and Koll did not disclose the purpose of their visit right away. Instead they enjoyed the hospitality and feasted with Balamir for the next three days. On the third day the princess, Hanund, made an appearance at the feast and greeted the guests with a little speech of welcome and was very friendly to them. Westmar stood up and made a light and jovial diplomatic speech in return. Everyone approved of his speech so much that he received a round of applause. He decided that this was a good time to state the purpose of their visit, so he announced that they had come to obtain the princess as a bride for Frode. This announcement was met with a stunned silence. After a moment the princess stood up and answered, "No, I can not consent to marrying Frode. He has no honour and he has no glory. No highborn woman would marry a man who has not won glory by admirable and heroic deeds."

The Danish envoys were surprised and confused, but Gotwar came up with a plan. She went over and sat with the princess, slipped some potions into her drinks, and told her about Frode's lineage and about the glory of his ancestors. The princess heard that Frode was young and had much potential. The next day, Gotwar sent Westmar, Koll, and their sons to the King and urge their mission again. She told them that if they were turned down, to challenge King Balamir to a fight.

Westmar left the hall and went with his warriors to the King's tent. He entreated Balamir to let him take his daughter back to Lejre as the bride of King Frode. He told Balamir that if he would not let his daughter go back with him, that he would have to challenge him to a fight. Westmar said. "I prefer to die fighting you than to go back in disgrace to Frode with my mission unaccomplished."

Then without another word Westmar drew his sword and threatened to aim a blow at Balamir.

Balamir looked Westmar in the eyes and replied, "It is unseemly for his royal majesty to meet an inferior in level combat, and it is not right that those of unequal station should fight as equals."

Westmar repeated his challenge so Balamir said, "Let us talk to my daughter and find out what she thinks about the matter."

The King sent for Hanund and asked what she thought about the affair. The King's daughter, now drunk and drugged, and full of stories about Frode's ancestors, replied, "Frode has no honour and no glory. But he has much potential. I expect that he will be a powerful leader who will win much honour and glory. He is descended from such a famous father. It pleases me that Frode is so young and has such a great and promising future. That is so much greater than his present lack of glory. I want to marry him and be a queen."

Balamir was astonished at his daughter's answer. But he was bound by his culture. His daughter had the freedom to choose her own husband.

With great pomp and ceremony, Balamir accompanied his daughter and Gotwar back to Lejre. There Frode married Hanund, the daughter of Balamir, King of all the Huns. After the wedding Frode gave Balamir much gold and Balamir went back to the land of the Huns.

In 378, the Romans sent envoys to the Hun King Balamir and made a treaty. The Huns also had a treaty with King Frode of Denmark, so they stayed out of Scandinavia and the Roman Empire and instead conquered tribe after tribe north of the Danube River.

After their treaty with the Huns, the Romans prepared to conquer the Visigoths. Valens, Emperor of the East, was unwilling to wait for Gratian, the Roman Emperor of the West to help them. Valens marched his army from Constantinople to attack the Visigoths ten miles outside the city of Adrianople. Before the battle began, the 20,000 men of the Roman cavalry and the 40,000 men of the Roman foot soldiers outnumbered the 50,000 Visigoth foot soldiers. Valens attacked the Goths while their cavalry was away on raids. The skilled and precise Roman legions and cavalry had the battle well in hand, when suddenly the Gothic cavalry, numbering 50,000 men, returned from their raids and charged the Romans at a thundering gallop. The Roman cavalry was then overpowered. This left the Roman foot soldiers powerless against the attacking Gothic horsemen. The Roman army was crushed and Valens fell. Roman casualties numbered over 40,000.

This defeat showed the Visigoths and the world that the Romans could be beaten. The last time Romans had been beaten that badly was during the battle of Teutoberger Wall, when they lost to the Saxons led by Herman in the year 9. The new Roman Eastern Emperor, Theodoseus the Great, negotiated an unstable peace with the Visigoths.

At Lejre, Frode lived in prosperity with Hanund. The sons of Westmar and Koll continued as before doing as they pleased and holding orgies. Day by day the actions of these courtiers became worse. They would catch some men and haul them up in the air on ropes and torture them as they hung, like tossing a ball on a string. They would put a piece of hide, attached to a rope, on the road and cover it with dirt. Then when someone walked on the hide, they would yank the rope making the person fall. With some people they would strip off their clothes and whip them so that they were full of red stripes. They would catch some men and burn off their beards with candles. Other men had their pubic hair burned off with brands.

Maidens were not allowed to marry unless they first had their chastity deflowered by the sons of Westmar and Koll. No man might give his daughter to wife, until he first had bought favour and consent with a bribe. Even after the marriages, the sons of Westmar and Koll came back to sleep with the wives.

Guests and strangers were treated with abomination. The sons of Westmar and Koll would pelt guests with bones, or force them to drink too much, sometimes until they burst. When guests tried to speak, they were mocked. The King did nothing to stop these activities and because of this the King became detested, not only by foreigners, but also by his own people.

Eventually Grep began to stalk Queen Hanund. He repeatedly trapped her and forced her to have intercourse with him. Grep punished those who even alluded to his activities with the Queen and thus kept it a secret from Frode. It was dangerous to accuse Grep yet whispers kept the rumours of Grep's crimes alive. Eventually Grep's relations with Queen Hanund became well known among all the people. All over Denmark people were whispering to each other about it. Grep kept himself close to the King and made sure that Frode would not find out about his affair with Hanund. It became so that people had to pay Grep in order to get an audience with King Frode. All the Danes thoroughly despised the ten year old, King Frode.

Grep was resentful of King Frode's sister Gunwar because she had rejected him but he hid his anger and hatred of Gunwar from everyone. Grep demanded the right to judge Gunwar's suitors, saying that the princess must make the best match possible. Gunwar had many suitors and Grep said that he would interview all the suitors of Gunwar all at once and he held a banquet for them all. The next evening when Gunwar entered her quarters, she found the heads of all her suitors neatly arranged on shelves.

King Gotar of Norway heard that the Danes were getting thoroughly disgusted with King Frode.

"Was Gotar King of all Norway?" asked Jorgen.

"No", replied the story teller, "In those days there were many small kingdoms in Norway. Gotar's kingdom was one of them. Norway was 'the north way' and was not a country. It was a route".

Gotar gathered his warriors and gave a speech. He told them that because of the situation in Denmark, that country would be easy to annex. He said that the Danes might even support King Gotar should he attack Frode.

After Gotar's speech, Erik, the warrior, made a speech. He said, "Men who covet other's belongings often lose their own. It takes a very strong hawk to take the prey from another. Although the Danes seem divided and hate their King, it will take only a threat from outside their kingdom to unite them and rally around their King. It would be wise to send some scouts to Denmark to determine the situation rather than risk all by approaching with a mighty army."

The speech of Erik amazed King Gotar because he had thought of Erik as a man of no importance. Gotar nicknamed Erik 'the Shrewd-Spoken'. Erik replied saying that a nick name should be accompanied by a gift. Gotar agreed and gave him a ship. The oarsmen called it "Skroter".

King Gotar picked Ravn to scout and make a raid on the Danes. When Ravn entered Danish waters with his fleet, he encountered Odd, Frode's nephew (Odd was the son of Ole Fridliefson) and was forced to fight them. Odd maneuvered his ships so that the Norwegians had to fight with the sun in their eyes. Ravn and many of his men were killed. Only six ships limped back to Norway.

Erik and Roller were sons of Ragnar the sea king, by different mothers. Roller's mother and Erik's step mother was named Kraka.

Roller made a vow to infiltrate the court of the Danes to see if the rumours about the Danes were true. Erik did not wish for his brother to go by himself, so he made a similar vow. King Gotar told the brothers to take whatever they needed for their journey.

First the brothers went to see their father, Ragnar who was an experienced old man to seek his advice. Since Ragnar was rich, he told them to take whatever cattle and gold they needed for the journey and they did.

Then Ragnar sent Roller to see his mother, Kraka, to see how she was doing. Erik went with Roller to visit Kraka, who lived in a little cottage deep in the woods. Kraka was a witch. She kept snakes and made potions from their venom. She welcomed the boys and gave them a meal. Along with the meal she gave them advice. She also entreated her step son Erik to always look after her son Roller.

Kraka accompanied the brothers back to Ragnar. Erik, Roller, Ragnar, and Kraka left for Denmark in a single ship, the Skroter. Soon after two more ships joined them.

As they were sailing down the coast of Jutland, they saw seven ships in the distance and knew this to be Odd's fleet. Erik had his ships lay at anchor while he consulted with Kraka and Ragnar about what to do. Together they came up with a plan. Erik had two of his men remove their clothes and ordered them to go to Odd and tell him that Erik had attacked them and had taken all their belongings. The two men went to Odd and were accepted by him as friends.

Odd had seen the three Norwegian ships and was planning an early morning attack because that was when he figured the Norwegians would be drowsy. Odd had filled his ships with stones to hurl during the sea battle. When most of the Danes had gone to sleep that night, the two men snuck back to Erik and reported all that they had seen and heard.

After consulting with Kraka, Ragnar, and Roller, Erik boarded a little skiff and rowed up to the Danish ships. There he bored holes in the planks of the Danish ships just under the water line. Then he rowed back to his own ships. He had not been seen nor heard by the Danes on watch.

While it was still night, Erik attacked the Danes with his three ships. Odd and his men were busy bailing out the water that was leaking in when Erik's ships bore down on them. Odd's flooding ships, full of stones, could not endure the battle. Odd and all of his crew perished.

After the massacre, Erik made a hasty retreat and landed on the island, Laeso.

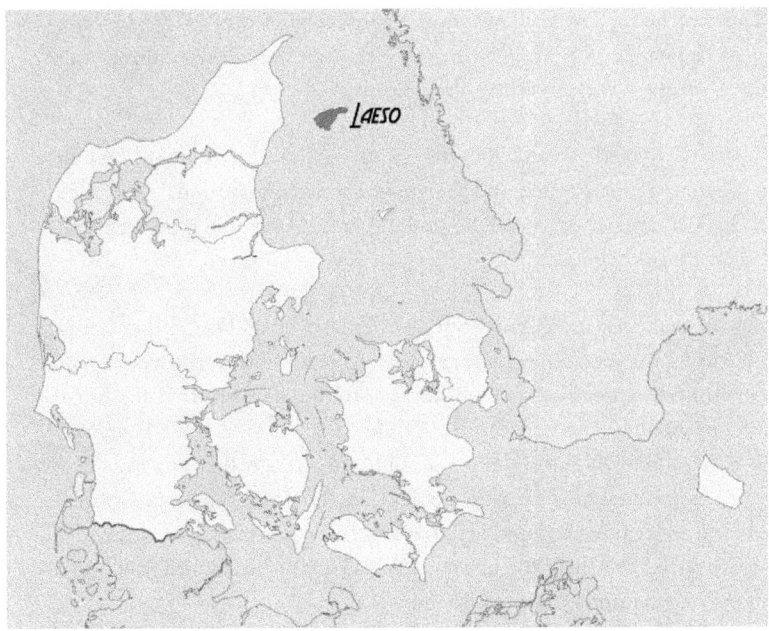

There was nothing to eat on the island and everyone was hungry. Since there was not enough food for everyone, Erik divided up the men and sent two of the three ships back to Norway with the spoils from their sea battle and tried to reach Lejre in a single ship. Ragnar and Kraka decided to go back with the two ships. The two ships were to return to Lejre later with provisions to last a whole year.

Erik sailed to Zealand and landed on the west coast. His warriors ran ashore and began to cut down cattle because they were famished. They killed a whole herd, skinned the carcasses and cast the carcasses on board. When the owners of the cattle found out what had happened they pursued the cattle thieves with a fleet.

When he saw the fleet pursuing him, Erik had the carcasses of the cattle tied with ropes attached to buoys and hid under water. When the Zealanders came up to his ship, he gave them permission to look about and search the ship. Unable to find the carcasses anywhere, the Zealanders apologized to Erik sailed off to look for new suspects. After the Zealanders had sailed off, Erik had the carcasses hauled out of the water and taken into the ship.

Meanwhile Frode had heard about the sea battle and that Odd and his men had perished. The news was spreading like wild fire. Nobody knew who had defeated Odd and his men. But people had seen three sails putting in to shore and departing again northwards.

Erik entered Roskilde Fjord and put in to the harbor of Lejre. As he stepped ashore, Erik tripped and fell tumbling on the ground. Erik took this as a good omen, because as he said, "there can be only a better result from such a poor beginning."

Grep heard that Erik the Shrewd-Spoken had arrived and hurried down to the harbor on horseback and attempted to insult Erik. However, Erik's retorts left Grep speechless. Grep became furious and spurred his horse back to the hall. He dashed inside, shouted that he had been beaten in words and roused all the warriors to fight to avenge this beating. But King Frode ordered the warriors to stay in the hall. Then he warned Grep that only a coward would attack a handful of men with an army and he forbade Grep to attack the visitors. But Grep persisted and finally got permission to attempt sorcery on them.

Grep went back to the harbor with a troop of wizards. One of the wizards carried a horse's head on a pole. Erik and his little band of men were coming up the road and saw the horse head on the pole with the band of wizards approaching him. Erik told his men to be wary and not to speak so that they should not be trapped by magic. Erik said that he was to be the only one to reply to the wizards.

They now reached a bridge crossing a river, with Grep and his wizards on one side and Erik and his band on the other side. Then Erik yelled out:

"May the weight of the burden crush the carrier! Let the gods bring us safety!"

Then it happened according to his prayer. The horse's head was shaken off the stick and crushed the wizard who had been holding it. The remaining wizards were so baffled that a single curse should be so effective that they immediately fled and dispersed.

It occurred to Erik as he proceeded towards the hall, that he should bring the King a gift. Therefore he picked up a piece of ice on the way and shoved it into a pouch and wrapped it into his robe.

As Erik entered the hall he stepped upon a hide, which had been placed, on the threshold. Some thralls yanked it from under Erik's feet and Erik would have fallen backwards but he fell into Roller who grabbed him and kept him upright.

Gunwar the Fair, Frode's sister, said that the King should not permit such a trick. But Frode said that a messenger should heed and expect treachery.

Havamaal:

"The man who stands

at a strange threshold

should be cautious

before he cross it"

It was mid-winter and inside the hall was a blazing fire. The fire ran the length of the hall. On one side of the fire sat the King and on the other side sat the champions. As Erik sat down with them, the champions made noises like dogs and howled. The King told the champions to stop the noise and that the sound of beasts should not be in the voices of men. Erik stated that it was in the way of dogs to all start barking when one of them started. He also added that all folk by their bearing betrayed their birth and revealed their race.

Koll, sitting on the side of the fire where the King sat, was the keeper of gifts given to the King. He asked Erik whether he had brought the king a gift. Erik produced the piece of ice hidden in his robe. When he handed it to Koll across the hearth he purposely released it into the fire making it look as if Koll had dropped it. All present had seen the shining fragment, and it seemed as though molten metal had fallen into the fire. Erik maintained that it had been jerked away by the carelessness of him who took it and asked what punishment was due to the loser of the gift.

The King consulted the Queen. She advised him that he must uphold the law, which he had passed. The law stated that all who lost presents, which were transmitted to him, were to be punished by death. Everyone else said that a penalty by law appointed should not be remitted. Therefore receiving advice that the punishment had to be inevitable, King Frode had Koll taken out and hanged.

King Frode proceeded to question Erik about where he came from and what his mission was. Erik answered that he was in the service of King Gotar but he was evasive so that no other real information was obtained. Then Frode asked Erik about his debate with Grep saying that Grep was not ashamed to openly avow himself vanquished. Erik said that Grep was riddled with shame for the adultery he had committed with the Queen.

Then Frode turned to Hanund and asked her whether this was true. Hanund gave a little cry, blushed and said that the charge was true. King Frode was astounded. Not knowing what to do, he stated that the Queen could choose her own punishment. Hanund hesitated not knowing what to say. Suddenly Grep ran forward with a spear intending to impale Erik. Instead Roller sprang between them with a drawn sword and killed Grep.

In response, the brothers of Grep sprang up and shouted that they would bring avengers on the whole fleet of Erik or fight him along with ten of his champions. Erik agreed to fight the brothers with ten of his champions provided Frode gave him the hide of an ox and three days to get ready. Frode laughed and taunted Erik by saying, "He who fell on a hide deserves a hide".

When Erik received the hide, he proceeded to cut it up and made sandals for himself and his men to fit over their boots. On the soles of the sandals he smeared a mixture of tar and sand. Then Erik negotiated the place for the fight. He said that he was unaccustomed to fighting on land and was not familiar with warfare of any kind. Therefore he wanted to fight on the ice of the open sea. To this all the parties agreed. Then Frode bade the sons of Westmar leave his lodging for the three days so that no fights would break out before the appointed day of the battle.

After the sons of Westmar had left, Frode turned his attention back to Hanund. He asked her what punishment she had come up with for herself for her infidelity. Hanund declined to give a punishment and begged the King to pardon her. Erik spoke up and said, "A woman's errors must often be forgiven. Punishment should not be given unless there was no other way to get rid of her fault." Seeing the wisdom in Erik's words, King Frode pardoned Queen Hanund.

Erik declared to King Frode that in the hall of King Gotar, when visitors arrived, a place at the table and rooms to sleep were always provided. So Frode gave Erik and his men the places of those champions who had just left. As Erik was eating, he wasted much food by casting it away and his men started to do the same. Then Erik would call for more food. Thus enough food for a whole banquet was consumed on a simple supper. The King was taken aback and said, "Do Gotar's warriors waste meat after once touching it, as if it were so many pared-off crusts?"

Erik replied, "Gotar maintains the highest manners and orderly conduct."

Frode said, "Your manners are not those of your lord, and you have proven that you have not taken your own wisdom to heart. He who goes against the example of his elders shows himself a rebel and a renegade."

Erik replied, "A wise man must be taught by someone wiser, for knowledge grows by learning."

Frode said, "You are making double talk, what will I learn from that?"

Erik said, "You will learn that a loyal few friends are a safer defense for a king than many traitors."

Frode asked, "Will you then show me a closer allegiance than my present advisors?"

Erik answered, "You have not yet had much experience. The hall of Gotar has not only drinking and feasting, but also the joy of celebrations."

Frode said, "Never before have I seen such a shameless beggar of food and drink."

Erik replied, "Nobody knows the wants or needs of the man who sits silent without speaking."

Then the King had his sister, Gunwar The Fair, bring a great goblet of mead to Erik. Erik caught hold of the goblet and Gunwar's hand at the same time. Then Erik asked Frode "Noblest King, have you granted me this gift? Is what I hold mine as an irrevocable gift?"

The King, thinking Erik spoke of the cup, said, "It is an irrevocable gift."

Erik drew Gunwar to him as if she had been given with the cup. Frode said "Erik, you are a fool Maidens are free and can not be given away like that."

Then Erik drew his knife and pretended he was going to cut off Gunwar's hand and said, "If I have taken more than you gave, at least let me keep some".

King Frode realized his mistake. But he could not take back his word. So he said, "I have indeed given Gunwar the Fair to Erik."

When it was time for the battle with the sons of Westmar and Koll, Frode decreed that no man should help either side. Then Erik and his men went down to the ships and on to the frozen sea. The sandals made by Erik for himself and his men kept their footing firm on the ice. The sons of Westmar and Koll were sliding on the ice on unsteady feet. Erik and his men were victorious without a single wound.

When Erik returned to the King's hall, he found an angry Gotwar eagerly wanting to avenge the death of her children whom Erik had just slain. She challenged Erik to a game of riddles. She wanted to wager her prized possession, the gold necklace, and she wanted Erik to wager his life. Erik accepted and won, so he got Gotwar's gold necklace.

Westmar then challenged Erik to a contest of strength in which the loser would forfeit his life. Again Erik accepted. The contest was to see who could drag away a plaited ring made of withy rope while they both held the ring. Erik wrested the ring out of Westmar's hands. Frode then said, "I think it is hard to tug at rope with a strong man".

Erik replied, "Hard indeed if there is a hunch on your back".

Then Erik swiftly kicked Westmar's crook on his back. Westmar's back broke and he died.

Frode drew his dagger, under the table out of sight, intending to throw it and pierce Erik. But Gunwar saw it and knew what he intended. She warned Erik who sprang from his seat and when Frode suddenly threw the knife, Erik side stepped. The dagger sat quivering in the wall where Erik had stood a split second previous. The whole hall was silent.

Erik broke the silence, "Gifts should be handed to friends, and not thrown. You would have made the blade acceptable had you given the sheath to keep the blade company".

Frode felt awkward and ashamed. To get past his awkward situation,

Frode at once took the sheath from his belt and gave it to Erik. Since the hour was late, Erik bade the King good night and went off to bed with his men.

Erik slept soundly and a little later woke slowly to someone shaking his shoulder. He became aware that it was the middle of the night. It was Gunwar who was shaking his shoulder. When she saw his eyes open she bent over him and whispered, "You must flee."

Erik woke his men and they all snuck down to the shore. There Erik cut away part of the sides of all the King's ships. He put the sides back on in such a way as that no one could see the damage to the ships. Then Erik and Gunwar, accompanied by Erik's men boarded the ship, Skroter, and put off from the shore a little ways. They could not sail completely out of the bay because of the ice.

King Frode gave chase in his ships, but soon the waves broke through the mutilated planks and all the ships started sinking. As the bows of the ships went under some of the men were swept into the sea by the waves and drowned. Some of the King's men did manage to get to land though. King Frode tried to swim off to the shore but was heavy with the armour he was wearing and quickly sank below the surface. Roller and Erik jumped into the water to save the King. Three times the waves dragged Frode under as Roller and Erik did their best to pull him back up. On the third try Erik dove deep and managed to catch a good hold of Frode by the hair.

Erik and Roller hauled Frode aboard their ship and had him sit by the fire. They removed his wet clothes and gave him fresh dry garments. After a while, when the numbness of the cold left him, Erik asked him whether he wished to sue for life and peace. Frode struggled to look up. Finally he did and said that he wished to die and that they had saved him in vain. Since the waves did not take him he would, instead, die by his own sword. He went on to list all the reasons that led up to this frame of thought. He stated that Erik had beaten him in wit; that he was terribly ashamed; his reputation was nonexistent; his people despised him; his men had done crimes behind his back; his wife was unfaithful; he had lost his sister; and that he was guilty of trying to kill Erik. At this point he was unable to hold back his tears. If Erik did not kill him, he would kill himself. But Erik talked to Frode about how fortunate he was being King of Denmark and about the things in life that he should be thankful for. He explained to Frode that he was there to help him.

After Frode had something warm to eat and drink, and conversed more with Erik, he regained most of his self-confidence and began to regard Erik as a friend.

With a new outlook on life, Frode ordered that they all go ashore. Once ashore Frode ordered that Erik and his men be taken in carriages to his hall where Frode called an assembly. Frode summoned Erik and under pledge of betrothal gave him his sister Gunwar the Fair, as well as one hundred warriors. He then announced that he was divorcing the Queen and wished to marry Alfhild, the daughter of King Gotar, and that Erik was to represent Frode as an embassy between the two kings to attain her hand for him. Next, he condemned Gotwar to death by stoning for her complicity in Grep's affair with the Queen. He announced that he would send Hanund back to her father because Frode would not have a traitor living amongst the Danes.

Erik voiced his approval of Frode's actions. Then he suggested, "Instead of sending Hanund back to her father, give her to Roller as wife. In Norway, Hanund will be no threat to you."

Queen Hanund then said "There is no need to grieve. I will accept this punishment."

She did not admit publicly that she and Roller had fallen in love. Frode had listened to Erik reverently, and said, "Let it be so."

The next day the two brothers were married, one to the king's sister, and the other to the king's ex-wife.

When the ice had melted off the Kattegat, Erik and Roller sailed off to Norway with their wives to bring back Alfhild to be Frode's wife. At home, they found that Ragnar had died and Kraka had remarried a man called Brak.

When King Gotar heard that Erik was back, he was not only afraid that Erik would be plotting against him, but he also wanted to marry Gunwar the Fair, despite the fact that Erik had already married her. Erik became aware of Gotar's intentions and called his group together and told them about it. He said that "a bundle not tied together would fall into little pieces". He reminded them that they had faced great trials before but were protected by the gods because of their innocence. Erik told them that their trials were not over yet and had to continue for a while, but that they would continue to persevere. He also instructed them to flee if they were ever attacked by Gotar.

When they were alone Erik asked Gunwar whether she had any love for Gotar. He explained to her his thoughts that Gotar was of royal lineage while Erik himself was not and it would be best for royal people to marry royal people. Thereupon Gunwar became upset and cried because she loved Erik and wanted to remain as his wife. Erik comforted Gunwar and told her that he loved her and that naught but death would ever sever them. Then he warned her that Gotar wanted to steal her away and pretend that it was done by Erik's good will. He told her that they would pretend to go along with Gotar's plan to marry her but that Gunwar was to hold back until Gotar had given Erik his daughter, Alfhild. Then he told Brak to lie in ambush not far from the King's hall with a chosen band of his quickest men.

Erik, Roller and Gunwar boarded Erik's ship, Skroter, with all their stuff, and fled. King Gotar, hearing that Gunwar was leaving with Erik, pursued them with his fleet. Erik's ship was slower because it was weighed down with his goods so when Gotar's fleet was close, Erik told his sailors to be ready.

Erik came about with his ship. Gotar came close and asked who the pilot of the ship was, and he was told it was Erik. Then Gotar asked if it was the same Erik who could silence the eloquence of other men by his speech. Erik replied that he had received the name "Shrewd-Spoken" and that he had not received the title for nothing. The ships beached at the nearest shore.

Erik asked Gotar for the hand of his daughter, Alfhild, for King Frode. Gotar agreed providing that it was a trade and that Gotar would marry Gunwar the Fair. Gotar suggested that Erik himself marry Alfhild and not go back to Frode. In this way, Gotar thought that Erik's loss of his wife Gunwar would not be the loss of a wife.

Erik praised the wisdom of King Gotar and said that the gods could not have shown better wisdom. Erik consented but asked Gotar to consult Gunwar on the matter. Gunwar told Gotwar that she would not marry him unless Alfhild was to marry Erik and she wanted the two weddings to occur at the same time. Erik negotiated some more with Gotar and was given the District of Leither as payment for going along with King Gotar's plan. Kraka, who had come with Erik, hid her head in her cloak so that no one could see who she was. When any one asked her, she said she was Gunwar's sister by the same mother but a different father.

The wedding feasts both took place in the same hall. But a wall had been erected to partition off the two feasts. The walls were all covered with tapestries. In one room sat Gotar beside Gunwar. In the other room, Erik sat between Kraka and Alfhild. As the party progressed, Erik worked a plank out of the separating wall large enough so that a human body could pass through. No one had observed him making the passageway.

During the festivities, Erik began to question Alfhild as to whether she would like to marry Frode instead of himself. She said that she would never marry against the wishes of her father. But Erik insisted that if she married Frode she would be Queen and, as Queen of the Danes be richer than any other woman. Kraka both assisted Erik in his persuasion of Alfhild and plied Alfhild with drinks containing her potions. Alfhild was at last persuaded to marry Frode because she wanted to be rich.

Gotar wanted to make sure the feasts went smooth and merry. He went from his feast hall over to that of Erik. As Gotar left his hall by the door, Gunwar slipped through the hole in the wall under the tapestry and took her seat next to Erik, where Kraka had been sitting. When Gotar saw Gunwar seated next to Erik, he wondered how that could be. Gunwar said that she was Gunwar's sister and that they resembled each other. Gotar hurried back to his hall to see if Gunwar was still there. When he got back to his own feast, Gunwar had slipped back through the hole in the wall and was seated at her seat. Seeing Gunwar in her seat, Gotar ran back to Erik's feast only to see Gunwar seated next to Erik again. As often as he changed from one hall to the other, he saw Gunwar in each hall.

When the feasting broke up for the night, King Gotar escorted Erik and Alfhild to their room. Then he went to his own bed, but he could not sleep because he was very suspicious of Erik and Gunwar. He got up and went out to examine the dividing wall in the hall of the feasts. But he found nothing because Erik had someone repair the wall earlier. Suspicious still, Gotar sent two men in the middle of the night to Erik's room to spy on him. Their orders were to kill Erik if he was with Gunwar.

While Gotar was fretting, Erik had put Alfhild in a different room and had gone to bed with Gunwar. After Erik and Gunwar were asleep, Gotar's two men crept silently into their room. When they heard Erik snoring, the two men stepped forward with drawn swords. They raised their swords to strike and Erik woke up. The startled Erik shouted his step mother's name, "Kraka!" as loud as he could. Erik's shield, which hung over head in the rafters, fell down with his shout and covered his naked body. The swords of the two men hit the shield. Erik caught up his sword from the floor and sliced both feet off one of the attackers. Gunwar, who suddenly had a lot of energy, ran a spear through the body of the other attacker.

Erik quickly gathered Kraka, Gunwar, Alfhild and his men. With the sound of Roller's horn alerting everyone to their escape, they ran down to the beach and sailed off in Erik's ship, Skroter. The sound of Roller's horn caused Gotar to think he was under attack and so he began to flee with his men. The sound of the horn meant something else for Brak and his men. It brought them out of the woods and they spent almost half the night pillaging and gathering up the goods of King Gotar and putting them on board Erik's ship.

In the morning, when Gotar discovered what had happened, he wanted to pursue Erik. One of the king's advisors warned him not to plan anything in haste. The advisor pointed out to the King that to pursue Erik to Denmark with so small a force and with such depleted supplies, because Erik had taken it all, would be a very unwise move.

But Gotar was furious and he pursued Erik with his small fleet anyways. When his fleet was just off the coast of Omni, the weather turned bad and a fierce storm blew in. The fleet turned and docked in the harbour of Omni.

While Gotar and his men waited for the storm to subside, they ran out of food. It was at that point that some of Gotar's men decided to mutiny and began to fight one another. King Gotar, with a few men, took to the cliffs and escaped.

Meanwhile, Erik and his small fleet had docked at Lejre where there was a big feast to celebrate the wedding of King Frode with Alfhild.

61 FRODE'S WAR AGAINST THE SLAVS

The Slavs were pillaging and plundering in the Baltic Sea, and were making raids against the Danes in greater and greater force as time went by.

A fleet of eight Slav ships were raiding in Denmark. King Frode commissioned Erik to suppress the Slavic raiders with eight ships. Erik had all but one of his ships covered with timbered parapets and covered with boughs of trees. Then he sailed up real close to the Slavs with just the one ship in order to get a good look. Since the ship looked somewhat like one of their own the Slavs didn't take notice of him right away. However, when they did finally realize that he was not one of them, the Slavs pursued him as Erik sailed back to the rest of his ships. Since they were covered in tree boughs, Erik's other ships looked like leafy woodland against the shoreline. Erik sailed into a narrow strait with the Slav ships close behind. The Slavs suddenly found themselves surrounded by Erik's fleet.

Erik put his ship in to shore and began to fling stones at the Slav ships. The Slavs tried to turn their ships to escape but they collided with the Danish vessels and were boarded. Most of the Slavs were killed.

On his way back to Lejre, Erik ran across a pirate ship stranded in the shallows. The pirates were trying to push their ship into deeper waters with poles. Erik took advantage of the situation and brought his ships in close and destroyed the pirates, taking all their loot as his own.

Now, King Frode had raised a mighty fleet of the Danes to go against the Slavs. Ships from neighbouring countries joined his fleet because the Slavs had been raiding those countries as well. King Frode also had a land army of horsemen from Jutland to fight against the Slavs. As the horsemen progressed they were joined by warriors from other countries bordering the Baltic Sea as they passed through those countries. As the land army accumulated warriors it became so huge that it had troubles making progress. So Frode had them build a road as they went. Trees were cleared, marshes were made passable and mountain chasms were filled with huge boulders and gravel.

Frode's fleet of ships also ran into difficulties. The sea was covered with such a throng of ships and crafts that there were not enough harbors on the east end of the Baltic where they were to land. The sailors set about building more docks. Erik split the fleet and sent some of the ships back for supplies and sent messengers to Frode to inform him of their progress.

When King Strunik of the Slavs heard of the huge Danish army working its way towards him, he became alarmed and sent envoys to ask for a truce. Frode refused and said that his enemy would not get a truce. Frode told the envoys that this would be his first war and he did not want to damage his luck since the man who conducts his first war successfully might hope for as good a fortune in the rest of his wars to follow. Erik applauded the King's answer, declaring that the Slavs had challenged the Danes with their raiding parties in the Baltic and deserved no truce. A furious battle unfolded between Frode's army and the Slavs.

When Strunik fell, the Slavs surrendered. At that time, Frode called a meeting of the Slavs. He said that any man among them who were experienced thieves, plunderers, or assassins should step forward and claim their highest rewards. Many of the Slavs stepped forward. Then Frode said, "Slavs these are the pests of whom you must rid yourselves". King Frode then ordered that the rest of the Slavs hang the men who had stepped forward.

Meanwhile, King Gotar still wanted revenge on Erik. He had spent his time collecting a great fleet of ships and he now sailed them towards Denmark. When Frode heard that Gotar's army was sailing towards Denmark, he equipped his own great fleet to go against them. The fleets arrived simultaneously at Renne's Island.

Gotar, who had underestimated the size of Frode's great fleet, became terrified at the sight of it and immediately sent ambassadors to negotiate peace. Erik told the ambassadors, "He who longs to win must struggle. Blow must counter blow. Malice must counter malice".

From these words, Gotar knew that there would be no quarter given, and he had his fleet attack Frode's fleet. King Gotar was unsuccessful and he fell in the battle.

After the sea battle with Gotar, Frode gave Gotar's kingdom, which stretched over seven provinces, as a gift to Roller. Erik also gave Roller the province, which had once been given to him by Gotar. Thus Roller became a king in Norway.

King Frode now spent several years in complete and tranquil peace. During that time he made laws for his people as follows:

Travelers Law:

(a) Seafarers may use what gear they find.

(b) No house is to be locked, nor coffer, but all thefts to be compensated threefold.

(c) A traveler may claim a single supper; if he takes more he is a thief.

(d) Thief and accomplices are to be punished alike, being hung up by a line through the sinews and a wolf fastened beside the thief.

Frode's Civil Law:

(a) The division of spoil shall be -- gold to captains, silver to privates, arms to champions, ships to be shared by all.

(b) No house stuff to be locked; if a man used a lock he must pay a gold mark.

(c) He who spares a thief must bear his punishment.

(d) The coward in battle is to forfeit all rights.

(e) Women to have free choice in taking husbands.

(f) A free woman that weds a slave loses rank and freedom.

(g) A man must marry a girl he has seduced.

(h) An adulterer to be mutilated at pleasure of injured husband.

(i) Where Dane robbed Dane, the thief to pay double and peace-breach.

(k) Receivers of stolen goods suffer forfeiture and flogging at most.

(l) Deserter bearing shield against his countrymen to lose life and property.

(m) Contempt of fyrd-summons or call to military service involves outlawry and exile.

(n) Bravery in battle to bring about increase in rank.

(o) When a pledge is promised, the one asking must pay a gold pound.

(p) Wager of battle is to be the universal mode of proof.

(q) If an alien kills a Dane two aliens must suffer.

62 FRODE AND BALAMIR

In the year 425, when Balamir heard that his daughter, Hanund, had been put away and given as a wife to Roller, he prepared to attack King Frode of Denmark. Balamir went about this by gathering, and equipping all the Hun tribes and groups. The Huns had been transformed because they had been assimilating the tribes they had conquered. They now consisted of not only the Mongoloid race but also Germanic, Ostrogoth, and many other tribes. This assimilation had made the Huns a stronger group to contend with.

Balamir sent ambassadors to Olmar; King of the Easterlings (Estonians) and after negotiations, Balamir and Olmar became allies. King Olmar had ports and ships at Ruthenia on the Baltic Sea, which Balamir needed to attack Denmark. Olmar started to equip his army and ships for the coming attack on Denmark and Balamir spent the year raising and equipping his army as well.

When King Frode heard of the preparations of Olmar and Balamir, he raised an army not only of Danes but also of Norwegians and Slavs. He sent Erik to spy on the enemy.

Erik went to King Olmar, who did not know who Erik was, and asked him, "Why have you equipped such a mighty war fleet?" Olmar replied, "We are going to attack the son of Fridlief. Who are you to ask such a bold question?"

Erik did not answer but instead he said, "Vain hope of conquering the unconquered has filled your heart. Against Frode, no man can prevail."

Olmar replied, "Whatsoever befalls must happen the first time. Often enough, the unexpected comes to pass".

Erik went south on horseback and after riding for many days came upon the Huns. He proceeded past the Huns and they proceeded past him in the opposite direction. Erik saw Huns as far as the horizon to both the east and the west. He asked some of the Huns, "Who has command of all these thousands."

Balamir heard about the man asking questions and rode up to Erik. He asked, "Who are you?"

Erik replied, "I am the man who comes from everywhere and is found nowhere."

The King of the Huns had an interpreter brought and asked, "What is Frode up to?"

Erik answered, "Frode never sits at home waiting for a hostile army. The wolf has never found its prey by lying asleep".

King Balamir perceived that Erik was a cunning speaker then said, "I think that you are that Erik who accused my daughter falsely".

Balamir ordered that Erik be taken captive. Erik said, "There is a lack of glory and honour to have one lone man dragged off."

Balamir was impressed and considered the matter. Then he let Erik go but not because of what Erik had said. He wanted Erik to go back to Frode to terrify him with reports of the vast Hun army.

When Erik arrived back at Lejre he reported that Olmar's fleet consisted of six kings each with his fleet. Each fleet contained five thousand ships. Each ship had three hundred rowers. Frode wavered in doubt as to what to do against so many. But Erik told him to raise his fleet and strike right away.

Frode and his fleet sailed off and subdued the islands lying between Denmark and the east. As they advanced towards Olmar's fleet they ran into a small Ruthenian fleet. Frode thought it shameful to attack such a small force with his huge fleet. But Erik said, "He who falls shall not fight against you again".

After hearing Erik's words, Frode was no longer ashamed of making an assault on the small fleet. Frode realized that advantage must be taken when possible. The small Ruthenian fleet was quickly wiped out.

Olmar's fleet was so large that it was hard to maneuver. Therefore, Olmar decided to wait for Frode to come to him. Frode's fleet began the assault by attacking the much larger fleet of Olmar. Although greater in numbers, the Easterlings did not have the skill and courage, which the Vikings possessed. The vessels of the Ruthenians were disorganized and because of their size were not easy to row. The small Viking ships outmaneuvered Olmar's large ships and the Viking warriors were more ferocious than Olmar's men. By the end of the day, Olmar was defeated.

All the Ruthenian Kings had fallen in battle except Olmar and Dag who, after defeat, swore allegiance to Frode.

Frode then summoned all the nations he had conquered and proclaimed new laws as follows:

(a) Every free householder that fell in war was to be set in his barrow with horse and arms.

A body snatcher was to be punished by death and the lack of sepulture. The body of a Jarl or king was to be burned in his own ship. Ten sailors may be burnt on one ship.

(b) Ruthenians to have the same law of war as Danes.

(c) Ruthenians must adopt Danish sale-marriage. (This involved the abolition of the Baltic custom of capture-marriage).

(d) A veteran, one of the Doughty, must be such a man as will attack one foe, will stand two, face three without withdrawing more than a little, and be content to retire only before four. (One of the traditional folk-sayings respecting the picked men, the Doughty or Old Guard, as distinguished from the Youth or Young Guard, the newcomers in the king's Company of House-carles.

(f) The house-carles (professional warriors) to have winter-pay. The house-carl receives three pieces of silver, a hired soldier two pieces, a soldier who had finished his service one piece.

King Frode asked Erik whether the army of Huns on land was as large as that of Olmar's fleet of ships. Erik replied, "I came upon a countless throng, a throng that neither earth nor wave could hold. Their campfires made it look as if there was a whole forest blazing. The flames told of numbers impossible to count. The earth sank under the fraying of horse hoofs. Creaking wagons rattled swiftly. The rumbling wheels of the chariots sounded like thunder. The earth hardly bore their weight. I thought that the air crashed and the earth was shaken, so mighty was the motion of the huge army. I saw fifteen standards flickering at once. Each of these had one hundred lesser standards. After each of these could be seen twenty and the captains in their order were equal to the number of standards".

Then Frode asked Erik how to resist so many warriors. Erik replied, "An army needs supplies. A huge army needs even more supplies. You must return home and allow Balamir's army to perish by its own hugeness as such a large force would need supplies in such proportions as they would be unable to find on their route."

Frode then left Ruthenia and sailed back to Lejre.

The Huns proceeded north and ran out of provisions. They could find food and supplies nowhere because they were passing through a huge swampy district. When they ran the risk of general starvation, they began to kill their beasts of burden for food. After consuming their beasts of burden they began to scatter, looking for food and supplies. Straying from the road caused some of their warriors to perish in the swamp. When they came to near starvation again, they killed some of their horses and all of their dogs for food.

At last the great army was worn out from hunger and the warriors started to die. Bodies were buried. Little by little, divisions started to desert Balamir. Then the army melted away by companies. Ygg, a man of unknown age, who had lived past the normal life span, also deserted Balamir.

As Frode's fleet sailed towards Lejre they ran into one hundred and fifty Norwegian ships fresh from the north. The commander of the ships, Hedin, a Norwegian prince, had his ships drop anchor. Then he cruised closer to Frode's fleet with twelve ships, signaling the approach of friends by a shield raised on the mast. Hedin joined Frode's army.

In the winter Frode distributed his warriors in the towns and carefully gathered in supplies needed to maintain his army. But a plague fell on Scandinavia and Frode's army suffered losses to match those of the Huns. Because of the plague, Frode took care to keep foreigners out. He sent a fleet, commanded by Revil and Mevil, to the Elbe River to see that nothing would cross.

Ygg arrived at Lejre. He was wearing grey clothes and a pale blue cloak. On his head he wore a wide brimmed grey hat."

"Odin", whispered Erik.

The story teller grinned at Erik, took a sip of beer, and continued, "Ygg told Frode what had been happening with the Huns.

Thirty kings followed Frode and were his friends or vassals. Frode saw that the cost of keeping his own army was getting harder to bear. He sent fleets out to get supplies. He sent Roller to Norway; Olmar to Sweden; King Onef and the sea king, Glomer to the Orkneys for supplies, each with his own forces. Hogni and Hedin decided to make some Viking raids together.

When Balamir heard that Frode's forces had been sent away, he mustered another great army.

In the fall Frode's fleets came back, not only with supplies and food, but also with a great number of more warriors. Roller had laid under him the provinces of Sundmor and Nordmor. Olmar had conquered Thor the Long, the King of the Jents and Helsings, and also had taken Estonia and Kurland with Oland. So Olmar brought back seven hundred ships, double those he had taken out. Onef and Glomer, Hedin and Hogni won victories and brought back an additional nine hundred ships. Revenue, food, and supplies gathered were adequate to maintain all the armies. They had also added twenty kingdoms to the sway of Frode in addition to the thirty, which he had before. All these kings were prepared to engage the Huns.

Hilda was the daughter of the Jutland Jarl, Hogni. Hedin and Hilda fell in love with each other and Hogni betrothed his daughter, Hilda to Hedin. Hodin and Hedin swore to each other that which of them should perish by the sword should be avenged by the other.

In 430, Frode and his army engaged the Huns in Russia. The fighting was fierce and continued for seven days. The three main rivers in Russia became so full of corpses that they formed a bridge. On the eighth day Balamir fell in battle and the line of the Huns gave way and was penetrated by Frode's army. The Huns surrendered to Frode. The massacre had been so great that for the space of a three days ride, the ground was strewn with corpses.

After the battle was over, King Frode called a meeting. He imposed a rule on the kings that they should all live under one and the same law. He set Olmar over Holmgard, Onef over Conogard and gave Revil the Orkneys. To Dimar, Frode gave the provinces of the Helsings, the

Janbers, and the Jemts, as well as both Laplands. Frode gave Estonia to Dag. Each king he burdened with fixed conditions of tribute. The realm of Frode now stretched all the way completely to the north, south to the Rhine, west to the Orkneys, and embraced Russia to the east.

In Jutland, people went to Hogni and accused Hedin of having bedded Hogni's daughter, Hilda before the marriage ceremony. At that time, this was an enormous crime in all nations. Hogni took his fleet to attack Hedin who was collecting the tribute from the Slavs. There was a fierce sea battle and Hogni was beaten so Hogni sailed back to Jutland.

King Frode heard about the battle and summoned both men. He inquired about the feud. Then he gave judgment according to the laws he had enacted. But this did not reconcile the two jarls. Hogni kept insisting that he should have his daughter back. Then Frode judged that the quarrel be settled by the sword since it seemed the only way to end the dispute.

The fight began and Hedin was grievously wounded. Hogni, who had an easy chance to kill Hedin, did not do so and instead he showed Hedin mercy. Hedin, with the help of his men, went back to his ships.

Hun Rua was chosen King of all the Huns. Hun Rua decided that it was futile to attack Denmark. In order to expand the kingdom of the Huns, Rua decided instead to go against Rome. But the Hun forces were much depleted after fighting the Danish Empire, therefore he first set about rebuilding the Hun army.

Frode decided to annex all the smaller kingdoms in northern Norway and attacked Norway with his fleet. Erik was in charge of the land forces. The Norwegians, when they heard that Frode was coming, fled and all gathered in Halogaland because they knew they had no chance of defeating Frode the Bold.

Frode pursued them and reached Halogaland with 3,000 ships. Here Frode battled them in a fierce and bloody battle. At nightfall both sides retreated. In the morning, Erik arrived from the mountains and the battle was renewed. The Norwegians suffered a mighty massacre. Frode had now annexed all of Scandinavia, but at a great cost. Of the 3,000 ships of the Danes that arrived for battle, only 170 returned.

63 OND THE CRUEL

When King Ond of Sweden was very old, he consulted a witch who told him that he would live another ten years if he sacrificed a son. Ond had ten sons so every tenth year he sacrificed a son. When he had only one son left, the people of Sweden refused to let him sacrifice his last son. Therefore that winter King Ond died in bed, a very old man.

Since this time, anyone who became old and feeble (including feeble minded) was said to be Ondsvag. Ond became a Scandinavian word for cruel. This is reflected in the song of the skald Thjodolf:

"In Uppsal's town the cruel king

Slaughtered his sons at Odin's shrine --

Slaughtered his sons with cruel knife,

To get from Odin length of life.

He lived until he had to turn

His toothless mouth to the deer's horn;

And he who shed his children's blood

Sucked through the ox's horn his food.

At length fell Death has tracked him down,

Slowly, but sure, in Uppsal's town."

64 EGIL

Tunne, a thrall, was King Ond the Old's treasurer. When King Ond died, Tunne took most of the treasure and buried it in the ground.

Egil was the surviving son of Ond the Old who succeeded as King of Sweden. Egil was no warrior and he mostly just sat quietly at home. When Egil became King, he had no respect for Tunne and he had Tunne sent back with the other thralls. Tunne resented his treatment so he organized a revolt and ran off with all the other thralls belonging to the King.

Tunne and his people began to live in the woods. They dug up the gold, which Tunne had buried. Sometimes they attacked farms, travelers, or small villages, killing and plundering. Outlaws and robbers flocked to Tunne, and his band grew.

When King Egil heard what Tunne was doing, he went out with his warriors to pursue Tunne's band of outlaws. One night, when the King had taken up night quarters, Tunne and his men attacked the King unexpectedly, killing many of Egil's men. King Egil set up his banner and organized his defense, but because Tunne's men were so bold and ferocious, most of Egil's men fled. The King had to run and try to hide in the woods with Tunne and his men right behind. Many of Egil's fleeing warriors were killed.

Because of his victory, Tunne became more popular with his men and more people joined him and they became bolder in raiding their own country.

Egil made his way back to Uppsala and raised another army. When he was ready, Egil again went searching for Tunne. They met in an open ferocious battle and Egil was once again defeated.

Eight battles were fought between Egil and Tunne's armies. Eight times Egil was defeated. Each time, Egil lost many warriors. Tunne became so bold that he attacked King Egil in Uppsala and drove King Egil right out of the country.

King Egil of Sweden went to Denmark and met King Frode the Bold at Lejre. Egil asked for Frode's help saying that he would pay tax to King Frode in return. Frode gave Egil an army and sent Erik with him.

Egil returned to Sweden with his new force. When Tunne heard about this he came out to meet him, unafraid. There was a great, ferocious battle and this time Tunne fell. Egil retook his throne in Uppsala and the Danes went home. Egil never did pay any tax to Frode. The two had become true, fast friends. Every year, Egil sent Frode great and good presents as a sign of his gratitude and friendship.

In the fall at Uppsala, a huge bull, destined for the fall sacrifice, escaped and ran into the forest and no one was able to recover it. The bull had gone rogue and began to kill unsuspecting travelers. King Egil was a great hunter and took it upon himself to track down the rogue bull. After a while Egil got separated from his men and eventually found himself alone and face to face with the bull. He began to ride up to the bull to kill it but the bull suddenly turned as the King struck it with his spear. The bull gored the King's horse and the spear was yanked free. The gored horse fell flat, throwing the King off. Egil sprang up and drew his sword but the bull gored Egil in his chest. At that moment the King's men then rode up and finished off the bull but Egil was gravely wounded and he lived for only a short time after. He was buried in a mound at Uppsala.

65 THE JUTES

When Angantyr, King of Reidgotaland died, his son Heidrek became King. Heidrek had two sons, Herebeald, and Heathcyn. It was expected that Herebeald would be King after his father but Heathcyn accidentally killed Herebeald with the sword, Tyrfing. Thus Hugleik was chosen as King after the death of Heidrek.

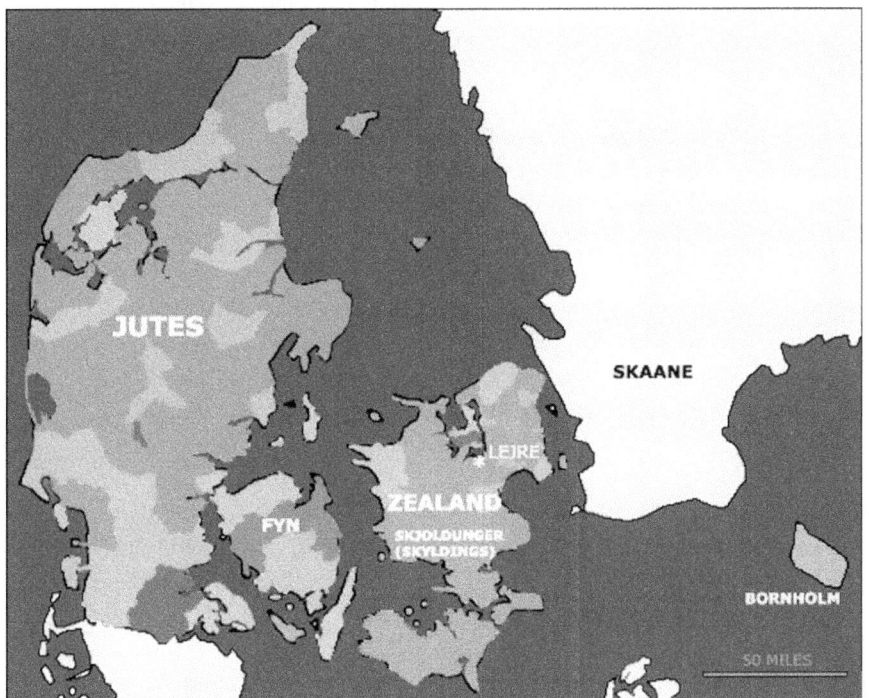

66 OTTAR VENDEL CROW

Egil had a son named Ottar who succeeded to the throne in Sweden. He was unfriendly to the Danes which bothered King Frode who had been good friends with Ottar's father.

Since there was no longer a friendship between the kingdoms, King Frode sent messengers to King Ottar, in Sweden, to demand the tax, which Egil had promised him. Ottar replied that the Swedes had never paid tax to the Danes and neither would he.

In response to this, Frode took a fleet to Sweden where he landed and ravaged the country. He killed many people, took many prisoners, took much booty, and burned a few towns.

After that, King Frode took a great fleet to the east to raid. King Ottar heard that King Frode was away, so he took a huge fleet to Denmark and ravaged there without opposition. When Ottar reached Zealand, he bypassed it because that is where Lejre was located. He had heard that there were many warriors on Zealand and he felt he was no match for them.

Ottar instead took his fleet westward to the Sound and proceeded along the coast of Jutland. When he reached the Lim Fjord he entered it and landed, plundering the Vend district (Vendsyssel). Ottar burned, laid waste, and desolated any area his army passed over.

The Jarls, Vatt and Faste had been charged with keeping Denmark safe while Frode was out of the country. When they heard that the Swedish King was laying Denmark waste, they gathered a fleet and proceeded up the east side of Jutland. Heathcyn had joined them in an effort to help keep Denmark safe. They entered the Lim Fjord and came unexpectedly upon Ottar. The battle began immediately. The Swedes fought ferociously. Many men died on both sides. Among the Danes who fell was Heathcyn Heidrekson.

The battle raged long and men continued to fall. But as Danish warriors fell, others took their place. Danish warriors were coming from all over the country. More Danish ships began to enter the Lim Fjord and take up the fight. The battle finally ended with the fall of Ottar and most of his warriors.

The Danes took Ottar's body and laid it upon a mound of earth in Vendsyssel (the Vend district). They let the ravens and wild beasts tear his body to pieces. Then they carved the figure of a crow out of wood. This they sent to the Swedes along with the runic inscriptions that their King Ottar was no better than the carved crow. Because of this, Ottar became known as "Ottar Vendel Crow".

Thjodolf, the skald sang of it thus:

"By Danish arms the hero bold,

Ottar the Brave lies stiff and cold.

To Vendel's plain the corpse was borne;

By eagles' claws the corpse is torn,

Spattered by ravens' bloody feet,

The wild bird's prey, the wild wolf's meat.

The Swedes have vowed revenge to take

On Frode's jarls, for Ottar's sake;

Like dogs to kill them in their land,

In their own homes, by Swedish hand."

67 ONELA

Ottar's brother, Onela seized the throne of Sweden. Ottar's sons, Edmund and Adils, were being fostered by King Gestiblind on the island of Gotland, east of Sweden. Onela wanted to kill Edmund and Adils and thus remove other claimants to the throne. However, he couldn't outright murder them so he devised to start a war with Gestiblind in hopes that Ottar's sons would die in battle. Onela raised a strong army and started a savage war with Gestiblind. It appeared to be only a matter of time until Onela would win, because Gestiblind was much weaker.

Gestiblind, who knew his army was weaker, sailed to Lejre and asked for Frode the Bold's assistance against Onela. Frode agreed and Gestiblind sailed back to the island of Gotland with a Danish fleet under the leadership of Skalk, the Skaanian and Erik. Gestiblind was determined to attack Onela with this fleet, but Erik thought it wiser to attack Onela's allies first.

Gunthion, Onela's son, was ruler of Wermland and Solongs (The Islands of the Sun). The Danish fleet attacked Gunthion first and Gunthion fell. Onela swore vengeance over the death of his son.

Onela summoned Erik secretly and implored him to refuse to fight for Gestiblind but Erik declined. Then Onela asked to settle the dispute with a duel between himself and Gestiblind. Erik said that Gestiblind was unfit for a duel because of his bad health and old age. Erik offered to fight in Gestiblind's place, explaining that it would be shameful to decline a duel on behalf of the man for whom he had come to make war.

Onela and Erik therefore fought a duel without delay. Onela was killed and Erik was most severely wounded. He did not heal for a very long time.

Gestiblind took Edmund and Adils to Uppsala where the Swedes hailed Adils as King of Sweden.

68 HALFDAN AND INGJALD

After the death of Frode, his two sons, Halfdan and Ingjald shared the Kingdom of Denmark. Halfdan lay at war with the Saxons. He had three children. The oldest was his daughter Signe who was married to the Jarl, Saevil. The two boys, Roar and Helge, were being fostered by Regin Jarl.

One night Ingjald surrounded Halfdan's hall with his warriors and burned it down with Halfdan and all his warriors inside. Thus Ingjald took Halfdan's half of the Kingdom as well as his own.

Ingjald wanted to get rid of any other claimants to the throne. Therefore he went to Regin to get Roar and Helge and have them killed. But Regin had heard of what befell Halfdan. So he had secretly brought Roar and Helge to the farmer Vifil. Vifil had an island with a little cave, which had been dug into a hillside to store vegetables in the winter. There he hid the two boys. The boys had the run of the island, which they thought was fun. The island was wooded and Vifil gave the boys coats made from wolf hides to wear. The hoods on the hides contained the ears of the wolves. Thus if anyone caught a glimpse of the boys, they would look like wolves or dogs. Vifil had two dogs called Hop and Hey. Vifil made it a signal with the boys, that if Vifil called his dogs, Hop and Hey, the boys were to run and hide in the cave.

Since the two boys were not found at Regin's place, Ingjald's men searched all over Zealand for Roar and Helge. Ingjald announced a great reward to anyone who could find them.

69 ROAR AND HELGE

After King Ingjald made a treaty with the Saxons, he had more warriors free to search for the two boys. Small bands of Ingjald's warriors roamed Zealand searching for Roar and Helge. Vifil had to call his dogs several times.

Very early one morning, Ingjald's men came to Vifil's farm. Vifil was already awake and saw them coming. He woke the two boys and sent them to the island. The warriors of Ingjald thoroughly searched the farm. They reported back to Ingjald that they had found nothing, but he was very suspicious of Vifil and sent his men back. Again they did not find the boys.

Vifil became very worried. He believed that next time Ingjald himself would come. He told the boys to stay on the island and to be sure to hide in the little cave if they heard him call his dogs.

In the afternoon, a long ship arrived at Vifil's beach. Ingjald had his men catch and hold Vifil, and demanded that Vifil tell him where the Halfdan sons were. Vifil told Ingjald that he did not know where the boys were and he begged that Ingjald release him so that the wolves would not eat his sheep. Then Vifil called his dogs, Hop and Hey. The King asked Vifil why he had called his dogs and Vifil said that he was just calling them so that they would now protect the sheep. Ingjald was angry and suspicious of Vifil and contemplated having him put to death. But he let Vifil go and left in his ship.

Vifil was now afraid to let the boys stay with him any longer. He sent them to their brother in law, Saevil Jarl. Roar and Helge called themselves Rane and Ham and obtained employment as servants of Saevil. They always wore hooded cloaks so that no one could recognize them. Even Saevil had not recognized them at first. Roar was twelve years old, and Helge was ten.

King Ingjald of Denmark invited Saevil Jarl to a feast. The invitation was sent mainly because Ingjald was suspicious that Saevil might be harboring Roar and Helge. Ham and Rane wanted to come with Saevil and Signe to the feast, like the other house servants. But Saevil said that they were to remain home.

After the entourage had left, Helge caught an untamed foal to ride and took off after the others. Roar caught another horse and followed Helge. Helge was sitting backwards on his horse laughing and carrying on. Roar rode his horse in a normal fashion.

Saevil and Signe were riding in a wagon. The boys caught up to them, and passed them. The Jarl could see that the boys could not manage their horses. As the boys rode by, Roar's hood blew from his head in the wind and Signe recognized him. She burst into tears and told Saevil what she saw. Saevil cautioned Signe to be quiet about it. Then he got on a horse and rode ahead to the boys and told them to turn back and go home, but the boys would not listen.

Ham and Rane showed up at the feast and ran about in the hall. Signe's warnings to them got no response.

There was an old witch at the feast. Ingjald asked her to divine the location of the Halfdan sons. The old witch-wife got out her rune stones and began to mumble things. At this point, Signe tossed a gold ring into the lap of the witch in hopes to bribe her for the safety of the boys. It worked and the witch then declared that her magic had gone wild and she could not go any farther. Ingjald was suspicious and threatened to torture the truth from the witch. The witch, who was terrified, gave in and announced that the Halfdan sons were in the hall disguised as Ham and Rane.

Ham and Rane immediately ran from the hall. Ingjald shouted to his warriors to grab the two boys. Regin, their foster father who was at the feast, now recognized them and quickly put out all the lights, while many of the guests moved forward and got between the warriors and the doors allowing Ham and Rane to escape. There was darkness and confusion.

Eventually, order and lights were restored in the hall. Ingjald thought that the Halfdan sons must have many friends and helpers to venture so boldly to his hall and he swore vengeance for this doing. Regin Jarl and his men now went about pouring more drinks for the King's guests. After a while most of the feasters were drunk and asleep.

Roar and Helge lay hidden in the woods near the hall. Later, Regin came out to them and pretended he was very angry and carried on as if he was going to beat the boys, in an attempt to get them to see the seriousness of their actions. However, Helge thought that Regin carried on like that because he had sworn an oath of allegiance to Ingjald. Thus Regin wanted to help but was bound by his oath. As Regin turned and walked back towards the hall, Roar and Helge followed. There was a small grove beside the hall that Regin walked passed. As he did so he said to himself "Had I something against the King, I would burn the grove".

From that Helge got the idea to set fire to the hall. They left only one exit. From this exit came Signe, Saevil, Regin and their men and many of the feast guests. Saevil promised to help the boys. They barricaded the only exit from the burning hall.

Inside the hall Ingjald woke up. He rushed to the door and begged peace with Roar and Helge. But nobody trusted him and nobody would let him out. Ingjald burned in his hall along with his warriors.

The Danes held a Thing and made Roar and Helge joint Kings of Denmark. Roar ruled the lands and Helge ruled the sea. At that time the Hardubards, a German tribe displaced by the Huns, was at war with Denmark. Helge's fleet kept the Hardubards out of Danish waters.

Roar built a trading town near Lejre. There were 24 brooks there and the town was called Roar's Kilde (Roar's Brook). It was later shortened to Roskilde.

70 HELGE

Helge went on Viking expeditions in the summers. One year he sailed his fleet to Stad in north Saxony where the ruler was a queen called Olof. Helge and his men went up to Olof's hall and invited themselves to a feast. Olof had not seen the ships pull into the beach and was completely taken by surprise. She had not had time to prepare her warriors in defense, therefore she put on a feast and entertained Helge and his men instead of making war with them.

During the feast Olof and Helge sat together on the high seats. Helge said that he thought the two of them should hold their wedding this very night. Olof was secretly reluctant and answered that she would have liked to have more friends about her on such an important occasion, but that because she had no time to invite them, she would have to do as Helge wanted. Olof ordered more drinks, and everyone drank most of the night away. So they were wed, but nobody at the feast could tell that Olof did not have the groom she wanted.

When most of the feasters had fallen asleep at the table, Helge and Olof went off to Olof's bedchamber. Helge was so drunk that he sank down onto the bed and immediately fell sound asleep. Olof took this opportunity to cut off all Helge's hair and covered his head in tar. Then she got some of her warriors to put Helge into a sack and had the sack put on his ship.

Olof went back into the hall and woke all Helge's men. She told the men that Helge had already gone down to the ships and wanted to sail right away while the tide was good. The men went down to the ships looking for Helge. They found him in the sack and released him. Helge was furious. He realized that his men were still drunk, and that Olof would have organized a defense of the hall by sending for more "guests". Therefore Helge sailed away.

About a month later, Helge sailed back to Saxony. He hid his ships a ways from Stad. He left most of his men at the ships and went into the woods with a small force. Then he dressed in old tattered clothes and went alone to Olof's place. In Olof's yard, Helge talked to the thralls. He heard from them about how Olof had been bragging about her insulting the Dan King Helge. Helge devised a plan. He selected one of the thralls and told him how he had found a treasure in the woods. The thrall followed Helge into the woods to a chest, which Helge had put there.

Helge opened the chest and the thrall could see that it was full of gold and silver. Helge offered to share the treasure with the thrall but the thrall said he was not allowed to keep it and that Olof would confiscate it. Helge then suggested that the thrall go to Olof and tell her about the treasure and that possibly Olof would reward him for finding so much treasure for her.

The thrall thought Helge's suggestion was a good idea so he ran back to Olof and told her about the treasure. Olof went alone with the thrall to the treasure because she did not want to share the treasure with anyone else. When she reached the place that the treasure was supposed to be , they found that it was gone. Instead, Helge's men jumped out from their hiding places, grabbed Olof and carried her off to the ships. At the ships, Helge apologized to Olof for his behaviour at the feast she had put on a month ago. He said that he wanted to make it up to her and give her a feast. They then took off in the ships with Olof. After keeping Olof with him for ten nights, Helge set her ashore near Stad, and continued on his Viking raids. Later Olof gave birth to a daughter. She called her Yrsa after her dog, and gave Yrsa to one of her thralls to raise.

In a battle between Helge's forces and the Hardubards, Frode, the King of the Hardubards fell. Ingjald, Frode's son became King of the Hardubards.

King Adils of Sweden had become very rich from his Viking expeditions. Adils went raiding against the Saxons that summer and went to Stad where Geirthjof was King. Geirthjof's wife was none other than Olof. Geirthjof and Olof were not at home at the time and so the warriors of Adils ran up to Geirthjof's hall and easily plundered it. Other warriors drove a herd of cattle attended by thralls, churls, and girls down to the beach. The cattle herders were also taken to the beach with the cattle and King Adils took them all to Sweden.

Among the girls was a remarkably beautiful girl called Yrsa. Everyone was impressed with Yrsa. She spoke well, was highly intelligent and very well behaved. Adils was also very impressed with Yrsa and decided that she could not be a slave girl, so he married her.

Helge Halfdanson came with his fleet to Uppsala. Helge's army was so great that Adils fled at once. Helge landed with his army, plundered and took booty. Helge caught Yrsa and took her back to Lejre where he married her, not knowing that she was in fact his own daughter. Helge and Yrsa had a son and they called him Rolf. They also had a daughter and called her Rut.

Queen Olof of Saxony one day sailed to Lejre. Olof sent a messenger to Queen Yrsa that she would like to meet with her and Yrsa agreed. Olof asked Yrsa if she was happy with her marriage. Yrsa said that she was the happiest woman in the world, and that she was married to the most famous King in the north. Olof then told Yrsa the story of Helge and herself and told Yrsa that not only was Helge her husband but also her father. Olof told Yrsa that she was Olof's revenge on Helge. Yrsa replied that she thought Olof was the wickedest woman in the world. Then she burst into tears and ran back to the hall.

Yrsa ran straight to Helge and told him what Olof had said. Helge was shocked. After thinking it over he decided that they should stay together. Yrsa, however, could not live in this relationship and went back to Adils in Uppsala.

Helge went into a deep depression and withdrew all contact from people. At night he slept in a little shed out in the back of the King's yard. Since Helge was inactive, the Hardubards became bolder and began raiding in Denmark again. Roar was quite worried about his brother who, after many months, still shunned contact with people and slept in the little shed.

At midwinter time during the Jule (Christmas) feasts, Helge was in bed and the weather outside was really bad. Someone came to the door of the shed and tapped weakly on it. Although Helge was avoiding contact with people, it occurred to him that it was unkingly of him to allow any person, however wretched to remain outside when he could help. Helge got up and opened the door. He saw someone or something poor and tattered standing outside.

The thing said, "You have done well, King" and went inside.

Helge said, "Take some straw and a bearskin for yourself so you will not freeze".

The visitor said, "Let me into your bed, Sire. I want to sleep next to you, for my life is at stake".

Helge replied, "You repel me, but if it is as you say, then lie down here along the side of the bed. Keep your clothes on, and you will not come to any harm".

She did as the king said. Helge lay down beside her and turned away. After a time, Helge woke. There was still light from the fire. Helge was curious and glanced over his shoulder at his visitor. What he saw was a sleeping woman so fair that he thought he had never seen anyone so beautiful. Her tattered clothes had come off her during the night. Quickly and tenderly he turned towards her.

In the morning, the visitor said, "Now I will leave. You have released me from a terrible bondage, which was my stepmother's curse. I have visited many Kings, but none of them accepted me because of my looks. I do not want to stay here any longer".

"No", said the King, "There is no possibility that you may leave so soon. We will not part that way. I will arrange a quick wedding for us because you please me well".

She said, "You are the one to make the decision, my lord".

That night they slept together.

In the morning, the woman said to Helge, "We have slept together because of your lust, and you know that we will have a child. Do now as I tell you King. Visit our child next winter at this same time down at your ships' landing. Unless you do so, you will pay for it".

The woman then went away. Since then Helge had lost most of his depression. Helge took his fleet out and battled the Hardubards until they had been driven out of Danish waters. Then he took up Viking raiding. Helge was now sailing his fleet and going on raids as before. That winter, Helge forgot to go down to his ships.

Although Helge was somewhat out of his depression, he still slept in the little hut. One midnight that winter, three people rode up to Helge's hut. They brought a girl child with them and put her down outside the hut.

Helge came out of his hut, and the woman who had been holding the child said, "You must know, King, that your kinsmen will pay for ignoring my request. Nevertheless you will reap a benefit for having released me from my curse. Be aware that the girl is named Skuld and is our daughter".

The three people then rode away. Helge never saw nor heard of the woman again. He concluded that she must be an elf woman. Skuld turned out to be a child with a vicious temperament.

The next spring, Helge planned to set out on a voyage to forget his sorrows, and asked his brother Roar to look after Rolf, Rut, and Skuld. Helge left Lejre with a fleet of ships. He decided to go to Uppsala and take Yrsa back with him. When Adils heard that Helge was on his way to Uppsala, he asked Yrsa how he should receive him. Yrsa told him to do what he wanted but to remember that there was no one to whom she was more related. Adils then had a big feast prepared. Yrsa wished that Adils and Helge could be friends, but Helge's love for Yrsa flared up. Helge talked only to Yrsa and at every opportunity and almost completely ignored Adils.

Adils had twelve berserkers. The berserkers just arrived from a Viking expedition. Adils had them hide in the woods and instructed them to attack Helge when he had left the hall.

After Helge and his followers left the hall, they were attacked on their way to the ships. While Helge and his men fought the twelve berserkers, Adils attacked Helge from behind with his army. Helge fought hard but fell with many wounds. All Helge's men were cut down. The few of Helge's men, who had remained at the ships, set sail for Denmark.

Yrsa did not know about Helge's death until Adils began to brag to his people about it. Yrsa was shocked and became furious. She said that she would never take his side in any doings with the Skjoldungers at Lejre. Adils gave Yrsa many presents to try to overcome her grief and anger. Yrsa did settle down a little, but from then on she was not on good terms with Adils and was always arguing with him.

The story teller paused and drained his mug of beer. Thorhild promptly refilled it. The story teller sipped his beer and then continued his story.

71 ROAR

Roar made peace with Ingjald the King of the Hardubards. To seal the peace treaty, Ingjald married Roar's daughter, Freyvor. She went to the land of the Hardubards with a small group of the Danish warriors.

When the Hardubard warriors saw the Danish warriors sit so close to their King, they did not like it at all. The Hardubard warriors complained loudly and argued with the Danes. Freyvor tried to calm the warriors down. She gave a ring to the greatest and loudest of the Hardubard warriors and spoke words of friendship to him. Instead this just angered the warrior and he became full of rage and hurled the ring away, yelling to Ingjald, "In your father's days, we never sat at the table drinking with our enemies and your father's killers. But you set your enemies higher in status than your own men. You sit calm in your chair while the Danes bear the weapons and rings in your own house that your father lost when the Danes cut him down and plundered his treasures!"

The warrior kept yelling and emotions boiled up amongst the men until one of the Hardubards cut down one of the Danes. Freyvor wanted vengeance and justice for the death of the Dane. But Ingjald protected the killer and let him escape.

The Hardubard warriors gave no peace to Ingjald. They did not want peace with the Danes. They wanted revenge. At last Ingjald gave in to his warriors and he assembled a great fleet and sailed to Lejre to take vengeance for Helge killing his father. Roar brought his army out in front of Lejre's gates to meet them in battle. There Ingjald died along with most of his warriors. The Hardubards no longer existed as a tribe.

72 BEOWULF (BJORNULV) (BEARWOLF)

Roar built a great hall at Lejre. It was the greatest and largest hall in Scandinavia. It was 48.3 meters in length and 11.5 meters in width. The beams were exquisitely carved and it was inlaid in gold and silver. The hall was named Hjort and was magnificent and beautiful in appearance.

A band of Jotuns arrived in Zealand and were killing the farmers at night. Roar sent out warriors to search for them but many of the warriors never returned.

A hush had fallen over the audience, and the story teller continued, "One night, the Jotun leader, Grendel, brought his warriors into Hjort. The next morning, the hall was soaked in blood and many of the King's best warriors were missing. Grendel came out of the marshes night after night. Finally Roar realized that he was powerless against Grendel, and sent envoys to King Hugleik's court in the land of the Geats (southern Jutland) for help. Hugleik's nephew, Beowulf gathered young warriors and sailed to Lejre to take up the fight against Grendel.

When it was darkest night, Grendel rose up from the swamp where he dwelt and went to Hjort where the Geats were waiting for them. In the first skirmish, Grendel lost an arm. In spite of this setback, more of Roar's men were killed and the hall was sprayed with blood. The next morning, the Geats followed the trail of the Jotuns. They found Grendel dead from the wound he had suffered. That night there was a feast in Hjort to celebrate the death of Grendel.

Soon Grendel's mother continued the raids and picked up where her son had left off. Roar was not free of the Jotuns yet. When the raids started up again, Beowulf went to the marshes and finally found the lair. It had an underwater entrance at the bottom of a lake. Here he killed Grendel's mother with her own sword. When Beowulf returned to Lejre, there was a great celebration, and Beowulf received great presents. The next day he returned home.

73 ROLF

Roar's son Horek expected to inherit the Kingdom of Denmark. Horek was jealous of his cousin Rolf's popularity and abilities. Since he was also afraid that during a Thing Rolf might get elected as King, he went to his father and told him that he was afraid that Rolf would make himself King after Roar died. He asked his father to show him favour by giving him the Skjoldung heirloom, a wonderful ring. But Roar would not agree to it because he felt that the ring possessed good luck. He said that he would wear the ring himself as long as he lived. Then Horek asked Roar to show him the ring. Roar took the ring from his arm and handed it to Horek. After a few moments of examining the ring closely, Horek said, "I have never seen a better ring and I can understand why you put great value on it. Now it is best that none of us have it and that no one else have it either". With that, Horek hurled the ring far out into the depths of the ocean where it sank to the bottom. This made Roar very depressed and he thought that the Skjoldung luck had been broken.

When Roar died, Rolf decided that it would not be in the interest of Denmark to oppose Horek's ascension to the throne. Instead Rolf went on Viking cruises and became a Sea King. Skuld, Rolf's half-sister married King Hjarvard of Oland, which is an island off the south eastern coast of Sweden.

One of King Horek's great loves was to accumulate gold. He sat at home in Hjort and raised taxes to build up his hoard of gold and silver and when his warriors came back from Viking raids he taxed their booty. The people grew tired of being taxed all the time and came to hate King Horek.

Horek's warriors grumbled that Horek was not like the old Skjoldungs who were quick with their weapons and generous with their riches. More and more of the Danish warriors sailed away to follow Rolf. The neighbouring countries began to laugh at Denmark with its gold hungry King who made the people poor.

The warriors, who joined Rolf, pleaded with him to go back to Lejre and take the kingdom. Finally Rolf sailed his fleet back to Lejre to have it out with Horek.

When Horek heard that Rolf was back, he went to wait for Rolf at the gates of Lejre with all his chests of gold. Rolf arrived at the gates to find

Horek with all his chests of gold wide open and gleaming in the sun. Horek told Rolf that he could take all the gold he wanted from the chests if he would only sail away and leave him in peace. Rolf replied that "men do not fight with gold but with weapons". He told Horek to either engage him in a fight or to leave Lejre in shame.

Horek packed up all his treasures and went back to Hjort to assemble his army. But no one wanted to go and fight for him. It was then that Horek realized that in order to save his dignity he had no choice but to challenge Rolf to a duel. He gathered his courage and went back to Rolf and challenged him. So there it was at the gates of Lejre, that Rolf felled his cousin Horek.

Rolf's first act after slaying Horek was to take all of Horek's gold and distribute it amongst the warriors. The warriors then hailed Rolf as King of all of Denmark. Rolf immediately lowered all the taxes and set up provisions for the care of the elderly and the sick. Thus began the golden age in Denmark.

Famous warriors began to show up at Lejre to go into service for Rolf. It wasn't long before Rolf had twelve berserkers serving as his bodyguard. One of his berserkers was Svipdag who used to serve the Swedish King Adils but had fallen out of favour with Adils. Svipdag wound up fighting King Adil's twelve berserkers and escaped them, but lost an eye while doing so.

Rolf's warriors were feared fighters who at times would bully weaker warriors. Rolf tried to stop them but it was in vain. The berserkers ridiculed Svipdag when he first arrived, thinking that he was of no significance. Svipdag, knew these types of men so he knew just what to do. He immediately confronted the mouthiest berserker claiming that he had insulted him and therefore must fight him in a duel. At the sound of this challenge all the berserkers rolled on the floor laughing.

The duel was short. Svipdag, who had fought Adil's twelve berserkers, quickly and easily killed his antagonist. With that Svipdag had earned the respect of the other berserkers and then took his place as one of Rolf's twelve berserkers.

74 ROLF KRAKE

One day, a poor youth, dressed in rags, wandered into Hjort. He looked at the very tall and thin Rolf sitting in his high seat. The young man burst out in poetry describing King Rolf. He called Rolf a "krake" (a very old tree standing with no branches on it, "a chico").

Rolf liked the youth and chose to adopt this name that had been bestowed upon him. From then on Rolf was known as Rolf Krake. Rolf asked the youth his name and was told that it was Viggo.

Rolf said to Viggo, "It is customary for the giver of a name to give a gift to go with it. But because you have nothing, I am giving you a present."

Rolf gave Viggo a gold arm ring. Viggo placed the ring on his right arm and proudly held his right arm up in the air while his left arm he hid behind his back. Rolf asked Viggo why he hid his left arm. Viggo answered that his left arm was ashamed to be seen because of the ring on his right arm. Rolf laughed at this in amusement and then made sure that Viggo's left arm was not ashamed by giving him a second gold arm ring. Viggo was so overcome by the generosity of Rolf Krake that he swore an oath that should Rolf fall in battle, he would avenge his death. The warriors hid their chuckles. They found it funny that so young a boy should make so lofty a vow.

75 HOTT

There was a farmer on Zealand who had many sons and the youngest was a handsome lad named Hott. He worked hard on the family farm and when Hott came of age, he considered his situation. As the youngest son, he would never inherit the farm. Therefore he must do something else with his life. After thinking about it for a long while he came up with a plan. Hott decided to go into service for the King.

One morning he rose from sleep and after breakfast shared his decision with his mother and father. His father was very understanding and his mother tearfully packed him a lunch. While it was still morning Hott left the farm and walked on the road leading to Lejre.

As he walked he listened to the meadow larks singing. The path led past many farm fields. In one of the fields a stork was hunting snakes. When it was noon, he was walking through a forest of oak where the song birds were whistling and warbling. He paused to eat his lunch.

After eating lunch, Hott walked until he came out of the forest. He paused and looked at the scenery. Fields of grains and grasses were everywhere. As he proceeded along the road, he saw some fields with grazing cows and some with goats. Here and there along the road were farm houses made of wood with thatched roofs. In the distance was the town of Lejre.

When Hott came closer to Lejre, he could see the magnificent Hall called Hjort. Hott entered Lejre and walked up the main street towards Hjort. People were moving in the street. Occasionally a horse drawn wagon passed him. The rows of houses stopped and a clear space of about one hundred yards separated the houses from the hall. The hall had intricate carvings in its structure and it was inlaid in gold and silver.

"It is the most magnificent hall in the North" said a female voice.

Hott turned slowly and found himself looking into the big blue eyes of a young woman in her teens. Hott was speechless at the beauty of the woman. The woman giggled and smiled at him. At last he said, "Oh my name is Hott and I have come to go into the service of the King."

"Ah" said the woman, "a mighty warrior! The greatest warriors of the north come to serve King Rolf."

Hott was embarrassed to be compared to the greatest warriors in the north. He was too shy to ask the woman her name.

"I have to get back to my work." said the woman. Then she turned and entered the nearest house.

Hott proceeded to the hall. At the entrance a guard asked him what his business was. Hott said, "My name is Hott and I have come to go into the service of the King".

The guard stared at Hott for a minute. Then he burst out laughing. Hott entered the hall which was deserted. He found a seat near the entrance and sat down.

In the evening, serving maidens brought food and put it on the tables. A short time later Rolf and his warriors entered the hall. They noticed Hott seated at the lowest bench. As the supper progressed, the warriors began throwing bones at Hott. At first it was small bones. Then the bones thrown were larger and larger. "Watch this" yelled a burly warrior and hurled a huge knuckle bone at Hott. It knocked Hott to the ground and the laughter of all the warriors echoed from the walls.

76 BJARKE AND HJALTE

Meanwhile, Bodvar, son of King Bjorn (Bear) Ringson in Norway, was restless and decided to wander. He obtained passage on a ship going south. Bodvar arrived at Zealand not far from Lejre. A cold rain was being driven by a strong wind and his horse was tired. Through the falling rain, Bjarke saw the outline of a farm house. He rode slowly up to the house, got off his horse and knocked on the door. When the farmer opened the door, Bodvar begged him for shelter for the night. The farmer invited Bodvar in and they stabled the horse.

During the evening meal, Bodvar explained that he was on his way to serve the King and asked about King Rolf Krake and his men. The farmer's conversation was very informative but his wife was crying as he talked. Bodvar asked her what the problem was. The woman replied, "Our youngest son, Hott has gone to Lejre to serve the King. But the warriors bully him and sat him in a pile of bones accumulated from their meals. They throw bones at him for target practice."

The farmer's wife sobbed some more. Then she said, "We do not know whether he is dead or alive anymore. I ask you as thanks for this supper that if he is alive and you see him there, that you throw only small bones at him."

Bodvar exclaimed, "As pay for the hospitality you have given me I will take care of Hott."

The next day, Bodvar went to Lejre, got his horse stabled, and entered the King's magnificent hall called Hjort. There were only a few men in the hall. Bodvar sat on the bench near the entrance. After he had been there a short time, he heard a noise coming from a huge pile of bones lying in a corner. A very black hand emerged from the huge pile of bones.

Bodvar walked over to the pile of bones, grabbed the hand and yanked Hott out scattering the pile of bones. Hott screamed, and exclaimed that he would now be killed during the next meal.

Bodvar told Hott to be quiet, picked him up, and carried him to a nearby lake. Bodvar washed Hott in the lake and when he was completely clean, he led Hott back to Hjort where he sat down in his previous seat. He had Hott sit down beside him. Hott was trembling with fright.

Late in the evening, Rolf's warriors entered the hall. They noticed that Hott was now seated at the table and thought that the man who had caused this was indeed brave. Afraid for his life, Hott tried to scramble back to his bone pile. But Bodvar held him tight so that he could not move.

As the supper progressed, the warriors gave in to their habit of throwing bones. They began to throw bones at Hott and Bodvar. At first it was small bones. Bodvar acted as if he did not notice. But Hott was so frightened that he neither ate nor drank. He expected to be hit by a large bone at any minute. The warriors were having a great time joking at Hott's expense and laughing so loud that their voices echoed from the rafters and the walls. Then a warrior said, "Watch this."

He aimed a huge knuckle bone at Hott and threw it with all his might. But Bodvar caught it in mid-air and hurled it back at the thrower. The bone hit the warrior so hard that he fell over dead. A dreadful silence followed. The King's men, struck with fear, stopped throwing bones.

A short time later, the King entered the hall with his berserkers. The King's men told him that the man in the corner had killed one of his men and that they wanted him put to death.

Rolf insisted on hearing the whole story and was informed about how his warrior had died. He did not want to put the stranger to death and declared that the dead warrior was not altogether innocent. Then he asked Bodvar for money to pay the vergeld for having killed a man. Bodvar explained that he did not have money to pay for that. So Rolf decided that the solution to this would be to take Bodvar into his service to replace the warrior who had been killed. Bodvar agreed but refused to be separated from Hott.

At the table Bodvar chose a place much closer to the king than before. When he pulled three men out of their seats and seated himself and Hott there, the men resented it but did not dare go against him.

When Jule tide drew near, the men became gloomy. Bodvar asked Hott if he knew the reason for it. Hott said, "A huge animal has been coming every year at about this time and feeds on the King's livestock. The men who have gone to hunt it have never returned".

One night the animal invaded the King's barn and carried off a heifer.

Bodvar took Hott with him as he followed the tracks of the animal into the woods. The tracks were those of a giant bear, the size of which they had never seen before. When they found the animal, it was the biggest bear Bodvar had ever seen.

When the bear saw them it lunged at them in an attack. Hott fell to the ground in fright but Bodvar killed the bear with his spear. Once the bear was dead Bodvar grabbed Hott from off the ground and forced him to drink of the bear's blood. When a shocked Hott had drunk enough blood according to Bodvar, he was told that now he was transformed because part of the spirit of the bear had entered him and that he now had the courage and strength of the bear. The thought of this gave Hott renewed confidence in himself and he started to feel a new sense of self-worth. Bodvar kept Hott several weeks in the forest and taught him the martial arts with various weapons.

After Bodvar and Hott returned to Hjort, Bodvar told Rolf that they had found the animal which had been killing the livestock, that it was a bear and it was now dead. Rolf looked at Hott and saw that the young man had changed. Hott stood tall and looked people in the eyes. Rolf said, "For this deed I will rename Hott. He shall now be known as Hjalte (sword hilt) and Bodvar shall be known as Bjarke (Bear)".

Then Rolf gave them each a gold ring and bade them sit next to himself. Bodvar Bjarke ever after sat on the King's right hand side and Hjalte sat on the King's left hand side.

77 BJARKE AND RUT

Agnar Ingildson arrived at Lejre to marry Rolf's sister Rut. During the wedding feast, Agnar learned that Bodvar Bjarke had killed his friend by throwing a bone at him. Agnar was furious and challenged Bjarke to a duel.

Everyone went outside and formed a circle for the combatants. At the outset of the duel there was a long dispute over which of them ought to have the chance to strike first. In those days in a ritual duel, men did not try to strike hard and fast. There was a definite pause and combatants would take turns striking after each pause, one stroke at a time. Those blows would be terrible. In this type of duel, victory usually went to the strong, because speed was not helpful. It was decided that Agnar, being of higher rank should strike first.

"No way!" yelled Erik, "Bjarke was the son of King Bjorn Ringson in Norway. He was a Prince."

The story teller looked at Erik for a minute and chuckled. "Indeed", said the story teller, "But Bjarke was in Denmark and did not want his Norwegian rank to be known. He just wanted renown as a mighty warrior. This could be achieved only by action and not by political posturing.

So inside the circle formed by Rolf's warriors, Agnar struck Bjarke a mighty blow. He cut through the front of the helmet and wounded the skin on the scalp. Bjarke wielded his sword, Lovi. To give the return blow, Bjarke leaned his foot against a rock in order to give more power to his swing. The stroke was so powerful that it cut through Agnar's armor and clove his body in two. It is told that Agnar, who was very brave, died with a smile on his lips. Three of Agnar's friends immediately challenged Bjarke to duels. None of them fared any better than Agnar.

After the fourth duel everyone went back to the feast minus the groom. Bjarke declared that in order to not spoil the festivities, he would marry Rut. This pleased Rut because in fact Rut had gotten to know Bjarke while he was there and had secretly fallen in love with him. Thus the festivities proceeded and Bodvar Bjarke became Rolf Krake's brother in law.

78 ROLF KRAKE AND KING ADILS

King Adils in Sweden was at war with King Ole of the Uplands. The two Kings agreed to settle their differences on the ice on Venner Lake in December. Adils discovered that his forces were much smaller than Ole's, therefore he sent a messenger to Rolf Krake for help. He promised to pay Rolf's berserkers 3 marks of gold each, pay Rolf's warriors 3 marks of silver each, pay Rolf 3 of his prized treasures of Rolf's own choosing.

Rolf lay at war with the Saxons and could not come, but he sent his twelve berserkers to King Adils in Sweden. With the help of Rolf Krake's berserkers, Adils won the battle on Venner Lake and King Ole fell. After the battle, King Adils refused to pay what was due to Rolf because Rolf had stayed at home. The berserkers refused their pay because they did not want pay unless Rolf was given his pay so they went home empty handed.

As part of his war booty, Adils took Ole's horse Raven. Adils was a lover of good horses and was famous for having the best horses. Ole's horse Raven was an excellent horse and Adils decided to breed him with his horse, Slongve. The resulting foal was also called Raven. Adils sent the young horse Raven as a gift to King Godgest at Omd in Halogaland. When King Godgest mounted the horse, he was not able to manage him and fell off and was killed.

Bjarke was convinced that if Rolf did not collect his due from Adils, his fame would be dimmed. Rolf chose one hundred warriors and twelve champions as well as his twelve berserkers and set out for Uppsala. Since it was winter they went across the frozen Ore Sound on horseback to Skaane and then north.

On the road they came to a farm. The farmer invited them all in to rest for the night. Rolf answered, "You are a bold man. But do you have the means for this? We are not so few and more than a small farm is needed to take care of us".

The farmer laughed and said, "Yes, I have at times seen no fewer men come to where I have been. You will lack neither drink nor anything else you will need for the night".

King Rolf said, "Then we will accept your invitation".

The farmer was pleased with the decision. The horses were taken care of and shown proper treatment. "What is your name?" asked Rolf.

"Some call me Rane", said the farmer.

The hospitality at Rane's place was good. Rolf could not remember such generosity anywhere. Rane answered every question he was asked. It was obvious that Rane was no fool.

Eventually they all went to sleep. In the night the warriors awoke feeling so cold that their teeth chattered. They fetched blankets and more clothes to try to get warm. The berserkers, however, slept on without feeling cold.

In the morning, Rane asked how everyone had slept. "Well", said Bjarke.

Then Rane said to Rolf Krake, "I know that your retainers found it cold in the hall, and so it was. They cannot be expected to withstand the trials King Adils will try on them in Uppsala if they found this trial difficult. Send half your company home Sire, if you want to stay alive. Because it is not with a large force that you will overcome Adils".

When they had readied themselves to go out, Rolf wished the farmer well. Then, on Rane's advice, he sent half his force home.

After traveling all day, Rolf and his companions came to a small farm. It looked identical to the farm where they had slept the night before. They all thought that this farmer looked like Rane. To their surprise they discovered that it was indeed Rane. It appeared that they had gone in circles.

The farmer greeted them well and asked why they came so often.

After feasting with the farmer, Rolf and his company once again fell asleep. In the middle of the night, the warriors awoke with an overpowering thirst. They went to a huge vat of wine and drank and drank. The berserkers slept soundly all night without waking.

In the morning, Rane spoke to the King, "Once again sire, matters are such that you might listen to me. I think there is little endurance in the men who drank during the night. You will have to endure trials more difficult than that when you visit King Adils".

Before they had a chance to leave again an unexpected blizzard sprang up and Rolf and his warriors had to stay in the farm house all day. When night came Rane built a huge fire. The men began to leave their seats at the benches and move back because of the heat, except Rolf and his berserkers.

Rane again spoke to Rolf, "Yet again Sire, you can cull your company. It is my counsel that no one should go except you and your twelve berserkers. Then there would be some hope that you would return. Otherwise there is none".

Rolf replied, "You impress me as so sensible, farmer, that we will take your advice".

They stayed the third night and in the morning, Rolf Krake sent his warriors home and rode out with his twelve berserkers.

When Rolf Krake and his berserkers reached Uppsala, they were well received. Servants took care of their horses and showed the men into the hall. The horses were taken straight to the stables, where the servants cut off their manes and tails as instructed by Adils.

Just outside the King's hall, Rolf and his berserkers discovered that their servants had deserted them. They were alone. Svipdag, who knew King Adils' hall, led them in. The hall was empty. Rolf and his men proceeded towards the high seat.

Suddenly, from behind the beams and benches, warriors sprang forward and attacked Rolf and his men. The berserkers formed a ring around Rolf. The fighting was furious and the Swedes began to fall. They could not stand against Rolf's berserkers. Suddenly, King Adils appeared and shouted for the fighting to stop. Then he scolded his warriors for attacking his guests.

King Adils ordered the hall to be cleaned, and the dead were carried out. Many of his men had been killed and a large number were wounded. King Adils invited his guests to be seated. Rolf and his berserkers sat at the benches with their weapons never letting them out of their reach. King Adils had a fire lit the length of the hall and called for a feast. Rolf and his men sat on one side of the fire. Adils and his men sat on the other side. Each group sat on a long bench and pleasant conversations were carried on across the fire.

The Swedes kept adding fuel to the fire, planks, branches, and pitch. Adils and his men kept pulling back away from the fire. The space occupied by Rolf and his men had gradually grown smaller. The Swedes continued adding more fuel to the fire. King Adils wanted to be sure which one was Rolf Krake so that it would be easier to kill him. King Adils said, "You champions of Rolf have the reputation of fleeing from neither fire nor iron. So I know you will not flee from this fire".

Bjarke and the other berserkers realized that Adils wanted Rolf Krake dead so they tried to protect Rolf from the intense heat with their bodies. Adils kept reminding them that they fled neither fire nor iron. Adils intended to burn Rolf and his berserkers on the spot or make them break their vow of not fleeing. The clothes of the berserkers were being singed and Adils had moved his seat right back against the outer wall.

Rolf realized that the fire would reach him and his men unless something was done. Their clothes had all been singed. King Rolf stood up and yelled, "He flees no fire, who jumps over it!"

Then he threw his shield on the fire and jumped over his shield. The twelve berserkers followed Rolf by throwing their shields on the fire and jumping over.

Then the berserkers each seized a Swede and hurled him into the fire.

The berserkers grabbed Swede after Swede and pitched them into the fire. The fire was so hot that no one could approach it. There came a stench in the hall of burned flesh and screams were heard as the Swedes were grabbed. The Swedes after being hurled into the fire had no time to scream. They were consumed in seconds. Soon there were no Swedes left in the hall. The berserkers intended to pitch Adils into the fire, but Adils had fled and was not to be found.

When Rolf and his men left the burning hall, Rolf's mother (the wife of Adils), Yrsa came to them. She gave Rolf a big hug and told them that she wished them as much good as Adils wished them evil. She showed them to a house where they could sleep.

In the middle of the night, Adils had warriors surround the house where Rolf and his men slept. Adils barred all the doors and set fire to the house. Rolf and his berserkers woke up. Bjarke told the berserkers to follow what he did and hurled himself against a wall. He repeated his action. Then the berserkers hurled themselves against the wall in unison until the wall broke and collapsed. The berserkers charged out in berserk frenzy and felled all the Swedes who were near them. A terrible battle raged. Rolf and his berserkers were victorious but once again, nobody knew where Adils was.

As Rolf and his men rested, Yrsa came to them. She gave Rolf a large horn full of Adils' best treasures, including his prized ring called Sveagris. She told them that Adils had left Uppsala. He had gone to raise a great army to defeat Rolf. Since Rolf's horses had been shorn of manes and tails, Yrsa had Adils' best horses brought to them. Rolf thanked his mother and wished her well. Then he and his berserkers mounted their new horses and rode south from Uppsala.

When Rolf and his berserkers were crossing the Fyris plains, they heard horns blowing directly behind them. And so the race began. Rolf and his twelve berserkers galloped across Fyris with the mounted Swedes in hot pursuit. Rolf dug into his horn and pulled out a handful of gold rings. These he strewed along his path and they lay there sparkling.

Adils forbade his men to stop and pick them up. Adils was riding Raven, the best horse in Scandinavia. He rode so fast that he outdistanced his army in no time. Rolf kept distributing gold on the ground but the Swedes kept pursuing. Then there was only one treasure left, the ring Sveagris. Rolf dropped Sveagris on the ground. Adils treasured Sveagris so much that he stopped to pick it up. When Adils stopped, his men all stopped and began to pick up the gold that Rolf had sown on the Fyris plains.

Rolf and his berserkers rode all day until they finally reached Rane's farm. There Rane wanted to give Rolf weapons; shield, sword, and chain mail. Rolf saw that they were old and full of rust, so he refused the presents. Rane was offended by this and became very angry. Therefore Rolf and his men rode on even though it was very dark.

Bjarke had noticed that Rane had but one eye and this reminded him of stories of Odin. He shared his suspicions with Rolf saying that he thought Rane was Odin himself. On hearing this Rolf decided to go back and apologize. But they could find neither Rane nor his farm again. They then went back to Lejre as quick as they could.

79 ROLF KRAKE'S LAST BATTLE

Skuld, Rolf Krake's sister, abhorred that her husband, King Hjarvard of Oland, had to pay tax to her brother Rolf. She had been filling Hjarvard's mind with plans of how to kill Rolf and assume the seat of Lejre.

Hjarvard and Skuld made annual trips to Lejre to pay the tax to Rolf. This year Skuld had hundreds of arms bundled up into packages to look like packages of tribute. These packages were loaded onto ships and the Olanders sailed to Lejre.

Rolf had a huge banquet for the Olanders and there was much drinking. The Olanders, usually heavy drinkers, drank very little, but the Danes drank much.

At night, while all the others were sleeping soundly, the Olanders slipped out of their sleeping quarters, opened the packages, donned armour and armed themselves. Then they entered the hall Hjort and started to kill the sleeping Danes. Many of the Danes woke to the dreadful carnage. But they were filled with the drowsiness of sleep and drink and were confused in the pitch dark of the hall. Not knowing friend from foe, their resistance faltered.

Hjalte was not in Hjort. He was sleeping with a woman in a nearby house. The faint but persistent din of battle woke him and he put on his armor and armed himself. Then he rushed out the door and ran to Hjort.

At Hjort, Hjalte plunged into the densest of the Olanders and moved down warrior after warrior. In the fierce battle, Hjalte could not find Bjarke. He hewed and fought his way out of the throngs of warriors and ran to Bjarke's sleeping quarters. There was Bjarke sound asleep. He woke Bjarke by shouting these words:

Awake, awake,

Friend troop band!

All you most excellent

Noble followers,

Wake not to vine,

The Saga Kings

And not to wise speeches,

Better to war's

Hard play

Bjarke woke and thought that guests had arrived at Hjort. When he got his senses, Bjarke called his servant, Skalk. He told Skalk to run into Hjort and stir the fireplace and find some embers. Then Skalk was to scatter the embers in the hall and fan as many as he could to fire so that there would be light in the dark hall.

Hjalte dashed back into the hall and fought hard. He still missed Bjarke and ran back to Bjarke's sleeping quarters. Bjarke had just finished dressing and was buckling on his armour. Hjalte scolded him for being so slow. Then Hjalte dashed back into the hall which was now lit by the fires Skalk had started. Hjalte organized a shield wall around Rolf.

Then Bjarke burst into the hall, went berserk, and wielding his sword with both hands, Bjarke waded forward into the Olanders and the Danes followed him. The Danes fought free of the hall just as the fires started to roar. Roosters started to crow as the sun began to rise. The berserkers formed a ring around Rolf and fought hard. They started to edge towards the forest where they might escape. But Hjarvard ignited the forest and it became a blazing inferno. The hall, Hjort, was now in full blaze as well. The Olanders closed in. The berserkers started to fall. Swords and battle axes swung and shields were cloven. There in front of the burning Hjort at Lejre, Rolf Krake fell with all his warriors.

Erik interrupted, "The Icelanders tell a slightly different story of Bjarke."

"Yes", said the story teller, "tell us about it."

"As told by the Icelanders, it was Bjarke who scolded Hjalte when Hjalte woke him. Bjarke's familiar spirit was a huge bear. When Bjarke was sleeping that bear fought for Rolf Krake in Bjarke's place. When Hjalte woke Bjarke, the bear disappeared. Bjarke thought that the Danes would have won if the bear was able to continue fighting." explained Erik.

The story teller continued, "As Rolf Krake lay dead, at his head lay Bodvar Bjarke. At his feet lay Hjalte. Skuld and Hjarvard were jubilant. That night they had a big celebration feast. Every one became drunk out of their wits. At the height of the celebration, Hjarvard gave a speech.

He praised Rolf's men because not one had tried to flee nor given up as a captive. He said he was sorry that no one was left alive because he would have liked to take them into his service. Then Viggo stepped forward and said, I am Viggo, the sole survivor of Rolf's warriors."

Hjarvard asked Viggo, "Will you take service with me?"

Viggo said, "Yes".

Hjarvard extended his sword so that Viggo could swear loyalty to him. Viggo said, "When we swore allegiance to Rolf Krake, Rolf held the blade and we held the hilt".

Hjarvard turned the sword around. Viggo took hold of the hilt. Then he drove the sword into Hjarvard's chest, and shouted; "Now I have fulfilled my vow, and avenged Rolf Krake!"

Viggo stood tall and stared at Hjarvard's warriors as they cut him down.

With Hjarvard dead, Skuld took the throne of Lejre.

Rolf Krake was the most famous of all the saga kings. When skalds wanted to honour their kings right up until the end of the Viking age, they compared their king to Rolf Krake.

The song the skalds used to honour Rolf Krake was called Bjarkemaal:

> **Sun is up, topping the forest**
>
> **Shining all like Gimle's roof**
>
> **Message it brings, rooster wings,**
>
> **Roosters crow as day breaks**
>
> **Wake, wake, Danish heroes!**
>
> **Jump up and buckle belts!**
>
> **Day and deed is warrior verse,**

The Saga Kings

Day and deed is warrior verse!

Loud it echoes, flames are calling

Warriors up at morning snap,

Posts creak, flames blaze,

Blazing over green grove.

Wake! Not to the high's speech,

Vine and smile in King's hall!

Hildur's play is now at hand,

Hildur's play is now at hand.

Wake! Plays castles arches

In the red bow shots!

Blaze resounds, Leire falls

Under Skuld's victory song

Hjarvard fire in forest ignites,

Leaves fade, beech trees burn,

Wake must even Dan and Skjold,

Wake must even Dan and Skjold!

Up now fight for Rolf Krake

Boldly lifting shield and sword!

For fire he does not dread

But for sight of small works

Ring with luster and sword with edge

Generously he gave with both hands,

Who dares form a ring about him?

Who dares form a ring about him!

In his home, comfortable and peaceful,

Slept so sweet that hero so bold,

Swedish flames he does not flee

With his wide Dane shield.

But ack! Though he stands on embers,

Magic sword and treachery he meets,

Who dares hold shield for him?

Who dares hold shield for him!

The one who called! Hjalte dares,

Zealand's farmer boy dares,

Bjarke dares, into the field

Even if the Fenris wolf itself was lose,

Lust has he with the heart of a lion

To reach Odin himself to slay,

Bodvar Bjarke strikes with his might,

Bodvar Bjarke strikes with his might!

Rolf pales, Bjarke falls,

Hjalte swims in his own blood,

Lejre's arches are in flames

Fallen down at Hjarvard's foot

The field can he not keep,

The Saga Kings

> **Before the embers are cold**
>
> **Slays he the last spark,**
>
> **Slays he the last spark!**
>
> **Sun is up, topping the forest**
>
> **Shining all like Gimle's roof**
>
> **Message it brings, rooster wings,**
>
> **Rooster crows as day breaks**
>
> **Wake, wake, Danish heroes!**
>
> **Jump up and buckle belts!**
>
> **Daybreak has gold in mouth,**
>
> **Daybreak has gold in mouth!**

Rolf Krake was mourned not just in Denmark but all over the north because Rolf was considered the ideal King. He was free and open handed with his riches and quick to give praise when it was due. He also inspired such a fierce loyalty among his warriors. For many years after, when Vikings were drinking they would give a toast to the memory of Rolf Krake. The reign of Rolf Krake was considered a golden age.

When King Adils heard that Rolf Krake fell at Lejre, he celebrated with a big feast at Disa. After the feast he showed off on his horse. As he rode around Disa Hall, his horse, Raven, stumbled and fell. King Adils was thrown forward on his head and his skull was split, and his brains dashed out against a stone. Adils was buried at Uppsala in a mound. The Swedes called him a great king. Thjodolf the skald sang thus of him: --

"Witch-demons, I have heard men say,

Have taken Adils' life away.

The son of kings of Frey's great race,

First in the fray, the fight, the chase,

Fell from his steed -- his clotted brains

Lie mixed with mire on Uppsala's plains.

Such death (grim Fate has willed it so)

Has struck down Ole's deadly foe."

80 ATTILA AND BLEDA

The Roman Emperor Theodoseus made Hun Rua a Roman general and began paying Rua a stipend of 350 pounds of gold per year. Rua continued to raise an army and plot against Rome.

In 434, Hun Rua had raised a huge army and proceeded towards Rome. Just before he reached the Roman frontier, he was struck by lightning and died.

Hun Rua's nephews, the brothers, Attila and Bleda became joint kings of all the Huns.

They proceeded on to Rome and instead of attacking they negotiated with the Romans. The results were that the stipend paid by the Romans was doubled and fugitives were to be surrendered. Also, free markets, open to Romans and Huns alike were to be instituted and any tribe, with which Attila might at any time be at war, was to be excluded from the Roman alliance.

In 435 A.D., Attila and Bleda pushed their armies westward conquering tribe after tribe.

The Romans were stretched in man power and resources with their dealings with the Huns and war with the Goths so they made peace with King Genseric of the Vandals. Then the Goths sacked the city of Rome.

In 441, the Huns under Attila and Bleda attacked the Roman town of Margus. Margus was seized and sacked. Then the Huns attacked the Roman town, Siriium, and it too fell and was sacked. Thus ended the treaty between Rome and the Huns.

81 UFFE (OFFA)

The first King of the Angles was Angul, the son of Odin and Frigg. His land was in southern Jutland and it was bordering on the land of the Saxons. The Saxon tribe along the border was the Murkings. When Angul died, his son Withlaeg became king. After the death of Withlaeg, his son Vermund became King.

When King Vermund was very old and had become blind, the Saxon tribe known as the Myrkings began to test the Angles defenses and skirmishes broke out along the border in Jutland. King Vermund the Old went with an army to the border between Saxony and Angul Land. Accompanying Vermund was his only son, 30 year old Uffe, called Uffe Den Spage (The Mild) because nobody had heard him speak, and nobody had any faith in him because all he had ever done was to sit near the fireplace and watch life go on about him. When Vermund had become old, he despaired of Uffe ever becoming King and had his sword Skraep buried so that no one would ever use it again.

Messengers from the Myrkings arrived at the court of Vermund the Old and demanded that Vermund deliver his kingdom to the King of the Myrkings because Vermund was too old to rule. They brought a challenge for Vermund to meet the King of the Myrkings in a duel to see who would get the kingdom. The King of the Myrkings, they said, realized that Vermund was too old for duels and offered the alternative of having the Myrking prince fight the Danish prince. The Danes realized that the Myrkings knew Uffe's condition and hung their heads. Then suddenly a loud voice was heard in the hall asking King Vermund's permission to speak. It was Uffe and the Danes were astonished to hear his voice. Vermund asked who had just spoken and when he was told that it was Uffe, his son, Vermund got angry and told the people to not make fun of himself nor his son. But the Danes persisted that it was his son, Uffe, who had spoken, and finally Vermund gave permission for Uffe to speak up. Uffe said that he was unhappy to meet just the Myrking prince by himself and that he would fight the Myrking prince and the best man the Myrkings could muster at the same time. The Myrking messengers laughed loud and long at Uffe's words. Then after an arrangement had been made for the time and place of the duel, the Myrking messengers left to bring this message to their King.

No chain mail could be found to fit Uffe, because they were all too small.

Finally Vermund ordered one set of chain mail to be cut open on the left and sewn together again, saying that Uffe could cover the open side with his shield. Uffe found the swords no better than the armour, since every sword Uffe tried to use broke. Finally Vermund had his old sword Skraep dug up, but he would not let Uffe try Skraep because he was afraid it would break. There were magical swords in Scandinavia and Skraep was one of them. These swords had been brought to Scandinavia by the Aesir and had been made by the dwarves who lived in the mountains north of Asgaard, by the Black Sea".

"Magical swords!" blurted Erik, "There are no such things!"

The story teller chuckled and said, "What makes you say that young fellow?"

Erik replied, "The Bishop says they have never existed".

The story teller laughed and said, "Tell that to the dwarves who dwell in the mountains north of Asgaard east of the Black Sea. They have made swords that cut through iron. They keep their craft a secret. But Skraep could cut through iron and that is enough magic for a sword.

At the appointed time of the holmgang, Uffe was put off alone on an island in a river, and the Myrking prince arrived on the island with his best fighter. People flocked to the river to watch the fight, Danes on one bank and Myrkings on the other bank. Vermund sat on a chair on a small dock, intending to drown himself if Uffe should be cut down. Both the Myrkings went ferociously after Uffe at the same time, and Uffe who was not sure of his sword, at first defended with his shield. Vermund, not hearing the sound which his sword used to make, edged his chair closer to the water. Uffe taunted the prince. He yelled at the prince, "You big coward, hiding behind your champion."

Uffe yelled at the champion, "Ha ha ha. You make me laugh! You are no champion. Champions do not stay behind their prince! You tiny coward!"

The champion became so angry that he charged ahead of the Myrking prince, Uffe swung Skraep and cut the champion into two pieces at the middle. Vermund could not see it, but he heard it.

> **"He heard a whistle in the air like the starling**
>
> **He heard a crackle like the lightning"**

Vermund heard the whistle Skraep made in the wind and recognized his old sword and asked where the sword had hit. When he was told that the Myrking champion was dead and in two pieces, he moved his seat back from the edge of the dock.

Then Vermund heard the whistle of his sword again and the Danes yell in triumph. Uffe had cut the Myrking prince into two pieces as well. The Danes triumphantly sent a boat to pick up Uffe, while the Myrkings collected the bodies of their two warriors.

When Vermund the Old died, the Angles called a Thing and chose Uffe as their King. Because Uffe loved peace and hated to fight, he kept his nickname den Spage (the Quiet).

82 ENGLAND

In 443, the Bretons sent emissaries to Rome and asked for assistance against the Picts. The Romans had no assistance for the Bretons because they were too busy fighting Attila the Hun.

Vortigern assumed Kingship of Britain. In 449, Vortigern invited the Jutes, the Angles, and the Old Saxons to Britain to help him consolidate his Empire. The leaders of the Jutes who came were two brothers, Hengist (Stallion) and Horsa (Horse, Hesten, Hastings), the sons of Hnaef (Kniv, Knife). Vortigern married the beautiful Rowena, the daughter of Hengist. The people of Kent are the descendants of these Jutes. From the Old Saxons descended the people of Essex, Sussex, and Wessex (East Saxons, South Saxons, and West Saxons). The Angles accepted Vortigern's invitation, went to Britain and received the territory called Mercia. From the Angles descended the East Angles, the West Angles, the Mercians and all those north of the Humber River. England got its name from the Angles, 'Angland'. The Celts had their strongholds in Wales.

83 ATTILA THE HUN

In 445, Bleda died and Attila became King of all the Huns. There were rumours that Attila had assassinated Bleda. Attila undertook campaigns against the Eastern Roman Empire. He pushed southwards to Thermopylae, Gallipoli, and the walls of Constantinople. The Romans bought peace by tripling the yearly tribute, which was now 2,100 pounds of gold. In addition, a heavy indemnity was paid.

In 453, Attila entered the land of the Gjukungs in Germany. There was a fierce battle in which King Gjuke fell. Eventually his sons Gunnar and Hogni were captured. There were rumours of the Andvar treasure hidden by the Gjukungs. Attila wanted the treasure and had Gunnar tortured to make him talk. During the torture, Gunnar was forced to watch Hogni have his heart cut out. Gunnar was tortured to death. The lineage of the Gjukungs became extinct. In the same year, Attila died on his wedding night. His bride, a Germanic princess, Ildico, was found sobbing beside his corpse.

Attila's heir was to be his son Ellac. But Ellac's brothers challenged his authority so that civil war broke out among the Huns. When the tribes in Europe realized what was happening they united in war against the Huns and in the year 454 almost wiped them out in the battle of Nedao where Ellac fell and his remaining brothers fled.

Because they were almost wiped out, the Huns were no longer a threat. They asked the Romans for land because they were no longer able to take land for themselves and afterwards they were gradually absorbed into the European tribes.

84 KING ARTHUR

In 474, the men of Kent, Jutes under Hengist moved west, driving the Britons before them.

In 476, Arthur was born in Wales, Britain's Celtic stronghold.

In 477, a Saxon Chief, Aella landed on the Sussex coast with his sons. The Britons engaged him as he landed, but the Saxon superior forces drove them into the weald. Over the next nine years, Saxon holdings expanded.

In 490, Hengist died in Kent, Britain. His son Aesc took over and ruled for 34 years.

In 495, the Saxon chief Cerdic and his son Cynric arrived in Britain with five ships. They fought with the Welsh the same day. Cerdic and Cynric established the kingdom of Wessex.

King Gwynllyw of Gwynllywg abducted Princess Gladys of Brycheiniog. War was avoided by the intercession of the new High King, Arthur of Wales. The couple was married".
"Wait" said Vagn, "Arthur was not a King, he was a warlord".

The story teller looked at Vagn and raised his eyebrows, "indeed and who told you that"?

"The Bishop said that was just part of a legend", replied Vagn.

The story teller chuckled and said, "Tell me something else. Did Arthur marry Guinevere?"

"Yes", said Vagn.

"Well", said the story teller, "Arthur and Guinevere were Celts. The Celts traced their family trees through their women. Guinevere was the High Princess of the Celts. Whoever she married would be the High King. Therefore, Arthur was indeed the new High King.

In 496, Arthur began to fight against the Saxons. Arthur fought the Saxons from 496 until 516 without losing a single battle. Twelve major battles were recorded. King Arthur gained a reputation of invincibility.

In the siege of Mount Badon, the British, under the High King, Arthur, defeated the Saxons under King Esla of Bernicia and King Cerdic of Wessex. Britain was now secure and Arthur lived at peace. He was a generous King who made good laws. This was called a golden age in Britain.

85 HUGLEIK

In 516 A.D., Hugleik, King of Reidgotaland, went with a fleet to raid in Frisia. He landed and took much booty. Then an army of Frisians, led by Theudobert, met him in battle. The battle was fierce and many Reidgots (Geats) fell. Hugleik fell with the famous magic sword, Tyrfing. The Frisians looted his armour and weapons. There were no more records of Tyrfing.

The Frisians pursued the fleeing Reidgot ships and overtook them because the Reidgots had too many rowers missing. The Frisians wiped out the raiders and recovered the booty. Beowulf alone escaped by swimming and made his way back to Reidgotaland.

The skeleton of Hugleik was preserved on an island at the mouth of the Rhine. Hugleik was so huge that at the age of twelve, no horse could carry him.

Hugleik's widow wanted to make Beowulf King of Reidgotaland. But Beowulf declined because he thought it was improper. He thought that Hugleik's son Heidrek should be King. At the Thing, Heidrek was chosen King of Reidgotaland and Beowulf was chosen as Heidrek's Champion.

86 FRODE AND HARALD

After the death of Rolf Krake, Bodvar Bjarke's brothers, the sea kings, Elk-Frode and Thorir Hound's Foot sailed to Zealand from Norway. When the Zealanders heard that Bjarke's brothers had landed, they flocked to them. Then they marched on Lejre and attacked Skuld's army of Olanders.

The Zealanders were furious and wanted to avenge Rolf and his men, while Elk-Frode and Thorir were furious over Bjarke's death. The fight was ferocious and all the Olanders fell. Among the dead lay the body of Skuld.

The Danes called a Thing to choose a King. Horek, Roar's son (killed by Rolf Krake), had four sons, three of whom had perished in war. The fourth was Olaf who had two sons, Frode and Harald. The Danes chose Frode and Harald as joint Kings of Denmark. One was to rule the sea, and the other the land. They were to take turns on a yearly basis.

After the Thing was over, Elk-Frode and Thorir Hound's Foot sailed back to Norway.

Frode was the first to have command of the sea. He would attack pirates to keep them out of Danish waters. But Frode's rowers were always defeated in rowing. The pirates would outdistance his rowers and get away. Frode became a disgrace at sea. It is thought that his problem was due to his warriors being newly married and preferred to be home with their wives rather than being at sea.

King Harald, the younger brother had control of the sea the next year. He chose warriors who were unmarried because he did not want to fare like his brother. Luck was with Harald and he triumphed over many pirates and sea kings.

Harald was married to Hildur, daughter of King Heidrek of Reidgotaland. Frode was married to Signe, daughter of king Siward of Skaane. Harald and Frode's wives did not get along. They were constantly quarrelling about who was the noblest. The royal household was therefore shattered because the two Kings gave more attention to the quarrels of their wives than to running the Kingdom.

Frode felt that his brother's victories at sea were a disgrace to himself.

When he discovered that the people held him in contempt, he began to hate his brother. Finally Frode ordered one of his warriors to secretly kill Harald. When the deed was done, he ordered another warrior to kill the assassin to cover his crime. Then he ordered a full investigation into the death of Harald.

Although Frode had covered his crime, he could not hide it from the common people. There were whispers among people that Frode had killed Harald. Later Frode asked Heidrek, King of Reidgotaland and Harald's father in law, "Who has killed Harald?"

Heidrek replied, "It is deceitful of you to ask a question about something which you know quite well."

Frode became afraid because he thought Heidrek had covertly accused him of murder. Frode ordered a warrior to secretly kill Heidrek.

Heidrek of Reidgotaland was buried in a great mound. At a Thing, the Reidgots chose Beowulf as King.

Frode was now determined to kill Gudrod and Halfdan, the sons of Harald. The foster parents of Gudrod and Halfdan cut off the claws of wolves and tied them to the feet of the boys. Then they had the boys run around many times near the dwelling. The ground, which was covered with snow, became full of wolf tracks.

The foster parents then killed two thrall boys and tore their bodies to pieces. These pieces they scattered about, and then claimed that Gudrod and Halfdan had been consumed by wolves.

87 FRODE

Frode was the only one who refused to believe that Gudrod and Halfdan were dead. He went to a witch and inquired where the two boys were. She declared to Frode that one named Ragnar had secretly taken it upon himself to rear the boys and had given the boys dog names to cover the matter.

Ragnar heard that Frode was coming and secretly had the boys transported to the island of Fyn. When Frode caught Ragnar, he confessed that he had secretly transported them to Fyn. He begged Frode not to kill the boys, whom he had already made fatherless. Ragnar also told Frode that it would not be good fortune to be guilty of two unnatural murders. When he heard this, Frode became ashamed. The two reached an agreement. Frode let the boys live, and Ragnar would let Frode know if they attempted any plots in their own land.

Frode now concentrated on peaceful pursuits. Frode bought two thralls, women Jotuns, from Sweden. He had a mill made with millstones so big that no human could use them. He set the two Jotuns, Fenja and Menja, at grinding grain in his mill.

Now are they come

To the house of the King

The prescient two,

Fenja and Menja,

There must the mighty

Maidens toil

For King Frode,

Brought to the mill

Soon they were;

The gray stones

They had to turn.

Nor rest nor peace

He gave to them:

He would hear

The maidens

Turn the mill.

Frode collected tax in the form of grain. Then he had the grain ground by Fenja and Menja. He sold the flour for gold.

88 RAGNAROK

"A wind age, a wolf age, an age of cloven shields"

(Voluspaa)

In 535, the Scandinavians heard a noise like a bass horn or distant thunder. Because it went on for hours, the people thought that only a god could blow a horn for such a length of time without pausing to draw a breath.

Voluspaa:

Loud blows Heimdal

His uplifted horn.

The people looked up and saw clouds working their way across the sky. The clouds took the form of a wolf. It engulfed the sun. As the sun was being engulfed, its reflection appeared in the cloud, a second dimmer sun. Then the sun was gone and only the second sun, much dimmer remained. The moon and stars had disappeared from the night sky.

Voluspaa:

A daughter

Is born of the sun

Ere the wolf swallows her.

She rides in her mother's course

When the mighty are no more

The sun grows dark,

The earth sinks into the sea,

The bright stars

From heaven vanish;

Meanwhile, Merlin the sorcerer in Britain described the clouds as dragon's fingers in combat.

Huge waves came crashing in on the coasts. The Viking ships at sea were lost. The coastal towns in Norway were hit with huge waves which caused many lives to be lost. The few survivors moved to higher ground in the mountains. They thought the giant waves were caused by Jormundgang, the huge serpent that surrounds the whole world, and is also known as the Midgaard Serpent or the World Serpent.

Voluspaa:

Jormundgang welters

In giant rage

And smites the waves

Thor (the descendants of Thor, i.e. The Norwegians) struggled with the Midgaard serpent.

Rain fell. It was red, the venom of the Midgaard serpent. Ashes fell from the sky.

The Saga Kings

All men

Abandon their homesteads

When the warder of Midgaard

In wrath slays the serpent.

Thor gets great renown for slaying the Midgaard serpent, but retreats only nine paces when he falls to the earth dead, poisoned by the venom the serpent blew on him. Poisonous dust killed many people.

Each day, the sun shone for about four hours, and still this light was only a feeble shadow. The temperature plummeted for a month and fell below freezing. Yellow dust fell like snow. It could be scooped up in handfuls. The poisonous dust filtered through the cracks in the timbers of houses.

Voluspaa:

I know a hall standing

Far from the sun

In Nastrand: the doors

To the northward are turned;

Venom drops filter

Down from the roof holes;

The hall is bordered

With backs of serpents.

The 536 winter was hard. The snow was yellow. Fierce winds would come from any direction. The sun remained dim and a fog was everywhere. The fog was strange because it was dry. When the moon could be seen, it was red as blood. The summer did not come. There were no crops. People were starving.

Frode had grain stored and he had the great Grotte mill. Therefore he grew rich selling flour

Menja sang:

> **We grind for Frode**
>
> **Wealth and happiness,**
>
> **And gold abundant**
>
> **On the mill of luck.**
>
> **He sits on gold!**

In 537, the winter was hard with winds from any and every direction. The Kattegat Strait and the Baltic Sea froze completely. The Black sea also froze completely. All the rivers were frozen including the Nile and Euphrates rivers in the south. Because the dry fog was everywhere, people could not see far.

89 STARVATION

For the next ten years, the winters were very severe and the summers were cool and short. It took the earth 400 years to warm back up. It has been calculated that the Fimbul winter and the following Ragnarok encompassing starvation, wars, and plagues, resulted in the elimination of 85% to 90% of the world population.

In Britain, people came out of the forests and mountains and sold themselves into slavery for food because they were starving. There was a mass migration of Celtic monks from England to France. The area where they settled is called Brittany. After the monks migrated to Brittany, other Britons followed. Many of these people migrated north from Brittany up to Anglia and the lesser Danish islands which had been left denuded of its inhabitants by starvation and food wars. Many of the Saxons living in Britain migrated back to the mouth of the Elbe from where they had originated.

Summer did not come. People were starving. In Norway, some people hazarded the dangerous ocean and took up fishing. In the Baltic Sea, people were going out on the ice and chopping holes for fishing with nets. Farmers went into the forests and hunted.

Frode had his mill working and was becoming rich. But the common people could not afford his flour.

Menja sang:

>Fire I see burning
>
>East of the burg,
>
>War tidings awaken.
>
>That is called warning:
>
>A host shall come
>
>Hither with swiftness
>
>To fire the dwellings

Of King Frode

You shall not hold

the stead of Lejre,

the red gold rings,

nor the gods' holy altar;

Now must we grind

With all our might,

No warmth will we get

From the blood of the slain.

The sea king called Myser went against Lejre and killed Frode. He took much plunder. Myser took the Grotte mill with him. He also took Fenja and Menja to work the mill. Myser's ship had become frozen into the ice in the Kattegat near the Sound. He had Fenja and Menja grind salt in an effort to get his ship lose. At midnight, Fenja and Menja asked Myser whether he was not weary of salt. He told them to grind longer. But the ice shifted and gave way, and the Grotte mill sank. Myser's ship, damaged by the ice also sank".

"And that is how the water in the seas became salty", interrupted Erik.

The old skald looked at Erik and smiled. Then he said, "That my young friend is how the myth goes. But no; the seas have always been salty".

The story teller sipped his beer and continued the story, "Jotunheim was the stronghold of the Jotuns. It was north of Halogaland along the shores of Gandvik. There dwelled the Jotuns, the children of Loke. They were starving. They started to come south, killing all in their path. Their leader was a child of Loke (descendant of Loke). He was called Fenris. Because his followers were dressed in the hides of wolves and ate the dead, he was called Fenris Wolf.

At first, the Norwegians fought Fenris Wolf, but they were too busy staying alive and keeping warm. They had to struggle with the ocean for food. The ocean was wild and windy. It kept rushing onto the land and submerging coastal villages.

Therefore the Norwegians built fortifications on top of hills and lived in them when Fenris migrated south in search of food. The Norwegians could make no progress against the forces of Fenris and Fenris could not overcome the Norwegians in their hill forts. Therefore the Jotuns kept going south.

Voluspaa:

Then Fenris Wolf gets lose;

Then the sea gushes forth upon the land,

Because the Midgaard serpent stirs in giant wrath

And advances up onto the land.

Odin goes forth against Fenris Wolf,

And Thor stands forward on his other side,

And is of no avail to him,

Because he has his hands full

Fighting against the Midgaard Serpent.

By 538, the dry fog had dissipated. But summer still did not come. Fenris Wolf reached the frozen Kattegat Strait and started across to Zealand. Odin (i.e. worshippers of Odin and also his descendants, the Danes) went out to meet him and a ferocious battle was fought on the ice. The field of battle on the frozen Kattegat Strait was called Vigrid. The plains of Vigrid were a hundred leagues wide each way. The leader of the Danes was Beowulf (Bolverk), King of Reidgotaland. There was a hard battle and the Danes were over run. Beowulf fell in battle and there was a great slaughter of the Danes

Voluspaa:

Vigrid is the name of the plain

Where the fight meets.

Odin rides first;

With his golden helmet,

Resplendent byrnie,

And his spear Gungner,

He advances against the Fenris Wolf.

The wolf swallows Odin

and causes his death.

"Wait a minute", exclaimed Erik.

The story teller paused and looked at Erik. "A dragon killed Beowulf, not a wolf", said Erik.

The story teller chuckled, took a sip of his beer, and said, "If you hear this story from the Angles or the Saxons, it is indeed a dragon which killed Beowulf. Their culture is steeped in dragons. But it really was the forces of the Jotun, Fenris Wolf which killed Beowulf. Bolverk was a name assumed by Odin when he went wandering in Midgaard and it is also a pronunciation of Beowulf (Bearwolf) in certain dialects. This then became the myth that during Ragnarok, Odin was killed by the Fenris Wolf.

The remnants of the Danes fled south to the mainland. Fenris overran Skaane and Halland. Then the Swedes with the help of the Jotuns took Zealand.

Garm, a chieftain from the east, led a great host of warriors into Saxony. The Saxons fought them on the shores of the Rhine. The two armies wiped each other out.

The Saga Kings

Voluspaa:

Even the dog Garm,

That was bound

before the Gnipa cave,

gets loose.

He contends with Tyr.

90 THE BATTLE OF CAMLAN

Euric, King of the Franks, raised a huge army of eighty to one hundred thousand troops. Then he crossed the English Channel and joined up with a warlord called Mordred and the Wessex King Cerdic to go against Arthur, High King of the Britons. Arthur assembled his armies and went out to meet them.

The two armies met at the River Camlan by the Antonine wall. Arthur's division assailed Mordred's battalion and killed him. In the chaos that followed Arthur and Cerdic both fell.

After the battle, remnants of Arthur's warriors found Arthur lying on the battlefield among the many corpses. He was still alive.

They took him to Avalon to heal. But his wounds were too great, and he died at Avalon. His sword Excalibur was returned to the Lady of the Lake and she hid it.

Voluspaa:

The bleak Fimbul winter arrived

Raging across the world

With a fury that defied the memory of man

Terrible wars were fought,

the like had never been seen

Men slew without a thought

The ties of kinship were no more

Brothers will fight

and be each other's banes;

cousins will betray one another;

men do suffer, whoredom is rampant;

The Saga Kings

it is the age of the axe, the age of the sword,

the age of cloven shields;

the age of storm, the age of wolves,

ere the world founders.

91 VIDAR

In the country, which is present day Austria, Halfdan collected the remnants of the Danish warriors as well as warriors who were migrating in from Britain, and prepared to retake Denmark from the Swedes. The Swedes who had taken over the land refused to budge and they called on the Jotuns to assist.

Fenris Wolf came south from northern Jutland across the ice of the Kattegat Strait towards Zealand where Halfdan was fighting the Swedes. Vidar, son of Beowulf, took an army out of Reidgotaland to meet the armies of Fenris Wolf. There on the plains of Vigrid was fought the most renowned battle of Ragnarok, called the Ice Battle. Vidar's warriors wore shoes of leather with the soles covered with a mixture of tar and gravel to keep from slipping on the ice.

Vidar arranged his warriors in the Svinfylking formation, as had been taught by Odin. The charge of the Reidgots broke the forces of Fenris in two and ripped it in half. There followed a great slaughter of the Jotuns in which Fenris Wolf fell.

Voluspaa:

Odin's son goes

To fight the wolf,

And Vidar goes on his way

To the wild beast.

Vidar, places one foot

On the nether jaw

With one hand seizes

The upper jaw of the wolf.

Vidar rends asunder

The jaw of the Fenris wolf.

> **Thus the wolf perishes.**
>
> **With his hand**
>
> **He thrusts his sword**
>
> **To the heart**
>
> **Of Loke's child**
>
> **And avenges his father.**

After Fenris Wolf had fallen, the enemy retreated as Halfdan's army attacked and made its way towards the north. The defeated Swedes were surprised to see that as the Danish army advanced, there came spring, accompanied by growing flowers and flocks of birds.

Voluspaa:

> Now do I see
>
> The earth anew
>
> Rise all green
>
> from the waves again;
>
> the cataracts fall
>
> the eagle flies,
>
> and fish he catches
>
> beneath the cliffs
>
> In wondrous beauty
>
> Once again
>
> **Shall the golden tables**
>
> **Stand mid the grass,**
>
> **Which the gods had owned**
>
> **In the days of old,**

The Swedes fled from Zealand. The Danes held a thing at Lejre and chose Halfdan as King of Denmark."

"What of Vidar after the ice battle?" asked Torval the White.

The story teller smiled and said, "Ah yes, Vidar was King of Reidgotaland. His son was named Havelock and he went to Britain where he married a Celtic princess called Goldborough. Their son was Hildebrand.

92 SOLVE

There was a sea king called Solve, a son of Hogne and Njardo who had their dominion in Jutland. Solve raided in the Baltic Sea.

Solve landed with his forces in Sweden in a district called Lofond. When King Eystein of Sweden was at a feast in the district, Solve came unexpected in the night and surrounded the house in which Eystein was feasting. Solve set fire to the house and burned Eystein and all his court.

Solve then went to Sigtun, a short distance from Uppsala, and desired that the Swedes should receive him and give him the title King. But the Swedes collected a great army and attacked Solve. There was a great battle that lasted eleven days. There king Solve was victorious and ruled Sweden for a long time.

Thjodolf, the skald sang of it thus: --

"For a long time none could tell

How Eystein died -- but now I know

That at Lofond the hero fell;

The branch of Odin was laid low,

Was burnt by Solve's Jutland men.

The raging tree-devourer fire

Rushed on the monarch in its ire;

First fell the castle timbers, then

The roof-beams -- Eystein's funeral pyre."

93 HALFDAN

Halfdan spent three years in Zealand and accumulated an army. At that time Hrym of the East countries began to raid in the Baltic. He ravaged territories in both Sweden and Denmark.

Halfdan handed over the sovereignty and rule of Denmark to his brother Gudrod. Then he took his fleet to Oland and the neighbouring isles, which are separated from Sweden by a sound. He proceeded to conquer Oland and the isles. This campaign lasted three years.

In 543, there was bubonic plague in Constantinople. It is said that about 10,000 people died there each day. The plague is described in Voluspaa as Nidhug. In 547, the yellow plague hit England and Ireland. The Saxons were immune and England was soon dominated by the Saxons.

Voluspaa:

From below the dragon

Dark comes forth,

Nidhug flying from Nidafjelde;

The bodies of men on

His wings he bears,

The serpent bright:

But now must I sink

When Solve was killed by the Swedes, Yngvar Eysteinson became King of Sweden.

After Halfdan completed the conquest of the isles, he attacked Sweden. King Yngvar of Sweden was a great warrior who often lay out with his warships. The forces of Halfdan and Yngvar had many battles, with victory shifting back and forth.

While Yngvar and Halfdan were tearing each other's countries apart, Hrym of the East was laying waste to both Sweden and Denmark.

Voluspaa:

From the east drives Hrym,

Bears his shield before him.

Jormundgang welters

In giant rage

And smites the waves.

The eagle screams,

And with pale beak tears corpses

Naglfar gets loose.

"What kind of beast is Naglfar?" asked Erik.

The story teller's eyes twinkled as he said, "Erik, it is not a beast. Naglfar is a ship. It is the ship which carried Surt and the Fire Giants to Scandinavia.

In 548, Yngvar and Halfdan made peace. Then Yngvar began to ravage the East country while Halfdan set out to retake Skaane. Halfdan sailed to Skaane and made war on its ruler, Erik, son of his uncle Frode.

Erik's champion, Haakon was skillful in blunting swords. Halfdan made a mace of wood. The head of the mace was round and had big iron knobs.

In the battle lines, Halfdan arranged his forces in Svinfylking formation, with himself at the front of the wedge. Halfdan covered his head with a helmet. Then without a shield, he used his mace with both hands and whirled it against the bulwark of shields before him. Nothing could stand before him. He overcame the champions who came at him in battle with the violent stroke of his mace.

Halfdan won many battles in Skaane. But eventually his army was defeated and he fled into Helsingland. He took refuge with Witolf who had been a warrior for his father Harald. Witolf lived in a lonely district far in the woods. Erik and his men went looking for Halfdan in the woods of Helsingland, but got lost in the mists.

When Halfdan's wounds were healed, he summoned the berserker Thore and again declared war on Erik. When Halfdan saw from a distance that Erik's forces were much greater, he hid part of his forces in ambush. But Erik saw from a distance that Halfdan was preparing an ambush, and left the road. He made his way into a mountain valley.

Halfdan brought his forces to the valley and the two armies joined in combat, force against force. The valley was deep and closed all around by lofty mountain reaches. When Halfdan saw that the battle was going against him he took Thore with him and climbed up a high mountain ridge. There they dislodged huge boulders and sent them rolling down the cliff side and into the lower columns of Swedish warriors. While dislodging boulders, Halfdan and Thore shouted back and forth to each other. When Halfdan yelled 'Thore', the Swedes thought he was yelling 'Thor'.

The Swedish warriors surrendered because they thought that Halfdan was the son of the great god Thor. When he visited Sweden in later times, people came and bestowed divine honours on him and treated him with devotion and divine respect.

Erik took a large force from Skaane and went into Zealand. There he ravaged and laid waste wherever he went. Gudrod took an army and went against Erik, but Erik won and Gudrod had to flee. Two more times Gudrod took an army against Erik, but each time, he lost and had to flee.

When Halfdan heard how it was faring in Zealand, he took his army out of Skaane and sailed back to Zealand. When Halfdan arrived in Zealand, Erik took his army back to Skaane and thus easily regained his land.

Halfdan went back to Skaane. He hid his fleet in a bay and sailed against Erik with two ships. Erik attacked Halfdan with ten vessels. Halfdan's ships fled into a narrow channel and into the bay where his fleet was hidden. Erik had pursued too far. The Danish ships came out to sea and surrounded Erik's ten ships.

Halfdan offered Erik his life in thralldom. But Erik could not bear a life like that. He said he would rather die as a free man. But Halfdan could not bear to kill so worthy an adversary. He had Erik made outlaw and took him to a land in the east where he was released.

Halfdan made Gudrod King of Skaane. Then he sailed back to Lejre and established his high seat there.

94 YNGVAR

Yngvar had a son Onund and Onund's son Ingjald was about six years old.

Yngvar's district Kings were spread widely over Sweden. Svipdag the Blind ruled over Tiundaland, the district where Uppsala was situated, and where all the Swedish Things were held. Here was also held the mid-winter sacrifices, at which many Kings attended.

Yngvar (same name as the King of all the Swedes), the district King of Fjadryndaland, had two sons, Alf and Agnar, who were at about the same age as Ingjald. In the winter, Yngvar came to Uppsala with his two sons for the mid-winter sacrifices. There was a great assembly and many Kings attended.

Alf and Ingjald, both six years old, were playing. Alf was stronger than Ingjald and Ingjald kept losing in the play. This vexed Ingjald so much that he was in tears and almost cried. Gautvid, Ingjald's foster brother came up and took Ingjald to his foster father, Svipdag, the Blind. Gautvid told Svipdag that it appeared ill that Ingjald was less manly than Alf, Yngvar's son. Svipdag agreed and said that it was a great shame.

The next day, Svipdag took the heart of a wolf, roasted it on a pair of tongs, and gave it to Ingjald to eat. From that time, Ingjald became a ferocious person with a bad disposition.

In the summer, Yngvar took his forces to Estland (Estonia), and plundered at a place called Stein. The men of Estland came down from the interior with a great army. There was a battle. The army of Estland was so brave that the Swedes could not withstand them. King Yngvar fell and his warriors fled. Yngvar was buried close to the seashore in Estland. After this defeat, the Swedes returned home.

Thjodolf sang of it thus:

"Certain it is the Estland foe

The fair-haired Swedish king laid low.

On Estland's strand, o'er Swedish graves,

The Saga Kings

The East Sea sings her song of waves;

King Yngvar's dirge is ocean's roar

Resounding on the rock-ribbed shore."

95 ONUND YNGVARSON

Onund was the name of Yngvar's son who succeeded him. King Onund went with his army to Estland to avenge his father. He landed in Estland and ravaged the country far and wide. Hrym fell in one of the battles. Onund returned to Sweden in the autumn with great booty.

In his time, there were fruitful seasons in Sweden, so Onund was one of the most popular kings. Sweden was a great forestland. There were such great, uninhabited forests that it was a journey of several days to cross them. Onund spent much wealth and hired people to clear land and make soil available for farms. He had roads made through the forests and had settlers brought in to cultivate the lands. In this way, great districts were settled.

Because Onund had roads made all through Sweden, through forests, morasses, and also over mountains, he became known as Onund Roadmaker. He also had a house made for himself in every district of Sweden.

Onund applied to King Algot for his daughter Gauthild to marry Ingjald. Algot was a son of Gotrek the Mild, and grandson of Got. From this line, Gotland got its name. King Algot thought his daughter would be well married if she got Ingjald as husband, so he sent his daughter to Uppsala

The sea kings, Toke and Anund were attempting to raid in Denmark. Halfdan met them at sea and attacked them. Toke and Anund were routed and sailed away.

At Uppsala, King Onund's son Ingjald married Gauthild, daughter of Algot. They had a daughter and called her Aasa.

Siwald, a Skaanian decided to take over the kingdom of Denmark. Siwald had seven sons and they set out in a fleet for Lejre. Halfdan heard of these things while out roving. The two fleets met and Siwald sent an envoy to Halfdan requesting that Halfdan meet himself and his sons in single combat. Halfdan sent the reply that single combat could not lawfully be fought by more than two men. Siwald sent the reply that it was no wonder a childless bachelor should refuse the offered conflict because he was void of heat. He also said that a man's children were a part of himself and were not different than the man who begat them, and that they were no different than one person. Halfdan was offended to the point that he was not thinking. He got very angry and accepted the terms for "single combat".

Halfdan went into a forest and found an oak tree. From the oak roots he made himself a mace. He put iron knobs on the mace. Then he put on his mail coat and helmet, leaving his shield behind. At the duel, he wielded the mace with both hands and attacked Siwald and his seven sons. Siwald and his seven sons were destroyed by the force of Halfdan's mace.

When Ingjald and Gauthild had a son, they called him Olaf.

Hardbeen from Helsingaland began raiding in the Baltic Sea. He had twelve berserkers with him at all times. He would come hidden ashore in kingdoms. Then he would kidnap and ravish princesses. The more noble and famous his victims, the more noble he thought himself. Men who tried to stop him were killed.

When the summer came, Hardbeen began raiding and ravishing again. Envoys came to Lejre from many Kingdoms. These envoys asked Halfdan to attack Hardbeen and his berserkers. Halfdan not only promised to fight but assured the envoys victory with confident words.

Word of Halfdan's boast came to Hardbeen and a time and place of meeting was arranged. When Halfdan arrived, Hardbeen began to consume his shield. He went into frenzy, drew his sword, killed six of his own berserkers, and then with the remaining six berserkers, charged Halfdan. Halfdan crushed Hardbeen and his six berserkers with an immense hammer which he was wielding with both hands.

Gauthild sent her son Olaf to his foster father, Bove, king of West Gothland. There Olaf was brought up with Saxe, Bove's son. Saxe was nicknamed Saxe Flette (Saxe Braid) because of his braided hair.

In the autumn, King Onund was traveling over one of his roads called Himmenheath. The road ran through some narrow mountain valleys with high mountains on both sides. There was a heavy rain at the time. There was an earthquake which caused a landslide of clay and stones to come down upon King Onund and his people. King Onund died and many of his people with him.

Voluspaa:

Then quivers the Ash Ygdrasil,

And all things in heaven and earth

Fear and tremble

The straight-standing ash

Ygdrasil quivers,

The old tree groans,

And the giant gets lose

All the earth trembles so,

And the crags,

The trees are torn up from the earth,

And the crags fall to ruin;

And all fetters and bonds

Shall be broken and rent.

96 INGJALD

(SURT THE FIRE GIANT AND FREY)

The Uppsala Kings were the highest in Sweden among the many district Kings. The family traced its lineage back to Frey himself. The dominions and kingly powers were spread among the branches of the family as these increased. Some of the Kings had increased their kingdoms by clearing great tracts of land and settling them.

Ingjald prepared a great feast to enter into his heritage after Onund, his father. He had a large hall made for the occasion. In it he placed seven high seats. The hall was called the Seven Kings Hall. Ingvar sent messengers throughout Sweden and invited kings and jarls to attend his feast. The district Great Kings invited were Algaut, his father in law, King of Gotland; Yngvar, King of Fjadryndaland, and his two sons, Alf and Algar; King Spornsjall of Nerike; King Sighvat of Aattundaland; and King Granmar of Sodermanland. All the people invited had places for them and their entourage in the new hall. Ingjald had appointed his own people and court to be seated at the Uppsala Hall.

When the guests had arrived they were all seated in the Hall of Seven Kings. Six Kings were seated in the high seats. But one of the high seats was empty. King Granmar of Sodermanland did not come. The Uppsala Kings were the highest in Sweden among the many district Kings. The family traced its lineage back to Frey himself. The dominions and kingly powers were spread among the branches of the family as these increased. Some of the Kings had increased their kingdoms by clearing great tracts of land and settling them.

It was the custom in those days that whoever gave an heir-ship feast after Kings or Jarls and entered upon his heritage, would sit on a foot stool in front of the high seat until the brag beaker was brought in. The brag beaker was a bowl full of strong mead. Then the heir would stand up, take the brag beaker, make solemn vows to be fulfilled afterwards, and drain the bowl. After draining the bowl, the heir would then ascend the high seat, which had been occupied by his father.

When the brag beaker came in, Ingjald grabbed it, stood up, and said, "I make this solemn vow to enlarge my dominions by one half towards all four corners of the world, or die."

He pointed the horn towards each of the four corners. Then Ingjald drained the horn.

The guests became drunk towards the evening. King Ingjald told Svipdag's sons, Gautvid and Hylvid, to arm themselves and their men. Gautvid and Hylvid went out, and came back with Ingjald's armed warriors from the Uppsala hall. Then they set fire to the Hall of the Seven Kings.

Voluspaa:

From the south comes Surt

With blazing fire-brand,

The sun of the war god

Shines from his sword.

Fire rages

Heat blazes

And high flames play

'gainst heaven itself.

Frey (the descendants of Frey) encounters Surt (the fire giant).

The hall was soon in a blaze, and the six kings, and all their people, were burned in it. Those who tried to get out were killed. Then King Ingjald laid all the dominions these kings had possessed under himself and took tax from them.

After this Ingjald became known as Ingjald the Bad. When King Granmar heard this news, he thought this would happen to him too if he did not take care.

97 HJORVARD AND GRANDMAR

In the summer Hjorvard, King of the Ylfings, came to Sweden. He brought his fleet into the Myrkva Fjord. When King Granmar heard that Hjorvard was in Myrkva Fjord, he sent a messenger and invited Hjorvard to a feast. Hjorvard had never raided in Granmar's dominions, so he gladly accepted the invitation.

When Hjorvard arrived at Granmar's hall, he was warmly welcomed. In the evening, the full bowls went around. It was the custom of kings, when they were at home, or at feasts which they had ordered to be made that they sat and drank together, a man and a woman with each other in pairs. The rest of the company sat and drank all together. It was the law among the Vikings that all who were at the entertainment should drink together in one company all around (That law has survived as a custom and today is called a 'toast').

King Hjorvard's high seat was placed right opposite King Granmar's high seat and on the same bench sat all his men. King Granmar told his daughter, Hildigun, who was a remarkably beautiful girl, to make ready and carry ale to the Vikings. Hildigun took a silver goblet, filled it and brought it to Hjorvard. She bowed before Hjorvard and said, "Success to all Ylfings: This cup to the memory of Rolf Krake!"

Hildigun drank out half the ale and handed the cup to King Hjorvard. He took the cup and took her hand, and said she must sit beside him. She replied that it was not Viking fashion to drink two and two with women. Hjorvard said that it was better for him to make a change, and leave the Viking law, and drink in company with her. Then Hildigun sat down beside him and they drank together. They spoke a great deal to each other throughout the evening.

The next day when King Granmar and Hjorvard met, Hjorvard spoke of his courtship and asked to have Hildigun in marriage. King Granmar laid this proposal before his wife, Hilda, and all the people of consequence. He told them they could trust Hjorvard and always have help. Every one approved the marriage and thought it very advisable. Hildigun was promised to Hjorvard and the wedding took place soon after. King Hjorvard stayed with Granmar, who had no sons, and helped him defend his dominions.

In the autumn, Ingjald collected a war force to go against Granmar, and Hjorvard. But Hjorvard and Granmar heard about it and also collected a war force. King Hogne of East Gotland, the father of Hilda, Granmar's wife, came to their assistance. Hildur, Hogne's son, also came to their assistance.

Ingjald landed with his army at Sodermanland. His army was by far the most numerous. A battle began, which was very sharp. Granmar's forces were ferocious. After the battle had lasted a short time, the chiefs, who ruled Fjadryndaland, West Gotland, Nerike, and Aattundaland, took flight with all their men from those countries and hastened to their ships. This placed Ingjald in great danger. As Ingjald fled to his ships, he received many wounds and Svipdag the Blind, Ingjald's foster father fell. Svipdag's sons, Gautvid and Hylvid, also fell. Ingjald managed to sail away to Uppsala.

King Ingjald was very displeased with his expedition and he thought that the army raised from the lands he had conquered had been unfaithful to him. There were now great hostilities between King Ingjald and King Granmar together with his son in law Hjorvard. When warriors from these realms met there were battles.

Egther, a Finlander was raiding in Skaane. Egther had three ships, and Halfdan attacked him with the same number. When night came, the battle had to stop. The next day Halfdan challenged Egther to a duel. Egther accepted and the two fought a holmgang which Halfdan won.

Grim was suing the chief Hather under threats for the hand of his daughter, Thorhild. Grim was known for his immense strength. Hather had sent word far and wide that whoever put Grim out of the way would have his daughter in marriage. Halfdan thought that he had been a bachelor long enough and desired to quit his roving and fighting. He set sail and went to Hather's dominion in Norway. When he landed, Halfdan disguised himself by smearing dirt on any mark he had by which he could be recognized. Then he went to Hather's hall and said he was there to challenge Grim.

When they came to the place of battle, Halfdan drew his sword and knew that it had been blunted. He cast his sword on the ground and drew another from a sheath and attacked Grim cutting through the mass on the side of the cuirass and slicing away the lower part of his shield. Grim said, "I cannot remember an old man who fought more keenly".

In his surprise, Grim's right arm hesitated in its stroke and Halfdan without wavering cut through it. Grim shifted his sword to his left hand and cut through the thigh of Halfdan. But the wound was slight and Halfdan felled Grim.

Halfdan married Thorhild and took her back to Lejre. Halfdan and Thorhild had a son and called him Ivar. The son was fostered out to the King of Northumberland.

Ingjald and Granmar met at the hall of a friend of both parties. Hjorvard came with Granmar. The meeting resulted in reconciliation between Ingjald and Granmar. Peace was the conclusion. It was agreed that the peace would last as long as the three kings should live. This was confirmed by oaths and promises of fidelity. In the spring, King Granmar went back to Uppsala and made offering for steady peace. Then he returned to his dominions.

In the autumn, King Granmar and his son in law Hjorvard went to their farm on the island of Sile and had a feast. When they were at the entertainment in the night, Ingjald arrived with his warriors and surrounded the house. Then he set fire to the house. Granmar and Hjorvard and all their men were burned inside the house. Ingjald then added the dominions of both these Kings to his own and appointed chiefs over them.

King Hogne and his son Hildur started to make raids on horseback into Ingjald's dominions, killing Ingjald's warriors. Hogne defended his kingdom against Ingjald to his dying day.

After King Gudrod of Skaane married Ingjald's daughter Aasa, she persuaded her husband to kill his brother Halfdan and thus become King of all Denmark. But after Halfdan was killed, the Danes held a thing and declared Rorik Eriksen, grandson of Frode, as their King.

98 RORIK FLING-BRACELET

After the death of Halfdan, the Skaanians, Kurlanders, Vends and other smaller kingdoms, which Halfdan had ruled, decided that they need not accept Rorik as their King. These rebellious countries resolved to attack Denmark. The Slavs joined them and also a number of other small countries.

Rorik summoned his country to arms. Then he brought his fleet out of the Roskilde Bay and sailed to where he could hide his fleet during the day. The leader of the rebel alliance had two thirds of the ships hide in a bay and set the rest to attack Rorik's fleet and then draw the Danes to the bay in which the two thirds of the ships lay in wait. Thus the Danes were to be surrounded.

The fleet, which was supposed to attack Rorik's fleet, sailed by the Bay in which Rorik's fleet lay hidden. Rorik's ships sailed out and attacked immediately. The fleet of the Danes was so swift that they quickly vanquished the enemy ships. The rest of the enemy, which had hidden in the bay, wondered what had happened to Rorik. The months rolled by and still they waited. At last they decided to sail out and attack the Danes.

As they approached the Danes, the fleet held back. An envoy was sent to Rorik. The envoy was an enormous man and renowned fighter. He said that in order to save many lives, it would be good to settle the dispute by a duel. He proposed that if he won, the countries represented in the fleet would be free from paying taxes. If the King won, the warriors would go home and the countries would pay tribute as usual.

A bold Dane stepped up to Rorik and asked what the reward would be if he beat the coalition champion. Rorik happened to have with him six gold bracelets intricately intertwined so that they could not be separated. He offered these bracelets as the prize to any man who beat the coalition champion. The young warrior agreed and went to meet the champion.

The battle started and the young warrior landed a blow on the champion. The first blow, that the champion landed, killed the young warrior. The Danes became very depressed and thought that they had lost. Rorik was vexed that his warriors could lose all their courage over the action of one man.

The next morning the champion came back and made the same challenge. It is possible that the champion thought he had fought the best man that the Danes had and was expecting Rorik to admit defeat or fight the champion himself. But Ubbe, an experienced fighter, stepped forward and accepted the challenge.

Ubbe also purposely asked the prize for the combat. Again Rorik offered the bracelets. Then Ubbe said, "How can I trust the promise when you keep the pledge in your own hands and do not deposit the pledge with a third party to hold? Let there be someone you can trust to hold it, so that you cannot take your promise back."

It was plain that Ubbe had said this in jest. But it was also a test of the new King. Rorik did not want to appear stingy in front of his men. It was a mark of a good King to be free handed with his wealth among his warriors. Therefore Rorik removed his six bracelets and hurled them across the water to Ubbe. But the distance was too far. The bracelets fell between the two ships and were lost in the depths of the sea. Ubbe went on to fight and beat the coalition champion.

From this event Rorik had earned the respect of his warriors and the name Fling-bracelet stuck with him for the rest of his life. But it had also won the hearts of the insurgents and they gladly started to pay tribute again.

99 IVAR VIDFADME

Gudrod in Skaane had become more depressed each year over having killed his brother Halfdan. Aasa became fed up with Gudrod and poisoned him. The Skaanians were upset over this and took up arms against Aasa. She fled back to her father, Ingjald, in Uppsala.

Ivar, Halfdan's son, was living with his foster father in Northumbria, Britain. When he heard about the death of his Uncle Gudrod, he raised an army and went to Skaane to avenge his uncle. The Skaanians flocked to him and made him their King. The Skaanian warriors joined Ivar's forces and they marched towards Uppsala. On their way, they were joined by Hogne and Hildur and their Goth warriors. They moved in all haste to Uppsala. But Ingjald was away at a feast in Raening.

At the feast in Raening, Ingjald heard that Ivar Halfdanson had come to Sweden with a huge army. Ingjald realized that he could not muster a force to go against Ivar. He also realized that if he tried flight, the Swedes would surround him from all over and kill him. Ingjald was famous for having killed twelve Kings. But each one he had killed with deceit. Each one would have been his ally. Each one would have wielded the sword of Frey on his behalf.

Ingjald conferred with his daughter Aasa and they both resolved on a plan. They drank until all their people were dead drunk. Then they set fire to the hall. The hall was consumed with everyone in it including King Ingjald and Aasa.

This was the end of the Ynglings in Sweden.

Thus sang Thjodolf:

"With fiery feet devouring flame

Has hunted down a royal game

At Raening, where King Ingjald gave

To all his men one glowing grave.

On his own hearth the fire he raised,

A deed his foemen even praised;

By his own hand he perished so,

And life for freedom did forego."

Voluspaa:

Frey contends with Surt,

And a hard encounter there is

Before Frey falls;

It is his death

That he lacks that good sword of his

That he gave to Skirnir.

The Swedes were happy to be rid of Ingjald and chose Ivar as their King. Thus Ivar Vidfadme became King of Sweden. Ivar declared Ingjald's son Olaf an outlaw.

All the Swedish people arose and drove out Ingjald's family and all his friends from Sweden. When Olaf heard of his father's death, he went to Nerike with the men who chose to follow him. Olaf's mother was Gauthild, and her mother was Alov, a daughter of Olaf the Sharp Sighted, king of Nerike.

Olaf married Solva, daughter of Halfdan Goldtooth, King of Soleyar. Soleyar was just west of Vermeland in Norway. Halfdan was a son of Solve Solvarson, who was a son of Solve the Old, who first settled on these islands. Olaf and Solva had two sons, Ingjald and Halfdan. Halfdan was brought up in Soleyar, in the house of his mother's brother, Solve.

Olaf Ingjaldson could no longer stay at Nerike because the Swedes had learned that he was living there. He went westward through the forest and crossed the river Klar that flows south into Venner Lake. There Olaf and his followers began to clear land, build houses and barns, burn and cultivate. After a few years there were great districts, which was called Vermeland and the people there made a good living.

When the Swedes learned what Olaf was doing, they laughed and called him the tree feller. Thus Olaf became known as Olaf Tree Feller.

Ivar spent the year securing the Swedish districts under his dominion. He spent another year in Skaane securing his kingdom. During this time, Ivar's daughter, Audrey was born.

100 HAMLET (AMLED)

Gerwendil, the Jarl of northern Jutland, died. His hall was on the island called Mors in the Lim Fjord. Rorik made Gerwendil's sons, Orwendel and Fenge, joint Jarls to defend northern Jutland.

Orwendel and Fenge decided that each should take turns governing northern Jutland for three years on an alternate basis. This would free the other up to go in Viking for three years. They decided that Orwendil should be the first to govern northern Jutland.

It became Fenge's turn to stay at home and govern Jutland. Because Fenge had no success in his raiding, he felt disgraced and inferior to his brother Orwendel.

Orwendel began his roving, and had great success. He did much pillaging and obtained great spoils.

Koller, a king in Norway, was very famous for his raiding. He became jealous of Orwendel's fame. Koller began cruising the seas in search of Orwendel's fleet and found it near an island. Each fleet landed on opposite sides of the island. The two chiefs agreed to fight in the center of the island with no witnesses. It was agreed that the fight was personal and that their warriors were to remain friends towards each other no matter what the outcome. It was also agreed that the victor would erect a mound over the fallen.

When the leaders met in the middle of the island, Orwendel went into berserker frenzy. He threw away his shield and grasping his sword with both hands rained blow after blow on his opponent. With the rain of blows he destroyed Koller's shield. At last he hewed off Koller's foot and then drove him lifeless to the ground.

Koller's sister, Sela, who was an experienced rover and warrior, attacked Orwendel, and he wound up slaying her as well. Then he raised a great mound over Koller's body.

The three years of roving was up for Orwendel. He sailed to Lejre. To gain favour with King Rorik Fling-bracelet, he gave the King the best trophies and the pick of the plunder. Orwendel met the King's daughter, Gerutha, and fell in love. He wooed Gerutha and won her. Rorik granted him her hand in marriage.

Orwendel then sailed home to Mors with his new bride.

Fenge now felt extremely inferior to Orwendel and was becoming jealous. He went out for his three years of roving, intent on becoming famous and successful.

Orwendel and Gerutha had a son and called him Hamlet.

Fenge returned to Mors. His three years of raiding had been as unsuccessful as the first three years, and he had grown more resentful of Orwendel.

Orwendel departed for his three years of roving and raiding. Then Fenge began to spend more and more time with Orwendel's wife, Gerutha.

Orwendel returned from his three years of pillaging. He was very successful again. The people of Mors celebrated and the two Jarls held a feast. Late at night after everyone was drunk, Fenge killed his brother Orwendel. The six year old, Hamlet saw his father being murdered.

Voluspaa:

Men slew without a thought

The ties of kinship were no more

Brothers will fight

and be each other's banes.

Fenge made up a cover story saying that Orwendel was killed to protect Gerutha from Orwendel's wrath and temper. But he also made a show of looking for the killer. Most people at court, including Gerutha, believed him. Fenge married Orwendel's widow Gerutha.

Hamlet observed everything and became afraid of Fenge. He began to believe that Fenge would kill him if he knew that Hamlet had seen the murder. To keep his uncle from suspecting him, he pretended that he was dull and utterly lacking in wits.

Every day Hamlet stayed at his mother's house utterly listless. He would fling himself on the ground and roll around in foul and filthy dirt. He smudged his face with slime to appear utterly mad.

Hamlet took to sitting by the fireplace. He would rake through the embers with his hands. He made wooden crooks and hardened them in the fire. When asked what he was doing, he would say he was making sharp spears to avenge his father.

Some of the people began to suspect that Hamlet was sane, because they recognized real craftsmanship in his crooks. When more and more people became suspicious of Hamlet, the matter came to the attention of the Jarl Fenge. The advisors of Fenge came up with a plan. A young woman was to be put in a secluded spot in the woods. Observers were to be placed out of sight. Then some of Fenge's men were to take Hamlet on a ride in the forest and ensure that he would happen to meet up with the young woman. It was agreed that if Hamlet's lethargy and state of mind were faked, he would yield straightway to violent delights.

One of the men chosen to ride with Hamlet was his foster brother. His brother warned Hamlet of the plan. When Hamlet was bidden to mount his horse, he did it backwards. He put the reins on the tail and sat on the horse facing the tail. Then he spurred the horse into a gallop. Everyone laughed at the ludicrous rider. When asked why he mounted the horse that way, Hamlet said that he wanted to be able to ride back home again.

As Hamlet rode on, a wolf crossed his path. The men with him told Hamlet that a colt had crossed his path. Hamlet replied that there were too few of that kind of stud in Fenge's stables.

The group rode by a beach and found the rudder of a ship that had been wrecked. They told Hamlet that they had discovered a huge knife. Hamlet said that this was the right thing to carve such a huge ham. By 'ham' Hamlet meant the 'sea'.

Hamlet's companions left him and he came across the maiden. There was a straw in the ground, which was fastened to the tail of a gadfly. Hamlet took this as a warning from his foster brother. He looked at the maiden, who was scantily dressed. The maiden knew Hamlet and wanted to lie with him as well. He caught her up and carried her off to a distant and impenetrable fern. When the two had lain together, he earnestly asked the maiden to disclose it to no one and she agreed.

When Hamlet was asked later whether he had ravished the maiden, he said yes that he had. When they asked about details, he talked about having rested upon the hooves of a beast of burden and a ceiling and that something had flitted by with a straw attached to it. At this answer, Hamlet's foster brother felt that Hamlet had thanked him for his warning. Fenge's men were frustrated that Hamlet had taken the girl to where they could not spy on him. They asked the maiden whether she had intercourse with Hamlet. She said that she had done no such thing.

One of Fenge's friends approached Fenge with another plan to test Hamlet's sanity. The plan was for Fenge to go on a trip. Hamlet was to stay in his mother's room while Fenge was away. Then the man would hide in Gerutha's room and listen to their conversations.

Fenge went on a pretend journey and had given orders that Hamlet was to quarter in his mother's room while he was gone. Fenge's spy sneaked into Gerutha's room and hid under a pile of straw.

When Hamlet entered his mother's room he was afraid of eavesdroppers, so he at first acted like an imbecile. He beat his arms as if they were wings and crowed like a rooster. Then he jumped up and down on the pile of straw. Feeling a lump there, he drew his sword and ran it through the lump. On discovering that the lump was a man, he pulled the man out of the straw and killed him.

Gerutha started to wail and berated her son for killing a man. But Hamlet scolded his mother for marrying her husband's murderer. He told Gerutha that he had seen the murder himself. Everything became clear to Gerutha, who now resolved to do everything she could to help Hamlet.

Hamlet cut the corpse into small pieces and boiled the pieces in water. When the pieces were cooked, he threw them out the window into the pigpen where the pigs ate them.

When Fenge returned from his trip, he could not find his spy anywhere. He searched all over. Fenge asked everybody but nobody had seen him. When he asked Hamlet, he said that the man had gone to the pigs and never came back.

Fenge now suspected that Hamlet was sane and knew that he had killed Orwendel. He could not do away with Hamlet because he feared that he would incur the wrath of his wife and Hamlet's grandfather, King Rorik Fling-bracelet. He came up with the plan of having the King of England kill Hamlet. He sent Hamlet and two messengers to Northumbria.

Before departing, Hamlet asked his mother to hang the hall with woven nets while he was gone. He also asked her to perform pretend memorial feast for him a year from this time. Then he promised to return after that.

On the voyage to England, Hamlet searched the belongings of the messengers and found a rune stick (a stick of wood with runes carved into it), which was addressed to a King in Northumbria. The message said to kill the prince and to take good care of the messengers. Hamlet altered the message and wrote for the king in Northumbria to kill the messengers and give the prince his daughter in marriage. There was marked on the rune stick, the rune signature of Fenge. Then he put the rune stick back where he found it. The messengers did not notice the changes. They were commoners and could not read.

The King in Northumbria greeted the party cordially. He read the runes and suspected that they were falsified. But he did not let on anything. In the evening he had a big feast prepared for the three guests.

Hamlet looked at all the splendours of the feast. But he refrained from eating anything. He even refused to drink. Everyone was curious as to why Hamlet touched neither food nor drink. The King sent a man to the room where Hamlet and his companions were to sleep. The man was to hide in the room and then report back on the conversations.

After retiring to their room, Hamlet's companions asked him why he had not eaten anything. He answered that the bread was flecked with blood and tainted and there was a tang of iron in the liquor, and furthermore that the meat reeked like a human carcass and was infected by a smack of the odor of the charnel. He also stated that the King had the eyes of a slave, and the Queen had in three ways shown the behavior of a bondmaid. Hamlet's two companions jeered him for saying those things.

When the King heard what Hamlet had said, he knew that Hamlet was either wise or mad. The King called his steward and asked where the bread had come from. The steward said that the bread came from the King's own baker. The King asked where the grain for the bread had come from. The steward replied, that not far off was a field with ancient bones of slaughtered men, and still bearing signs of the ancient marks of carnage. The steward had himself planted the grain in the field in the spring time because he thought that the extra fertilizer would produce a good crop.

The King learned that Hamlet had spoken the truth about the bread, so he asked about the meat. It turned out that the pigs had escaped from their pen and had consumed the carcass of a robber. The king then asked about the brew. He went to the well where the water had come from. He had the well dug up and found several rusted swords in the ground. Also the bees, that had made the honey, which produced the mead, had been nesting in the pouch of a dead man.

After learning these things, the King began to worry about his own lineage. He held a secret meeting with his mother. His mother would not tell him at first. But at last she admitted that the King's father was a thrall.

Though ashamed of his lowly birth, he admired Hamlet's perceptiveness and was now ready to believe anything Hamlet told him. He asked Hamlet what he had seen about the Queen to call her mother a bondmaid. Hamlet replied that, first she had covered her head in her mantle as bondmaids do, second she had gathered up her gown for walking, and third she picked her teeth with a splinter and then chewed up the remnants of food from between her teeth.

The King now admired Hamlet and gave him his daughter for wife. Then he had the two messengers executed. Hamlet pretended that he did not want the messengers dead and grieved. Therefore the king paid Hamlet gold for the loss of his servants and explained that the Jarl Fenge had so decreed. Hamlet took the gold, melted it down and poured the molten gold into two hollowed sticks of wood,

Hamlet spent a year with the King, enjoying life at court and his new wife.

When a year had gone by, Hamlet asked the King leave to go on a journey. Then he sailed home to Jutland taking the two sticks with him. When he reached Jutland he changed his clothes and dressed as a beggar. He rolled himself in filth and grime. Then Hamlet made his way to Fenge's hall.

In the Jarl's hall people were feasting in a memorial to Hamlet's death a year ago. Then suddenly, there was the mad prince at the door! The people were terrified to see him until they discovered that he was alive. When he was asked where his two companions were, Hamlet pointed at the two sticks he was carrying and said, "Here are both the one and the other".

Then Hamlet helped the cup bearers serve drinks. He changed the position of his sword so he could walk better. He drew his sword several times, each time pricking his fingers. The bystanders took his sword and scabbard and ran a nail through them, fastening the sword firmly inside the scabbard. Hamlet kept plying the lords with drink until it became apparent that they were too drunk to walk away from the hall. One by one the revelers fell asleep in the hall during the night.

Then Hamlet went to his old quarters and got the hooks he had made by the fireplace. When he entered the hall again, all the warriors and nobles were sound asleep. Hamlet took down the nets his mother had hung on the walls during his absence. He put the nets over the sleepers and fastened them down so tight with his hooks that the men could not get up. After this he set fire to the hall.

Then Hamlet went to Fenge's quarters. When Hamlet entered Fenge's quarters, Fenge was sound asleep. Hamlet exchanged his sword with that of Fenge. Then he shouted that the nobles and warriors were perishing in the burning hall and that Hamlet was here with his crooks to avenge his father. On hearing this, Fenge sprang from his bed. Hamlet cut him down with Fenge's own sword while Fenge was trying to draw the strange sword of Hamlet. Meanwhile the hall burned up with all the nobles and warriors inside.

Hamlet hid because he did not know what the people would say about his deeds. The whole neighborhood had watched the blaze during the night. In the morning, they gathered and discussed the matter. Some of the people were angry, others grieved and others yet were delighted to be free of Fenge.

After overhearing the various groups talking, Hamlet left his hiding place. He called a meeting of those whom he knew were faithful to his father Orwendel. Then he gave a speech and told everyone about his witnessing Fenge killing his father Orwendel, and how he played insane to stay alive. The people were deeply moved by his speech. They all voted for Hamlet to replace Fenge as their leader.

Hamlet left Mors in a ship and sailed to Lejre. He explained to King Rorik what had happened. Rorik appointed Hamlet as Jarl of Jutland.

Hamlet equipped three vessels and prepared to sail back to Britain to see his wife and father in law. He had chosen the best young warriors of Jutland to come with him to England. For his warriors he had the best weapons and armor made. Hamlet wore the finest clothes there was to buy and his armor, helmet, and shield were gold plated. Hamlet's shield was inlaid with the story of his life. The shields of his warriors were also all gold plated.

When all was ready, Hamlet sailed the three ships to Northumbria. The King of Northumbria received them very generously, and threw a big feast in honour of Hamlet's return. The Queen had died the past winter of illness, and Hamlet expressed his regrets.

The King asked how his friend Fenge was faring. Hamlet told the King the whole story of Orwendel and Fenge and how Hamlet had avenged his father and had slain Fenge. When the King heard this he was shocked because he and Fenge had made a vow to each other that if one of them was killed the other would be his avenger.

The King was torn between his love for his daughter and Hamlet, and his need to fulfill his vow. The King decided that he would not break his tie to hospitality and he could not himself have his daughter's husband killed. He decided to send Hamlet on a mission which would cause his death.

Ermontrud was Queen in one of the districts in Scotland. She was unmarried and hated her wooers. Everyone who had sought her hand in marriage wound up dead. The King told Hamlet that he wished to marry Ermontrud. He asked Hamlet to go to Ermontrud and ask her to marry the King. Hamlet agreed to go and the King gave Hamlet a rune stick with a message to Ermontrud.

Hamlet marched to Scotland with his men and some of the King's men. On the way to the Queen's hall, they camped by a stream. When Queen Ermontrud heard of Hamlet's approach, she sent out ten warriors to scout out Hamlet's band of men. One of Ermontrud's men slipped by Hamlet's guards and found Hamlet asleep with his head on his shield. He took Hamlet's shield and the rune stick, which he was carrying. Ermontrud's scout then slipped back out of Hamlet's camp without being seen.

When Ermontrud's patrol returned, she read the rune stick. Hamlet's shield was engraved with the story of his life. After reading the shield and the stick, she knew all about Hamlet. Ermontrud abhorred her suitors because they were all old men. She resolved to have a closer look at the young prince Hamlet. Therefore she changed the runes on the stick so that the writing said that she was asked to marry the one who brought the message. She also added the story of Hamlet as written on the shield. Thus it looked as if the one confirmed the other. She then told her patrol to return the stick and the shield.

When the man with the shield and the rune stick came back to Hamlet, he was seized and bound, because Hamlet had woken up and missed his shield. The next day, Hamlet and his men reached Ermontrud's stronghold. Hamlet greeted the Queen in the name of the King and presented the rune stick. Ermontrud took the stick and read it out loud. Then she praised Hamlet for outwitting Fenge and avenging his father's murder. She marveled that such a mighty hero could have made a marriage in mistake. She said her scepter and her hand went together. She said that Hamlet should put away his wife and marry herself. Then she fell on Hamlet in a close embrace and kissed him tenderly.

Hamlet was overjoyed at the speech of the young Queen Ermontrud and kissed her back. Friends were invited, the nobles gathered, a banquet was held, and the wedding rites were performed. A few days after the wedding Hamlet went back to Northumbria with his new bride. A band of Scottish warriors followed behind them.

The daughter of the King, to whom he was still married, came out to meet them. She told Hamlet that she loved him and would not hold it against him that he married Ermontrud. She said that she wanted to stay with him and that their son might hate Ermontrud, but she would love Ermontrud. Then she said that her father would try to kill Hamlet. While they spoke, the King came to them and invited them to a feast. Hamlet graciously accepted the invitation.

Hamlet put on a mail shirt under his regular shirt. Then he had the Scottish warriors wait in the woods, and took his own warriors to the banquet. As he entered the gate, the King attacked him and thrust a spear at his chest. The spear glanced off the mail shirt and Hamlet was slightly wounded. Hamlet and his warriors fled to where the Scottish warriors were hidden. The king pursued Hamlet with haste and a fierce battle was fought at the edge of the woods. Most of Hamlet's forces were killed in the battle. Night put an end to the fighting.

During the night Hamlet put stakes under the bodies of many of his dead warriors and propped them up to look alive. He put other bodies on horseback like living men. Still other bodies he tied to large stones. He had put the dead corpses up in battle formation. Between the dead corpses, he stationed the living of his warriors.

In the morning, the King came back with his army, and was terrified, because the light from the rising sun reflected off the armour of the warriors of Hamlet. Hamlet's forces looked as big as the night before and the King's forces were now much smaller. The King ordered his forces to flee. Hamlet and his men pursued the King and cut down most of his warriors. The King also fell.

Hamlet triumphantly looted the King's hall. Then he sailed back to Mors with his two wives.

101 RORIK AND HELGE

Helge, the brother of the Dan King Rorik Fling-bracelet, wished to marry Audrey, the daughter of King Ivar of Sweden. Helge sailed to Sweden and asked Ivar for Audrey's hand in marriage.

King Ivar of Sweden was a mighty warrior who harried often, far and wide in other lands. Because of these exploits he was nicknamed Vidfadme (Far Reacher, or Far Grasper). When Helge asked for Audrey's hand in marriage, Ivar went to his daughter to hear what she thought. Audrey would like to marry Helge, but Ivar said, "I see that it is necessary in this case, that there be spoken little about men wooing you. In the olden days, King's daughters never took the first suitor, but let three or more wooers come. There are other well raised kings than Helge".

Audrey answered, "It makes no difference whether you ask me about this or not, because I know that you have ahead of time resolved completely that this wedding will not take place. It will not go as I wish. It is possible that you will withhold such a good match from me because you have someone else in mind for my marriage".

King Ivar said, "You have guessed correct. You shall never be married to King Helge, whether you want to or not".

Ivar went back to his hall and sought Helge. He told Helge that he had spoken with his daughter about Helge's case. He said that he had approached her with care but that her answer seemed that it was not worth pursuing. He said that the more he talked with his daughter it seemed that this she thought the match was not good enough for her. He said that her sights were set much higher. Ivar told Helge that he would not press forward his suit because as things stood now, it would amount to nothing. Helge sailed back home.

Rorik Fling-bracelet's wife had died a few years ago. Because Rorik sat at home in his Kingdom, his friends pressed Rorik to marry Audrey. The more Rorik thought about it, the more he liked the idea. But Rorik was unsure about his suit because his brother Helge was much more outgoing and had failed. His friends said that Rorik would never marry if he did not woo the girl and that there was no shame in being turned down.

Rorik asked Helge to go to Sweden on his behalf to ask for Audrey's hand in marriage. Helge said that he was willing to go but that chances of success were not good. Then Helge sailed back to Sweden where he was well received. At the feast that night, Helge put forth his brother's suit. King Ivar said that it was unwise and that there was no hope for it. He said that since Audrey is unwilling to marry you she would be even less likely to marry someone less worthy than yourself.

Helge replied that Rorik was in no way inferior to himself. He said that Rorik was not as famous because he stayed at home in his Kingdom and therefore did not have as many battle victories for bards to sing about. He begged Ivar to go to his daughter with the suit. Ivar said that he was unwilling to do so and that he expected the same answer as before.

The next day, Ivar summoned Audrey and told her that Helge had come on behalf of his brother to ask her hand in marriage. He said that Helge wished to hear her answer. Audrey answered that it should not go like the previous time and that she would marry Rorik.

Ivar was unhappy that his daughter would not follow his advice. But Ivar then went to Helge and promised his daughter to Rorik. Audrey spent the day packing and the next morning she sailed off with Helge. On the trip to Lejre, Helge and Audrey talked about how this situation came about. They talked about what Ivar had said to each of them.

When they arrived at Lejre, Rorik met them with horses and a large number of followers. A big feast was prepared and Rorik was wedded with Aud. That winter Helge sat at home on Zealand.

When summer came, Helge went on Viking raids as usual.

Rorik and Audrey had a son. They called him Harald.

In the summer, Ivar Vidfadme came from the east with his fleet from Sweden. He was on his way to Reidgotaland. Ivar's fleet put in at Zealand, and Ivar sent a messenger to Rorik to come and see him. Rorik told his wife Audrey about the message. She asked him if he wished to seek Ivar out and invite him to a feast on land.

That evening Audrey prepared Rorik's bed with new sheets and new pillows and blankets. Then she moved the bed to the middle of the room. When Rorik went to bed, she slept in a different bed. In the morning she asked Rorik if he had dreamed that night.

Rorik had dreamed that he was beside a forest and beside the forest was an even beautiful prairie. He saw a buck standing on the prairie. Then he saw a leopard run out of the woods. The pelt of the leopard shone like gold. The buck stuck the leopard's side with its antlers and the leopard fell dead. Next a flying dragon swooped down on the buck and rent it into little pieces. Then a she bear came out of the woods with a little cub. The dragon tried to take the cub, but the she bear protected it. Audrey said that it was an important dream and to be careful of her father.

That day Rorik took many men and went to Ivar's ships. He went aboard Ivar's ship and went forward to Ivar who was standing under the dragon prow. He greeted Ivar, who did not answer and pretended that Rorik was not there. Then Rorik said that he was having a feast prepared and invited Ivar to come.

Ivar's reply was full of anger. He said that Audrey and Helge were playing behind his back, and that the common folk said that Harald was Helge's son. Ivar said that he had come to tell Rorik about the deceit, and that he thought that they should not have Audrey together. He advised Rorik to give his wife to Helge.

Rorik said that he had not heard about this, but that he would under no circumstance give up his wife. Then he asked Ivar for advice. Ivar said that the only advice he could give was for Rorik to slay his brother, because the way things were was not tolerable. Rorik said that he would never give up his wife, and that he would rather seek revenge.

Rorik and his men rode back to Lejre and Ivar sailed with his fleet south to Reidgotaland.

When Helge came home from his Viking raids in the fall, Rorik was in a deep depression. No one could get Rorik to talk about it. Audrey had a big feast prepared for Helge's return. There were many guests and many games were played. Helge thought it a great shame that Rorik was so depressed, so he invited Rorik to take part in the games. Rorik said that the way things were he had no desire to play. But Helge persisted and wanted to do some jousting on horseback like they used to do.

Rorik sprang up without a word and went out to his men. He took his helmet, mail shirt, sword, and spear, and rode out. The other men rode with lances. Helge and Rorik rode at each other, Helge with a lance, Rorik with his spear. Rorik stuck the spear under Helge's arm penetrating through his body, so that he fell dead from his horse.

All the men rode to the spot and asked Rorik why he did this ill deed. Rorik said there was good reason for it. He said that he had received the information that Helge had robbed him of his wife.

Everyone denied what Rorik said. They told him it was a big lie. When Aud heard the news, she told Rorik that she knew it was her father's advice he had acted on. She said that not all he has planned has yet come to pass, but will soon happen.

Audrey took her son Harald and rode away with many warriors. But Rorik went back to the hall and continued with the feast.

A few days later, Ivar Vidfadme came from the south with his fleet and landed at Zealand. When Ivar heard that Helge had been slain, he declared that it was a deceitful act. He told his men to arm themselves and avenge his friend Helge. He sent his warriors ashore and into the nearby woods.

When Rorik heard Ivar had come, he rode out with his men to meet him. When Ivar got news that Rorik was coming to the coast to meet him, he had the men who had remained with the ships go ashore. Then he set up his standard and went against Rorik when he arrived. When the warriors in the woods heard Ivar's war horn blowing, they rushed out and ran at Rorik's warriors from behind. When the forces collided Rorik's forces were caught in the middle of Ivar's warriors. Rorik was surrounded and fell with all his men.

King Ivar Vidfadme demanded that the Kingdom of Denmark be given to him. The people in the neighborhood were made to swear allegiance to him.

The next day Audrey, Ivar's daughter, arrived with a big army, which she had gathered. Ivar's forces were much smaller, so he had his men board the ships and sailed away to Sweden.

That winter Audrey collected all the gold and treasures which had belonged to Rorik and packed it up. When the spring came, Audrey prepared to leave Lejre. Many Jarls and great warriors went with her and they sailed to the island of Gotland.

The Saga Kings

In the summer, Ivar took his fleet to Lejre and added Denmark to his kingdom. Ivar appointed Wiglek as Jarl in north Jutland. Wiglek sailed to Mors where he harassed Hamlet's mother, Gerutha, daughter of Rorik. He stripped her of her wealth. He said that her son had usurped the power in Jutland and defrauded the King of Lejre, who had sole privilege of giving and taking away office.

In the fall Hamlet returned from his Viking raids. He submitted to Wiglek and gave him the most of his spoils.

In the spring, Audrey and her warriors left the island of Gotland and sailed to Frisia. King Radbard (Red Beard) of Frisia received them well.

When Hamlet got the chance, he attacked Wiglek. There was a great battle. Wiglek lost and had to flee.

Hamlet now took the offensive. He took a fleet to Skaane and attacked the Jarl, Fjaller. Hamlet was victorious and Fjaller was driven into exile in Undensakre.

Wiglek recruited warriors in Skaane and Zealand. Then he sent envoys to Hamlet and declared war.

Hamlet knew that he had no hope of surviving if he went to war. He was worried about his wife, Ermontrud. But Ermontrud declared that she had the courage of a man and would not forsake him. She said she was prepared to die alongside him on the battlefield.

The forces of Hamlet met the forces of Wiglek on a big field. When Hamlet fell in battle, Ermontrud surrendered. She presented herself to Wiglek as the conqueror's spoil and bride. Wiglek accepted Ermontrud's offer and married her. Wiglek's rule in Jutland was long and peaceful. Hamlet was buried in a great mound.

102 AUDREY AND KING RADBARD

Audrey and her people left Gotland and sailed to Frisia where the King of Frisia invited Audrey to stay with him. Radbard of Frisia was a mighty King, and Audrey thought Harald needed a father. Radbard and Audrey became married.

When the news reached Ivar that Audrey had married Radbard, he was insulted that Radbard married his daughter without his permission. He gathered a great army from Denmark and Sweden. His fleet was so large that it was impossible to count his ships. Ivar Vidfadme declared that he would lay waste Radbard's kingdom and burn everything in it. Then he led his fleet eastward towards Frisia.

Ivar brought his fleet into the bay where King Radbard's Kingdom began and waited for favourable conditions for his attack on Radbard. One night Ivar had a dream as he slept on a raised part of his ship. He dreamed that he saw a huge dragon fly in from the ocean, and he thought that its colour was gold. He saw a huge flock of birds of all kinds follow the dragon.

When Ivar looked to the northeast he saw hard rain and heavy winds. Thunder and lightning was in the rain and winds. Then he saw the dragon and the birds fly over the land and into the storm until he could see them no longer. Then he heard the sound of the storm and it moved southwest and over all his lands. When he looked at his ships, they turned into porpoises and swam off.

Ivar woke up and summoned his foster father, Hard. He told Hard his dream and asked Hard to interpret it. Hard stood on a cliff opposite the ship where Ivar stood on a raised part. Ivar was in a bad mood and wanted Hard to come aboard, and interpret the dream.

Hard said that he would not board the ship and said "It is not necessary to interpret the dream because you know very well yourself what it means. It is certain that you will die and your enemies will obtain the power."

Ivar was very angry at Hard for foretelling his death. He wanted to kill Hard and sprang down from the raised part of the ship. But he was so mad that he went too far, out over the railing and into the water. Hard jumped off the cliff and into the ocean. That was the last anyone saw of them. They never came up to the surface. The guards on the King's ship were the last to see them.

The ships in the fleet all beached. All the warriors went onto the land and held a Thing. They conferred on what to do with the huge army. They all agreed that since Ivar was dead, they had no suit against King Radbard. A chief suggested that they return home as soon as possible when they had good sea weather. Everyone agreed. The army disbanded and each ship sailed home to its own country.

103 HARALD WARTOOTH

When King Radbard of Frisia heard what happened to Ivar Vidfadme and his fleet, he gave Harald a portion of his warriors. Harald took the warriors and sailed to Zealand with the jarls and heroes who had accompanied Audrey to Frisia. When they arrived in Zealand, the Zealanders held a Thing and chose Harald as King of Denmark.

Harald had the deeds of Halfdan recorded in runes on a rock as a memorial in Bleking. Then he set out to re-conquer the territories which Halfdan, and after him, Ivar had owned. First he took the isles of Denmark. Then he took Skaane and Gotland. He established jarls in all the areas and had them pay tribute or tax. He placed the Ylfing, Hjormund over Sodermanland. Hjormund was the son of Hervard, who was the son of Hjorvard who had ruled Sodermanland with King Granmar. He also gave Hjormund East Gotland.

Harald was notable on the battlefield because he fought as a berserker, without shield and armour. Harald retook northern Jutland in battle against Hather. During the fierce fighting, Hather fell. Then he went to Reidgotaland, where King Hildebrand swore him allegiance.

Harald was now called Harald Wartooth because of his constant battles. He continued to subjugate more small kingdoms.

Asmund, King of the Wikars, was exiled by his older sister. Asmund sent a messenger to Harald Wartooth for help to regain his Kingdom. Harald sailed to Norway in a single ship. When the battle began, Harald went forward in a purple robe, no armour and no shield. He wore a coif, braided with gold, and his hair bound up. When the other side saw him fighting unarmed they made an attack. But Harald Wartooth, fighting as a berserker, made whoever came against him take flight. Finally the whole opposing army fled and Asmund regained his throne. Asmund's sister fled in a ship. Asmund pursued her with a fleet and killed her.

Alver, King of the Swedes died. His sons Olaf, Ing, and Ingjald, split the Kingdom. Ing was not satisfied with his part of the Kingdom. He declared war on the Danes to enlarge his territories. Olaf joined Ing in his war on Denmark. There were several battles between the Swedes and Harald Wartooth.

In the land battles, Harald arranged his army into three squadrons, each of which was arrayed in twenty ranks. The center squadron was extended further than the rest by a number of twenty men. The center squadron was also arranged in svinfylking formation. The front rank of this squadron consisted of two men. The succeeding ranks were increased by only one in each rank. Thus there were three men in the second line, four in the third line and so on, until the end of the wedge was made. At this junction the wings were formed.

Each wing was drawn up in ten lines. After these ten lines, there were young men armed with lances. Behind the lancers were aged men, veterans of valour. These men advised and encouraged their younger fellows. After these were wings of slingers and archers, who attacked the enemy with missiles from a distance. After these came men of any age or rank indiscriminately, including the inexperienced. Behind them the warriors were arranged like the previous ranks except in reverse. This way if attacked from the rear, the squadron was just as strong as if attacked from the front.

When fighting on the sea, Harald would withdraw a portion of his ships from the engagement. This portion would circle the enemy and weave in and out, attacking in unexpected places.

Using these tactics, Harald Wartooth won every battle in which he engaged. In one of the battles in the autumn, both Olaf and Ing fell. Ingjald sent a message to Harald asking for truce, which Harald granted. Ingjald then swore allegiance to Harald and became the sole King of Sweden.

The two shield maidens, Stikla and Rusla, demanded the Kingdom of the Tronds from its ruler, King Olav, who had sworn allegiance to Harald. Harald fought Stikla and Rusla in a holmgang and felled them both.

Ubbe, a Frisian, was harrying in Jutland. Harald challenged Ubbe to a duel. Ubbe fought so well that Harald could not beat him with weapons. He managed to strike Ubbe so that he fell to the ground. Harald had his men tie up Ubbe. Then Ubbe swore allegiance to Harald Wartooth and married his sister.

Harald Wartooth made the nations along the Rhine tributaries to his Kingdom. Then he levied warriors from the bravest of these countries and attacked Slavonia. The Slavonian generals, Duk and Dal were mighty warriors and brave fighters, but their armies were defeated and Duk and

Dal were taken as captives. After having Duk and Dal swear allegiance, Harald combined the Slav warriors with his army and invaded Aquitania, which he annexed to his kingdom.

Harald Wartooth was now so famous that warriors came from many parts of the world to join him. Harald formed these warriors into bands of mercenaries. No one dared to assume any sovereignty over the sea without Harald's consent.

Harald's mother Audrey was married to King Radbard of Frisia. Their son Ranver was on a raid in England when he was killed in battle. Ranver's son was called Sigurd. Harald appointed Sigurd guardians and put him over the kingdom of Sweden. Harald assured that the Swedish warriors were well trained. King Sigurd of Sweden became known as Sigurd Ring. He spent a lot of time with Harald Wartooth.

At this time Hildebrand was King in Reidgotaland. He was a mighty warrior. His son was Hilde and his daughter was Hild. Sigurd Ring married Hild.

104 OLAF TREE FELLER

There were many people who had moved out of Sweden because of Ivar Vidfadme. Many of these refugees had heard that Olaf Tree Feller had good lands in Vermeland, and went there. So many went there that the land could not support them. The Swedes ascribed good harvests and famines to their kings. The Swedes in Vermeland ascribed the land not being able to support them to their King, Olaf Tree Feller. They thought that Olaf had not made enough sacrifices.

The Swedes gathered together warriors and went to Olaf's house by Venner Lake. They surrounded his house and burned him in it, giving him to Odin as a sacrifice for good crops.

Thus sang Thjodolf:

"The temple wolf, by the lake shores,

The corpse of Olaf now devours.

The clearer of the forests died

At Odin's shrine by the lake side.

The glowing flames stripped to the skin

The royal robes from the Swedes' king.

Thus Olaf, famed in days of yore,

Vanished from earth at Venner's shore."

Voluspaa:

"Frey contends with Surt,

And a hard encounter there is

Before Frey falls;

It is his death

That he lacks that good sword of his

That he gave to Skirnir."

Olaf's son Ingjald was chosen as King in Vermeland.

Many Swedes in Vermeland realized that it was not the King who produced good crops. They realized that there were too many people for the land in Vermeland to support. These people banded together and crossed the Eida forest. They came unexpectedly into Soleyar. They attacked King Solve. After a fierce battle, which the Swedes won, they captured King Solve and put him to death. They took Halfdan, son of Olaf Tree Feller, prisoner.

The Swedes in Soleyar made Halfdan their chief and called him their King. Halfdan then subdued Soleyar and made its people swear allegiance to him. Halfdan became known as Halfdan White Legs.

105 KING SKJOLD OF VARNA

King Eystein of Westfold and Raumarike took a fleet to Varna and made war. He plundered there and carried of clothes, valuables, and livestock. King Skjold of Varna gathered an army and went after Eystein. They reached the shore in time to see the sails of Eystein's ships departing in the distance.

King Eystein was sitting at the helm and his ship was passing another ship. The waves caused the boom of the other ship to sweep Eystein overboard. Eystein drowned. Eystein's men fished up his body, and carried it into Borre where a mound was thrown up facing the sea at Raden near Vodle. It was told that Skjold had killed Eystein by witchcraft.

Song by Thjodolf: --

"King Eystein sat upon the poop

Of his good ship: with sudden swoop

The swinging boom dashed him to hell,

And fathoms deep the hero fell

Beneath the brine. The fury whirl

Of Loke, Tempest's brother's girl,

Grim Hel clutched his soul away;

And now where Vodle's ocean bay

Receives the ice-cold stream, the grave

Of Eystein stands -- the good, the brave!"

Halfdan, Eystein's son succeeded Eystein as King of Westfold and Raumarike. Halfdan became known as Halfdan the Mild. He was a great warrior and went often on Viking expeditions. He was married to Liv, a daughter of King Dag of Westmar.

106 HALFDAN WHITE LEGS

Halfdan White Legs took his army into Raumarike and plundered there. After subduing Raumarike and adding it to his Kingdom, he took his army into Hedemark and plundered. The ruler of Hedemark, Eystein the Severe, King of the Uplands, went against him and there were fierce battles. When Eystein and Halfdan decided to make peace, Halfdan had subdued a great deal of Hedemark.

Halfdan also conquered Toten, Hadeland, and Westfold adding them to his kingdom

107 ISLAM

During the reign of Harald Wartooth, the religion called Islam was born. In 632, the prophet, Mohammed died at Medina. The very next year, the Arabs took Yemen and raided in Iraq. In 634, the Arabs crossed the Jordan River and made war in the name of Allah and Islam. Anyone who did not accept Islam and learned Arabic was put to death.

The Islamic conquests came fast and furious. In 635, the Arabs conquered Damascus, and in 636, they took all of Syria. In 637, the Arabs took Jerusalem, and in 638, they conquered Jazirah. In 639, they conquered Khuiszistan and then invaded Egypt which they conquered in 641. Then in 642, the Arabs fought battles in Persia.

By the year 711, the Arabs had conquered all of North Africa. Then in 712 A.D. the Moslems, under Omayyad, crossed the Straits of Gibraltar. They defeated the Visigoth army commanded by Roderic and conquered Spain. Omayyad made Abd-er Rahman the governor of Spain.

108 CHARLES MARTEL (THE HAMMER)

In 687, Pepin of Heristhal had conquered Neustria and united all the Franks. When Pepin died, his son Charles became King of the Franks.

In 732, Abd-er Rahman, Islamic governor of Spain took his army across the western Pyrenee Mountains. He then proceeded towards the Loire River. Records number his army between 60,000 and 400,000 soldiers. Charles raised an army and sent out messages to neighbouring kingdoms for assistance. The Danish prince Holger brought an army of Vikings to France to assist Charles. Holger was called Holger the Dane by his Norwegian warriors and the name had stuck. The Franks could not pronounce Holger's name so they called him Ogier le Danois or sometimes Ogier de Danemarche (Holger of Denmark).

Charles met the Moslems between Tours and Poitiers. Charles set his forces up into a phalanx, in the style of the old Roman army. The invading Moslems rushed forward at a gallop. They were relying on the slashing tactics and overwhelming number of horsemen, which had brought them victories in Syria, Egypt, North Africa, and Spain. The French were armed with only swords, shields, axes, javelins, and daggers. The Moslems were armed with large swords and lances. But the terrain was unsuited for a cavalry attack. The French army withstood the ferocious mounted attacks again and again. This was one of the few times that foot soldiers were able to withstand mounted attacks.

During the battle on the seventh day, the French captured and killed Abd-er Rahman. Night came and the battle stopped. The French waited to resume the battle at dawn, expecting a surprise attack in retaliation. The next day, October 10, was peaceful. The Moslems had slipped away during the night. The fall of their leader was a sharp setback. They recrossed the Pyrenees and went back to Spain. After this battle, Charles was called Charles Martel (Charles the Hammer). Holger the Dane became recognized as a national hero ever after.

The battle of Tours stopped the Moslem invasion of Western Europe. But it did not stop the Arabian holy war. They went on to take southern Italy, and they harried the coasts of north Italy and southern France. There were no fleets, which could withstand the Arabian ships. The western Mediterranean had become an Islamic sea.

109 THE BATTLE SLAUGHTER ON THE BRAAVALLE PLAIN

Harald was now very old. He conferred with Sigurd Ring on the method of Sigurd inheriting Harald's Kingdom. Harald Wartooth wanted to put an end to all the blood feuds and wars, which had been ravaging the North since the Fimbul Winter. Harald did not want to die on his sick bed. He wanted to die in battle and go to Valhalla. To meet these goals, Harald and Sigurd Ring came up with a plan of one big battle which would involve all of the fighters in the North, especially the ones involved in feuds. Harald and Sigurd would each collect a huge army so that the feuding parties could be allied on opposing forces. Then they would fight in one huge battle to end all the feuds. This was the plan to end the days of Harald, transfer the rule of all the North to Sigurd Ring, and put an end to all the blood feuds of Ragnarok by staging one great final battle. Brune was Harald's only advisor. The others had gradually died off. Harald Wartooth and Sigurd Ring used Brune as a courier to carry secret messages to each other on rune sticks.

Harald was so old that he found it difficult to move and he was going blind. Vikings were harrying in Denmark and there was fighting throughout the north. It now appeared that Harald was too old to check the pirates and sea rovers. People began to talk about Sigurd Ring taking over from Harald. It appeared that Harald and Sigurd Ring had a falling out. But they kept passing messages through Brune.

Harald Wartooth and Sigurd Ring declared war. The Scandinavians were surprised because Harald had named Sigurd Ring as his successor. For the next seven years Sigurd Ring and Harald Wartooth went about raising armies.

Sigurd Ring gathered warriors from all of Sweden and West Gothland. A huge army from Norway joined him. The Swedes and Norwegians went out through Stocksund in 2,500 ships.

Sigurd Ring rode with his army over land around the Oresund to the forest of Kolmark which lay between Sweden and East Gotland. When he came out of the woods onto the plain at Braavalle, Sigurd's sea army met him there and they set up camp on the plain between the woods and the Vik, to wait for the forces of Harald.

Harald gathered an army from the Danish Kingdoms. A great army came to him from the eastern kingdoms, and also from Konegaard and Saxony. He led his armies to Zealand, the part called Sygia. The ships there reached from Lanor to Skanor, and were packed so tight that you could walk on the ships dry footed between Zealand and Skaane. Harald selected Herleif and his Saxons to seek out Sigurd Ring and tell him they were coming to war.

Harald led his armies for seven days and at last reached the Braavalle plain.

An unknown skald sang this song:"

Suddenly Erik started singing. Everyone listened quietly as Erik's clear voice reverberated around the room. It was obvious that he was very familiar with the song.

> **"There stands a smithy on Helgoland**
>
> **So lonesome it stands by the white strand**
>
> **Here swings Taarmod the Smith with power**
>
> **His heavy hammer in the midnight hour.**
>
> **But, as he thus by his anvil stands**
>
> **A strange clatter on his ears lands.**
>
> **It is as if two fiery steeds are trotting**
>
> **Though the sound comes from the wild ocean.**
>
>
> **He runs to the door, looks out, and dreads**
>
> **For frightful is the sight he beholds.**
>
> **It is like a cloud of murk and lightning**
>
> **Which swerves on the ocean's grayish waves.**

The Saga Kings

It comes closer and closer towards the land.

At last he makes out a horse and a man

And the man a flaming glavind swings

And the horse on four pairs of feet springs.

One eyed like a sun clear day he was.

On his silver gray head a gold helmet he wore

About his mighty shoulders swings

Two screaming ravens on coal black wings.

"Up Smith", thus spoke the frightful guest,

"Take hammer and tong and shoe my horse.

One shoe is broken. Be good and quick.

It is very late. My time is scarce.

Before the day flows from the east side

I have well a hundred miles to ride".

And the Smith his mighty hammer swang

And the iron sparked and the anvil rang.

Soon was shoed the fiery horse.

Into the saddle swung the frightful guest.

But before the next sun had set,

Stood the battle slaughter on the Braavalle plain."

The story teller thanked Erik for the song. All the people applauded. When it became quiet, the story teller continued in a clear voice, "The two leaders set up their armies on the plain of Braavalle. Sigurd Ring told his warriors to stand their ground until Harald was ready. Harald was blind and could not walk so he rode in a wagon. He selected Brune to set up his army.

Brune set up the different chiefs under their own standards. King Harald's standard was set up in the middle of the svinfylking formation. The armies were assembled about his standard. These warriors came to follow Harald: Svend, Sam, Gnepe the Old, Gaard, Brand, Blaend, Teit, Tyrving, Hjalte. These were Harald' skalds and warriors. Among Harald's own fighters were: Hjort, Borgar, Bele, Barre, Beigad and Toke.

The shield maidens, Visna and Heidi, both came with a big army to King Harald. Visna was Harald's standard bearer. Visna had a great army of Vends. They were easy to recognize because they had long swords and long shields, not round like the others".

"Vends!" exclaimed Erik, "the Vandals?"

The story teller chuckled and said, "yes Erik, the Vandals had migrated north and had land on the south east coast of the Baltic Sea. Here in the North we call them Vendels or Vends.

Another shield maiden who came to Harald was Vebjerg from south of Gotland. She brought many champions with her.

On the right wing, Brune put the shield maiden, Heidi in charge. She had one hundred warriors, and the berserkers, Grim, Geir, Holmsten, Osaddel, Heden the Small, Dag and Harald Olafson. There were many chiefs in that wing. The left wing was commanded by Haakon and contained the chief, Hage Hugginkind, and there was a standard borne in front of him. This wing also had Alvar, and Alvarin, the sons of King Gandalf.

Harald asked Brune how Sigurd Ring had arranged his army. Brune told him that Sigurd had set up a svinfylking. Harald was surprised because he thought that only Odin could teach this formation. Then Harald asked

Brune who had taught Sigurd how to set up that formation, because Harald said that he knew only Odin could teach how to do that. Brune did not answer. But Sigurd had spent a lot of time with Harald and it was only natural that he therefore knew the formation.

Sigurd Ring had many kings and chiefs in his army. The most famous was Ole the Vigorous. Many Kings had come from Norway to Sigurd Ring: Aage, Ejvind, Egil Skjalge, Hilde, Got, Gude Tolleson, Sten from Vaernern, and Styr the Strong.

In the middle of the fylking, Sigurd placed Starkad, said to be a descendant of Starkad the Old. Sigurd's warrior chiefs from Norway included Thrond the Trondske, Tore the Morske, Helge the White, Bjarne, Havr, Fin from the Fjords, Sigurd, Erling Snog from Jaeren, Saga-Erik, Holmsten the White, Einar from Agder, Rut Vave, Odd Vidforle, Einar Trug, and Ivar Skage.

When both armies were arranged and ready, the trumpets were blown. Then the warriors beat on their shields with their swords or axes and the archers rattled their quivers. The sound was deafening, and then the two armies moved forward with shouts and war cries. The name of "Odin" was shouted again and again.

The two forces came together. The sky and the ground seemed to merge and become one. When the spear throwing began, the sun was darkened by the numbers of flying spears. The clash of arms echoed like thunder across the field and a mist arose from the steam from wounds.

When all the spears were spent, the two armies waded into each other with slashing swords, cleaving axes, and iron shod maces. In Harald's army, Ubbe the Frisian fought forward in berserker gang. He advanced where the fylking point was in Ring's army. He first assailed Ragnvald Radbard. Terrible blows were exchanged. Ragnvald fell and Ubbe went after Tryggve and gave him a deadly wound.

The Alrek sons were nearby and saw Tryggve fall. They went after Ubbe for revenge. But so great a fighter was Ubbe that he cut them both down. Then he cut down Yngve.

Next Ubbe came against Starkad. This became a fearsome duel with powerful sword strokes. Ubbe received a great wound from Starkad. But Starkad received six from Ubbe. Then the press of the armies forced them apart.

Ubbe had cut down sixteen of the Swedes and Goths who were in the wedge of Ring's fylking. Next Ubbe went against the Teles (the warriors from Telemark). These warriors started to give way and avoided meeting him head on. Thus Ubbe went wading through the Teles cutting down man after man.

Ubbe had cut down twenty-five warriors when he reached the center of Ring's army and there were no warriors nearby. He looked around and saw only archers. The archers were led by Had the Hard and Roald Taa. Ubbe fell to the ground with one hundred and forty five arrows in his breast.

The shield maiden, Vebjerg, attacked the Swedes and Goths very hard. She met the warrior, Sokne Sote. They exchanged huge blows and she cut the chin from Sokne. Vebjerg and her followers cut a huge path through the Swedes and Goths. Then Vebjerg came against Torkel Traa from Telemark. The fight was long and hard, but Vebjerg fell with many wounds and great courage.

Many great events were happening in a short time. Sometimes one army was advancing and sometimes the other. Many warriors got stranded in the wrong army and were cut down.

Starkad was determined to reach King Harald and attacked the Danes. He went against the warrior, Hun and killed him. Elle attempted to avenge Hun but was cut down by Starkad. Then there was a hard fight between Starkad and Borgar. Borgar fell.

Starkad then ran between the two armies to reach Harald. He cut down man after man as he ran. When he reached Visna, Harald Wartooth's standard bearer, his arms were red with blood. They engaged in a fight. Hjort came between them and engaged Starkad. It was a fierce fight until Hjort fell. The fighting became fierce around Harald, and Visna lost a hand from a chopping cut by Borge.

Gjnejpe then attacked Starkad. Starkad gave him a deadly wound and was immediately attacked by the berserker, Hake. Hake fell but gave Starkad many wounds. Starkad's neck had been cut at the shoulder and his chest had been sliced open so that his lungs fell out. He was also missing a finger from his right hand.

Harald said to Brune, "I will ask Odin for victory. If he does not grant it, I wish to fall with all the warriors in my army. But all who fall on this battle field, I give to Odin".

Brune did not answer, but ripped the mace from Harald Wartooth's hand and hit him in the head. Harald tumbled from his wagon and lay dead. In the battle, twelve thousand kings and jarls had fallen on Ring's side and thirty thousand on Harald's side. This was not counting common men.

When King Ring saw that Harald's wagon was empty he called for peace and for the warriors to cease fighting. When the fighting ceased, Sigurd asked that Harald's corpse be found. A half day passed by before they found the corpse. It was lying with Harald's mace by his side. Brune however was never seen again and therefore it was rumored that Brune was Odin in disguise. This was the last battle of Ragnarok.

Sigurd Ring remembered his friendship with Harald Wartooth and wanted to honour him. Sigurd had Harald's ship dragged onto the shore. He laid the corpse on it and set the ship on fire. The ashes from Harald's funeral pyre were transferred to Lejre and buried in a mound along with riches and weapons.

By honouring Harald Wartooth in such fashion, Sigurd Ring won the hearts of the Danes. With the Danes as his friends he won time to organize his new Kingdom.

110 SIGURD RING

Sigurd Ring established his new Kingdom. He put his cousin Ring from Norway in charge of Jutland. Then he set kings and jarls in all the territories.

Sigurd Ring gathered a great fleet and sailed to the colony in England called Northumbria, which Harald Wartooth had owned, and also Ivar Vidfadme before him. Sigurd demanded that the Northumbrians recognize him as King and pay tribute. There were English Kings in Northumbria and many swore allegiance to Sigurd.

The King of Northumbria, Ingjald, came with an army against Sigurd. They fought several battles. In the last great battle, King Ingjald fell. His son Ubbe and a large number of their warriors fell also. Then Sigurd established a king called Olaf. He was the son of Kinrik who traced his line to Ivar Vidfadme's mother's brother. King Sigurd then departed and went back to his country.

Because Jutland belonged to Ring and Zealand and the islands to Sigurd, Denmark was split and weakened. Sea rovers and pirates began to raid in Denmark. Sigurd took his fleet to protect Denmark and to make incursions in the lands of the raiders.

Ring saw the raids on Denmark as an opportunity and began to lay Danish lands under himself. Each year, Ring gained more and more territory belonging to the Danes.

In 737, King Sigurd was away on a war expedition. Ring came to Zealand and demanded that all the Zealanders swear him allegiance. The Zealanders were faithful to Sigurd and held a Thing. They decided that to show support for Sigurd they would declare Ragnar, Sigurd's son as King of Zealand. Thus Ragnar, at the age of two years, became King of Zealand.

111 RAGNAR

When Ring heard that Sigurd was back home in Sweden, he again attacked the Zealanders. He proclaimed that all the Zealanders would be put to death if they did not surrender and swear allegiance to Ring. The Zealanders called for a truce to consider the matter. Ring granted the truce.

During the meeting, the young King Ragnar wandered in and listened. Ragnar spoke up and said, "Swear allegiance to Ring falsely."

There was silence in the meeting hall. Someone said, "What?" Then Ragnar said, "Swear allegiance and not mean it."

The Zealanders marveled at the wisdom of their young King. They did as Ragnar advised.

The Zealanders called a Thing to consider Ragnar, because they feared for the boy's life. They all agreed to send him away for his safety. Ragnar was sent to Norway to be fostered by Siward Jarl of Westfold.

In Northumbria, Ubbe's son Eave came into power. He had many battles with Olaf who reigned there under Sigurd Ring. Eave was victorious and became King of Northumbria. Olaf fled to Sigurd Ring in Sweden who proclaimed him Jarl in Jutland.

Sigurd assembled a great army and sailed to Norway where he attacked Ring. He slew Ring but in the battle he received a mortal wound and died a few days later.

Ragnar returned to Zealand as King. Then Ragnar conquered the Danish islands and added them to his Kingdom. Ragnar defeated Olaf in Jutland and added Jutland to his Kingdom.

The Swedish King Fro sailed a fleet to Norway and attacked Ragnar's foster father Siward. Fro was victorious and killed Siward. The women of Siward's kin were put in bonds in a brothel.

When Ragnar heard what had happened to Siward, he assembled a fleet and sailed to Norway to avenge his foster father. When he landed in Norway he made a camp.

Many women from Fro's brothel went to Ragnar's camp. They arrived in male attire and wanted to fight Fro. Regnar gave the women weapons and armor. Then with his warriors and the women he went against Fro and his army. Among the women warriors was Ladgerda who fought courageously at the front. She hewed down warrior after warrior. Ragnar and his men marveled at the sight of Ladgerda fighting with her long hair loose over her shoulders. Fro fell in the battle and his warriors fled.

After the battle, Ragnar asked his men about Ladgerda and learned that she was of noble birth. Ragnar proceeded to court Ladgerda. She pretended that she was interested in Ragnar. But when she got home she had a bear and a dog set on her porch to keep him out.

Ragnar departed with his fleet but had his ships put to port near Gaurladal where Ladgerda lived. He left his men behind and proceeded alone to the valley of Gaurladal. When he reached Ladgerda's dwelling, the bear and the dog attacked him. He managed to kill the bear with his spear and he wrestled the dog down and choked it. Then he wrung its neck. Ragnar proceeded into the dwelling. Ragnar married Ladgerda. Ragnar and Ladgerda had two daughters and a son called Fridlief.

Ragnar conquered southern Norway up to the Oslo Fjord and added it to his Kingdom. Olaf in Jutland thought that Ragnar would stay in Gaurladal with his wife. Therefore he made an alliance with Skaane and attacked Zealand. When Ragnar heard of the attack on Zealand, he equipped thirty ships. With favourable winds he sailed to Skaane and crushed the Skaanians in a big battle at Whitby. Winter came and Ragnar over wintered at Lejre.

As soon as spring came, Ragnar took his thirty ships to Jutland and entered the Lim Fjord. There a great battle was fought with Olaf and his warriors, which Ragnar won. Then Ragnar sailed back to Skaane and fought the Skaanians and Hallanders successfully. The Skaanians and Hallanders fled, but Ragnar pursued them and another big battle resulted. Finally the Skaanians and Hallanders surrendered.

112 RAGNAR LODBROK

Thora, the daughter of Herod Jarl in Gotland, had been given some snakes as pets when she was a little girl. The snakes turned out to be adders. The adders grew to be very big and Thora arranged for the adders to be fed an ox a day. The vipers were large and now were pests in the country. One of the snakes was so huge that it normally slept wrapped around Thora's house with its head touching its tail. Herod proclaimed that whoever would rid his country of these pests would have his daughter as wife.

Ladgerda refused to leave Gourladal and move to Denmark. Ragnar did not trust Ladgerda and the memory of her setting beasts to destroy him would not go away. He divorced Ladgerda and made a plan to marry Thora.

Many warriors had tried to rid Herod's country of the adders and failed. But now warriors did not try any more. Ragnar made himself some hairy pants and a hairy mantle with a hood to repel the bites of the snakes.

Ragnar sailed to Gotland and landed in a vik near Jarl Herod's home. Ragnar exhorted his men to be loyal to Fridlief if he did not return. He put on his hairy pants and mantle, tied his sword to his side and lashed his spear to his right hand with a thong. Then he proceeded alone to Thora's house.

As Ragnar approached Thora's house, an enormous serpent glided forward to meet him. As Ragnar started to fight the serpent another, just as big, glided up behind the first one. Herod and his men came and watched the fight from a distance as Ragnar killed the two serpents with his spear.

Herod came forward to Ragnar and looked closely at his shaggy pants. Then he laughed and in jest called him Ragnar Lodbrok (hairy pants). The name stuck. From then on Ragnar was known as Ragnar Lodbrok.

Herod invited Ragnar Lodbrok to a feast in his honour. Ragnar accepted and went to his ship to get his men. At the ship, Ragnar changed his clothes to regal attire. He had all his men dress regally and they went to Herod's feast. At the end of the feast, there was a wedding ceremony for Ragnar and Thora.

A few days later Ragnar Lodbrok and Thora sailed to Lejre. Ragnar and Thora had a son and called him Erik. Ragnar and Thora's second son was called Agner.

Meanwhile in Westfold Norway, Halfdan the Mild became sick. He died on his sickbed in his house. Gudrod, Halfdan's son, known as Gudrod the Hunter, became King after his father.

In Denmark, Thora became sick and died. Ragnar was heartbroken and became very depressed. He decided to give up his kingship and become a Viking rover again.

Ragnar called a Thing and proclaimed new laws. He decreed that every father of a family should devote to Ragnar's service whichever of his children he thought most contemptible, and any slave who was lazy at work or of doubtful fidelity. He said that the feeblest of Danes were stronger than the men of other nations and that each of those chosen would have a chance to wipe out bad reputations in his service. Ragnar was raising an army.

Ragnar then proclaimed that any man who had a suit against another must not present it himself at a Thing, but have a representative do so, and that the defendant also must have a representative instead of defending himself. The accuser would be forbidden to charge and the accused would be forbidden to defend. He also decreed that the judgment on these suits be decided by a group of twelve peers. Then Ragnar announced that he was giving up the throne to his younger brother Sigfred (Sigurd Ring II), and that he would take his army on Viking raids and would defend Denmark from attackers. Ragnar then moved his home to Fyn so that Sigfred could have his High Seat at Lejre.

113 THE VIKING AGE

Most of Viking society consisted of farmers and fishermen. The food wars of Ragnarok had shown that raiding was profitable. It was now a common belief that raiding could do away with poverty and hunger.

Just as neighbours would band together to cut fire wood for the winter, they now also would band together, build a ship and go raiding in the summer to insure that hunger and poverty would not happen. Material things captured in raids could be used as trade goods thereby increasing the status of the participants.

In 789, three Norwegian Viking ships arrived in Portland, England. They set up tables and began to trade with the people. The King wanted to see the newcomers and sent officials to escort them into his presence. The Vikings refused to accompany the officials. Then the officials drew their weapons and attempted to take the Vikings by force. The Vikings killed the officials and sailed away. Because they did not want to go home empty handed, they proceeded to loot several towns in southern England.

In 790, Viking ships sailed up the Thames River and sacked London. Then Vikings made raids in the English midlands. At this time Ragnar Lodbrok also made raids along the British coast.

The Christian missionaries in Frisia decided that it was useless to attempt to Christianize the Danes.

In 791, Vikings made raids in Northumbria, but had to withdraw because the resistance was too strong.

In 792, Ragnar Lodbrok came back to England and raided the coastlands.

In 793, Vikings attacked the monastery at Lindisfarne, killing the monks and seizing the treasures.

In 794, Vikings went to the Orkney Islands. There they set up a stronghold at Scapa Flow, which became their permanent base.

In 795, Vikings raided along the Scottish coast and looted the monastery in Iona Scotland, which had been founded by Saint Columba. There were also raids in the Hebrides.

Vikings then sailed across to Ireland and harried along the coast. They attacked Rathlin north of Dublin. This was the first recorded Viking attack in Ireland.

"The Bishop said that the Vikings were cowards because they killed defenseless monks", said Helga.

The story teller chuckled. Then he picked up his mug and drained it. Grete hurried to refill his mug with more beer. "Defenseless monks!" said the story teller. "That Bishop would have us think that the monks were like little children sitting around singing praises to their god while the Vikings cut them down.

The monks were also warriors. In Ireland the warrior monks raided neighbouring monasteries. The monasteries went to war against each other. Some monasteries even went to war against the Irish Kings. The idea that Vikings cut down defenseless monks is not reality. Raiders of monasteries were not all Vikings. In Ireland there were more raids on monasteries by the Irish themselves than by Vikings. The monasteries were used to store the riches of the nobles. That is enough reason alone for enterprising warriors to raid them. The securities of the riches of the nobles were the warrior monks.

The monasteries had smithies in which armour and weapons were crafted. These monasteries attracted raiders because of their hordes of treasure and their fine crafted weapons. The monasteries in France made the best swords at this time. Those swords alone made it worthwhile to raid a Frankish monastery. The Vikings were not the only people raiding and plundering. Every country in those days had their raiders. Those were violent times.

In 798, Vikings raided Scotland. Then they proceeded to Ireland where the Vikings rustled the cattle tribute, which the Irish Kings paid to the High King every year.

114 THE SAGA OF RAGNAR LODBROK

In the summer, Ragnar Lodbrok sailed along the coast of Norway and landed his ships in a little port near the farm Spangerhede. In the morning the cooks went ashore to bake bread. They saw the farm and thought it would be easier to bake bread there.

At the farm the cooks met an ugly crone called Grima. They told her that they were in the service of Ragnar Lodbrok and asked for help in baking bread. Grima said that her hands had become too stiff for that kind of work. But she said that she had a daughter called Kraka who would be able to help and that she would be home soon.

Kraka had gone out early that morning to tend sheep. When she saw that there were many ships in the harbor, she bathed herself. The crone had forbidden Kraka to wash herself because she did not want anyone to see how beautiful she was. Her hair was like silk and it reached the ground.

Just when the cooks had made a fire for the baking, Kraka came home and saw the men whom she did not know. She looked at them and they looked at her. The cooks thought that Kraka was the most beautiful woman they had ever seen. They asked Grima if Kraka was really her daughter. Grima insisted that she was. Then the cooks said, "Yet you are so unlike each other. You are so very ugly and your daughter is the most beautiful woman we have ever seen. Your daughter is so beautiful and nice to look upon and you are frightful to look upon".

Grima said that the years had not been kind to her appearance.

The cooks and Kraka agreed that Kraka should knead the dough and they should bake the bread. Kraka did her work very well, but the cooks could not take their eyes off Kraka and burned the bread. When the cooks were finished baking, they took the bread back to the ships. The Vikings thought that the cooks should be punished for ruining the bread. Ragnar asked them why they had made bread in this fashion.

The cooks apologized and explained that they had burned the bread because they could not take their eyes off the most beautiful woman in the whole world. Ragnar argued that it was impossible for any woman to be more beautiful than Thora had been. But the cooks insisted that Kraka did not stand second to anyone.

Ragnar thought about the matter and called his wisest man to him. He instructed the man to go and see for himself whether Kraka was as beautiful as reported. If she was, Ragnar wanted to meet her. But he wanted to test her intelligence and wisdom, so he instructed his man to tell Kraka to meet Ragnar neither dressed nor naked, neither full nor fasting, neither lonesome nor accompanied by any human.

The messenger went to the farm the next day. He found Kraka as beautiful as had been described and therefore delivered the instructions. Kraka pondered the matter and Grima declared that the messenger's chief was mad. But Kraka told the messenger that she would come to the ships the next day.

Kraka slept at home that night. The next day she got up and over her naked body she threw a fish net and over the fish net she put her long hair. Thus she wore no clothes yet was not naked. Then she took an onion to bite on so that she had not eaten yet was not fasting. For a companion she chose her dog.

Thus Kraka came to the ships. Ragnar found her very beautiful and delightful and asked who she was. She replied that she did not want to hurry over his message and oh, by the way would not come aboard his ship without free board.

Ragnar talked with Kraka and said she should come with him. She told him no. He asked her to stay on the ship overnight with him and again she told him no. That shall not happen she told him until he had finished the quest he was on. "Maybe", she told him "you will have forgotten me by then".

Ragnar offered Kraka a beautiful dress which had belonged to Thora. Kraka refused to accept it. Then she told him that when he came back on his return journey from his quest he could send for her if he had not forgotten her. Then she would come with him she said. Having said that, Kraka walked back to the farmer and Grima. Ragnar Lodbrok continued his journey north along the coast of Norway.

On his journey home, Ragnar Lodbrok landed in the same vik near Spangerhede. He sent messengers to the farm to ask Kraka to come and sail away with him as she had promised. Kraka promised to come the next day.

In the morning Kraka went to Grima and the farmer and said that she knew they had killed her foster father, Heimer, and that now she would leave. Then she went to the ships and was well received. At bedtime, Ragnar told her that he wanted to go to bed with her. She said that must not happen and that she wished to have the wedding drink with him when they reach his home. Ragnar did as she wanted.

When they reached Fyn, there was a big wedding celebration as Ragnar married Kraka. After the wedding Ragnar wanted to bed Kraka. She said that he must wait three nights or their child resulting from their union would have no knuckles. Ragnar this time did not abide by her wishes. He did not wait.

Ragnar's sons Erik and Agner had their own fleets and went on Viking raids during the summer. In the fall when they came home they met their new mother whom they grew to love.

When Kraka bore a son, he was called Ivar but he had no knuckles. He became known as Ivar the Boneless. Later Kraka and Ragnar had twin boys. They were called Bjorn (Bear) and Halfdan. Halfdan was also known as Hvidsaerk (White Shirt). The next son was called Ragnvald.

115 THE LODBROK SONS

Ivar had been watching his two half-brothers leave every spring to go on Viking raids and return in the fall. He had also watched his father leave on Viking expeditions. This year he declared to his brothers Halfdan and Bjorn that they should all go out and earn honour and fame. His brothers agreed and they went to Ragnar who gave them ships and warriors. Ragnvald wanted to come with them, so they took him along.

Ivar decided that they should take Hvitaby, a city many Vikings including Ragnar himself had tried to take and failed. They reached Hvitaby and prepared for the assault. Ivar, Bjorn and Halfdan decided to let Ragnvald who was the youngest stay with the ships as guard to keep him safe.

Ivar arranged the warriors in the svinfylking formation and they went against the city. Ivar could not walk and was carried on a shield into battle. The town's people had some wild cows (aurox), which they released against the Vikings. After Ivar had shot the cows with arrows, the worst was over.

At the ships, Ragnvald was unhappy to be left behind. He told his men that his brothers had left him behind because they wanted all the fame for themselves. "Let's all go up and fight, every one of us", said he.

They all went up and joined Ragnvald's brothers. Ragnvald went courageously forward in the battle but fell after a short while. His brothers fought their way into the city and put the people to flight. After pursuing the people for a while they went back and burned the town and knocked down its walls. They gathered up all the coins they could find, went back to their ships and sailed away

116 RAGNAR LODBROK AND EYSTEIN

Eystein, rich and mighty, was King of Sweden with his High Seat in Uppsala where the greatest cult-offerings in the north took place. The Swedes there worshipped a cow (aurox) called Sibilja and sacrificed much to it. During battles, the King had the cow lead the wedge in the svinfylking formation.

King Eystein had a daughter, Ingeborg, who was the most beautiful of all the women in the land. He was friends with many chiefs and jarls including Ragnar Lodbrog. Eystein and Ragnar took turns every summer to hold a feast for each other.

It was Eystein's turn to be host and Ragnar and his men were well received in Uppsala. Eystein had his daughter Ingeborg pour the ale for Ragnar. Ragnar's men talked about Ingeborg and concluded that Ragnar should set aside Kraka, a mere farmer's daughter, and marry Ingeborg. When the night was done, Ragnar and Ingeborg were engaged.

When the feasting was ended, Ragnar and his men sailed home to Fyn. Before they reached the castle Ragnar held a meeting. He told his men that any who talked about Ingeborg would be put to death.

When Ragnar reached home, his people greeted him with great joy. After he had sat in his High Seat for a long time drinking ale, Kraka came and sat in his lap. She put her arms about his neck and asked him about his adventures. But he said that he had nothing to tell.

After the evening's drinking bouts, people sought their beds and Kraka lay down beside Ragnar. She again asked him about news and his adventures, and he answered, as before that he had nothing to tell.

Then Kraka said that she would tell him the news. "This I call news", she said, "that a king engages himself to a woman when he already has a wife".

Ragnar asked who had told her this, but she answered that his men could keep their lives and limbs. "You saw the three birds in the tree, when you held your meeting with your men. They have told me the news", she said.

Kraka advised Ragnar to break his engagement with Ingeborg and drive it from his head. She told him that she was not a simple farmer's daughter but a King's daughter whose ancestors would be remembered for all times. She told him that she was an Ylfing, daughter of Sigurd Fafnirsbane and Brynhild Bundlesdatter. Then she related to him the Volsung saga. She told him that her real name was Aslaug.

Aslaug said, "I was raised by Brynhild's foster father, Heimer. When my parents died, Heimer began to worry about my safety. Therefore he built a harp which was so big that I could hide myself inside it."

"Heimer then went wandering about making a living as a skald", continued Aslaug, "We arrived at Spangerhede one night. We went to Grima and Aake's farm and they took us in for the night. For our safety, I was hiding in the harp. Grima talked Aake into killing Heimer. Grima expected the harp to contain treasure, silver and gold. But when she broke it to pieces, she found only me. They kept me and gave me the name 'Kraka'. I was Grima's slave until you came to Spangerhede."

Ragnar could hardly believe what Aslaug told him. But she reminded him that she was with child. She told him that she would give birth to a boy and that it would be recognized that he came from the line of Sigurd in that there would be a mark in his eye, which would look like a snake. She said, "If you find the mark in his eye, he shall be called up after Sigurd Fafnirsbane".

After some time passed, Aslaug gave birth to a baby boy. She asked her servants to carry the boy to Ragnar. When the boy was carried to Ragnar and laid in his lap, the people asked Ragnar what the boy should be called. Ragnar looked into the baby's eye, saw the snake in his eye, called him Sigurd, and gave him a gold ring as a naming present. Sigurd became known as Sigurd Snake-eye.

But in Uppsala, king Eystein considered himself and his daughter insulted. Therefore he broke his old friendship with Ragnar Lodbrok.

When Ragnar Lodbrok's oldest sons, Erik and Agner, discovered the hostility of Eystein, they gathered men and ships and sailed, though warned, to Sweden and harried in the land. Eystein took a great army against them with the cow, Sibilja.

The battle went terribly bad for the Lodbrok sons and the cow trampled their best warriors. Most of their warriors fled. The remaining warriors fought on until Agner fell and Erik was captured.

King Eystein called a halt to the battle. Then he offered Erik the choice of marrying his daughter or death. Erik refused to marry Ingeborg and asked that his men be set free to go where they would. For his death, Erik chose to be cast onto spears.

The spears were set firmly in the ground. Erik took a gold ring from his hand, threw it to his men, and asked them to bring it to Aslaug. Then he was thrown on top of the spears. Erik's men went to their ships and sailed home without stopping. When they got home Ragnar was away in the east on a Viking expedition and his sons were also away. The warriors went straight to Aslaug and told her that Thora's sons had fallen, gave her Erik's greeting, and Erik's ring.

Then they saw Aslaug cry, for the first and last time, heavy, sobbing tears.

Ivar, Halfdan and Bjorn came home long before Ragnar. Aslaug went to see them and took Sigurd with her. They asked each other what news there was and Aslaug told them about the death of Thora's sons and said they should avenge their half-brothers.

Ivar was immediately against going to Sweden to fight Eystein. He asked her why she did not cry when Ragnvald, her own son, fell. She answered that Ragnvald died an honourable death in battle and went straight to Valhalla, but Erik had been cast on spears. When Aslaug persisted, Ivar told her about the cow Sibilja.

Aslaug gave up all hope of having her sons seek revenge and prepared to go back home. Just then the three-year-old Sigurd Snake-eye recited a verse with the story that in three nights he would travel to Uppsala and battle Eystein for his mother. When the brothers heard this, they decided to go against Eystein and began planning how to outfit the fleet and man it with warriors. Then Aslaug went home.

The Ragnar sons each gathered a separate fleet and army. Aslaug also gathered an army and had Sigurd's foster father help Sigurd collect an army. Ivar decided where they would meet in Sweden. Ivar, Halfdan, and Bjorn took their fleet and sailed for Sweden, while Aslaug took Sigurd and an army over land through Skaane.

When Eystein heard there were warriors come to fight him, he knew who had come. He gathered all his men who could bear weapons. In front of his army ran the wild cow (aurox) Sibilja.

When Ivar saw the cow he commanded that all his warriors yell their war cries and clash their weapons against their shields. While the warriors were making the loud noises, Ivar Boneless who could not walk had himself carried on a shield closer and closer to Sibilja. He sat on his shield and used his bow to fire arrow after arrow at Sibilja. Arrows hit each of Sibilja's eyes and the cow was terribly angry, running faster forwards than before. But when the cow came forward towards Ivar, he told his bearers to throw him at the cow. The bearers hurled Ivar at the cow.

When Ivar fell on the cow, its back broke and it died. When the cow was dead, the worst of Eystein's defenders was gone and a terrible battle took place. Under Ivar's directions, the Lodbrok sons obtained the victory and Eystein fell Ivar called for a cease in the fighting and let Eystein's men go free.

Bjorn had himself declared as King of Sweden and stayed on in Uppsala. Aslaug took Sigurd and journeyed back to Fyn, while Ivar and Halfdan took their armies and went on Viking raids.

When Ragnar Lodbrok returned from raiding in the east he was angry that Aslaug and his sons had not waited for him before going against Eystein. But after Aslaug said, "Erik sent his ring to me, not to you". The matter was never spoken about again.

117 CHARLEMAGNE

In 768, Pepin died. Pepin's two sons Charles and another divided the Kingdom of the Franks.

In the year 771, the brother of Charles died, leaving Charles as king of all the Franks.

In 772, border friction between France and the Saxons turned into open warfare when King Charles destroyed the Saxons' holy tree, Irminsul. The war lasted thirty-three years. The Saxons were heathen and worshipped the old gods while the Franks were Christians.

Charles the Great (Charlemagne) of France had made the Abrodites and Frisians his allies by conquest, which left only the Saxons in Northern Germany to oppose him there.

In 777, Ibn al Arubi sought the help of Charlemagne to combat the Moslems in Spain.

In 778, Charlemagne summoned warriors from all his provinces and invaded Spain. The army was split into two divisions. One crossed the west Pyrenee mountains and the other the east Pyrenee mountains. As the armies advanced, many well-fortified castles surrendered at once because they recognized that Charles had superior forces. Charles attacked both Christian and Moslem cities.

Charlemagne attacked Saragossa and Saragossa fell. While the Franks were fighting Saragossa, the Christians under Ibn al Arubi united with the Moslems to fight Charlemagne. The new force set up an ambush in the Pyrenees and attacked when Charlemagne came through. The ambush destroyed the entire rear end guard of the Franks and Charles's nephew Roland fell.

In 781, Charlemagne conquered Italy and set his son Pepin as the ruler.

In 782, Charlemagne went back to Saxony. In the town of Verden in north Saxony he had 4,500 Saxons beheaded in one day. They were first baptized so that they could find their way to heaven. The Saxon Chief, Widukin, fled to Denmark for asylum and Ragnar's brother King Sigurd Ring II (Sigfred) took him in.

The Saga Kings

In 783, just south of Denmark, Charles the Great of France fought a long protracted battle against the Saxons on Mount Osning at Detmold. One month later Charles fought another battle against the Saxons at the River Hase. Charles forced the conquered Saxons to accept Christianity. Then he attacked Frisia.

In 785, the Christianization of Frisia was complete. Then in 786, Charles the Great conquered Britanny on the seacoast of western Gaul. He compelled the inhabitants to give hostages and to do his bidding.

On Christmas day in the year 800 at St. Peter's Church in Rome, Pope Leo III crowned Charles the Great as Emperor of the Holy Roman Empire. This revived the Roman Empire with the Pope in authority. The Pope authorized Charlemagne to make the heathen into Christians and to conquer in the name of the Holy Catholic Church."

Charles now had several titles: Holy Roman Emperor, King of the Franks, Conqueror, The Butcher of Saxons, Charles the Great, Charlemagne.

In 801, Charlemagne forced the conquered Saxons to accept Christianity and forced them to be baptized. In northern Saxony, people were fleeing to Denmark where they were protected.

In 802, Vikings attacked the monastery in Iona and looted its treasures.

In 804, Charlemagne finished his conquest of the Saxons. His border to the north was now at the Elbe River and his northern neighbours were the Danes. He took ten thousand Saxon families living on the banks of the Elbe and relocated them to various districts in Gaul and Germany.

The Abrodites received the eastern half of Holstein from Charlemagne.

118 GODFRED

When King Sigurd Ring II (Sigfred) of Denmark died in 804, the Danes held a Thing and chose Sigurd's son Godfred as King.

King Godfred of Denmark took his fleet and all his cavalry to the border between Jutland and Saxony in anticipation of an invasion by Charlemagne. The Danes knew that it was just a matter of time before Charlemagne would try to invade Denmark.

Charlemagne sent word to Godfred to surrender the Saxon refugees. Godfred refused to give up the refugees and sent word to Charlemagne that the territories of Frisia, Northern Saxony, and the country of the Abrodites belonged to Godfred. He demanded that Charlemagne withdraw from these territories, which had been paying taxes to the Danish King.

Charlemagne sent word to Godfred that he would like a meeting at the Elbe River. Godfred agreed. Charlemagne went with his army to the Elbe, but Godfred did not come because he did not trust Charlemagne.

In 806, Vikings attacked the monastery in Iona Scotland for the third time. After the raid, the resident abbot and the monks relocated to Kells in Ireland. The monastery in Iona lay abandoned for more than a century.

The King of the Juns asked Charlemagne for help against the Slavs called the Bohemians. Because the King of the Juns was a Christian, Charlemagne assembled an army and assigned his son Charles to lead it against the Bohemians. Charles attacked the Bohemians and lay waste all their lands. In the battle with the Bohemians Charles killed their Prince, Becho.

In 807, Godfred's brother Halfdan went to Charlemagne with a large following and swore allegiance to him. Charlemagne gave Halfdan the island of Walcheren in Frisia.

War was waged between the Franks and Linolia, which ended when Charlemagne conquered Linolia.

In the spring of 808, Charlemagne went to Aachen. Then Godfred the Dan King crossed into the territory of the Abrodites with an army. Charlemagne sent his son Charles with an army to the Elbe in case

Godfred attacked. Thrasco, a duke of the Abrodites hung another duke, Godelaib because Godelaib wanted to join Godfred.

Charlemagne sent his son Charles to go after the Danes in the country of the Abrodites. Charles took an army to the Elbe River and waited.

After camping on the shoreline for a considerable time Godfred brought his army against the Abrodites. He captured castle after castle. In the final great battle, Reginald, Godfred's brother's son fell. Thrasco was driven from the territories of the Abrodites and Godfred took two thirds of the territory. Charles still waited. "What was he waiting for?" asked Ejvind.

The story teller smiled and said, "He was afraid of the Danes".

Godfred destroyed the trading town of Reric. Then he took the merchants aboard his ships and transported them to Hedeby, a trading center just north of Danevirke. There he built them shops and homes and set them up in business. Thus Hedeby became the main trade center of northern Europe.

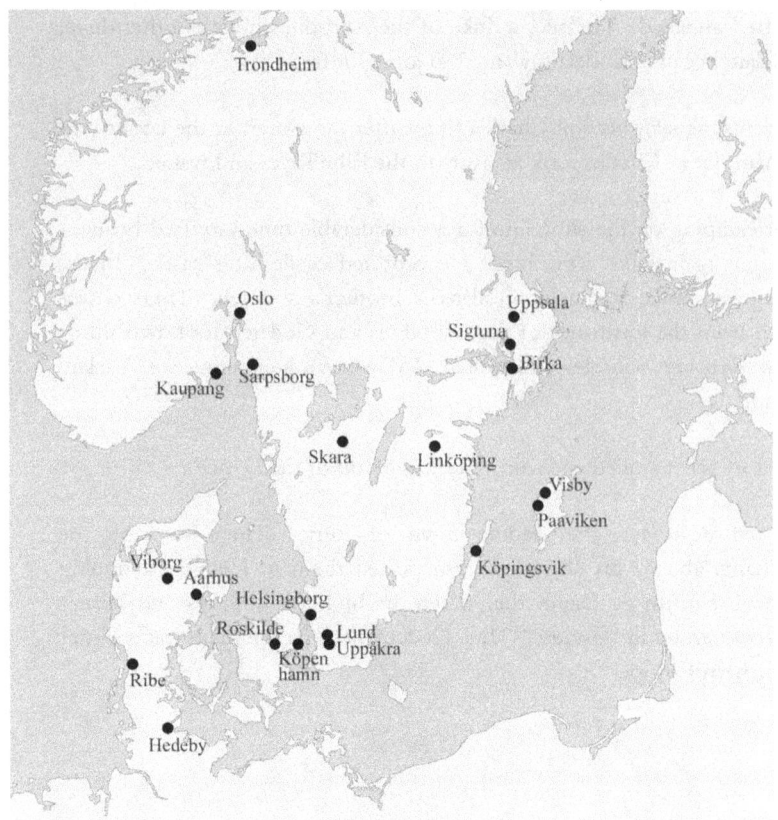

Instead of attacking the Danes, Charles waited until Godfred had left the Abrodite country. He then threw a bridge across the Elbe and with speed moved his army to the territories of the Abrodites. There he massacred the Linones and the Smeldingi for surrendering to Godfred. Then he lay waste their fields and returned across the Elbe with his army unscathed.

Godfred did more work on Danevirke. He built on the rampart and made a protected single gateway so that horses and wagons could pass through it. The rampart now stretched from the gulf on the eastern seaboard along the entire bank of the river Eider all the way to the ocean on the west. When he had assigned the work to his warriors, he returned home to Lejre.

Eardwulf, King of Northumbria was driven out of his Kingdom. He made a journey to see the Pope. Charlemagne sent two abbots with him.

The Pope authorized Eardwulf as King of Northumbria and sent legates back to ensure his reinstallation. On the way back, they were attacked by Vikings, who captured Eardwulf's deacon Ealdwulf.

In Northumbria, Eardwulf was reinstated as king. Then the Vikings showed up and demanded ransom for the deacon Ealdwulf. One of King Cenwulf's nobles paid the ransom.

Charlemagne built two castles on the Elbe River bank and posted garrisons there.

In 809, Godfred sent a message to Charlemagne calling for a meeting. The two met beyond the Elbe on the day chosen and negotiated with no conclusion.

Thrasco, Duke of the Abrodites assembled and army and called for the Saxons to help against the Wilzi. They lay waste the land of the Wilzi and fired their towns. There was also much slaughter. Thrasco then made a treaty with Godfred, giving his son as hostages.

When he returned to his own land, Thrasco raised a great army again and asked the Saxons for more help than before. Then he went into the land of the Smeldingi and destroyed their most important city.

Thrasco's victories made him very arrogant and he forced those who had abandoned him to come back under his rule. Then Godfred's men killed Thrasco in the town of Reric.

In 810, Charlemagne decided to attack Godfred and began to gather an army. Charlemagne could not get past the Danish wall, Danevirke to attack Denmark. When he sent a fleet of ships to bypass the wall, Ragnar Lodbrok with a fleet of Viking ships defeated Charlemagne's fleet.

Godfred with a fleet of 200 long ships arrived in Frisia and ravaged all the islands off the coast of Frisia. The Frisians made friends with Godfred by paying him 100 pounds of silver. Then Godfred landed on the mainland of Frisia and the Frisian warriors joined him. Three battles were fought by the Frisians and Danes against the Franks. Godfred was victorious in each one and drove the Franks out of Frisia.

Godfred talked about conquering all Germany. He stated that Frisia and Saxony were provinces of Denmark, and the Abrodites were Godfred's tax men (Jones, 2001). He also stated that he would be coming soon to Aix-la-Chapelle itself to beard the Emperor in his court and to water his horses at the palace well.

When he received word that Godfred was in Frisia, Charlemagne was greatly disturbed at the news and sent runners through all the provinces of his Empire to assemble an army. He also gave instructions for a fleet to be built. He gathered all the men he could and went across the Rhine. When his army had gathered he moved it to the Aller River in east Frisia thinking that Godfred was still in Frisia. But Godfred had left.

Godfred returned to Lejre where he was assassinated by one of his own men. There was civil war and the sons of Godfred had to flee into exile. Hemming the son of Godfred's brother Halfdan became King and immediately made peace with Charlemagne.

119 HEMMING

In 811, Hemming and Charlemagne each brought chiefs and had a meeting about the peace. Hemming brought his brothers Hankwin and Angandeo, along with Osfrid Turdimulo, Warstein, Suomi, Orm, Osfrid Heiligenson, Osfrid of Skaane, Hebbi and Aowin. It was agreed that the Eider River would be the border between the Kingdom of the Franks and Denmark.

In 812, Hemming died. Civil war broke out between Godfred's nephew, Sigfred, and Anulo, a descendant of Harald Wartooth. Many battles were fought between Sigfred and Anulo. In the last battle both Sigfred and Anulo fell. But the forces of Anulo won. The Godfred sons fled to the island of Fyn and took refuge with Ragnar Lodbrok. From Fyn, the Godfred sons went to exile in Sweden. Harald Klak and Reginfred, the sons of Anulo became joint Kings of Denmark

120 HARALD KLAK AND REGINFRED

In 813, Harald Klak renewed the peace treaty with Charlemagne and declared himself in alliance with the Franks. The Skaanians and the Jutes supported Harald Klak and Reginfred.

The people of Westfold, where Ragnar Lodbrok had ties, refused to submit to Harald and Reginfred. Therefore Harald and Reginfred took a fleet to Norway and subdued Westfold.

While Harald and Reginfred were fighting in Westfold, Ragnar Lodbrok sailed to Sweden where the Godfred sons lived in exile. Ragnar accompanied the Godfred sons to Zealand where the Zealanders declared Godfred's son Horik as king of Denmark. Ragnar then sent envoys to Norway for help.

The exiled Danish Jarls returned from Sweden to join King Horik and Ragnar Lodbrok against Harald Klak and Reginfred. Ladgerda arrived from Norway with her husband and son. They brought one hundred and twenty ships. Ragnar rallied the Zealanders and many men joined his ranks including very young boys and very old men.

With these forces, Horik and Ragnar attacked the Skaanians. Ragnar dispersed the old men and the young boys between wedges of the strongest fighters in his army. The two armies clashed on the Laenus plains in Skaane. The battle was fierce and Siward Jarl fell wounded. This made his warriors look around for flight or surrender. But Ragnar Lodbrok, with yells of "Odin" and encouragement went forward with his forces. The army of Horik and Ragnar rallied and held.

Ladgerda was not to be seen on the battlefield. She had taken her army unseen around the opposing army and suddenly attacked Harald's forces from the rear. The lines of Harald's warriors became slack and his warriors started to fall. Then Harald was routed. In the slaughter, which followed, Harald's brother Reginfred fell. Harald Klak fled to Frisia with a small fleet.

Siward Jarl was taken to a nearby town where he stayed until he was healed. Ladgerda sailed home with her fleet. When she reached her home she murdered her husband by driving a spear point into his neck and took over his throne. She then ruled alone.

121 HARALD KLAK

Charlemagne died in January, 1814 and his son, Louis the Pious succeeded as Emperor of the Holy Roman Empire. Harald Klak sent a messenger to Louis the Pious for help against Ragnar Lodbrok who wanted to drive Harald out of Denmark. Louis promised help if Harald would confirm his Christianity. Harald traveled to Mainz where he was baptized in the presence of Louis the Pious at St. Albans Church. Harald dipped himself three times in the holy water and swore to never again worship heathen gods. Louis then gave Harald Klak the country of Rustringen in Frisia.

In 827, Harald Klak journeyed back to Jutland with Saxon auxiliaries given to him by Louis the Pious and with the missionary Ansgar. Horik received Ansgar well, gave him permission to build a church in Hedeby, and listened intently to Ansgar's words of Christ.

Ragnar Lodbrok was very angry with Harald for bringing the Christian religion into Denmark. He gathered a great army and attacked Harald driving him out of Denmark. Harald Klak fled to his new country Rustringen in Frisia with 60 ships.

The Christian missionary, Ansgar went to Sweden and met with King Bjorn Lodbrokson now called Bjorn Ironsides. Then Ansgar went to Birka, built a church in Malaren, and won the friendship of Bjorn Ironsides.

122 HORIK

In 815, Louis the Pious, King of the Franks, decided to add Denmark to his Kingdom and Christianize the Danes. He gathered an army of Franks, Saxons, Slavs, and Abrodites. Then he called Harald Klak and his Vikings from Frisia to lead the attack.

The Frankish army moved against Danevirke. At the same time Harald's fleet of ships attacked from the Baltic Sea. The walls of Danevirke held until the gate of Danevirke was breached and the warriors of Louis poured through it. Horik and his forces retreated and went to the island of Fyn. The Danish Knights, commanded by Glum, counter attacked the invading forces and drove them back beyond Danevirke.

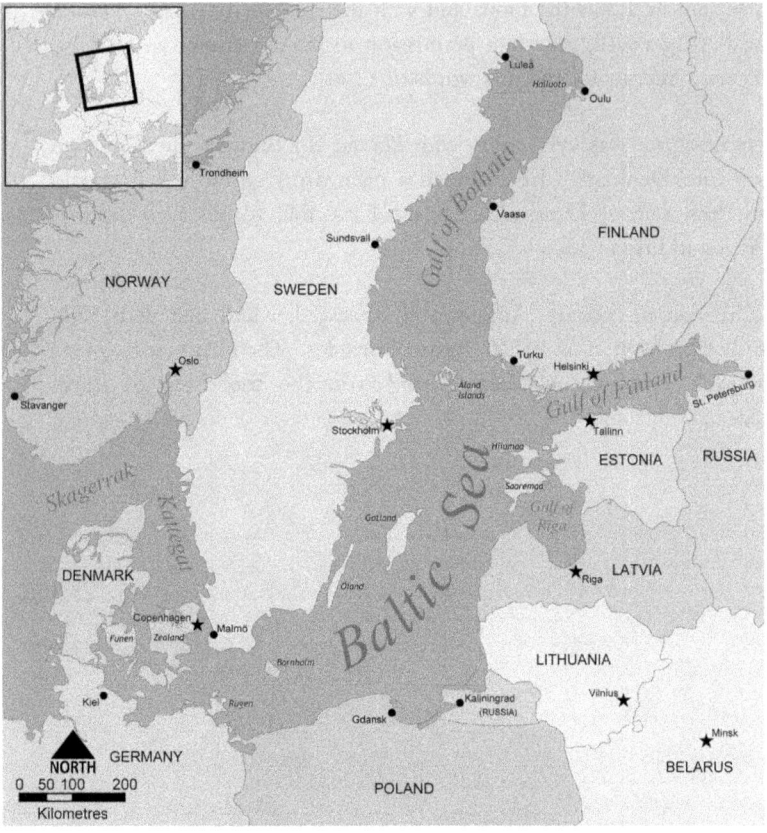

The fleet attacking from the Baltic ran into a Danish fleet commanded by Ragnar Lodbrok. The battle started immediately. The Frankish fleet was beaten by the Danish fleet. The invasion had ground to a halt.

Glum took his knights south of Danevirke and attacked the town of Itzehoe north of the Elbe. He failed to take the town and retreated back to Danevirke.

In 816, an army of Danes was on the north side of Danevirke while an army of Franks was on the other side. But there were no battles.

In 817, Horik established Glum as border Jarl at Danevirke to free his time for other matters. A fleet of 200 Danish long ships arrived at Hedeby to tend the border and the Abrodites switched sides and joined the Godfred sons. Louis withdrew his armies from the Danish border.

In 818, the border between the Saxons and the Vends was established.

In 819, two of Horik's brothers were jealous and wanted a part of the Kingdom. Horik refused to share saying that it would weaken the country. He sent a third brother to Frisia and formed an alliance with Harald Klak. The brother returned with Harald and his warriors. The result was that Horik and Harald Klak chased out the two rebellious brothers and became co-Kings

123 VIKING RAIDS

In 820, Thirteen Viking ships sailed along the coast of Britanny, France. The Vikings landed and attacked Flanders but had to withdraw. Then they sailed to the mouth of the Seine and attempted another raid but had to withdraw again. They sailed on to Aquitaine in southern France. There the raids were successful and good booty was obtained.

Ebo, the Archbishop of Louis the Pious, entered Denmark and set up a mission. Harald Klak came with his wife and children and 400 followers and converted to Christianity.

Danish Vikings sailed into the Thames River mouth and began raiding in south England. These raids lasted thirty years. The Anglo-Saxons fought the Vikings and sometimes won victories against them. But the Vikings established strongholds on the islands of Thanet, out from Kent, and Sheppey, in the mouth of the Thames, and were not to be stopped.

124 IRELAND

In 835, the Norwegian Viking, Turgeis captured the city of Armagh, capital of Ulster and established his Viking kingdom in Ireland. Then he made raids into Meath and sacked the capital city of Brega. That year he established fortified harbours, which grew into towns. Around one of these the city of Dublin came into existence in the same year. A fortified harbour of Turgeis developed into the town of Waterford and another became the town of Limerick. The Moors sent ambassadors to the court of Turgeis in Dublin which resulted in trade agreements.

In 837, Several Viking fleets commanded by the brothers of Turgeis raided Ulster, Leinster and Munster. In 845, The Irish tricked Turgeis and captured him. Then they drowned him in Lough Owel. With the death of Turgeis, the Viking kingdom in Ireland collapsed.

In 849, a fleet of 140 Danish long ships landed in Ireland. They had come to take Dublin from the Norwegians. There were many battles between the Danes and the Norwegians.

The Danes and Norwegians fought a great battle at Carlingford Loch which lasted three days. The Danes were victorious and took over the Viking areas of Ireland. In 853, Olaf the White, a descendant of Halfdan White Legs of Westfold, arrived with a fleet from Norway and attacked the Danes. Olaf was victorious and became King of Dublin. Some of the surviving Danes took service with Olaf the White, but most left and raided in England.

125 THE KINGS OF DUBLIN

In 856, Ivar the Boneless and Olaf the White's brother Ivar arrived in Dublin and negotiated with Olaf the White. After the negotiations, Ivar the Boneless and Olaf the White were joint Kings in Dublin and Olaf's brother Ivar the White was King of Limerick.

Aed Finnlaith the High King of Ireland brought his army against Olaf the White's warriors. He carried the battle to the gates of Dublin. The three Kings of Dublin made peace with Aed Finnlaith and Olaf the White married Aed's daughter.

126 BRITAIN

Two Viking brothers Halfdan and Sigfred defeated the Anglo-Saxon Bretwalda, Egbert at Carhampton in Somerset, England. There they made their headquarters.

In 838, Egbert defeated Halfdan and Sigfred in a battle at Hingston Down and drove them out of England.

In 839, Halfdan and Sigfred invaded Scotland with a large force and slew the Pict King Uven.

After Egbert died in 841, Halfdan and Sigfred invaded England and did great destruction in Lindsey, East Anglia, and Kent.

In 850 the Danish King Horik sailed into the Thames River with 350 ships and attacked England. They made a winter headquarters at Thanet. From there they raided and plundered Canterbury and London and over wintered in Thanet.

In 851, King Aethelwulf of Wessex, son of the mighty King Egbert, ruled most of South England. He took his army against Halfdan and Sigfred. There was a fierce battle at Oakley in Surrey, which Aethelwulf won. Aethelstan, son of Aethelwulf put a fleet to sea and pursued the fleeing Vikings. Halfdan and Sigfred sailed to the Viking stronghold at Thanet.

127 WESTERN EUROPE

In 833, The Emperor Louis the Pious was captured by his sons Lothar, Louis, and Charles who set themselves up as Emperors. The brothers could not agree and Louis the Pious was reinstated, but the nobility of the Franks were now divided which caused the Frank defenses to be weakened.

In 834, Harald Klak and his brother Rorik supported Lothar. They took their Viking fleet of 40 long ships and defeated and looted Dorestad in Frisia. Harald Klak and Lothar defeated and looted Dorestad again in 835.

King Horik of Denmark sent diplomatic messengers to Louis the Pious with the message that he had no responsibility in the sacking of Dorestad and Walcheren. Furthermore the diplomats explained that Frisia and the land of the Abrodites belonged to the Danes and they should be given back to Horik. Louis sent back word to Horik that he could not have Frisia or the land of the Abrodites.

In 836, Harald Klak and Lothar yet again defeated Dorestad. Louis the Pious made peace with his son Lothar. Then he gave Dorestad to Rorik and Walcheren to Harald Klak.

In 840, Ragnar Lodbrog and Rurik were freebooting in Frisia. The Kingdom of the Franks was formally divided into three pieces. Louis wound up with the German territories east of the Rhine. Charles the Bald wound up with France, and Lothar got Frisia, the Netherlands, and Italy. Ragnar Lodbrok took a fleet up the Seine and raided Rouen.

In 846, Harald Klak died and Lothar drove Rorik from Frisia. Rorik fled to Louis and from there journeyed to Denmark.

In 850, Rorik collected a big fleet and with the Lodbrok sons led by Hastein raided Frisia and in 851, Rorik and the Lodbrok sons again raided in Frisia. Louis the Pious died and his sons went to war against each other.

128 RAGNAR LODBROK SAGAS

Bjorn Ironsides, like his father Ragnar Lodbrok, decided that he preferred to be a sea king to being King of a country. He gave Sweden to his son Anund and sailed home to Fyn.

Ragnar Lodbrok collected a group of carpenters and had them build two ships bigger than any seen in the north. When the Kings in the north heard that Ragnar was building ships, they collected more warriors and set up more guards in case Ragnar had their kingdoms in mind.

Aslaug asked Ragnar where he had in mind to go, and he answered that he would go to England in the two ships with as many warriors as they would hold. She told Ragnar that the plan was unwise. She counseled him to take more long ships and many more warriors. But Ragnar did not heed her words.

When Ragnar prepared to depart with his two ships, Aslaug saw him off. She hugged and kissed him and then gave him clothes made from a bearskin, which was tough as armour. All the warriors could feel that Aslaug was very depressed.

King Horik of Denmark abhorred undisciplined Viking raids. Were there to be Viking raids from Denmark, he would do them himself. Horik took his fleet of 600 ships up the Elbe River. At the same time Ragnar Lodbrok reached the Seine River with several fleets of long ships that had joined him. Ragnar's force now numbered 120 long ships and 5,000 Viking warriors.

Horik's fleet of long ships sailed up the Elbe River where he looted and burned Hamburg. The missionary, Ansgar, managed to slip away with his life.

Ragnar Lodbrok took his fleet into the Seine River and proceeded towards Paris. Charles the Bald collected an army to stop him. The army of Charles was posted on both sides of the river in anticipation of Ragnar's approaching fleet. But the army of Charles was now split in two and Ragnar's Vikings attacked the smaller force and defeated it, taking 111 prisoners. Ragnar took the prisoners to a small island in the river and hanged them in full view of the second Frankish army. This so terrified the Franks that they could make no effective opposition.

Ragnar Lodbrok continued up the Seine with no further resistance. On Easter Sunday, March 28, Ragnar's Vikings entered and plundered Paris. Then Ragnar stayed in Paris until Charles the Bald paid him 7,000 pounds of silver to leave in peace. This was the first incidence of a Viking being paid to leave. March 28 became known as Ragnar Lodbrok day.

After making the 200 mile Seine River journey back to the Ocean, Ragnar's fleet dispersed. Ragnar took his two ships to England but ran into a storm and both ships were lost. Ragnar and all his Vikings managed to make it ashore.

King Aella of Northumbria heard that Vikings had landed in his Kingdom. He took his army out against them. When he saw Aella's army approach, Ragnar set up his battle standard and prepared for the battle. He wore neither shield nor armour but was dressed in the bear skin outfit which Aslaug had made for him. He had with him the spear, which he had used to kill the serpents at Thora's house.

Ragnar's force was much smaller than Aella's and were exhausted from swimming ashore. They were also wet and chilly. It took but a short time for many of Ragnar's men to be cut down. No weapon could damage Ragnar because of the bearskin tunic and pants, which he wore. He received no wound but killed many of Aella's warriors. This was the only battle Ragnar ever lost. When all Ragnar's men had fallen he was pressed between shields and was taken alive.

They asked Ragnar who he was but he would not answer. Aella had him thrown into a pit of snakes to make him talk. There sat Ragnar in the pit of snakes and was being struck by poisonous vipers, but he received no harm because of his bear skin outfit. Aella told his men to remove the clothes from the aged Viking.

When Ragnar was naked in the pit, the snakes attacked him from all sides. Ragnar said,

"Grunt would the pigs,

if they knew,

what the boar suffers".

Now Aella knew from Ragnar's words that he had Ragnar Lodbrok in his pit. In fear of vengeance from Ragnar's many sons, he had Ragnar quickly pulled from the pit, but it was too late. Ragnar Lodbrok was dead.

Aella decided to send word to Ragnar's sons and pay coins for their father's death. He selected some good warriors for the task and asked them to observe the sons when they were told the news.

When Aella's messengers arrived at Ragnar's stronghold on Fyn, Ivar the Boneless was in the high seat, Sigurd Snake-eye and Halfdan were playing chess, and Bjorn Ironsides was sanding a spear shaft. The messengers went before Ivar and were received well. They said that they were messengers from King Aella and that they were English men sent to inform the brothers about the death of Ragnar Lodbrok.

Sigurd and Halfdan dropped the game and listened. Bjorn stood leaning on the spear shaft. Ivar asked about all the details about their father's death and the messengers related it all.

When the messengers got to the part when Ragnar said, "Grunt would the pigs..." they saw Bjorn grip the spear shaft so that his hand left a mark on the shaft. When they said that Ragnar was dead, Bjorn swung the shaft against the ground so that it broke into two pieces. Halfdan, who was holding a chess piece, crushed the piece so that blood sprang from his finger nails. Sigurd, who was holding a dagger cleaning his fingernails, rammed the dagger into one of his hands without feeling it. Ivar became pale.

Halfdan said that revenge could start by putting the messengers to death. But Ivar said that the messengers should return unharmed and not wanting anything. He said that they should go in peace and take with them whatever they needed for the journey back.

When the messengers had returned to Aella and told their story of their journey, Aella said that the only one they needed to fear was Ivar. From then on he doubled all the coastal watches.

129 HORIK THE YOUNGER

In 854, Rorik raided in Frisia and Hovi Jarl, who was in charge of the Danevirke wall, chased the Christian priests out of Denmark.

A sea king relative of King Horik decided that it was his turn to be King of Denmark and took his fleet home. There was a great battle and all Horik's family was wiped out except for his son Horik the Younger who was then proclaimed King of Denmark.

In 855, Horik the Younger displaced Hovi as Jarl of the border with someone else and gave the missionary Ansgar permission to ring the church bell. The Christian priests came back to Denmark. The Pope sent a message to Horik the Younger offering him a baptismal service in the Carolingians' land. Horik sent the message back, "No Thanks".

Lothar gave Dorestad to Rorik in order to stop the raids on Frisia. Rorik settled down, ruled Dorestad and defended it from Vikings. Lothar gave Godfred, Harald Klak's son, a territory in Frisia and paid him to keep Viking pirates away.

130 BJORN IRONSIDES

In 857, Bjorn Ironsides raided up the Seine River. Bjorn and his Vikings established a base on the river island, Oissel. Charles the Bald laid siege to Oissel. Bjorn and his Vikings fought back. They were surrounded and could not get away, but it looked as if they could hold out indefinitely. Internal French strife caused the siege to be lifted for twelve weeks and during the twelve weeks, Bjorn Ironsides raided along the Seine again obtaining food and supplies.

Another Viking fleet commanded by Weland arrived on the Seine. Charles the Bald offered Weland 3,000 pounds of silver to get rid of the Vikings on Oissel. It took a long time to collect the silver. Then Weland was paid not 3,000 pounds but 5,000 pounds of silver and provisions of grain and cattle. Weland then laid siege on Oissel.

When the Vikings on Oissel ran short of food, Bjorn Ironsides called a truce and paid Weland 6,000 pounds of silver to let him and his men go. Then Weland entered the service of Charles the Bald and was baptized. Later Weland was challenged to a duel by one of his Viking followers and was killed in the duel.

131 RUSSIA

In Gardarike the small tribes were being raided by the Varangians. They were also being raided by each other constantly. During a truce some of the tribes pointed out that the Varangians were mighty warriors and proposed that Vikings be invited to come and be their ruler so that they would have some security and order. They sent envoys to Sweden and asked different tribes to come and rule over them. The Varangians and the Goths turned them down.

In 858, Rurik, the Chief of the Swedish tribe accepted the invitation to be ruler in Gardarike. Rurik brought his whole tribe to Novgorod. He proceeded to subdue and unite the land. Rurik's people became known by the tribes in Gardarike as the Rus (the Rowers). After this event, the land became known as Russia (Rus Land or Land of the Rus). Two of Rurik's jarls Askold and Dir proceeded south to Kiev and took the rulership there. Askold and Dir attacked Constantinople in 860 A.D. but were repulsed.

132 LODBROK SONS SAGAS

In 859, the Lodbrok sons Bjorn Ironsides and Hastein sailed to Loire and the Vikings there joined them. With 62 ships they sailed to Spain and Portugal where they harried the coasts. Then they sailed into the Mediterranean Sea and fought the Arabs in North Africa. They over wintered at the mouth of the Rhone River.

Bjorn Ironsides and Hastein plundered up the Rhone River. From there they sailed to Italy. When they reached a very beautiful fortified town, they thought it was Rome. The defenses of the town were so strong that Hastein judged they could not take it with an assault.

Hastein sent messengers to the town who told the townsfolk that Hastein and his men were exiled from their own country and had been driven by storms to the town. They said they needed provisions and that their sick chief was almost dead. The next day, the messengers went back to the town and told the towns folk that their chief had died in the night and needed a Christian funeral. The town's folk agreed to provide the funeral.

A long procession of mourning Vikings followed the pall bearers carrying the coffin. After the funeral service, Hastein rose from his coffin, impaled the presiding Bishop with his sword and led his Vikings on a raid inside the town. Hastein was jubilant about conquering Rome. But later in the day he discovered that the town was not Rome but a town called Luna. Hastein was enraged and ordered the men of the town to be massacred.

In 861, Bjorn and Hastein's fleet sailed back near Gibraltar where a Moorish fleet attacked and defeated them. The survivors escaped north and reached Navarre. There they went inland and captured Pamplona. They held the prince captive until they had collected a ransom for him.

In 862, Bjorn and Hastein's fleet of 21 ships returned to the mouth of the Loire.

133 THE GREAT ARMY

In 865, a huge Viking army led by the Lodbrok sons Ivar, Ubbe, and Halfdan, and their brother in-law Guthorm Sigurdson, landed in East Anglia in Britain and made peace with the people (by accepting tribute). Then they took up winter quarters and obtained horses.

In 866, the great army led by Ivar the Boneless went north into Northumbria and attacked York and York fell after a hard battle both inside and outside the city walls. Aella had just driven out King Osberth. The arrival of the Vikings caused Aella and Osberth to unite their armies against the Vikings. In 867, the armies of Aella and Osberth went against the Vikings. In the fierce battle, Osberth fell and Aella was taken captive. The English army was scattered. Ivar had the Vikings carve the blood eagle on Aella's back in revenge for the death of Ragnar Lodbrok. Aella's ribs were separated from his spine and his lungs pulled out so that they could be seen flapping like an eagle's wings as he died. Halfdan was made King of York.

Sigurd Snake-eye sailed back to Denmark with Aella's daughter, Heluna. When he reached Denmark, he married Heluna.

134 THE LODBROK SONS IN ENGLAND

Ivar the Boneless took the great army into Mercia and routed the Mercians down the Trent valley to Nottingham. The Vikings seized Nottingham and remained there. King Burhred of Mercia appealed to King Aethelred of Wessex for help. Aethelred and his brother Alfred arrived in Mercia with a big army and laid siege to Nottingham. The end of the siege happened when the Mercians paid the Vikings to leave. The Vikings then went back to York where they over wintered in 868 – 869. Ivar the Boneless went back home to Dublin.

In the spring of 869, the great army, led by Halfdan, rode through Mercia to East Anglia where they went against Peterborough and Ely. The earls of East Anglia were defeated and King Edmund was captured and executed. King Edmund was later proclaimed a Saint and a Martyr. East Anglia became part of the Danish Deira. Halfdan and Ubbe established winter quarters in Thetford.

In 870, Halfdan took the great army into Wessex and seized the town of Reading. The Vikings fortified the town and used it as their base of operations.

In 871, King Aethelred brought his army against Halfdan. The two armies fought five battles within a very few days. With Aethelred was his younger brother Alfred and the Earldorman Aethelwulf. At Ashdown on January 8, 871, the English won a victory. It was not decisive. Three months later on April 15, Aethelred lost his life in a ferocious battle. Alfred became King of Wessex and paid the Vikings to leave. The Vikings left and over wintered in London in 871 – 872.

In 872, Halfdan led the army into Mercia where the Mercians negotiated peace and paid the Vikings to leave. Halfdan's army over wintered in Reading.

Olaf the White took a fleet out of Dublin and sailed to Norway to fight in a battle. He never returned. Ivar the Boneless then became sole King of Dublin. When Ivar the Boneless died, Eystein, Olaf the White's son, became King of Dublin.

In 874, Halfdan took his army back into Mercia and drove King Burhred out of Mercia. Burhred journeyed to Rome and stayed there for the remainder of his days. Halfdan had the Thane Ceolwulf swear allegiance and service to him and set him up as King of Mercia. Halfdan gave half of Mercia to Ceolwulf. The other half he divided up to his men who took up farming. Halfdan's army over wintered at Repton.

In 875, the great army split. Halfdan took one part to Northumbria and made war on the Picts and Welsh while Guthorm became leader of the second part. Guthorm took his army into East Anglia.

In 876, Halfdan gave land in Northumbria to his men who took up farming.

In 877, Halfdan went raiding in Ireland. At Strangford Loch there was a battle between the Norwegians and Halfdan's Vikings in which Halfdan fell.

135 GUTHORM AND ALFRED

Guthorm went into Wessex from the north and Ubbe Lodbrokson took a fleet of ships from Kent to Wessex to attack Alfred from the south. They utterly defeated Alfred's army and his warriors scattered. Alfred fled into the woods and swamps of Somerset and became a lone wanderer.

Guthorm continued his conquest of Wessex and many Saxons fled from England and went to France.

Alfred wandered through the wilds of Somerset, living off the land and begging food from farmers. One day he was sitting at the hearth in the house of a cow herder. The woman had cakes baking and was preparing to make bread. The cakes started to burn and the woman ran up to Alfred and scolded him for letting the cakes burn. She did not know that the wandering adventurer was King Alfred himself.

Alfred gradually gathered an army again. His chiefs and earls who had fled rejoined him. Guthorm took his army into Essex to go against Alfred. A fleet of Viking ships under Ubbe was to arrive and also engage Alfred.

The Viking fleet got lost in a dense fog and 120 ships perished near Sandwich. The armies of Guthorm and Alfred clashed and Guthorm had to flee. Alfred's men rode after the Vikings as far as Exeter but could not catch them. The Vikings entered their stronghold.

Ubbe finally landed in Essex with 23 ships. The warriors of Alfred went against them and during the fierce battle Ubbe fell and 800 Vikings with him. Ubbe's war flag, 'the Raven' was taken as a souvenir. The Raven had been the war standard of Ragnar Lodbrok and had been made by his daughters.

In 878, Alfred took his army to Edington where Guthorm had his stronghold. Alfred entered Edington and decisively beat the Danes. The Danes fled to their stronghold and held out for 14 days. Then suffering from hunger, cold, and despair, the Danes surrendered. Alfred took pity on them and accepted the surrender on condition that they give hostages, immediately leave the Kingdom and accept Christianity. Guthorm accepted the conditions.

Guthorm took his Vikings north into Dane law. After seven weeks

The Saga Kings

Guthorm came with thirty men to Aller near Atherney and were received by Alfred. After eight days, Guthorm and his thirty men were baptized and Alfred became Guthorm's godfather. Guthorm's Christian name became Aethelstan. Then Guthorm remained with Alfred twelve days after his baptism.

Alfred gave Guthorm and his nobles many houses.

In 879, Guthorm left Chippenham and took his army to Cair Cori in Wiccii where they stayed one year. A large fleet of Vikings under the leadership of Hastein Lodbrokson entered the Thames River and joined Guthorm. They over wintered at Fulham.

Sigfred brother of Godfred, the Viking King of York attacked Wessex but was decisively defeated by Alfred. Sigfred fled and sailed to Dublin where he expelled its King Sigtryg. Sigfred then ruled as King of Dublin.

In 880, Hastein and his Vikings who had over wintered in Fulham sailed away to France.

When Guthorm, King of East Anglia, died, he was buried at Hadleigh twelve miles from Stowmarket. Guthorm's son Eric became King of Northumbria and his son Helge became King of East Anglia.

136 SIGURD SNAKE-EYE

Horik the Younger died and Sigurd Snake-eye Lodbrogson was chosen King of Denmark.

In 881, Sigurd Snake-eye brought his fleet to Frisia and raided at the Rhine River.

In 882, Sigurd continued his raids in Frisia, and Oleg son of Rurik of Novgorod took a great fleet to Kiev, conquered the city and established himself as the ruler. Thus northern and southern Russia was united.

In 885, Sigurd Snake-eye brought his fleet to Lowen. From there he sailed up the Seine with his brother Hastein and 700 long ships and went against Paris. Count Odo of Paris established firm defenses and kept the Vikings out. Sigurd offered to leave Paris if he was allowed to go unhindered back the 200 miles on the River Seine. The offer was refused.

The Vikings assaulted Paris but the City held. Warriors came from all over France to help the city. The Vikings destroyed the bridges on the Seine and went on past Paris to raid the countryside. King Charles the Fat of France came with a great army to Paris and Odo was poised to wipe out the Vikings.

Charles the Fat reopened negotiations with Sigurd Snake-eye. He gave Sigurd permission to go unhindered down the Seine provided he raid Burgundy where his subjects were not loyal. He sealed the contract by offering to pay Sigurd 700 pounds of silver. Sigurd took his fleet down the Seine and raided in Burgundy.

Sigurd Snake-eye brought his fleet to Neustria for his payment of 700 pounds of silver. Odo who was now ruler of west France refused to pay Sigurd. This resulted in a battle, which Sigurd won. Odo was then forced to pay Sigurd his 700 pounds of silver.

In 890, Sigurd Snake-eye and Hastein invaded Britanny but they were defeated and sailed north.

In 891, Sigurd Snake-eye and Hastein sailed to the Dyle near Louvain. King Arnulf of the East Franks took an army against them. During the fierce battle Sigurd and his son Erik fell. The Danish survivors fled to Burgundy.

In 892, the Danish army in Burgundy under Hastein Lodbrogson sailed to Kent England in 250 ships. Many Danes in England joined Hastein's army.

137 HELGE

When Sigurd Snake-eye died, Helge, son of Aethelstan (Guthorm), left East Anglia to be King of Denmark. Helge's son Guthorm ruled in his place in East Anglia. Guthorm was just a boy and was called King Svend (boy or apprentice). Because of his large feet, King Guthorm became known as King Svend Langfod (Long foot).

Helge ruled over a weak Denmark because many warriors had fallen in England and France in the past years. He was constantly battling to keep out the Swedes.

Helge ruled over Jutland, Zealand, and the islands. The Swedes raided in Denmark and King Ring of Sweden was taking districts in Skaane.

138 GUDROD THE HUNTER

Gudrod the Hunter sent some of his men west into Agder to King Harald Redbeard to sue for his daughter's hand in marriage. King Harald declined the suit.

Gudrod launched a fleet of warships and sailed to Agder, where he beached his ships. In the night he came unexpected to King Harald's house. Although greatly outnumbered, Harald took the warriors he had about him out against Gudrod. There was a great battle in which King Harald and his son Gyrd fell. Gudrod took great booty and carried away Aasa, King Harald's daughter, and had a wedding with her. King Gudrod and Aasa had a son and called him Halfdan.

King Gudrod lay with his ship in Stiflesund. Gudrod and his warriors had a drinking bout and they were all very drunk. In the evening, just before dark, King Gudrod, left the ship. As he was walking on the gangplank and was just about to step on shore, a man ran down the gangplank and drove a spear through his body. Gudrod died and the man was instantly cut down. In the morning when it was light, it was discovered that the killer was Aasa's page boy. When questioned about it, Aasa did not deny it.

Thjodolf sang of it: --

"Gudrod is gone to his long rest,

Despite of all his haughty pride --

A traitor's spear has pierced his side:

For Aasa cherished in her breast

Revenge; and as, by wine opprest,

The hero staggered from his ship,

The cruel queen her thrall let slip

To do the deed of which I sing:

And now the far-descended king,

At Stiflesund, in the old bed

Of the old Gudrod race, lies dead."

Aasa took her son Halfdan and sailed to Agder where her father had been King. There Halfdan became known as Halfdan the Black because of his black hair.

Olaf, Gudrod's son became King after his father. He became known as Geirstad-Alf. He was very handsome, and was a great warrior.

King Alfgeir went into Vingulmark and did battle with Olaf Geirstad-Alf. Alfgeir won, took Vingulmark and placed his son Gandalf over it.

139 HALFDAN THE BLACK

Halfdan the Black, now 18 years old took his Kingdom in Agder. Then he went to Westfold and divided that Kingdom with his brother Olaf. Halfdan got the southern part.

Halfdan the Black married Ragnhild, the daughter of Harald Goldbeard who was King in Sogn.

In the autumn, Halfdan the Black took an army to Vingulmark against King Gandalf. There were many battles and sometimes Gandalf won and sometimes Halfdan won. In the end they agreed that Halfdan should have half of Vingulmark as his father Gudrod had it before him.

Eystein subdued Hedemark, Toten, and Hadeland and laid these districts under him. This left Olaf Geirstad-Alf with Westfold, Vermeland, and Raumarike.

Halfdan the Black took his army to Raumarike and subdued it. Eystein's son Sigtryg, King of Raumarike had his residence in Hedemark. When he heard that Halfdan the Black had taken Raumarike, he brought his army against Halfdan. There was a fierce battle, which Halfdan won. As Sigtryg turned to flee an arrow struck him under the left arm and he fell dead. Halfdan then laid the whole of Raumarike under his power.

Eystein's second son, also called Eystein, was King of Hedemark. As soon as Halfdan the Black had gone back to Westfold, Eystein invaded Raumarike and laid the whole district under him.

Halfdan the Black gathered his army together, went into Raumarike and attacked Eystein. After a great battle, Halfdan won and Eystein fled north to Hedemark pursued by Halfdan. Another battle took place and Halfdan was victorious. Eystein fled north to into the Dales and the Jarl Gudbrand where his army was strengthened with new warriors.

King Olaf Geirstad-Alf died of a disease in his foot. He was buried in a mound in Geirstad.

Thjodolf sang of it:

> "Long while this branch of Odin's stem
>
> Was the stout prop of Norway's realm;
>
> Long while King Olaf with just pride
>
> Ruled over Westfold far and wide.
>
> At length by cruel gout oppressed,
>
> The good King Olaf sank to rest:
>
> His body now lies under ground,
>
> Buried at Geirstad, in the mound."

Olaf was succeeded by his son Rognvald. Rognvald was called Rognvald the Mountain High.

In the winter, Eystein took his army south towards Hedemark. Halfdan the Black met him on a large island in Mjosen Lake. A fierce battle took place in which many warriors on both sides fell including Guthorm who was son of the Jarl Gudbrand and was considered one of the finest men in the area. Halfdan was victorious and Eystein fled north up the valley.

Eystein sent Halvard Skalk to Halfdan to beg for peace. Halfdan the Black declared peace and gave Eystein half of Hedemark, which Eystein's ancestors had held before. Halfdan kept Toten, the district called Land, and Hadeland. Thus Halfdan the Black had become a mighty King.

One spring Harald Halfdanson died. Halfdan the Black took a great army to Sogn to claim the kingdom. He was well received by the people and they proclaimed him King. Halfdan made Atle the Slender, Jarl of Sogn district.

In the autumn Halfdan the Black was in Vingulmark. One night at midnight a man rode up and said that a large force was approaching. Halfdan ordered his men to arm themselves and went out and arrayed his warriors up in battle order. Then Gandalf's sons, Hysing and Helsing appeared with a large army. The battle was fierce. Halfdan was overpowered by superior numbers and fled leaving many of his men behind. During the battle, Halfdan's foster father Olver the Wise fell.

People now flocked to Halfdan and he went after Gandalf's sons. He met them at Eid near Lake Oiren and there was a great battle in which Hysing and Helsing fell. Their brother Hake fled to Alfheimer. King Halfdan took all of Vingulmark as part of his Kingdom.

140 SIGURD HART

Sigurd Hart was King in Ringerige. His father was Helge the Sharp and his mother was Aslaug, daughter of Sigurd Snake-eye whose father was Ragnar Lodbrok. Sigurd had two children Ragnhild and Guthorm. His wife was Ingeborg whose mother was Thorny, a daughter of Harald Klak of Denmark. Sigurd rode into the forest one day and came across some cleared land. The Berserker Hake attacked him with thirty men. Sigurd Hart fell after killing twelve of Hake's men and cutting one hand off Hake.

Hake and his men then rode to Sigurd Hart's house and carried away Ragnhild and Guthorm and much booty. They then rode to Hadeland where Hake lived. Hake intended to marry Ragnhild but he waited because of his great wounds.

Halfdan the Black was celebrating Yule feast in Hedemark when the news of the fall of Sigurd Hjort reached him. The next morning he called Horik Jarl to him and told him to go to Hake's house and bring back Guthorm and Ragnhild.

Horik took 100 men and made the journey to Hake's house. In the early morning before any one was up, Horik and his men crossed the lake to Hake's house and barred all the doors and windows. They broke in to where Hake slept and took Guthorm and Ragnhild and much treasure. Then they set the houses on fire and left. They put Ragnhild and Guthorm in a covered wagon and crossed the ice of the lake.

Hake got up and pursued Horik to the lake. There he set his sword in the ground with the point up and let himself fall upon it and died.

When Horik returned to Hedemark there was a great feast and Halfdan the Black married Ragnhild. Halfdan and Ragnhild had two sons, Harald and Eystein.

141 HALFDAN THE BLACK'S YULE FEAST

Halfdan the Black held a Yule feast in Hadeland. But when the guests were to sit around the table in the evening, all the food and ale had disappeared. All the guests were disappointed and went home. Then Halfdan had a Fin captured and had him tortured to tell what had happened. The Fin begged for mercy but Halfdan would give him none. Harald, Halfdan's son begged his father for mercy for the Fin. But Halfdan refused to show mercy.

Harald helped the Fin to escape and went off with him. They came to a place where a group of Fins were having a great feast. They were well received and joined in the feast.

Halfdan the Black returning home from Hadeland went over a lake called Rand. It was spring and there was a thaw. As the King crossed the lake the ice broke, and Halfdan and many with him drowned.

Halfdan the Black had been loved by his people. His body was floated to Ringerige for burial. But the people of Raumarike, Westfold, and Hedemark came and intercepted it. They all wanted the body to be buried in their own district because they believed that it would bring them good crops.

At last it was agreed to divide Halfdan's body into four parts. The head was laid in a mound in Stein in Ringerige. Each of the other parts was laid in mounds in the other regions. These mounds are called Halfdan's mounds.

142 HARALD

Harald Halfdanson stayed with the Fins until spring. Then the chief of the Fins said to him, "Your father was very upset in the winter when I took some provisions from him. Now I will repay you with some good news. Your father is dead and now you shall go home and take possession of the whole kingdom, which he had. With it you shall lay the whole of Norway under you".

Because King Harald was ten years old, his mother's brother Guthorm was head of the government and commander of the army. Many of Halfdan's chiefs coveted the Kingdom. Among them were King Gandalf; Hogne and Frode the sons of King Eystein of Hedemark; and Hogne Karuson of Ringerige.

Hake the son of Gandalf took 300 warriors and marched towards Westfold to take Harald by surprise while Gandalf sat at home with his army prepared to cross the fjord into Westfold once Hake had engage Harald. When a messenger told Guthorm what was happening he took Harald and an army and marched up towards the oncoming Hake. The two armies met in a valley and a ferocious battle took place. There fell Hake and most of his warriors. The valley became known as Hakedale.

When Guthorm and Harald came back to Westfold, they found Gandalf there with his army. In the fierce battle most of Gandalf's warriors were cut down. Gandalf fled with the remnants of his army and reached his kingdom.

When the news of Harald's victories reached Hedemark, the sons of Eystein expected war and sent messengers to Hogne Karuson and Herse Gudbrand to meet them at Ringsaker in Hedemark.

Guthorm and King Harald gathered all the warriors they could and marched back north through the forests and into the Uplands because they had found out where the Upland Kings were meeting. They reached the meeting place at midnight without the watchmen spotting them. They found the houses in which Hogne Karuson and Gudbrand slept. They barred the doors to these houses and set them on fire. Hogne and Frode, the sons of Eystein came out and battled against Harald and Guthorm until Hogne and Frode both fell.

Harald and Guthorm subdued Hedemark, Ringerige, Gudbrandsdal, Hadeland, Thoten, Raumarike, and the whole northern region of Vingulmark.

King Harald and Guthorm made war on King Gandalf. Many battles were fought and finally Gandalf was killed in a battle. King Harald took Gandalf's Kingdom as far south as the Raum River.

King Erik of Hordaland had a daughter named Gyda who was being fostered by a farmer in Valdres. King Harald of Norway had seen that Gyrda was a remarkably beautiful girl and wanted her as his concubine, so he sent messengers to her. Gyrda replied that she would not throw herself away even to a king who had no greater kingdom than a few districts. She said, "It is wonderful that no King in Norway will make the whole country subject to him in the same way as Frode the Bold did in Denmark, or Erik at Uppsala".

The messengers thought Gyrda's answer was very haughty. They told her that King Harald should be good enough for her. They judged that they did not have enough warriors to take her by force so they prepared to leave. As they were leaving, Gyda said to them, "Tell King Harald that I will only agree to be his lawful wife upon the condition that he shall first subject to himself the whole of Norway for my sake. Then he may rule over his kingdom as freely and fully as did Erik in Upsala and Frode in Denmark. Only then can he be called the King of his people".

The messengers returned to King Harald and told him what Gyda had said. They told him that the King should send warriors to get the foolish, haughty girl and inflict some punishment on her. The King answered, "The girl has done nothing for which she should be punished. I should rather thank her for reminding me of something I think wonderful which seems to have slipped my mind. Now I make a solemn wow and take God for witness. Never shall I cut nor comb my hair until I have subdued the whole of Norway with tax, duties and dominion. This will I do or die in the attempt".

Guthorm thanked Harald for his wow and said that it was royal work to fulfill a royal wow.

King Harald of Norway and his foster father Guthorm gathered an army of warriors and went into the Uplands and reached the valley Gudbrandsdal. Then they went north to Dovrefjeld. There Harald ordered that all the men there be killed and everything burned. The men fled into the forests. Some begged for peace and got it on the condition that they swear allegiance to Harald and join his forces.

When he came to Orkadal, King Gryting came against him with an army. In the battle most of Gryting's men fell and King Gryting was taken prisoner. King Gryting swore allegiance to Harald and Orkadal was added to Harald's Kingdom.

King Harald made laws over his lands. The King was to own all the lands and each farmer was to pay Harald land dues for their possessions. The

Jarls were to collect the land dues and keep one third for themselves. Harald had increased the land dues so much that the Jarls had a greater income than the kings did in the districts before them. Because of the increased dues, many great men in the land joined Harald and entered his service.

One of the men to enter Harald's service was Ragnvald. Ragnvald was the son of Eystein who was son of Halfdan the Black.

Jarl Haakon Grjotgardson came to King Harald from Yrjar and entered his service. Harald and Haakon went into Gaurladal and there was a great battle. During the battle the Kings of Gaurladal and Strind districts fell. Harald gave the district Strind to Jarl Haakon to rule over.

Harald entered Stjoradal and conquered it, adding it to his Kingdom.

In the Trondheim district, the Kings of Veradal, Skaun, Sparbygja, and Eyna districts brought their armies together to go against Harald. Harald entered Trondheim and in the mighty battle the four Kings were defeated. Two fell in battle and two fled. Harald had eight battles in Trondheim district and killed eight kings. Harald laid the whole of Trondheim under him.

In Naumudal reigned two brothers Herlaug and Roller. During the past three summers they had been raising a mound of earth and wood. When they heard that King Harald was coming upon them with an army, Herlaug had a great quantity of food and drink put into the mound. Then he entered the mound with eleven companions and ordered the mound to be sealed up. But Roller went to the summit of the mound and had his high seat placed there. Then he ordered feather beds to be placed on a bench below which was used for his Jarls to sit on. Then sitting on his high seat, Roller threw himself on the bench below and gave himself the title Jarl. Roller went out and met Harald and told him the whole story about his mound. King Harald fastened a sword to Roller's belt, gave him a shield, and gave him the title of Jarl of Naumudal.

King Harald went to Trondheim for the winter. There he built a great house called Lade, which he made his home. Then he married Aasa, daughter of Jarl Haakon Grjotgardson. During the winter Harald picked men of renown and berserkers for his personal bodyguards. He caused a great dragon ship to be built, which would be manned by only his elite warriors.

From the poem "Glymdrapa" by Hornklofe:

"O'er the broad heath the bowstrings twang,

While high in air the arrows sang.

The iron shower drives to flight

The foeman from the bloody fight.

The warder of great Odin's shrine,

The fair-haired son of Odin's line,

Raises the voice which gives the cheer,

First in the track of wolf or bear.

His master voice drives them along

To Hel -- a destined, trembling throng;

And Nokve's ship, with glancing sides,

Must fly to the wild ocean's tides. --

Must fly before the king who leads

Norse axe-men on their ocean steeds."

King Harald moved his army from Trondheim south to More. King Hunthiof of More, his son Solve, and his brother in law King Nokve of Raumsdal brought a great army against Harald. There was a great battle at Solskel.

Hornklofe told of the battle:

"Thus did the hero known to fame,

The leader of the shields, whose name

Strikes every heart with dire dismay,

Launch forth his war-ships to the fray.

Two kings he fought; but little strife

Was needed to cut short their life.

A clang of arms by the sea-shore, --

And the shields' sound was heard no more."

The two kings fell in battle and Solve fled to South More. King Harald laid both districts under his power. Harald made Ragnvald Jarl of North More and Raumsdal.

In 868, Solve Klofe was raiding in North More, burning, pillaging, and killing many of King Harald's men. In the spring, King Harald sailed from Trondheim to South More with a great fleet to go against Solve. When King Arnvid of South More heard that King Harald was coming, he gathered many warriors and Solve went south to ask King Aurdbjorn of Firdafylke for help. Aurdbjorn gathered a great army and went to King Arnvid.

King Harald's fleet met the fleets of Arnvid and Aurdbjorn at Solskel and a fierce sea battle started. Many men fell on both sides. Then Harald laid his ship against the ship of Arnvid and they were lashed together. Harald went to the foredeck in berserk fury and slew so ferociously that Arnvid's men were driven back to the mast. Then Harald boarded Arnvid's ship and began to clear its deck. Arnvid fell and many of his men tried to flee. In the battle King Aurdbjorn had fallen. Solve fled and became a sea king who often raided in Norway.

Hornklofe sang of it:

"Against the hero's shield in vain

The arrow-storm fierce pours its rain.

The king stands on the blood-stained deck,

Trampling on many a stout foe's neck;

And high above the dinning stound

Of helm and axe, and ringing sound

Of blade and shield, and raven's cry,

Is heard his shout of 'Victory!'"

King Harald subdued South More and added it to his kingdom. Ragnvald, son of Eistein Glumra, became the Jarl of all of More and Raumsdal. Vermund, Aurdbjorn's brother succeeded Aurdbjorn as King of Firdafylke.

During these times of King Harald many Norwegians, wishing to avoid the battles and Harald's harsh rule, went to live in Iceland.

Ragnvald Jarl went south with many warriors to Firdafylke. They learned that Vermund was staying at Naustdal and went there in the night. They surrounded Vermund's house and burned him in together with 90 of his warriors. The berserker Berdlukare came to Ragnvald and took all Vermund's ships and many possessions. Berdlukare and Ragnvald sailed together to Trondheim and reported to Harald that Firdafylke was taken. Berdlukare then entered Harald's service.

Harald went to Firdafylke to take possession of the district. While he was gone Jarl Haakon of Lade sent word to Jarl Atle Mjove of Sogn that he should leave Sogn and be Jarl of Gaular instead and give Sogn to Haakon. Atle disagreed and raised an army. Haakon also raised troops. The two sailed to Stravenger fjord in Fjalar where they had a fierce battle. Haakon fell in the battle. Atle received a mortal wound and his men took him to the island of Atley where he died.

Eyvind Skadaspiller sang of it:

He who stood a rooted oak,

Unshaken by the swordsman's stroke,

Amidst the whiz of arrows slain,

Has fallen upon Fjalar's plain.

There, by the ocean's rocky shore,

The waves are stained with the red gore

Of stout Earl Haakon Grjotgard's son,

And of brave warriors many a one."

In 883, King Erik Eymundson of Sweden attacked and conquered Vermeland and West Gotland. He then set Hrane Gautzke as Jarl of the country. It was told to King Harald of Norway that Erik would not rest until he had as vast a kingdom in Viken as Sigurd Ring or his son Ragnar Lodbrok used to have. Many districts in Viken had gone over to Erik Eymundson. When Harald heard this he became very angry. He went through the districts of Viken and called a Thing. At the Thing he accused the farmers of treason. Some farmers defended themselves against the accusation, some paid fines, and some were punished.

In late fall, Harald heard that King Erik was in Vermeland in a guest hall. He marched his army east through the Eid forest and came into Vermeland where he demanded a feast. Ake, a farmer in Vermeland who had served Halfdan the Black invited Harald to a feast. He also invited King Erik to the feast. Both kings came to the feast. Ake placed King Harald in a new hall, which had just been built, and Erik feasted in the old hall.

Ake gave Harald his son Ubbe age 12 to enter his service and gave Harald great gifts. Then he went to the Swedish king Erik and gave him great gifts. King Erik and his men mounted their horses and rode towards the woods and Ake followed and talked with Erik. At the edge of the woods

Erik asked Ake why he had treated King Harald better than himself. Ake answered that he had made no difference between the two. Then Erik drew his sword and struck Ake.

King Harald made ready to depart and wished to see Ake. A man ran out to get him and found Ake dead by the edge of the woods. Harald and his warriors mounted their horses and pursued Erik. When he saw Erik and his men enter the woods dividing Gothland from Vermeland, he halted pursuit. King Harald went back and laid Vermeland under him and killed all the Swedes he could find there.

King Harald of Norway raided and looted in Gothland. The Goths brought an army against him but Harald was victorious.

In 887, all the Norwegians who opposed to Harald's rule in Norway gathered and brought their dragon ships into one big fleet. The leaders were King Erik of Hordaland, King Sulke of Rogaland and his brother Sote, King Kjotve the Rich of Agder and his son Thor Haglang, and King Hroald Hryg and his brother Had the Hard of Telemark.

143 THE BATTLE OF HAFERS FJORD

When Harald heard that all his enemies were getting together, he gathered his warriors and launched his fleet. He took his fleet south gathering ships and warriors as he proceeded. When King Erik brought his fleet to Hafers fjord, Harald was there with his fleet waiting for him. A great hard long battle began. King Erik fell and so did King Sulke and his brother Sote. The berserker Thor Hagland laid his ship against Harald's and a fierce hand-to-hand fight began. When Thor fell his whole ship was cleared of warriors.

King Kjotve fled and after that all his men fled and sailed southwards.

Hornklofe sang of the battle:

>"Has the news reached you? -- have you heard
>
>Of the great fight at Hafersfjord,
>
>Between our noble king brave Harald
>
>And King Kjotve rich in gold?
>
>The foeman came from out the East,
>
>Keen for the fray as for a feast.
>
>A gallant sight it was to see
>
>Their fleet sweep o'er the dark-blue sea:
>
>Each war-ship, with its threatening throat
>
>Of dragon fierce or ravenous brute
>
>Grim gaping from the prow; its wales
>
>Glittering with burnished shields, like scales
>
>Its crew of udal men of war,
>
>Whose snow-white targets shone from far

And many a mailed spearman stout

From the West countries round about,

English and Scotch, a foreign host,

And sword men from the far French coast.

And as the foemen's ships drew near,

The dreadful din you well might hear

Savage berserks roaring mad,

And champions fierce in wolf-skins clad,

Howling like wolves; and clanking jar

Of many a mail-clad man of war.

Thus the foe came; but our brave king

Taught them to fly as fast again.

For when he saw their force come o'er,

He launched his war-ships from the shore.

On the deep sea he launched his fleet

And boldly rowed the foe to meet.

Fierce was the shock, and loud the clang

Of shields, until the fierce Haklang,

The foeman's famous berserker fell.

Then from our men burst forth the yell

Of victory, and the King of Gold

The Saga Kings

> Could not withstand our Harald bold,
>
> But fled before his flaky locks
>
> For shelter to the island rocks.
>
> All in the bottom of the ships
>
> The wounded lay, in ghastly heaps;
>
> Backs up and faces down they lay
>
> Under the row-seats stowed away;
>
> And many a warrior's shield, I ween
>
> Right on the warrior's back be seen,
>
> To shield him as he fled amain
>
> From the fierce stone-storm's pelting rain.
>
> The mountain-folk, as I've heard say,
>
> Ne'er stopped as they ran from the fray,
>
> Till they had crossed the Jadar sea,
>
> And reached their homes -- so keen each soul
>
> To drown his fright in the mead bowl."

Harald had defeated all opposition in Norway. His opponents fled the country and went to Iceland, the Faeroe Islands, the Shetland Islands, the Orkneys and the Hebrides.

In 888, King Harald of Norway took his fleet on an expedition to search out and destroy his enemies. He first went to Shetland where he killed all the Vikings who were unable to get away by flight. Then he went south to the Orkney Islands and cleared them of Vikings. From the Orkneys Harald went to the Hebrides and killed many Vikings there. Some of the Vikings fled to Scotland and Harald pursued them into Scotland where he plundered far and wide. An army came against him but Harald was victorious. Then Harald took his fleet west to the Isle of Man. But the

Isle was deserted because all the people had fled to Scotland. On this expedition fell Ivar son of Ragnvald Jarl of More.

As compensation for his loss Ragnvald received the Orkney and the Shetland Islands. Ragnvald gave these islands to his brother Sigurd.

The Franks considered Charles the Fat not fit to rule and deposed him.

In 889, Sigurd Jarl of the Orkneys made an alliance with Thorstein the Red, a son of Olaf the White and they raided in Scotland. They conquered Caithness and Sutherland as far as Ekkjalsbakke (Ekkjals hill). During the conquest, Jarl Sigurd killed the Scottish Jarl Melbridge Tooth. Sigurd cut off Melbridge's head and hung it on his stirrup leather. The teeth of Melbridge's head scratched Sigurd's lower leg. The leg became infected and Sigurd died from the infection. Sigurd's son Guthorm became Jarl of the Orkneys.

King Harald of Norway was at a feast in More. He took a bath and washed and combed his hair. Ragnvald Jarl of More cut Harald's hair to shoulder length. People were amazed at Harald's beautiful and abundant head of hair. He had not cut his hair in over ten years. Harald became known as Harald Fairhair.

Harald remembered Gyda, the girl who would not marry him until he was King of all Norway. He sent men to fetch Gyda and took her to his bed.

Harald had many sons with many wives. His children were fostered out with their mothers' families.

King Harald's son Guthorm was responsible for defending the Vik for Harald Fairhair. He sailed by the islands on the Vik coast and came to the Got River. While he lay at anchor there, the sea king Solve Klofe arrived and immediately attacked. During the battle Guthorm fell.

144 TURF EINAR

Ragnvald was married to Hild, a daughter of Rolf Nefia. Their sons were Ivar who had fallen in the Orkneys, Thorer and Rolf called Ganger (Walker) because he was so large that no horse could carry him. Ragnvald had three other sons Hallard, Einar, and Rollaugh.

Guthorm Sigurdson died and Vikings from Norway and Denmark began to take over the Orkneys. Ragnvald sent his son Hallard to take over as Jarl of the Orkneys. Hallard took many warriors and established himself as jarl. Vikings would come in the fall, winter, and spring to cruise around the headlands and raid the coasts of the Orkneys.

Hallard became tired of ruling the Orkneys and returned home and his father told him he was a disgrace. Ragnvald's son Rollaugh had immigrated to Iceland, and Thorer was out on Viking raids. Einar told Ragnvald that if Ragnvald would give him a strong enough force he would go west and be Jarl of the Orkneys. He told Ragnvald that if he did so Ragnvald would never see him again. Ragnvald replied that he would be glad if Einar never came back because there was little hope that he would obtain honour among his friends, because all the people on his mother's side were thralls.

Ragnvald gave Einar a long ship completely equipped and Einar sailed west in the fall. When he reached the Orkneys two Viking ships barred his way. One was commanded by Thorer Treskeg (Tree Beard) and the other by Kalf Skurka. Einar attacked them immediately and was victorious. Both Thorer and Karl fell in battle.

Einar became the Jarl of the Orkneys and was considered a great man. He was blind in one eye and considered ugly to look upon but he was very wise. Einar was called Turf Einar because he burned peat for fuel. There were no woods on the Orkneys.

Harald Fairhair had many sons with many wives. These sons were beginning to be jealous of the Jarls and thought that the Jarls were inferior to themselves in birth. The sons all wanted to be rulers.

Two of Harald's sons, Halfdan Haleg and Gudrod Ljome, set out one spring with a great army. They went into More and surrounded Ragnvald's house and set fire to the house and burned it down with Ragnvald and sixty men inside it.

Halfdan Haleg took three long ships, outfitted them and sailed west. Gudrod set himself up as ruler over the districts, which Ragnvald had.

In 894, when Harald Fairhair heard what had happened to his good friend Ragnvald, he became furious. He gathered a huge army and went to More. Gudrod surrendered because that was his only choice. Harald sent Gudrod to Agder.

Harald then made Ragnvald's son Thorer Jarl of the districts his father had and he gave him his daughter Alof as wife.

Halfdan Haleg came with his three ships to the Orkneys and Turf Einar immediately fled to Scotland.

In the early fall, Turf Einar sailed back to the Orkneys with many warriors. After a short battle, Halfdan fled in the night. Turf Einar waited till dawn and kept watch with his warriors. In the morning's early light they searched the islands and killed every man they could find. Then on the isle of Rinansey they saw a man get up and then lie down again. They went onto the isle and found that it was Halfdan Haleg whom they took prisoner. Turf Einar cut the blood eagle on Halfdan's back. Einar drove his sword through Halfdan's back and divided the ribs from the backbone. Then he pulled out Halfdan's lungs so that he died.

Einar then composed a song, which went:

> **"Where is the spear of Hrollaug? where**
>
> **Is stout Rolf Ganger's bloody spear!**
>
> **I see them not; yet never fear,**
>
> **For Einar will not vengeance spare**
>
> **Against his father's murderers, though**
>
> **Hrollaug and Rolf are somewhat slow,**
>
> **And silent Thorer sits and dreams**
>
> **At home, beside the mead-bowl's streams.**
>
> **For Ragnvald's death my sword is red:**

The Saga Kings

> Of vengeance it cannot be said
>
> That Einar's share is left unsped.
>
> So now, brave boys, let's raise a mound, --
>
> Heap stones and gravel on the ground
>
> O'er Halfdan's corpse: this is the way
>
> We Norsemen our tax duties pay."

"Many a stout udal-man, I know,

    Has cause to wish my head laid low;

And many an angry udal knife

    Would gladly drink of Einar's life.

But ere they lay Earl Einar low, --

    Ere this stout heart betrays its cause,

Full many a heart will writhe, we know,

    In the wolf's fangs or eagle's claws."

King Harald Fairhair raised a great army and sailed to the Orkneys. Einar Jarl fled to Caithness in Scotland. Many messages were passed between Harald Hair Fair and Turf Einar. At last a meeting was organized.

Turf Einar committed his case to King Harald for judgment. The King committed Jarl Turf Einar and all the Orkney people to pay a fine of sixty marks of gold each.

The farmers were too poor to pay sixty marks each. Turf Einar volunteered to pay the fines if the farmers would give him their lands. The farmers agreed because they would be able to buy their lands back by making payments over time. Thus Einar paid the fines to Harald Fairhair who then sailed back to Norway.

145 THE KINGS OF YORK

Sigtryg returned to Dublin with a huge fleet of Norwegian Vikings and battled Sigfred. Sigfred fled back to York. In 895, Sigtryg raided in northern England in retaliation of being chased out of Dublin. Godfred went against Sigtryg and fell in battle. Then Sigfred became King of York.

When Sigfred in 896 did not support Hastein in his war on Alfred the Great, he was deposed by the Jarls and the Viking army in England declared Hastein King of England. King Alfred the Great took his army against King Hastein Lodbrokson. The armies met at Benfleet in Essex. The battle was fierce and long. Alfred was victorious and Hastein fell in battle.

Hastein's army dispersed and some of his Vikings went to East Anglia and some to Northumbria where they settled. The rest went back across the sea. Sigfred was restored as King of York and the Danes submitted to Alfred the Great as their King.

Alfred the Great died on October 26, 899. He was buried at Winchester. Alfred's son Edward the Elder became King England. Edward's cousin Aethelwold wanted to be King and a rebellion broke out. Edward won the battle and Aethelwold went north to York where he was proclaimed King.

Svend Langfod, son of King Helge of Denmark, was King of Danish Deira in East Anglia. Svend Langfod accepted King Aethelwold as his King. In 900, Aethelwold and King Eric of Northumberland with an army of Danes from East Anglia and Northumberland attacked Mercia and took it.

146 ROLF GANGER (ROLF THE WALKER)

Rolf, son of Ragnvold, was called Rolf Ganger (Rolf the Walker) because he was so big that no horse could carry him. He raided often in the East Sea. Rolf was returning from the east and his men were very hungry. Rolf landed his fleet in the Vik and went on a cattle raid. Harald Fairhair just happened to be in the Vik at the same time and was in a rage that Rolf Ganger would raid in Norway. The King called a Thing and had Rolf Ganger declared an outlaw in all Norway. When Rolf's mother Hild heard what had happened she went to Harald to plead Rolf's case. Hild said the following:

> "Think'st thou, King Harald, in thy anger,
>
> To drive away my brave Rolf Ganger
>
> Like a mad wolf, from out the land?
>
> Why, Harald, raise thy mighty hand?
>
> Why banish Nefia's gallant name-son,
>
> The brother of brave udal-men?
>
> Why is thy cruelty so fell?
>
> Bethink thee, monarch, it is ill
>
> With such a wolf at wolf to play,
>
> Who, driven to the wild woods away
>
> May make the king's best deer his prey."

Rolf Ganger sailed west to the Hebrides. Then he became a sea king and started to raid the coast of France. His Viking fleet gradually became larger and most of his Vikings came to him from Denmark.

Rolf took his fleet to France and stopped at Rouen. The people at Rouen were terrified when the Vikings went ashore and examined the fortifications and the town and the church. The archbishop of the area approached the Vikings in an attempt to make a treaty. Rolf told the archbishop that they intended to make this site their headquarters. When the archbishop related this to the people, they were greatly relieved but still uneasy. They considered that this was not welcome news but was much better than having the Vikings pillage and loot the countryside.

The Vikings built a great camp and fortified it. Then they all sailed away to Bayeux and assaulted it. They took Bayeux and the Count of Bayeux, Berenger fell in the battle. The Vikings took much loot and Rolf Ganger took Berenger's beautiful daughter Poppa. When he arrived back in Rouen, Rolf married Poppa.

King Charles of France at this time was at war with several pretenders to the throne. Rolf and his Vikings helped him in some of his battles. They also went raiding in the territories of these pretenders. The people of Neustria grew to love Rolf and his Vikings. They called him 'Rollo'.

Charles considered his situation. He was fighting pretenders to his throne. His dukes and counts who swore him allegiance sometimes defected to his enemies. There was an army of Vikings in one of his coastal territories. Charles knew that the Vikings had a very great sense of honour. A Viking who had given his word would never break it. A Viking who had sworn allegiance would always be faithful.

In 911, King Charles the Simple of France met with Rolf Ganger. Charles offered Rolf the dukedom of Neustria and land for his warriors if he would pledge allegiance to King Charles, accept Christianity, and defend Neustria from other northern raiders. Rolf Ganger accepted. The inhabitants of Neustria felt safe with Rolf's Viking army and were very happy with the arrangement. In 912, Rolf Ganger swore allegiance to King Charles the Simple of France. Rolf was then baptized and received the Christian name of Robert. Most of Robert's Vikings accepted Christianity and were also baptized. Some of them were baptized many times because of the wonderful gifts received with baptism. Although Robert was now a Christian, he still kept up his sacrifices to Thor.

Robert received the title of Duke and Neustria was his Duchy. Robert kept his word to Charles and drove other Vikings away from Neustria. He also helped Charles with the fighting in France. Rolf and his Vikings were very popular with the inhabitants of Neustria. The Vikings and the Neustria natives intermarried and became the people of Neustria. In time Robert's territory was expanded and became known as Normandy.

147 ERIK BLOOD AXE

In 905, Harald Fairhair divorced nine wives and married Ragnhild the Mighty, a daughter of King Erik of Jutland. Harald Fair Hair and Ragnhild the Mighty had a son and called him Erik.

When Erik turned twelve years old, Harald Fairhair gave him five long ships and Erik went raiding in Denmark and in the Baltic Sea. Then he went west and raided in Saxony and Frisia. From these raids, Erik Haraldson became known as Erik Blood Axe. He also raided Scotland, Britain, Ireland, and Valland.

In 920, Erik Blood Axe raided in Bjarmaland and Finland.

In 921, Erik Blood Axe spent the summer on Viking raids.

In 922, Erik Blood Axe married Gunhild daughter of King Svend Langfod (Guthorm), (Gorm) of East Anglia. Svend's wife Thyra was daughter of Aethelred, the Lord of Mercia, and brother of Alfred the Great. Erik and Gunhild's children were Gamle, Guthorm, Harald, Ragnfrod, Ragnhild, Erling, Gudrod, and Sigurd Sleva.

Harald Fairhair wanted his son Erik Blood Axe to rule Norway after him. He set all his other sons as rulers over the various districts.

Harald heard that his son Ragnvald who ruled in Hadeland allowed himself to be trained as a warlock. Harald sent a message to the warlock Vitgeir that he should give up witchcraft. Vitgeir sent word back that witchcraft was respectable because Harald's own son and ruler, Ragnvald, was a warlock. Under orders from Harald Fairhair, Erik Blood Axe went to Hadeland and burned Ragnvald in his house along with eighty other warlocks.

In 924, Gudrod Ljome was visiting his foster father Thjodolf in Hvin and wanted to sail to Rogaland. Thjodolf warned Gudrod to wait till the storm subsided but Gudrod would not wait. While sailing off Jader the long ship was swamped and sank. All on board were lost.

Thjodolf of Hvin sang of it:

> "Wait, Gudrod, till the storm is past, --
>
> Loose not thy long-ship while the blast
>
> Howls over-head so furiously, --
>
> Trust not thy long-ship to the sea, --
>
> Loose not thy long-ship from the shore;
>
> Hark to the ocean's angry roar!
>
> See how the very stones are tossed
>
> By raging waves high on the coast!
>
> Stay, Gudrod, till the tempest's o'er --
>
> Deep runs the sea off the Jadar's shore."

In 925, Harald Fairhair's son Bjorn ruled over Westfold. He did not go on war expeditions but was a trader. He had a fleet of merchant vessels with which he used to trade in the Vik, Denmark, and Saxony. While Bjorn was in Tunsberg, Erik Blood Axe came to him with a fleet of warships and demanded the tax from Westfold, which Bjorn normally paid to his father. Bjorn normally delivered the taxes to his father himself and refused to pay Erik. The two brothers quarreled about it. Erik also wanted provisions, tents, and liquor. Erik got nothing and left.

In the evening Bjorn went to Saeheim. Erik came to Saeheim just as Bjorn was engaged in drinking with his men. Erik's warriors surrounded the house and Bjorn and his men went out and fought Erik's warriors. During the battle Bjorn and most of his men fell. Erik looted and proceeded north.

King Bjorn was laid in a mound at Saeheim. The people of the Vik hated Erik for this deed and it became known that King Olaf, who succeeded Bjorn in Westfold, was waiting for an opportunity to avenge his brother Bjorn.

In 926, Erik Blood Axe went to More and was at a feast in Solve.

Halfdan the Black heard about it and brought an army to Solve in the night. He surrounded the house and burned it with everyone inside. But Erik slept in a small hut set apart and escaped into the forest with four of his men.

Erik went to his father and told him what had happened. Harald Fairhair was very angry, assembled a great army, and prepared to go against the Throndheim people. When Halfdan heard the news he gathered men and ships and sailed to Stad in Thorsbjerg. King Harald lay in at Reinsletta and people tried to go between them and negotiate peace. One of the negotiators was Guthorm Sindre, a skald who was friends with both Harald and Halfdan. Since each had told him that any request he made they would do, Guthorm now used his requests by requesting of each that they be reconciled with the other. Because of Guthorm the reconciliation took place and Halfdan was to keep the Kingdom, which he had before, and to leave Erik Blood Axe in peace.

In 930, Harald Fairhair had become so heavy that he was unable to travel throughout the country on the King's business. Therefore he brought his son Erik Blood Axe to his high seat and gave him the power of ruler-ship over all Norway.

When the news spread over Norway, the people of Throndheim took Halfdan the Black as their King because they did not want to be ruled by Erik. The people of Westfold took Olaf, Bjorn's brother, as their King for the same reason. Olaf's son was called Tryggve and Olaf fostered Bjorn's son who was called Gudrod. The two foster brothers were about the same age.

When the people of the Vik heard about the districts that had chosen their own King, they did the same and chose Olaf as their King.

Erik Blood Axe was very upset at the districts that had fallen away from him.

148 HARALD FAIRHAIR AND AETHELSTAN

Harald Fair Hair had a son with one of his servant girls called Thora. When Thora was about to give birth she was with her mother at Moster. Sigurd Jarl of Lade took her in his ship and they sailed north to meet Harald who was at Saeheim. But Thora did not make it to Saeheim because the baby would not wait. They anchored close to the land and Thora gave birth to a son. Sigurd poured water on him and called him Haakon after his own father.

Sigurd Jarl was married to Bergljot the daughter of Thorer Ragnvaldson Jarl of More who was married to Alof daughter of Harald Fairhair.

Harald Fairhair was on good terms with Aethelstan King of all England. They had made it a habit of sending each other great gifts. At one time, Harald sent Aethelstan a long ship. This year, Aethelstan sent messengers to King Harald in Norway with a gift. The gift was a sword, which had the hilt gilded and the sheath was inlaid with gold and silver and inlaid with precious jewels. The messenger presented the sword to Harald and Harald took it by the handle. The messenger then said, "now that you have taken the sword according to our King's desire, you are therefore his subject".

When Vikings swore allegiance to a King they held the King's sword by the handle. Therefore Harald Fair Hair felt deeply insulted and became enraged, because he in no way felt inferior to Aethelstan. Harald consulted his advisors and they told him to let the messengers go home and take time to think things over. Harald allowed the messengers to leave.

Harald Fairhair sent Hauk Habrok to England with Haakon, Harald's youngest son. When Hauk's long ship arrived in London, King Aethelstan was there. Hauk took thirty men and went up to the King and greeted him. King Aethelstan bade Hauk welcome. Then Hauk placed the young boy Haakon in Aethelstan's lap and said, "Harald the King asks you to foster his servant girl's child".

Aethelstan was in great anger, drew his sword and made as to kill Haakon. Hauk said that since Aethelstan had the child placed on his knees he could do with him as he wished. Hauk and his men left immediately and sailed back to Harald Fairhair who was very pleased because the man who fosters another's child is considered to be less than the other.

King Aethelstan had Haakon baptized and brought up in the Christian faith. He grew to love Haakon above all his relations. Haakon grew to have good manners and was loved by all people wherever he went. He became a great skald (bard) and became larger and better looking than most men. Aethelstan gave Haakon a sword with a gold hilt and handle. When the sword was tested it bit into a millstone to the center eye. Its name became Quernbite and Haakon carried it with him until his death.

In 932, Halfdan the Black died suddenly at a feast in Throndheim. It was rumored that Erik's wife Gunhild had paid a witch to give Halfdan a death drink.

The Throndheim people called a Thing and chose Sigrod to be their King.

Rolf the Ganger died and his son William Long Sword became Duke of Neustria.

In 933, King Harald Fairhair died on his sick bed in Hogaland   He was 83 years old

When King Olaf and King Sigrod heard that Erik Blood Axe intended to make himself King of all Norway, they went to Tunsberg in the Vik and raised an army. When Erik heard that the two kings were in Tunsberg, he took a great fleet and sailed to Tunsberg. The gale was strong and steady and was with him so that he arrived at Tunsberg faster than the news of his coming.

Olaf and Sigrod took their forces out of Tunsberg and set up a battle array on a plain. The battle was fierce and many men fell. Erik won because he had many more warriors than Olaf and Sigrod who both died in the battle.

When news of the battle reached Westfold, the young boys Tryggve Olafson and Gudrod Bjornson fled to the Uplands.

149 HAAKON THE GOOD

When Haakon Aethelstan's foster son heard of his father, Harald Fairhair's death, he prepared to sail to Norway. Aethelstan gave him ships and warriors. In the fall Haakon reached Norway and heard of the death of his brothers. Haakon sailed north to Throndheim and was well received by Sigurd Jarl of Lade.

Sigurd Jarl called a Thing and recommended Haakon as King of Norway. Haakon gave a speech offering himself as King and asked for help and warriors to defend the Kingdom. He also promised to give the farmers their land back, which had been confiscated by Harald Fairhair so that once again the farmers would be free men. The speech was met with overwhelming applause and the people cried out that Haakon was their King.

Haakon took some warriors as bodyguards and proceeded through the country with his speech. Word of Haakon spread from mouth to mouth and soon the whole of Norway had heard about him. Men began to flock to him, first from the Uplands and then from the other districts.

In 935, Haakon went into the Uplands and the people called a Thing and declared him King. Then with Tryggve and Gudrod he went to the Vik where the people called a Thing and declared him King. This happened where ever Haakon went and Haakon was now called Haakon the Good. Then Haakon gave Tryggve and Gudrod the title of King and gave them the districts which their fathers had.

Haakon tried to introduce Christianity to Norway, but the people resisted.

Haakon collected warriors and ships and prepared to go against Erik blood Axe. Meanwhile Erik also collected warriors and ships, but not many would go with Erik. When Erik realized that he would have no chance of defeating Haakon, he sailed west and landed in the Orkneys.

From the Orkneys, Erik Blood Axe raided in Scotland and in North England.

150 OLAF, GNUPA, AND GURD

Olaf of Sweden brought a fleet of long ships to Hedeby and attacked the Danes. King Helge resisted with an army but Olaf won the battle. Olaf declared himself King. Olaf's sons were called Knud and Gurd".

"Oh!" exclaimed Erik, "I heard they were Gnupa and Gurd".

The story teller chuckled and took a drink of his beer. Then he said, "Gnupa is Swedish for Knud, the Danish pronunciation and the Saxons say 'Canute'. Hedeby was the richest trading town in Denmark, so Olaf and his family became very rich and controlled most of the foreign trades.

King Gnupa Olafson of Hedeby raided in Frisia. In retaliation King Henrik the Fowler of Saxony attacked and conquered Hedeby. Gnupa was captured and forced to be baptized. Hedeby then belonged to the Saxons and paid tax to Henrik the Fowler.

151 GORM THE OLD

In 936, when King Helge of Denmark died Gorm left England and sailed to Zealand in Denmark to claim the throne. At the same time Hardegon Svendson came from Northmania, arrived with a fleet at Hedeby and attacked the Swedes. Gnupa's son Sigtryg battled against Hardegon but lost and had to flee".

Erik could contain himself no longer. He burst out, "Who was Hardegon Svendson?"

The story teller smiled and said, "A good question Erik, Gorm's son was Hardegon and his last name was Svendson because in England Gorm was known as Svend. The English name Hardegon was used because they could not pronounce 'Hardeknud' which was his real name. He was called Knud for short".

"Wait a minute", said Ole, "The abbot told us that Hardegon was the father of Gorm."

The story teller looked at Ole, took a sip of beer and chuckled. Then he said, "There is great confusion about where Gorm came from and who his father was. Some say that Hardegon was his father and some say that Guthorm was. Some say that Sigurd Snake-eye was his grandfather or his father. Some say that Helge was his father. But this is my story. In my story, Gorm was the son of Helge who was the son of Guthorm Sigurdson who was married to Ragnar Lodbrok's daughter. Gorm was King in East Anglia and he married Thyra, the daughter of Aethelred, Alfred's brother. She was also the sister of the mighty King Aethelstan of England. Hardegon was the son of Gorm and Thyra. Hardegon was a very famous warrior in England having fought in many battles. When he took Hedeby from the Germans and chased out the Swedes, he did not become King of Denmark. Why not? It was because he was fighting for Gorm, his father who became King."

"What happened to Sigtryg?" asked Erik.

"Ah", said the story teller "Sigtryg became a Sea King and took up raiding. He sailed his fleet to Normandy. There he took service with Duke Hugo of the Franks who invaded Normandy and Sigtryg fought in the battles against Duke William Longsword. Eventually he died fighting in Holland."

The story teller continued, "King Gorm (Svend Langfod) moved the Danish royal court from Lejre to Jelling near Hedeby. On his arrival the Danes called him the Englishman because he came from England.

Svend Langfod (Guthorm) and his son Hardegon (Knud) conquered Jutland. In one of the battles in Jutland Gnupa fell. During a battle in Skaane King Ring of Sweden fell and Skaane was retaken by Gorm who became king of Jutland, Zealand, the islands and Skaane.

After Gorm had secured the country and was firmly established as King of Denmark, Thyra organized work on Danevirke (the wall between Denmark and Germany) to strengthen it and extend it. She was a common sight walking around supervising the construction. She insured that lots of food was available for the workers. Thyra cared for the Danish people and the Danes grew to love her very much. They called her Thyra Danebod (Thyra Denmark's Blessing).

Henrik the Fowler died and Otto I became King of Saxony. The German Kings looked upon themselves as Emperors of the old Roman Empire restored the same as Charlemagne had done. The Pope encouraged this view. In Germany Gorm was known as Vurm. Vurm means "Dragon" and Guthorm means "good dragon". Thus in Germany King Gorm was known as the Dragon King.

Because he could speak and write Latin, King Svend (Guthorm) (Gorm) was considered very wise and people called him King Frode (the wise). As well as his son Knud, Gorm had a younger son called Harald and a daughter called Gunhild who was married to Erik Blood Axe.

Gorm was a Christian and had been baptized in England. Thyra was a devout Christian. King Gorm sent a message to the Pope asking that Bishops be sent to Denmark to Christianize the Danes. Three Bishops went to Denmark. One was established at Aarhus, one at Hedeby, and one at Ribe. But it is rumored that Gorm reverted to the worship of Odin.

Many Vikings, who were not Scandinavians, roamed the Baltic Sea at this time, Estonians, Slavs, Vends, and Saxons. The most feared of these were the Vends".

Haakon the Good set up coast watches and a system of beacons in Norway as a defense against Viking attacks. The beacons were fire wood piled very high and covered with pitch. If a section of Norway was attacked, the wood was to be ignited and anyone seeing a burning beacon was to ignite the next one. Viking attacks against Norway came to almost a standstill.

Danish Vikings raided in the Vik and Haakon met them with a great army. The Danes fled to Jutland with Haakon in pursuit. Haakon chased the Vikings way into Jutland killing many. When the Jutes banded together and came after him, Haakon retreated to his ships. From there he sailed to Zealand and raided in Zealand. Then he raided in Skaane.

King Gorm's two sons Knud and Harald went on Viking expeditions each year. On one expedition, Harald was hit in the mouth by a blunt object and some of his teeth turned black. From then on he was called Harald Bluetooth.

King Gorm loved his son Knud so much that he swore the oath that he would kill who ever brought him word of Knud's death. The Danish people also loved Knud and called him Knud Dane Fryd (Danish Delight). They also called him Dane Aesa in recognition that he was of Aesir descent.

In 941, Knud Dane Fryd and Harald Bluetooth decided to conquer Dublin which was held by Norwegian Vikings. They gathered a great fleet, sailed to Ireland, and lay siege on Dublin. Olaf Godfredson was King of Dublin. When night fell he went with some archers near the Danish camp where the Danes were playing at games. The archers began to shoot and Knud was hit. Knud told his men to continue the games so that the Norwegians would not know that the Danish leader had been hit. Knud died during the night and Harald Bluetooth took command.

In the morning Harald attacked Dublin and after a fierce fight Olaf fled to Britain. Olaf was attacked by the English and he died in battle.

Harald returned to Jelling with Knud's body. Nobody knew how to tell King Gorm that his son Knud had fallen because Gorm had once declared, "I will put to death anyone who brings me the news that Knud has died."

Finally Thyra came up with a plan. She told everyone not to say a word.

Then she decked the King's hall in black tapestry. That night when the King entered the hall, he wondered what the black decorations meant. Then Thyra said, "Your Majesty, King, you had two falcons, one white the other gray. The white flew far away and was overcome by many birds that plucked the feathers off it. But the gray still catches birds for your table".

King Gorm understood what Thyra said. After a moment he yelled, "My son Knud is dead since all Denmark is in mourning!"

Thyra answered, "It is true. You said it yourself, not me".

152 ERIK BLOOD AXE IN ENGLAND

In the year 936, King Aethelstan of England sent a message to Erik Blood Axe that he had been a good friend of Erik's father Harald Fairhair and because of that offered Erik a fief in Northumberland if Erik would consent to becoming a Christian and defend Northumberland from Vikings. Erik accepted the offer and moved his family to York where he was baptized and installed as King of York.

In 939, King Aethelstan of England died and his son Edmund became King.

William Long Sword, Duke of Normandy, died in 943. His son Richard the Fearless succeeded him.

In 946, King Edmund of England died and his brother Eadred became King of England. Eadred hated Erik Blood Axe and brought pressure on the Northumbrians so that they expelled Erik Blood Axe by the end of the year.

In 952, Erik Blood Axe went back to York and became King of Northumbria.

In 954, King Eadred drove Erik Blood Axe out of York. Then when Erik went on a raiding spree in England, Eadred gathered a great army and went after him. A dreadful battle took place at Stainmore. Many warriors fell. During the battle more and more Englishmen arrived to fight Erik. Towards the evening the battle was over. Among the fallen were Erik Blood Axe and his sons Guthorm, Sigurd, and Ragnvald. After the battle of Stainmore King Eadred was crowned the first King of all the English.

When Gunhild and her sons heard that Erik had fallen they gathered up their belongings and much treasure. Then they took some warriors and Erik's ships and sailed to the Orkneys where Thorfin was Jarl. Thorfin was the son of Turf Einar. Erik's sons subdued the Orkneys and took the taxes for themselves.

In 955, when Gunhild heard that there was raiding between the Norwegians and the Danes, she married her daughter Ragnhild to Thorfin Einarson and sailed with her sons to Denmark. Thorfin reestablished himself as the Orkney Jarl.

153 HARALD BLUETOOTH

Harald Bluetooth received his sister well and gave her sons fiefs in Denmark so that they could maintain themselves with taxes. The sons of Erik Blood Axe took up Viking raiding in the Baltic Sea with Danish warriors.

In 956, Erik's sons began to raid in the Vik. King Tryggve of the Vik kept an army of foot soldiers to repel raiders and they fought the Erik sons. In retaliation Tryggve raided in Zealand and Halland.

In 957, Harald Bluetooth and Gunhild reached an agreement that Harald help Erik's sons conquer Norway. Erik's sons took a fleet of many ships and sailed north.

A message came to Haakon the Good that the sons of Erik Bloodaxe were lying with a very large fleet south of Stad. Haakon did not think that he could raise enough warriors to meet them in time. Egil Ulserk an old man, who had been Harald Fairhair's banner carrier, advised King Haakon that in the olden days Harald Fairhair was always victorious whether outnumbered or whether he had superior forces. Haakon sent a war arrow throughout Norway.

Erik's sons sailed north around Stad with 20 ships and Haakon had 9 ships, which he lay in at Freedaberg in Freysund. King Haakon sent a message to the sons of Erik to meet for battle on a field at Rastarkalf. Egil Ulserk asked Haakon to give him ten men with ten banners. Egil got his ten men with banners and took them behind a low ridge. Haakon set up his battle standard on the plain and arrayed his warriors.

Egil Ulserk arranged his ten men far apart and when the Erik sons and their warriors approached he had his ten men advance. The Erik sons saw Haakon and his army on the plain and they saw the tops of the ten banners approaching behind the ridge. They thought that a huge army was coming to join Haakon so they all fled. Haakon the Good pursued the warriors of the Erik sons and killed many.

Gamle Erikson fled from the south of the Ridge to the plain. All his brothers and many of his warriors assembled there. The Norwegians came upon them led by Egil Ulserk. Egil and Gamle exchanged blows and Egil fell and many warriors with him. But Gamle was seriously wounded.

Then Haakon clashed with the Erik sons with his warriors and the warriors of the Erik sons started to fall. The Erik sons and the remaining warriors fled to the ships but the warriors who had not made a stand had pushed the ships off into the water and were sailing away. The few ships remaining were so far up on shore that they could not be pushed off before Haakon would be upon them.

The Erik sons and their warriors rushed into the sea and began to swim. Gamle who was seriously wounded drowned. The rest reached their ships and sailed for Denmark.

When Haakon's warriors had assembled from all over Norway, they sailed for Denmark. Haakon's fleet arrived in Jutland and attacked the Jutes. Haakon fought boldly and went forward before his banner in berserk fury without helmet or coat of mail. Haakon subdued northern Jutland. Haakon then took his fleet to Zealand and overran Zealand. He added Zealand to his Kingdom and made the Zealanders pay tax to him.

From Zealand Haakon took his fleet to Skaane and raided far and wide. After taking great booty he entered Gothland and raided there as well.

In 958, Harald Bluetooth was very depressed. He was depressed because his father was dying, his Danish Kingdom was broken, and the sons of Erik Blood Axe were losing his warriors in Norway. During the winter Gorm the Old died. His son Harald laid his body in a mound.

Harald considered his Kingdom and became very angry. Any attack on Denmark was an attack on himself. He sent word throughout Denmark and gathered a mighty army and went to Zealand where he drove out the Norwegian Jarls.

In 959, Harald Bluetooth's war ships patrolled the Danish waters and drove out the foreign Vikings and then he went into Vend land and conquered the Vends.

In 960, Harald went to the Lim Fjord and assembled a great fleet. Then he and the Erik sons took his fleet to Norway.

King Haakon the Good was at a feast in Hordaland on the island of Stord when Eyvind Finson burst into the hall and said:

> "Up king! The avengers are at hand!
>
> Eirik's bold sons approach the land!
>
> The Judgment of the sword they crave
>
> Against their foe. Thy wrath I brave;
>
> Tho' well I know 'tis no light thing
>
> To bring war-tidings to the king
>
> And tell him 'tis no time to rest.
>
> Up! Gird your armour to your breast:
>
> Thy honour's dearer than my life;
>
> Therefore I say, up to the strife!"

Haakon ordered the tables removed and went out to look at the approaching ships. He saw that they were numerous Danish dragon ships. He pondered whether to go and fight or take his ships and flee north because the Danish ships outnumbered his small fleet. His men told him that they would rather die fighting than flee. They said that they had fought Gunhild's sons before and always gained the victory even when outnumbered Haakon thanked his men and ordered them to arm themselves. Haakon set his warriors in battle formation and set up his standard.

The Danish ships drew up to the island and the warriors came ashore.

They outnumbered the Norwegians six to one. Both sides hurled their spears and then the warriors rushed forward and came together in a ferocious battle.

Eyvind Skadaspiller sang of it:

> "The body-coats of naked steel,
>
> The woven iron coats of mail,

> Like water fly before the swing
>
> Of Haakon's sword -- the champion-king.
>
> About each Gotland war-man's head
>
> Helm splits, like ice beneath the tread,
>
> Cloven by the axe or sharp sword blade,
>
> The brave king, foremost in the fight,
>
> Dyes crimson-red the spotless white
>
> Of his bright shield with foemen's gore. --
>
> Amidst the battle's wild uproar,
>
> Wild pealing round from shore to shore."

Eyvind Skreya and his brother Alf came against Haakon. Eyvind swung his sword hard at Haakon but Thoralf thrust his shield at Eyvind who tottered with the impact. Haakon wielding his sword Kvernbite with both hands sliced Eyvind through his helm and head down to his shoulders and Thoralf slew Alf.

After the fall of the two brothers, Haakon pressed so hard that all the Danes gave way before him. Many arrows were flying and one struck Haakon in the arm. The Norwegians fled, boarded their ships and sailed away.

When Haakon went to his ship, he had his wound bound up but the men could not stop the bleeding. When he knew he was dying, he had his ship put to land and he sent messengers to Erik Blood Axe's sons telling them that they should be Kings of Norway. He also said that if he did not die he would go away to a Christian land and do penance for what he had done against God. Haakon died at the hill on the shore of the island Stord where he was born. His warriors took his body to Saeheim in North Hordaland and buried him in a mound in full armour but with no other possessions.

Eyvind Skadaspiller composed a poem about the death of King Haakon the Good:

"In Odin's hall an empty place

Stands for a king of Yngve's race;

'Go, my Valkyries,' Odin said,

'Go forth, my angels of the dead,

Gondul and Skogul, to the plain

Drenched with the battle's bloody rain,

And to the dying Haakon tell,

Here in Valhal shall he dwell.'

"At Stord, so late a lonely shore,

Was heard the battle's wild uproar;

The lightning of the flashing sword

Burned fiercely at the shore of Stord.

From leveled halberd and spearhead

Life-blood was dropping fast and red;

And the keen arrows' biting sleet

Upon the shore at Stord fast beat.

"Upon the thundering cloud of shield

Flashed bright the sword-storm o'er the field;

And on the plate-mail rattled loud

The arrow-shower's rushing cloud,

The Saga Kings

In Odin's tempest-weather, there

Swift whistling through the angry air;

And the spear-torrents swept away

Ranks of brave men from light of day.

"With batter'd shield and blood-smear'd sword

Slits one beside the shore of Stord,

With armour crushed and gashed sits he,

A grim and ghastly sight to see;

And roundabout in sorrow stand

The warriors of his gallant band:

Because the king of Dags' old race

In Odin's hall must fill a place.

Then up spake Gondul, standing near

Resting upon her long ash spear, --

`Haakon! The gods' cause prospers well,

And thou in Odin's halls shalt dwell!'

The king beside the shore of Stord

The speech of the Valkyrie heard,

Who sat there on his coal-black steed,

With shield on arm and helm on head.

Thoughtful, said Haakon, `Tell me why

Ruler of battles, victory

Is so dealt out on Stord's red plain?

Have we not well deserved to gain?'

'And is it not as well dealt out?'

Said Gondul. 'Hearest thou not the shout?

The field is cleared -- the foemen run --

The day is ours -- the battle won!'

Then Skogul said, 'My coal-black steed,

Home to the gods I now must speed,

To their green home, to tell the tiding

That Haakon's self is thither riding.'

To Hermod and to Brage then

Said Odin, 'Here, the first of men,

Brave Haakon comes, the Norsemen's king, --

Go forth, my welcome to him bring.'

Fresh from the battle-field came in,

Dripping with blood, the Norsemen's king.

'Methinks,' said he, great Odin's will

Is harsh, and bodes me further ill;

Thy son from off the field to-day

From victory to snatch away!'

But Odin said, `Be thine the joy

Valhalla gives, my own brave boy!'

And Brage said, `Eight brothers here

Welcome thee to Valhalla's cheer,

To drain the cup, or fights repeat

Where Haakon Eirik's earls beat.'

Quoth the stout king, 'And shall my gear,

Helm, sword, and mail-coat, axe and spear,

Be still at hand! 'Tis good to hold

Fast by our trusty friends of old.'

Well was it seen that Haakon still

Had saved the temples from all ill;

For the whole council of the gods

Welcomed the king to their abodes.

Happy the day when men are born

Like Haakon, who all base things scorn. --

Win from the brave and honoured name,

And die amidst an endless fame.

Sooner shall Fenris wolf devour

The race of man from shore to shore,

Than such a grace to kingly crown

As gallant Haakon want renown.

Life, land, friends, riches, all will fly,

And we in slavery shall sigh.

But Haakon in the blessed abodes

For ever lives with the bright gods."

Harald Bluetooth built a castle at Jomne in the Land of the Vends at Wollin Island also called Vineta. The castle was called Jomsborg (Joms Castle). The harbour was made so that 360 long ships could dock at the same time. Palnatoke was made Jarl of Joms castle and oversaw its construction. The Castle had a marine gate in the harbour and a stone bridge went to the castle.

The fellowship of the Joms Vikings attracted the most famous Vikings and the Joms Vikings became the most feared of all the Vikings. Indeed, they were the most feared Vikings of all times. The purpose of the Joms Vikings was to keep the Danish waters safe from foreign pirates and invaders.

The rules of the Joms fellowship were very strict:

1. A Joms Viking must be no younger than 18 and no older than 50.
2. A warrior must not flee an enemy who is less strong and no better armed than himself.
3. Everyone must avenge another as a brother.
4. A Joms Viking must not run down a companion with words and quarrelling is forbidden.
5. If anything new happens the Jarl is to be told about it.
6. Private hate and vengeance is to be put aside. If any one's father or brother was killed it was to be presented to the Jarl for him to decide.
7. Women were not allowed. Joms Vikings were to be wifeless.
8. No one is allowed to be out of the castle more than three days without the permission of the Jarl.
9. All war acquisitions and property is to be shared out by

drawing lots between warriors.
10. **It is forbidden to offend another with words and to humiliate another with words.**
11. **Nobody can be accepted as a Joms Viking because of wealth, relationship, or friendship. Only those who have done an honourable deed may be accepted.**
12. **Whoever breaks one of the laws will be thrown out in disgrace.**

The priest Poppo came to Harald Bluetooth's court and gained an audience with Harald. He challenged Harald to accept Christ. He told Harald that Christ was stronger than the old gods. Harald believed that the old gods were stronger than Jesus and challenged Poppo to prove it. Poppo had two choices of a trial. He could either fight the King's champion or elect trial by ordeal. Poppo elected the ordeal.

Poppo carried a heated, glowing plowshare nine steps and dropped it. Then his hands were bandaged. After nine days the bandages were removed revealing that Poppo's hands were healed. If they had not healed it would have proven that the old gods were stronger than Christ. Thus Harald Bluetooth became a Christian and now went about persuading his subjects to convert to Christianity.

154 THE SONS OF ERIK BLOOD AXE

In 961, Gunhild and her sons sailed to Norway to take over the Kingdom. Sigurd was Jarl of the Throndheim district and lived in Lade. Gudrod Bjornson ruled Westfold and Tryggve Olafson ruled the Eastland. The sons of Erik Bloodaxe took over the middle of the country and did not go into the other districts because they did not feel safe where the people hated them.

The skald Glum Geirson made a song about the fall of Haakon:

"Gamle is avenged by Harald!

Great is thy deed, thou champion bold!

The rumor of it came to me

In distant lands beyond the sea,

How Harald gave King Haakon's blood

To Odin's ravens for their food."

Eyvind Finson made a song in retaliation:

"Our dauntless king with Gamle's gore

Sprinkled his bright sword o'er and o'er," etc.

King Harald Erikson was upset about the song and threatened to kill Eyvind. Some people mediated the quarrel and Eyvind Finson was reconciled with Harald and became Harald's skald. Eyvind then composed a song to Harald Erikson:

"Guardian of Norway, well we know

Thy heart failed not when from the bow

The piercing arrow-hail sharp rang

On shield and breastplate, and the clang

The Saga Kings

Of sword resounded in the press

Of battle, like the splitting ice;

For Harald, wild wolf of the wood,

Must drink his fill of foeman's blood."

The sons of Erik Blood Axe negotiated with Jarl Sigurd, King Tryggve, and King Gudrod. The result was that Sigurd, Gudrod, and Tryggve were to keep the districts that they had under King Haakon the Good.

Eyvind Finson continued to offend King Harald Erikson and eventually left Harald and went home to Iceland.

The Erik sons made Viking raids every year, sometimes by themselves and sometimes together.

Gunhild was displeased with the Kingdom. She wanted all Norway and wanted her sons to take the other districts. She wanted to take the Throndheim district but Harald told her that it would not be easy to do away with Jarl Sigurd.

Sigurd Jarl had a younger brother called Grjotgard who had no title and very little respect among the people. He went on Viking raids every summer.

Harald Erikson sent a message to Sigurd saying that he wished to be friends with Sigurd and establish the same relationship that Sigurd had with Haakon the Good. The messengers invited Sigurd to come and visit Harald. Sigurd sent back many great presents and the word that he was happy and grateful for the words of Harald but because of his many affairs he could not come.

Because Sigurd would not come, Harald Erikson sent his messengers to Grjotgard with the same message. Grjotgard came to Harald for a visit. An agreement was made with Harald and Grjotgard that if Grjotgard would be a spy in Sigurd's domains and help the Erik sons overpower Sigurd, Grjotgard would be the Jarl in Lade. Grjotgard was to send word when there was a favourable opportunity to attack Sigurd Jarl. Grjotgard returned home with many good presents.

In the fall of 962, Sigurd Jarl went to Oglo in Stjoradal for a feast. Because of the friendly words from Harald Erikson, he felt safe and had only a few warriors with him. Grjotgard sent word to Harald that he would never find a better opportunity to surprise Sigurd.

Harald and Erling sailed immediately to Throndheim Fjord where Grjotgard came out to meet them. Late that night they came to Oglo where Sigurd Jarl was at his feast. The warriors of Harald, Erling, and Grjotgard surrounded the house and set it on fire. The house burned up along with Sigurd Jarl and all his men who were with him. In the morning Harald and Erling sailed south to More.

155 HAAKON JARL

Haakon son of Sigurd Jarl was in the interior of Throndheim when he heard of his father's death. All the Thronds gathered together and launched their ships. They took Haakon to be their Jarl and they all sailed out of the harbour and set their course south.

"Jarls were appointed by the King" said Eyvind.

"Indeed yes" said the story teller, "But the Thronds refused to recognize any son of Erik Blood Axe as King. They had no King. Their leader was their Jarl. They took the son of their Jarl to be their leader and called him their Jarl.

When the sons of Erik Blood Axe heard of Haakon's fleet coming they sailed south to Raumsdal and South More.

In the fall, Jarl Haakon went to the Uplands and met Tryggve Olafson and Gudrod Bjornson. The three agreed to be friends with each other.

The Erik sons heard of the meeting and suspected that Haakon, Tryggve, and Gudrod Bjornson were plotting against them.

In the spring of 963, Harald and Gudrod stated that they were making their usual Viking trip into the Baltic or the West Sea. The night before the departure Harald and Gudrod drank with their men. Some of the Vikings compared the Erik sons and they said that Harald was greater than any of his brothers. Gudrod became angry and said that he was in no way inferior to Harald and that he was ready to prove it. Some of the warriors who had drank less than others stepped in and stopped the conflict.

In the morning Gudrod took his fleet east along the land while Harald sailed his fleet out into the ocean. Gudrod sailed through the channels to the Vik and then east to the Fold. There Gudrod sent a message to Tryggve inviting him to come along on a raid in the Baltic Sea. Tryggve accepted the invitation and hearing that Gudrod had only a few warriors with him came to the Fold in a single ship.

They met at Veggen and Tryggve landed. Just as Tryggve and his men were going up the beach, Gudrod's men ran down and killed Tryggve and twelve of his warriors.

After Harald Erikson had sailed far west, he turned and set a course for the Vik. He came to Tunsberg and heard that Gudrod Bjornson was at a feast in the country. Harald went in the night to the house where Gudrod was feasting. King Gudrod Bjornson went out with his warriors to meet Harald, but after a short ferocious battle he fell and many warriors with him.

King Harald joined his brother Gudrod and after subduing the Vik, they went about collecting many warriors. Then they set sail for Throndheim to do away with Jarl Haakon. When Haakon heard the news he went about collecting warriors, got together a fleet, and sailed south to meet the Erik sons. Along the coast of More Haakon went pillaging and raiding wherever he came. But word reached Haakon that Harald and Gudrod had an overwhelming force waiting south of Stad for a favourable wind. Haakon then sent the farmers of Throndheim home and kept only his experienced warriors with him.

When the farmers had left, Haakon took his ships west into the ocean so far that his sails could not be seen from the land. He then turned eastward in a line towards Denmark and sailed until he reached Denmark. From there he sailed into the Baltic Sea and raided all summer.

When the winds were favourable, the sons of Erik Bloodaxe sailed to Throndheim and they remained there and collected tax from the people. After a while they left Sigurd Sleva and Gudrod behind and sailed east.

In the fall Haakon Jarl landed his ships in the Bothnian Gulf where he drew his ships up onto the land. Then he took his warriors overland through Helsingland and Jamtland, then over the mountain ridge and down into Throndheim where the people flocked to him. When Sigurd Sleva and Gudrod heard about it they went to their ships and sailed out of the Fjord.

156 THE FUGITIVES

Gudrod Bjornson's son Harald Grenske was being fostered by Hroe the White. Hroe's son Hrane was the same age as Harald. When Harald Grenske heard the news about his father he fled to the Uplands. Hrane and a few warriors went with him.

Tryggve Olafson was married to Astrid daughter of Erik Bjodaskalle. When she heard of Tryggve's death she was very pregnant. Astrid fled. Her foster father Thorolf Lousebeard went with her with a few warriors. Because she was so pregnant, Astrid was unable to travel fast and could not go very far. The little party hid on an island in a lake. There Astrid gave birth to a son and she called him Olaf after his grandfather. They remained there all summer.

In the fall when the weather grew colder, Astrid's small party left the lake and traveled by night. They avoided houses and people. After many days they reached Oprustader where Astrid's father lived. Her father Erik took them to a small cottage in the back and gave them a feast. Astrid stayed there all winter and her escort left her except for Thorolf Lousebeard and his six year old son Thorgils.

In 964, Gunhild sent men to the Uplands and down to the Vik to search for Astrid and her son. The men came back saying they did not find Astrid and that she must be at her father's place. Gunhild then sent her men to Erik in Oprustader with orders to bring Astrid's baby back to her.

When Gunhild's men appeared in Oprustader, they were recognized. Erik gave Astrid guides and a few warriors and told her to make her way to Sweden to stay with his friend Haakon the Old. Astrid left in the night with her small group. They were all dressed in poor clothing. They reached the house of the farmer Bjorn Eiterkveisa who was very rich, but he drove them away. The next farm was in Vidar and belonged to Thorstein who took them in.

In the morning Gunhild's men went to Erik and asked about Astrid. Erik told them that she was not there. The men asked everyone where Astrid had gone. Late in the afternoon they found someone who was willing to tell them and they rode out after Astrid on fast horses.

They reached Bjorn's house who told them that he had drove some people away in the night. One of Torstein's men was at Bjorn's house on business and he hurried to Thorstein and told him Gunhild's men were coming. Thorstein received the news in the middle of the night, woke his guests, and told them they had to hurry away because men were after them.

Astrid's guide took the party to a lake and out upon an islet covered with cattails. There they hid while Gunhild's men went by. The men had to go back to Gunhild and tell her that they could not find Astrid. Astrid reached Haakon the Old in Sweden and stayed with him.

People told Harald Grenske that he should get out of Norway because the sons of Erik Bloodaxe were hunting down and killing all who had stood in their way. Harald and his foster brother Hrane went to Sweden to become Vikings. They went to the home of Toste, a famous Viking chief and became his warriors. Toste had a daughter called Sigrid.

For the next five years Harald Grenske and Hrane went on Viking raids with Toste in the summers.

157 HARALD GREY CLOAK

King Harald Erikson was in Hardanger when a boat docked from Iceland. The boat was loaded with skins and pelts. Nobody would buy the skins from the Icelander. The steersman was acquainted with King Harald and complained about his bad luck in trading. Harald promised to come down and visit him at his ship.

The next morning Harald went with a fully manned ship to the docks and visited the Icelander. He observed that the pelts were all of good quality and asked the Icelander if he would give him a present of one of the grey skins. The Icelander said, "I will give it to you willingly".

Thorvald said, "How come Harald did not buy the pelt? Surely he could afford it."

The story teller said, "If a King accepted a present which you offered, you would be in favour with the King. That is worth much more than a present would cost.

Harald obtained a grey pelt, which he wrapped about himself. Before he left each of his crew had bought a pelt. Within a few days people flocked to the Icelander to buy pelts and he was soon sold out. From then on Harald Erikson was called Harald Grey Cloak.

Haakon Jarl had many battles with the Erik sons and many warriors fell on both sides. But the Erik sons could not gain a foothold in Throndheim.

In 965, Haakon maintained an army in Throndheim to keep out the sons of Erik Blood Axe. He sometimes went overland to Helsingjaland and took his fleet into the Baltic and raided.

The Joms Castle construction was finished and manned with Danish and Vendish Vikings. Harald Bluetooth established a trade center right next to the Joms Castle.

Harald Gray Cloak took his warriors north to Bjarmaland and fought a great battle on the shores of the Vina River. Harald was victorious and went plundering throughout the land. He burned many buildings and killed many people.

King Sigurd Sleva went to the house of Herse Klyp in Vors. Herse was not at home, but his wife Alof gave Sigurd a good reception and put on a feast. In the night Sigurd took Alof to bed against her will. In the morning Sigurd continued his journey.

In the fall Harald Grey Cloak and his brother Sigurd Sleva went to Vors and called a Thing. The farmers attacked them and there was a great battle. The farmers would have killed Harald and Sigurd but they escaped by different routes. Harald went to Hardanger and Sigurd went to Alrekstader.

Herse Klyp heard where Sigurd was and assembled all his relatives. They went into Alrekstader and attacked Sigurd. Herse ran his sword through Sigurd Sleva so that he died. Erling Gamle killed Herse at the same time.

In 966, the Erik sons and Haakon Jarl negotiated a peace.

158 HARALD BLUETOOTH AND HAAKON JARL

Harald Bluetooth continued to strengthen the Danish defenses. He began to build great castles of timber and earth. They were Trelleborg near Slagesle in west Zealand, Aggersborg on the Lim Fjord in northern Jutland, Fyrkat near Hobro in east Jutland, Nonnebakken in Odense on the island of Fyn and Borgeby and another Trelleborg in Skaane.

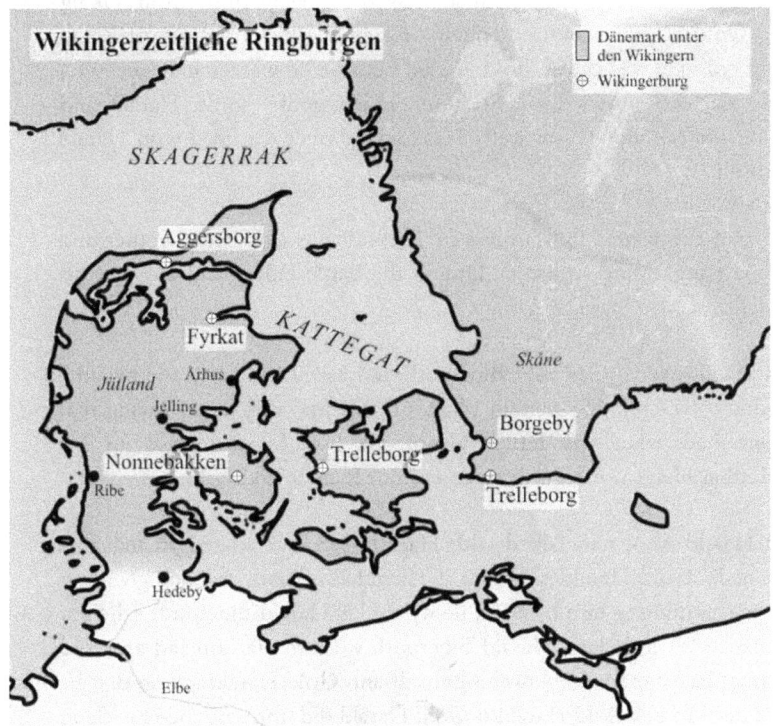

In 969, Harald Grey Cloak and his brother Gudrod gathered an army in the east and set out towards Throndheim. When Haakon heard about it, he knew he was no longer safe in Norway. He gathered his warriors and sailed south to More where he plundered. Grjotgard the brother of Haakon's father was Jarl in More and he brought an army against Haakon. During the battle, Grjotgard fell.

Haakon sailed west until his sails could no longer be seen from the land. Then he sailed to Denmark to seek asylum with Harald Bluetooth. Harald Bluetooth received Haakon well. He had grown displeased with the activities of Erik's sons in Norway.

Harald Grey Cloak and his brothers arrived in Throndheim. They took heavy taxes from the farmers and levied many fines. They had not received any income from Throndheim for years because of Haakon Jarl.

In the fall Harald Grey Cloak went south with most of the warriors. His brother Erling stayed behind to rule Throndheim.

In the fall the Viking, Gold Harald arrived at Jelling fresh from Viking raids. Gold Harald was the nephew of Harald Bluetooth, son of Knud Dane Fryd. He was called Gold Harald because he was such a successful Viking that he always brought home much gold. Gold Harald and Haakon Jarl got along very well. Haakon Jarl over wintered with Harald Bluetooth.

In 970, in the winter the farmers in Throndheim gathered together and attacked King Erling Erikson. During the battle Erling and most of his men fell.

Gold Harald went to Harald Bluetooth and asked his uncle for half the Kingdom of Denmark. Harald Bluetooth became very angry saying that no one had asked his father Gorm for half his Kingdom or his grandfather Helge nor Sigurd Snake-eye nor Ragnar Lodbrok.

Gold Harald went and talked with Haakon Jarl and related all that had happened. Gold Harald said that if Harald Bluetooth did not give him what was coming to him by right, he would kill Harald Bluetooth if he got the chance. A little later Harald Bluetooth went to Haakon Jarl and told him what had happened between himself and Gold Harald saying that he would have to kill Gold Harald if Gold Harald did not renounce his claim to the throne. But he was aggravated because he did not really want to kill his own nephew. Haakon said that they should wait a few days and think the matter over.

A few days later Harald Bluetooth and Haakon got together again and Haakon said that he had come up with a plan. He said, "Give Gold Harald another Kingdom outside Denmark".

Harald Bluetooth was puzzled and replied, "What other Kingdom could I possibly conquer and give to gold Harald?"

Haakon said, "Norway, where the people are oppressed by the Kings and pay too much tax".

Harald replied, "Norway is a large country and its people are fierce. Attacking Norway would be a bad decision and Harald Grey Cloak is my foster son whom I have held on my knees".

Haakon Jarl replied, "I have known for a long time that you have helped the sons of Erik Blood Axe to take Norway. But you have got nothing from it in return. We can conquer Norway by stealth. Invite Harald Grey Cloak to Denmark by offering to give him land and fiefs in Denmark. Then when he arrives, Gold Harald can win his own Kingdom".

Harald Bluetooth did not like to deceive his own foster son. But Haakon Jarl persuaded him and ended by saying, "It is better to kill a Norwegian Viking than your own brother's son".

Harald Bluetooth finally went along with Haakon Jarl. The two went to Gold Harald and told him the plan of luring Harald Gray Cloak into the Lim Fjord. Then Harald Bluetooth sent messengers to Harald Grey Cloak.

Harald Bluetooth's messengers arrived at the home of Harald Grey Cloak and told him that Haakon Jarl was in Denmark and that he was very sick, close to dying. They then invited Harald Grey Cloak to come to Jutland and receive the fiefs in Denmark which the Erik sons had held before.

Gunhild was suspicious about the message and some of Harald's friends advised him not to go. But there was a famine in Norway and Denmark was well off in food. Harald Grey Cloak decided to go because lands in Denmark would alleviate the food shortage in Norway. Harald Grey Cloak sailed from the Vik into the Lim Fjord in Denmark in three long ships. Herse Arinbjorn from the Fjord district commanded one of the ships. Harald Grey Cloak's ships lay in where the Dan King was expected to meet him.

Haakon Jarl was outfitting his twelve ships for an expedition when the news arrived that Harald Grey Cloak was lying with three ships in the Lim Fjord. Gold Harald proceeded with nine ships to the Lim Fjord.

When Gold Harald arrived in the Lim Fjord he challenged Harald Grey Cloak to fight. Harald took his warriors on to the land, arranged his men and set up his battle standard. Gold Harald landed with his warriors and the battle was fierce. In the battle Harald Grey Cloak and Herse Arinbjorn fell.

Glum Geirson sang of the event:

> "On Lim Fjord's strand, by the tide's flow,
>
> Stern Fate has laid King Harald low;
>
> The gallant Viking-cruiser -- he
>
> Who loved the isle-encircling sea.
>
> The generous ruler of the land
>
> Fell at the narrow Lim Fjord strand.
>
> Enticed by Haakon's cunning speech
>
> To his death-bed on Lim Fjord's beach."

Haakon Jarl sailed into the Lim Fjord shortly after the fall of Harald Grey Cloak and immediately attacked Gold Harald. Haakon won the battle and took Gold Harald prisoner. After erecting a gallows and hanging Gold Harald, Haakon sailed back to Jelling and paid Harald Bluetooth a fine for killing his nephew.

Harald Bluetooth collected warriors and with a fleet of 600 long ships and with Haakon Jarl and Harald Grenske sailed to Norway. When Harald Bluetooth arrived in the Vik, all the people surrendered to him. When he reached Tunsberg, the people there flocked to join him.

When Gunhild and her sons Gudrod and Ragnfred, the only sons of Erik Blood Axe still alive, heard that Harald Bluetooth was on his way north they gathered warriors and ships, but not very many would join them. They then decided that they could not hope to defeat Harald's fleet and sailed west with whomever would join them. When they had come to where their sails could not be seen from the land they sailed south to the Orkneys where Hlodver, Arnfrid, Ljot, and Skule, the sons of Thorfin Turf Einerson were Jarls.

King Harald Bluetooth gave Haakon Rogaland, Hordaland, Sogn, Fjord district, Raumsdal, More, and Throndheim to rule over as Jarl of Harald Bluetooth of Denmark. He made the agreement with Haakon Jarl that Haakon keep all the taxes he would collect and that Haakon was to supply help should Harald Bluetooth need it. To Harald Grenske, Harald Bluetooth gave Vingulmark, Westfold and Agder and also gave him the title King. Harald Bluetooth then took his fleet back home to Denmark. Thus Harald Bluetooth was in control of southern Norway and Haakon Jarl had all of northern Norway.

In 971, Ragnfred spent his time in the Orkneys collecting warriors. In the spring he sailed to Norway with large dragon ships and fierce warriors. When he heard that Haakon Jarl was in Throndheim, he sailed north around Stad and plundered in South More.

When Haakon heard that Ragnfred was raiding in South More he collected warriors. People were eager to join him so he had a large force and he sailed south. Haakon's fleet ran into Ragnfred's fleet at the north corner of More and the battle began immediately. The ships fought bow to bow. Haakon had more men but fewer ships and in the battle Haakon lost more men than Ragnfred.

The current and wind drove the ships towards land. Haakon landed his ships where the beaching was easiest and had his men draw the ships so far up the land that they could not easily be launched again. Then Haakon drew up his battle lines on a grassy field and dared Ragnfred to land and battle. Ragnfred laid his long ships close to land and the two armies fired arrows at each other for a long time. Ragnfred did not dare land because he was afraid that warriors would come flocking to Haakon's help. Therefore he sailed his fleet south. Haakon did not pursue Ragnfred because he had no hope of winning a sea battle.

Haakon sailed back north to Throndheim, while Ragnfred went through Fjord district, Hordaland, Sogn, and Rogaland collecting many warriors.

In 972, Haakon Jarl ordered all the men of the north who could bear arms to gather. Then he put together a fleet and sailed south around Stad. Haakon heard that Ragnfred was in Sogn and went to meet him there. Haakon and Ragnfred met on the border of Sogn and Hordaland and Haakon who had the most warriors won the battle. After more than 300 of his warriors had fallen, Ragnfred and his remaining warriors fled to their ships and sailed away from Norway.

Einar Skalaglam sang of the battle:

"In the fierce battle Ragnfred then

Met the grim foe of Vinland men;

And many a hero of great name

Fell in the sharp sword's bloody game.

The wielder of fell Narve's weapon,

The conquering hero, valiant Haakon

Had laid his war-ships on the strand,

And ranged his warriors on the land.

Sharp was the battle-strife, I ween, --

Deadly and close it must have been,

Before, upon the bloody plain,

Three hundred corpses of the slain

Were stretched for the black raven's prey;

And when the conquerors took their way

To the sea-shore, they had to tread

O'er piled-up heaps of foemen dead."

159 ERIK HAAKONSON

Eleven year old Erik the son of Haakon Jarl received a ship manned with 15 benches of rowers from his foster father Thorleif. Erik sailed south to Denmark.

Erik Haakonson stayed with Harald Bluetooth all winter. In the spring Harald Bluetooth made Erik Jarl of Vingulmark and Raumarike in southern Norway.

Eyjolf Dadaskald sang of the event:

> "South through ocean's spray
>
> His dragon flew away
>
> To Gormson's hall renowned.
>
> Where the bowl goes bravely round.
>
> And the Danish king did place
>
> This youth of noble race
>
> Where, shield and sword in hand,
>
> He would aye defend his land."

160 OTTO II
OTTO II'S ATTACK ON DENMARK

The Emperor Otto II took an army of Saxons, Franks, Vends, and Frisians and attacked directly against Danevirke, the wall separating Germany from Denmark. Harald Bluetooth sent to Haakon Jarl and Joms Castle for help. The fight was fierce and the wall held.

The Joms Vikings arrived and helped defend Danevirke. Otto II laid a siege and settled down for a long fight.

Haakon Jarl arrived from Norway with a great fleet. He took his men up onto Danevirke and they helped in the defense.

Einar Skalaglam sang of the battle in the "Vellekla":

> "Over the foaming salt sea spray
>
> The Norse sea-horses took their way,
>
> Racing across the ocean-plain
>
> Southwards to Denmark's green domain.
>
> The gallant chief of Hordaland
>
> Sat at the helm with steady hand,
>
> In casque and shield, his men to bring
>
> From Dovre to his friend the king.
>
> He steered his war-ships o'er the wave
>
> To help the Danish king to save
>
> Mordalf, who, with a gallant band
>
> Was hastening from the Jutes' wild land,
>
> Across the forest frontier rude,

With toil and pain through the thick wood.

Glad was the Danish king, I trow,

When he saw Haakon's dragon's prow.

The monarch straightway gave command

To Haakon, with a steel-clad band,

To man the Dane-work's rampart stout,

And keep the foreign foemen out."

"Thick the storm of arrows flew,

Loud was the din, black was the view

Of close array of shield and spear

Of Vend, and Frank, and Saxon there.

But little recked our gallant men;

And loud the cry might be heard then

Of Norway's brave sea-roving son --

'On 'gainst the foe! On! Lead us on!"

"They who the eagle's feasts provide

In ranked line fought side by side,

'Gainst lines of war-men under shields,

Close packed together on the fields,

Earl Haakon drive by daring deeds

The Saxons to their ocean-steeds;

And the young hero saves from fall

The Danevirke -- the people's wall."

Danevirke held against Otto II's army. Eventually Otto II withdrew his army and left. Then Haakon and his warriors returned to their ships and sailed north. The Joms Vikings also left. Haakon had intended to return to Norway but a great storm came up and he entered the Lim Fjord where he was wind locked.

When Harald Bluetooth's extra help had departed, Otto II came back. This time he came in a fleet of ships and entered the Fjord of Slee and landed at Hedeby. The fight was now in Jutland. Harald's forces were outnumbered and he fought a retreating battle as he fled north in Jutland. When he reached the Lim Fjord, he made a stand on the island of Mors. Haakon Jarl was still in the Fjord and Otto II could go no farther.

Harald Bluetooth negotiated with Otto II and an agreement was reached. Harald Bluetooth was to have all his Jarls baptized. Otto II would withdraw from Jutland but keep the trading center of Hedeby.

Haakon was a staunch worshiper of Odin and refused to be baptized, but he was forced. When enough of the nobles were baptized, Otto II took his army south to Hedeby where he built a castle and manned it with Saxons to keep the Danes from retaking the trade center.

Haakon was very angry about his forced baptism, and relations between him and Harald Bluetooth became very bad. When the wind became favourable to him he sailed out of the Lim Fjord east through Oresund and ravaged the lands on both sides. Then he sailed east along Skaane and ravaged the land wherever he went.

Haakon landed in East Gothland and made a great blood sacrifice to Odin. When two ravens flew by, he knew that his sacrifice was accepted and that he was now in Odin's good graces again.

Haakon then set fire to his ships and went ravaging through Gothland. The Jarl Otto who ruled in Gothland brought an army against Haakon. In the battle Otto and a large number of his warriors were killed.

After ravaging East Gothland, Haakon took his warriors in to West Gothland and ravaged there as well until he came to Norway. Then he went over land to his home in Throndheim.

When Harald Bluetooth heard that Haakon Jarl had plundered in the Danish lands he gathered a great fleet and sailed to Norway. He took his fleet up the Norwegian coast until he reached the lands ruled over by Haakon Jarl. He laid waste the whole of northern Norway. All the Norwegians took their movable belongings and fled into the mountains and forests. In Laeradal only five houses were left standing. After Harald's foray into Norway, Haakon Jarl kept to his own lands.

In 975, King Edgar of England died and his oldest son Edward became King. In 979, in England King Edward was murdered by the attendants of Aethelred's mother Ælfthryth. Aethelred, Edward's half-brother, then became King of England at the age of about 10.

161 PALNATOKE

In 981, while at a feast which Harald Bluetooth hosted, Palnatoke bragged about his skill in archery. He said that he could with one arrow shoot an apple off a post. Harald demanded that he should demonstrate at once by shooting an arrow off his son's head. Palnatoke became very angry but set up his son and took three arrows from his quiver. With the first arrow, he shot the apple from his son's head.

Harald asked Palnatoke why he had taken three arrows from the quiver. Palnatoke replied, "If my first arrow failed, I would have avenged my innocent son's death on you".

From then on Palnatoke and Harald Bluetooth were bitter enemies.

Harald Bluetooth deposed Palnatoke as Jarl of Joms Vikings and set Sigvald, son of King Strut Harald in Skaane, as Jarl of Joms Castle. Other Joms Viking leaders were Sigvald's brothers, Hemming and Thorkel the Tall, Styrbjorn Staerke (Big Bear the Strong), son of Olaf Bjornson, Bue Dige of Bornholm and Sigurd his brother, and Vagn son of Aage. Vagn's mother was Thorgunna who was a sister of Bue and Sigurd.

Styrbjorn Staerke was married to Thyra, Harald Bluetooth's daughter.

162 STYRBJORN STAERKE

Styrbjorn Staerke, a Joms Viking chief, took a fleet of Joms Vikings to Sweden and went against his uncle Erik, King of Sweden. Erik and Styrbjorn set up their battle lines on the Fyris plains close to Uppsala. Erik set his warriors in the svinfylking formation. When Styrbjorn saw Erik's battle formation, he burst out laughing because he thought it was old fashioned. While Styrbjorn was laughing, the ritual spear cast hit him in his beard and he fell backwards, dead on the spot. Thus it was told that Styrbjorn died laughing. There was a fierce battle and Erik was victorious. After this battle, King Erik of Sweden was called Erik the Victorious.

The surviving Joms Vikings sailed their ships to Oland. There they raised a rune stone to commemorate their fallen comrades. Then they continued their journey to Joms castle.

163 HARALD BLUETOOTH'S MEMORIAL STONE

Harald Bluetooth's son was called up after his grandfather. He was not called Gorm but Svend, the nick name by which the Danes called Gorm the Old when he was alive. This was the first time a son of a King had the real name of Svend. Until Harald Bluetooth's son, svend meant a boy child or apprentice. Svend Haraldson was given the name Forkbeard because before a battle he would braid his beard into two pigtails to keep the wind from blowing the beard into his eyes.

In 983, Svend Forkbeard took some warriors and attacked Otto II's castle at Hedeby and set it on fire. While the castle burned to the ground, Svend entered Hedeby and attacked the Germans. The Germans fled south and Denmark was again in possession of Hedeby.

Svend Forkbeard asked his father for half the Kingdom of Denmark. Harald Bluetooth told him 'no'.

In 984, Svend Forkbeard set up a high seat in Lejre, the old Danish seat of power, and made that his headquarters. There he gathered followers to take over the Kingdom.

Harald Bluetooth had a memorial stone inscribed. On the 3-meter high stone were the runes:

"Harald King bade the making of this memorial stone after Gorm his father and after Thyra his mother. Harald who won himself Denmark whole and Norway, and made the Danes Christian"

On the other side of the stone was carved a picture of the crucified Christ.

Harald Bluetooth had oxen and men drag his memorial stone to his mother's grave and had the stone raised. Then he proudly asked one of his men if he had ever seen a heavier burden being dragged by men. His man answered, "I have seen Svend drag all of Denmark from you; judge for yourself which burden is the heaviest".

In 986, Harald Bluetooth lay with ships in the harbour of Lejre gathering ships for an expedition against Svend. Svend Forkbeard was also gathering warriors and ships in the Lim Fjord. Palnatoke came and joined Svend. When all his warriors were assembled, Svend sailed to Zealand and attacked Harald Bluetooth in Isa Fjord.

The battle was fierce and many people ran to assist Harald so that Svend's forces became outnumbered and Svend had to flee. Harald was wounded in the battle and went to Joms Castle to recuperate.

When Harald Bluetooth was starting to recover, he took daily walks. He liked to walk in the woods close to Joms Castle. One night when he was walking in the woods, he was struck in the back by an arrow. This caused the death of Harald Bluetooth. His body was buried at Roskilde.

164 SVEND FORKBEARD

Svend Forkbeard was hailed as King of Denmark. Svend held a wake for his father at Roskilde and much beer was drunk. While everyone was sitting around drinking beer the arrow, which had killed Harald was brought forth. The warriors were asked one by one if they recognized the arrow. When Palnatoke was asked the question he said, "Why would I not recognize my own arrow? Hand it over. It is mine".

Svend asked Palnatoke when he had last seen this particular arrow and Palnatoke replied, "I parted with this arrow last time when it flew from my bowstring to penetrate your father".

"Then the friendship between us is over", yelled Svend and commanded his warriors to seize Palnatoke.

But Palnatoke clove the head of the first man who tried to lay hands on him and escaped with a small following of warriors. Svend Forkbeard declared Palnatoke an outlaw.

The Joms Vikings refused to acknowledge Svend Forkbeard as their King. Svend assembled a fleet in Green Sound to force Sigvald Jarl to acknowledge him as King. Early one morning, Sigvald came sailing in a small ship and lay in alongside the King's ship. Believing it was the night watch with something to report, Svend leaned out over the railing. One of Sigvald's men said, "The jarl is very sick. He is in the cabin and wants to speak with you. Svend boarded the little ship and entered the cabin. Sigvald was lying on a bed and whispered to Svend. Svend could not hear Sigvald and leaned closer. Sigvald Jarl grabbed Svend around the neck and hung on tight. While Sigvald held Svend tight about the neck, his men quickly rowed the small ship away from Svend's fleet.

Sigvald Jarl carried Svend to Joms Castle, where he dictated terms for the release of the King. He sent messengers to Denmark that he wanted the King's weight in gold and twice his weight in silver. With Svend he negotiated that Svend Forkbeard negotiate peace with Boleslaw, King of the Vends and that Boleslaw's daughter Gunhild was to marry Svend; Boleslaw's daughter Astrid was to marry Sigvald Jarl; Styrbjorn's widow the sister of Svend, Thyra was to marry King Boleslaw. If Svend did not agree to the terms, Sigvald would hand him over to Boleslaw.

Svend Forkbeard was so popular and loved by the women of Denmark that they all sent their jewelry to be ransom for the King. Svend returned to Jelling with his new wife Gunhild. Svend Forkbeard, overcome by the generosity of the Danish women changed the law of inheritance so that a sister, who at that time had no inheritance right, would inherit half against a brother. The law of inheritance used to be equal for a brother and a sister. This all changed when the Vikings were Christianized. He also restored all the freedoms which the women had lost under the Christian laws.

Svend Forkbeard held a succession feast during the Yule season. Strut Harald in Skaane had just died, and also Vesete in Bornholm who was father to Bue Dige and Sigurd. Therefore Svend had invited the jarls of the Joms Vikings to his feast, and they came with 40 ships from Joms Castle and 20 from Skaane.

165 THE JOMS VIKINGS

The first day of the feast, Svend drank the brag cup before he went up into the high seat. He drank to his father's memory and made the solemn vow that before three winters had passed he would take his army to England and kill King Aethelred or drive him out of the country. They all drank to that so that the bowls were empty. Then the bowls were filled and they all drank Christ's health. Svend, a heathen, was tolerant of his Christian warriors, and the third bowl was drunk to St. Michael. Then Sigvald Jarl drank to the memory of his father Strut Harald and made the solemn vow that before three winters had passed he would sail to Norway and kill Haakon Jarl or drive him from the country. Thorkel the Tall made the solemn vow that he would go with his brother Sigvald to Norway and would not flee as long as Sigvald was fighting. Bue Dige drank to the memory of his father Vesete and made the solemn vow that he would go with Sigvald to Norway and not flee as long as there were Joms Vikings fighting. Vagn Aagesen of Fyn made the solemn vow that he would go with Sigvald to Norway, kill Thorkel Leira and take his daughter Ingeborg to bed without any one's consent. Many other leaders also made solemn vows.

The next morning when the Joms Vikings became sober, they thought about what they had vowed and that maybe it was too much. They thought that they should fulfill their vows as soon as possible because news travels fast. Therefore they prepared to sail as soon as spring would arrive.

In the spring of 987, the Joms Vikings assembled a fleet of long ships in the Lim Fjord. A messenger came to Erik Jarl in Raumarike and told him the news.

Thord Kolbeinson sang of it:

> **"News from the south is flying round;**
>
> **The bonde comes with look profound,**
>
> **Bad news of bloody battles bringing,**
>
> **Of steel-clad men, of weapons ringing.**
>
> **I hear that in the Danish land**

> Long-sided ships slide down the strand,
>
> And, floating with the rising tide,
>
> The ocean-coursers soon will ride."

Erik immediately gathered warriors and went to the Uplands, then over the mountains to Throndheim. The Jarls Haakon and Erik split up war arrows and sent them around the country to Throndheim, North More, South More, Raumsdal, Naumudal and Halogaland. All of Norway was ordered to provide warriors and ships.

In the words of Thord Kolbeinson:

> "The skald must now a war-song raise,
>
> The gallant active youth must praise,
>
> Who o'er the ocean's field spreads forth
>
> Ships, cutters, boats, from the far north.
>
> His mighty fleet comes sailing by, --
>
> The people run to see them glide,
>
> Mast after mast, by the coast-side."

A fleet of 60 long ships glided out of the Lim Fjord and turned northwards. They reached the coast of Agder and turned north towards Rogaland. As soon as the Joms Vikings reached Haakon Jarl's territories they began to plunder and burn along the coast.

From Rogaland a man named Geirmond sailed a light boat with a few men north until he reached the place in More where Haakon Jarl was at supper. Geirmond burst into Haakon's hall and announced that the Danes were raiding along the coast. Haakon asked if Geirmond had certainty of the event. Geirmond stretched out an arm with his hand missing and said, "Here is a token that the enemy is in the land".

Haakon asked particulars about the composition of the Danish army. Geirmond said, "They are all Joms Vikings and are ferocious and in a hurry. They will be here soon".

Haakon sent watchmen south and north along the coast then collected his warriors and hastily went north to meet up with Erik Jarl.

The Joms Viking ships glided north around Stad and came to the Herey Isles where they raided and burned. They drove cattle down to the beach and killed all men able to bear weapons. A farmer walked down to the shore to Bue's warriors and said, "You are not acting like warriors. Instead of chasing cows and calves around you should be hunting the bear since you are coming close to its den".

The warriors asked the old farmer what he could tell them about Haakon. The farmer said, "The Jarl sailed yesterday into Jorund's Fjord with one or two ships and does not know you have come".

Bue and his men ran to their ships leaving their booty behind. Sigvald Jarl called to them asking what was going on. Bue yelled back, "The Jarl is in Jorund's Fjord".

Then the whole Joms Viking fleet sailed into Jorund's Fjord and rounded the island Hod. Haakon and Erik lay with their fleet at Halkelsvik in Jorund's Fjord and seeing the Joms Vikings long ships enter the Fjord from the sea, they rowed out to meet them. The Norwegian fleet numbered 180 ships.

The fleets met each other at Hjorungavag. Sigvald's banner flew from his mast and Haakon arranged his fleet to go directly against him. Sigvald himself had 20 ships and Haakon had 60. Bue Dige was on one side of Sigvald with 20 ships and Vagn Aagesen was on the other side also with 20 ships. Erik Jarl went against Bue Dige with 60 ships and Svend Haakonson went against Vagn Aagesen with 60 ships.

The fleets came together and a sharp battle began. Many warriors fell on both sides but more Norwegians fell than Joms Vikings. Outnumbered the Joms Vikings fought desperately and their arrows pierced right through the Norwegian shields. In spite of being outnumbered, the Joms Vikings were winning.

Many spears were thrown and Haakon was hit so often that his armour became split into pieces. He finally discarded his armour.

Tind Helkelson sang of it:

"The ring-linked coat of strongest mail

Could not withstand the iron hail,

Though sewed with care and elbow bent,

By Norn, on its strength intent.

The fire of battle raged around, --

Odin's steel shirt flew all unbound!

The Jarl his ring-mail from him flung,

Its steel rings on the wet deck rung;

Part of it fell into the sea, --

A part was kept, a proof to be

How sharp and thick the arrow-flight

Among the sea-steeds in this fight."

Haakon Jarl went back to shore and sacrificed his eight year old son for victory.

Vagn Aagesen laid his ship alongside that of Svend Haakonson and was about to board it when Svend pulled his ship away and took to flight. Then Erik laid his ship next to Vagn's but Vagn pulled his ship away. Svend came back and the original battle positions were resumed.

Erik laid his ship alongside that of Bue Dige and two other Norwegian ships laid in on Bue's other side. Bue's ship had become surrounded. Bue's ship was being boarded and the combat there became fierce hand-to-hand. Just then a severe hailstorm sprang up which blew directly into the faces of the Joms Vikings.

Thorkel the Tall was hit in the head by a stone and fell unconscious to the deck. Sigvald Jarl turned his ship around and fled. Thorkel's men, thinking that Thorkel was dead, turned their ships and followed Sigvald. 35 ships followed Sigvald Jarl in flight leaving 25 ships still fighting. Vagn yelled for Sigvald to stay. When Sigvald kept going Vagn threw his spear at him. It missed Sigvald but hit Sigvald's helmsman.

On Bue's ship Aslak Holmskalle, Bue's foster brother and forecastle commander, went berserk. No weapon could touch him and he laid killing blows to both his left and his right. For a long time Aslak held back the Norwegians. Then Vigfus, a very strong man, picked up an anvil lying on the deck and hurled it at Aslak so that the sharp end pierced Aslak's skull into his brain.

Erik's men boarded Bue's ship and gradually the ship was being cleared. Erik's men came aft where Bue stood. Thorstein Midlang cut Bue's nose so that the nosepiece of his helmet broke in two and Bue received a great wound that knocked out all his front teeth. Bue cut Thorstein's side so that his sword went halfway through Thorstein's body. Bue picked up two chests full of gold and yelled, "overboard all Bue's men". Then Bue Dige, holding a chest under each arm, threw himself overboard. Many of his warriors leaped overboard with him. The rest were cut down because there was no quarter given.

One by one the Joms Vikings' ships were boarded and cleared. On each ship a few Joms Vikings were captured by pinning the last few remaining alive between shields so that they could not move. Finally only Vagn's ship remained. Erik Jarl laid his ship against Vagn's and another ship laid in on the other side of Vagn's ship. Vagn's ship was boarded and the hand-to-hand fighting was ferocious. Gradually Vagn's ship was cleared and Vagn was pinned by shields so that he could not move.

Tind Helkelson sang of it:

"Many a Viking's body lay

Dead on the deck this bloody day,

Before they cut their sun-dried ropes,

And in quick flight put all their hopes.

He whom the ravens know afar

Cleared five-and-twenty ships of war."

The captured Joms Vikings were taken to land. Vagn and thirty Joms Viking were seated on a long log, bound together in one chain by the ankle but had their hands free. Thorkel Leira walked up to Vagn and said, "You made a solemn vow Vagn to kill me, but now it seems more likely that I will kill you".

Haakon Jarl left for Throndheim leaving his son Erik in charge of executing the Joms Vikings. As Haakon Jarl was getting ready to sail an arrow flew from Bue Dige's ship and hit Gissur from Valders who was standing right next to Haakon. Haakon and some of his men boarded Bue's ship and found Havar Hoggande on his knees because his legs had both been severed at the knees. Havar had a bow in his hands. Havar asked, "Who fell by my arrow?"

The Norwegians answered, "A man called Gissur".

Havar said, "Then my luck was not with me".

The Norwegians answered, "Your luck was good enough, but you shall not make it greater".

Then they killed Havar.

After Haakon had departed, the executions began. Thorkel Leira took an axe and swung at the Viking sitting out most on the log. The Viking's head fell clean off. Thorkel walked along the log beheading one Viking after another. There was a very handsome young Joms Viking with long blonde hair. He gathered his hair, held it over his head, stuck out his neck, and said, "Do not make my hair bloody".

A warrior stepped up and took his hair in his hands and held on tight. As Thorkel swung the axe, the young Joms Viking lurched forward so hard that the man holding the hair was jerked into the path of the axe and both his hands were cut off. Then Erik Jarl stepped forward and said, "Who is that handsome man?"

The young Viking replied, "I am called Sigurd and I am the son of Bue Dige. Are all the Joms Vikings dead?"

Erik Jarl said, "I can see now that you are certainly Bue's son. Will you accept freedom and go in peace?"

"That depends", replied Sigurd, "on who is doing the offering".

"The one with the power to offer it", said Erik, "Erik Jarl".

Sigurd replied, "I will accept freedom and peace from Erik Jarl".

Sigurd was freed from the chain. Thorkel Leira yelled, "Even if all these men receive life and peace, Vagn Aagesen shall never come away from here alive!"

Then Thorkel ran at Vagn with a raised axe, but the Joms Viking Skarde twisted in the chain and threw himself at Thorkel's feet so that Thorkel tripped over him and went sprawling. Vagn caught up the axe and buried it in Thorkel's skull so that he died.

Then Erik said, "Vagn, will you accept life from me?"

Vagn replied, "I will accept on condition that you give it to all of us".

"Free them all from the chain", said Erik Jarl and they were all freed. Eighteen Joms Vikings had been executed and twelve went free.

Jarl Haakon was displeased that Erik had freed some of the Joms Vikings, but he returned home to Throndheim.

Erik Jarl returned over land to his home in the Vik and took Vagn Aagesen with him. Erik married Ingeborg, Thorkel Leira's daughter, to Vagn and gave Vagn a ship and men. Thus Erik had developed friends among the Joms Vikings.

166 OLAF TRYGGVESON

In 967, Astrid's brother Sigurd had been away serving as a warrior with King Vladimir of Gardarike. Astrid decided to travel to Gardarike to live with him. Haakon gave Astrid a ship and warriors and they sailed out into the Baltic Sea.

In the Baltic they were attacked by Estonian pirates and taken prisoner. Olaf was separated from his mother and a man called Klerkon got Olaf, Thorolf Lousebeard, and Thorgils as his booty. Klerkon thought that Thorolf was too old to be a thrall and killed him. Klerkon sold the two boys for a ram to a man named Klerk.

A man called Reas bought Olaf by giving Klerk a good cloak. Rea had a wife called Rekon and a son called Rekone.

Sigurd came from Novgorod to Estonia to collect King Vladimir's tax and rent. In the market of one of the towns he saw a handsome young boy who was a foreigner to Estonia. He asked the boy his name and the boy told him that he was Olaf son of Tryggve Olafson and that Astrid daughter of Erik Bjodaskalle was his mother. Sigurd asked Olaf how he came to be there and Olaf told him. Sigurd then bought both Olaf and Thorgils from Reas and took them with him back to Holmgaard in Russia. But he did not tell Olaf that he was his mother's brother.

In 973, Olaf Tryggveson was in the market place of Holmgaard when he recognized Klerkon who had killed his mother's foster father, Thorolf Lousebeard. Olaf grabbed a little axe and ran to Klerkon and buried the axe in Klerkon's skull. Klerkon sank down dead and Olaf ran home to Sigurd and told him what he had done. Sigurd immediately took Olaf to Queen Allogia, told her what had happened and begged her to protect Olaf. Queen Allogia replied that the boy was too good looking to be put to death and ordered all her warriors to arm themselves in his defense.

People learned that Olaf was in the Queen's castle and came to storm it to put the murderer to death. King Vladimir arrived but he would not allow the boy to be taken. He named a fine for the deed and the Queen paid it.

It was a law in Holmgaard that no man of royal descent was allowed to stay without the King's permission. Therefore Sigurd told Queen Allogia who Olaf was and asked her to speak to King Vladimir about Olaf staying on. The Queen told King Vladimir Olaf's story and begged him to help

Olaf. King Vladimir received Olaf into his court and treated him as a King's son.

In 980, with the help of Olaf Tryggveson and the Varangians (Vikings), Vladimir, a descendant of Rurik, became sole ruler of Russia.

Vladimir's advisors told him that Olaf Tryggveson would eventually be dangerous to him because he was very popular and he had developed his own group of warriors. King Vladimir grew steadily colder towards Olaf.

Olaf became aware of what was happening between Vladimir and his advisors. Therefore Olaf went to Queen Allogia and told her he had a desire to see his homeland and wanted to travel. The Queen wished him a prosperous journey and Olaf set out with a small fleet.

When Olaf came to Bornholm he landed and raided. The people of Bornholm came down to the shore and a battle was fought. Olaf won the battle and plundered the island.

After leaving Bornholm, Olaf's fleet ran into a storm, which drove him south and he had to land in the land of the Vends. He found a good harbour and disembarked.

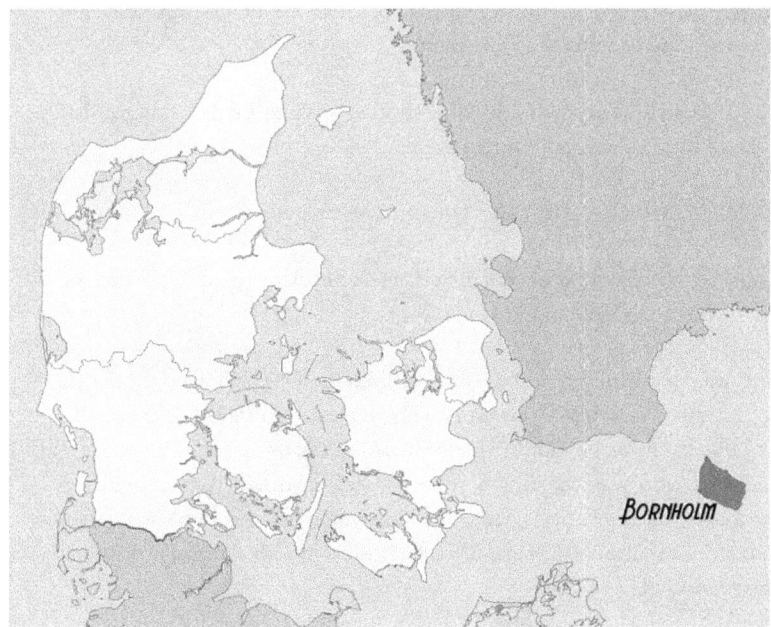

King Boleslaw of the Vends had three daughters Geira, Gunhild, and Astrid. Geira ruled over the area where Olaf had landed and her chief advisor was Dixen. When Geira heard that there were noble looking strangers in the area she sent Dixen to them and invited them to stay in her castle for the winter because it was so late in the fall that the storms might not subside. Olaf accepted the invitation. During the winter, Olaf courted Queen Geira and married her.

Geira, Olaf Tryggveson's wife became sick and died. Olaf no longer wanted to stay in the land of the Vends. He took a fleet and raided in Frisia. Then he raided in the land of the Saxons and in the fall he went to Flanders and raided. Olaf spent his next four years as a sea king raiding in many places including Northumberland, Scotland, the Hebrides, and Ireland.

In 988, Olaf Tryggveson was in Scilly where he became a Christian and was baptized. From Scilly he sailed to England.

In England, a Thing was called and Olaf went to it. Queen Gyda also came to the Thing. She was the sister of King Olaf Kvaran of Dublin and had been married to a great Jarl who had recently passed away. A famous warrior called Alfvine was courting Gyda but she did not want him. The Thing was assembled so that Gyda could select a suitable husband and she went around looking at all the men.

Olaf was dressed in his rough weather clothes. When Gyda came to Olaf she asked him, "What kind of man are you?"

Olaf said, "I am called Olaf and I am a stranger here".

Gyda asked if he would accept her if she chose him and Olaf said he would. After a while Olaf and Gyda were engaged.

Alfvine was displeased about Gyda and Olaf so he challenged Olaf to a duel. Each was to bring 12 warriors who were also to fight. Olaf told his men to do exactly as he did. At the time of the duel, Olaf took an axe and met Alfvine who was wielding a sword. Olaf disarmed Alfvine with his axe and then tied him up. Each of Olaf's men did the same with their opponents. Alfvine left England. Olaf took over all Alfvine's property and married Gyda.

167 THE BATTLA OF MALDON

In 991, Thorkel the Tall lay with a fleet twenty three ships of Joms Vikings in the Lim Fjord waiting for a favourable wind. A fleet of twenty eight Norwegian long ships glided into the Lim Fjord. Thorkel yelled to the leader to join him if he wished adding that if he came to fight he would have one. Thorkel also said that if there were a fight the Danes would certainly win. Olaf Tryggveson, the Norwegian leader pointed out that he outnumbered Thorkel's fleet by five ships. Thorkel replied that his men were well rested while the Norwegians were exhausted from hard rowing to get out of the wind and high waves. When Olaf learned that Thorkel was making a raid on England he joined up with him.

A few more ships arrived to join Thorkel the Tall's expedition so that when the wind was favourable, a fleet of 55 long ships rowed out of the Lim Fjord and set sail for England. Thorkel raided Stone, Sandwich, and Ipswich. The second week in August, the fleet came to the mouth of the Panta River just below Maldon and landed on Northey Island where they spent the night.

In the morning the Maldon Earl Byrthnoth had brought an army, which was lined up on the main land, across from Northey Island. The Vikings lined up along the shore of the island and faced Byrthnoth's army. Thorkel the Tall's herald yelled out across the water:

"I say to you from these bold seamen,
Give us silver and gold. Then we give you freedom.

You are richer than us and it is better for you to purchase peace with

Treasures than to meet folk like us with spears and swords.

If you are rich enough there is no need for us to kill one another.

And when you have bought your freedom and won peace for yourselves and your

Families and farms and all that belongs to you,

Then we will be your friends and leave in our ships with the silver and gold.

We will sail away and keep our promise."

Byrthnoth stood forward in front of his warriors and raised his shield high and brandished his spear. Then he replied:

"Listen, pirates, to what we answer.
These are the presents we will give you. Spear points and sharp swords.
It would be shameful if a Jarl like me,

Byrthnoth son of Byrthelm whose honour is unblemished

Should not defend my country and that of my King.

Between us there will be only weapon and shield

And hard will you have to fight before you find anything else here."

Then Byrthnoth ordered his warriors into formation at the river's edge. The two armies waited. The tide gradually receded and a small path of shallow water appeared in the river. The Vikings began to cross at this narrow ford.

Byrthnoth placed his best warrior, Wulfstan to defend the causeway. Aelfere and Maccus joined Wulfstan to defend at the ford. The first Viking to reach the shore was quickly killed and Wulfstan easily kept the Vikings from reaching shore through the narrow ford.

The waiting continued and the tide went out so that the river became shallow to waist deep. Then Thorkel the Tall's herald again went forward and shouted.

"Now we have waited long enough.

Come over to us and we will give you room to arrange your warriors.

Or give us room on your beach.

Then we will come over to you."

Jarl Byrthnoth considered it unwise to wade across through the water. The river water was cold and his men would become stiff with the cold and their clothes would become heavy with the water.

Byrthnoth then arranged his warriors in battle formation and taunted the Vikings to come across. The Vikings responded:

> Then advanced the war wolves - for water they feared not.
> The troop of Vikings, waded west over Panta.
> Over the shining water they carried their shields
> Seamen towards shore, they advanced their linden shields.
> There against the raiders ready stood
> Byrthnoth with his band and with the shields bade
> Form the shield wall, and make firm the ranks
> fast against the foes. Then was fighting nigh,
> Fame in battle - now was the hour come
> When doomed men must fall.

Spears flew, bows twanged, arrows soared and the air was filled with battle cries. The two armies collided and clashed. Shields were cloven, axes swung and swords hewed. Byrthnoth yelled encouragements to his men. A spear struck Byrthnoth's shield so that the spear shaft broke and the blade bounced off.

Byrthnoth was wounded in the arm by a Viking spear and another spear went through his body. Byrthnoth fell but exhorted his warriors from the ground. Byrthnoth said a prayer and died.

The English jarls Godwin and Godwig grabbed horses and fled. With them fled their warriors and the English shield wall was broken. Byrthnoth's elite warriors formed a ring around his corpse and defended it to the last man.

For the English it was a source of shame to have survived the battle of Maldon while Byrthnoth and his personal warriors became heroes.

Thorvald said, "The bishop has said that Byrthnoth was over courageous and foolish in letting the Vikings across the Panta River and up on the mainland."

The story teller laughed and laughed. Finally he said, "He could not stop them. When the tide was higher and there was only a narrow ford he could prevent them from reaching his side of the shore which he did. When the tide went out and the river became shallow to waist deep, the Vikings could reach his side all along the river bank. There would be no stopping them. It is not fair of the Bishop to criticize Byrthnoth in this fashion.

After the battle of Maldon, Thorkel the Tall and Olaf sailed their fleet to London. King Aethelred talked with Olaf Tryggveson and then paid him 10,000 pounds of silver to prevent an attack on London. Thorkel the Tall and Olaf Tryggveson made some more raids in England and Aethelred sent for Olaf Tryggveson. King Aethelred negotiated a peace for three years and paid more tribute. The total tribute collected by Olaf and Thorkel was 22,000 pounds of gold and silver.

King Aethelred negotiated with Richard the Fearless, Duke of Normandy, and agreed to not harbour each other's enemies.

In Sweden, Erik the Victorious died and his son Olaf Scotking became King. "That is a strange name", said Bjarne "Why was he called Scotking? He was not a king in Scotland just in Sweden".

The story teller smiled and said, "The English mispronounce the word Scotking. It should be pronounced Skat King (Tax King). He was called Olaf Scotking in his later years when he was paying taxes to Knud the Great.

In 994, King Svend Forkbeard of Denmark sailed a fleet of ships to Normandy where Olaf Tryggveson joined up with him. With a fleet of 94 long ships they sailed to southeast England where they raided. The three years of peace with Aethelred was up and Olaf Tryggveson was back in England.

Svend's fleet entered the Thames River and attacked London. London held and the attack turned into a siege. Then King Aethelred called for a truce and sent Bishop Aelfeah and Earldorman Aethelweard to bring in Olaf Tryggveson. Svend Forkbeard held hostages while Olaf went to confer with Aethelred. King Aethelred met Olaf Tryggveson at Andover and gave him royal gifts, stood by him at confirmation (that Olaf was a Christian), and paid 16, 000 pounds of silver in Dane geld. For his part of the contract, Olaf vowed to leave England and never again return.

Thorer Klakka was sent to Ireland by Haakon Jarl to find out whether Olaf really was the son of Tryggve and of Harald Fairhair's lineage. Thorer told Olaf that he should sail immediately against Haakon because the farmers were up in arms against him for having intercourse with their daughters. Olaf did as Thorer advised and sailed night and day for

Norway with 5 ships.

After leaving Ireland, Olaf sailed his fleet of five ships to the Orkneys. There he ran into the Orkney Jarl, Sigurd the Stout with a fleet of three ships. Olaf called Sigurd onto his ship and said to him, "I want you and all those who serve you to be baptized. If you do not agree to this, you will die here on the spot and I will kill everyone on the islands and fire all the houses."

Sigurd agreed because his force was outnumbered. This was the beginning of the Christian faith in the Orkneys.

168 HAAKON JARL AND OLAF TRYGGVESON

Haakon Jarl was at a feast in Gurladal. He sent some thralls to a farmer called Orm with instructions to bring him Orm's wife, Gudrun who was known to be the most beautiful woman in the district. The thralls arrived at Orm's farm and told Orm of their errand. Orm fed the thralls supper and then told them that he would not send Gudrun with them. Gudrun said to the thralls that she would go to the Jarl only if Thora his mistress came and fetched her. The thralls threatened Orm and his wife and said they would be back another time and finally left. Then Orm sent out the war arrow to all the farmers with the message of what had happened. The farmers in the district had suffered from Haakon borrowing their wives and daughters and were very hostile. They armed themselves and gathered at Orm's house.

When Haakon heard about the farmer's revolt he sent his men into the woods and told them to go to Orkadal. He told them that no one would molest them if he was not with them. Then he sent a message to his son Erland, who was watching the ships, to take the ships out of the fjord and meet him in More. Then with the thrall Kark, Haakon went into the woods and hid in a hole. The farmers set up roadblocks on all the roads watching for Haakon Jarl.

The next day Haakon made his way to the house of Thora and asked her to hide him. She told him that the farmers would search her place all over because they knew she would hide him. She thought that the only place safe was in the pigsty. Kark dug a great hole in the pigsty and carried away the dirt. Then he covered the hole with wood and he and Haakon hid in the hole. Thora covered the hole with more wood, piled pig dung on it and drove the pigs over top of it.

Erland was rowing 3 ships out of the fjord of Gurladal when Olaf Tryggveson's fleet of 5 long ships was entering it. Erland perceived that the fleet might be enemies and steered towards land. Olaf gave pursuit because he thought Haakon might be on one of the ships. Erland's ships ran aground before they reached the land and he and his men sprang overboard. Olaf's ships came up to them and Olaf threw his tiller at the swimming Erland. The tiller struck Erland on the head and killed him. Of Erland's men some were killed, some taken prisoner, and some escaped.

Thora brought the news to Haakon that Erland had been killed in the fjord. Meanwhile Olaf Tryggveson landed and the farmers declared him their King.

Then they all went to Thora's house and searched it for Haakon Jarl. Olaf held a Thing and standing on a great stone next to the pigsty he promised riches to the man who killed Haakon Jarl. Haakon and Kark heard the speech.

During the night Kark and Haakon kept each other awake. Towards morning Haakon fell asleep but he did not sleep well. He had a nightmare and woke up screaming. Terrified, Kark slit Haakon's throat. When Haakon was dead, Kark cut off his head and ran away.

Kark went up to Lade, approached Olaf Tryggvesson and gave him Haakon Jarl's head. Olaf had Kark taken out and beheaded.

Olaf had the heads of Kark and Haakon taken to Nidarholm gallows where thieves and murderers were hung. There the two heads were hung on the gallows. The Throndheim farmers came and threw stones at Haakon's head and called him Haakon the Bad.

A general Thing was called in Throndheim and Olaf Tryggveson was chosen as King of all Norway. Olaf went through Norway and was hailed as King wherever he went.

Many people fled from Norway because of Olaf Tryggveson. Most of them joined Erik Jarl in Sweden. Erik outfitted ships and gathered warriors. Then Erik took his fleet to Gotland where he lay in wait to seize merchant vessels and attack Vikings. In the fall Erik returned to Sweden where he over wintered.

Olaf Tryggveson went into the Vik and into the Uplands. Wherever he went he was hailed as King of all Norway. Haakon Jarl's sons Erik Jarl and Svend Jarl fled to King Olaf Scotking in Sweden, and their territories, which had belonged to Denmark, now was part of Olaf Tryggveson's Kingdom of Norway.

Lodin, a merchant who lived in the Vik, was out on his trading expedition. In the summer he landed in Estonia and went to a market place. There he recognized a woman slave up for sale. Lodin recognized her as Astrid, the mother of Olaf Tryggveson. Lodin bought Astrid and took her home with him and after a while married her.

Olaf Tryggveson spent most of the summer in the Vik visiting his mother and his relatives whom he had never seen before. He had his relatives agree to become Christians and had them baptized. Then he went north and Christianized the people of the northern Vik. Some of the people of the northern Vik opposed him and he dealt with them by killing some, mutilating some and driving some into exile.

The Duke of Normandy, Richard the Fearless, died. He was succeeded by his son, Richard the Good.

Erik Jarl sailed from Sweden to Denmark and courted Gyda, the daughter of Svend Forkbeard. After marrying Gyda, Erik over wintered with Svend Forkbeard.

In the spring of 997, Olaf Tryggveson went north to Agder and proclaimed that everyone should be baptized. Nobody dared to oppose Olaf so all the people in Agder became Christians. In Rogaland the people called a Thing when Olaf arrived. Olaf proclaimed that all the Rogalanders were to be baptized. Some farmers tried to speak against baptism but they were unsuccessful and all the people at the Thing were baptized.

The most powerful Jarls of Norway were at the Gula Thing and could have caused Olaf great problems, but Olmod the Old arose and addressed the King. He said, "We have considered at length upon this matter. If you force us to break with the old ways and accept Christianity, we will fight you with all our might and let fate declare the winner. But if you will give your sister in marriage to Erling Skjalgsson we will do as you wish and serve you faithfully".

Olaf spoke to his sister Astrid but she refused the marriage wishing for a better match. Later Olaf took Astrid's falcon and had all its feathers plucked off. When Astrid saw her bird, she said, "The King is angry".

Then Astrid went to her brother and told him she would leave it to the King to determine her marriage. Shortly after, Astrid was wed to Erling Skjalgsson and the people of Gula were baptized.

Olaf sent the Saxon priest Thangbrand to Iceland to proclaim Christianity. Thangbrand converted many Icelanders to Christianity, but many people resisted him. Among Thrangbrand's critics were the skalds Thorvald Veile and Veterlide who composed satirical verses about

Thangbrand. For these verses, Thangbrand killed the two skalds. In one of his conversion speeches Thangbrand insulted the goddess Freya and called her a 'bitch'. This made the Icelanders extremely angry. They banded together and drove him out of Iceland and threatened to kill him if he came back.

169 ERIK THE RED
THE VINLAND SAGAS

In Jadar, Norway lived a man named Thorvald. His son was named Erik. Thorvald and Erik had some disputes with neighbours. They wound up killing those neighbours. To avoid reprisals, Thorvald and Erik left Norway and sailed to Iceland where they settled.

After Thorvald died in Iceland and Erik married Thorhild, the daughter of Jorund and Thorbjerg the ship breasted. Erik and Thorhild's three sons were Thorvald, Thorstein and Leif. Their daughter was called Freydis.

Thorhild's cousin, Ari Marsson, was caught in a storm near Iceland. His ship was blown westward to Greenland.

Erik's thralls caused a landslip on the estate of Valthjof. For this landslide, Eyjolf the Foul slew the thralls. In return Erik slew Eyjolf the Foul. In that process he also wound up slaying Hrafn the Dueller, at Leikskalar.

Erik, now known as Erik the Red was made an outlaw for 3 years at a Thing in Iceland for the series of killings. Because there was a chance that his enemies might kill him in Iceland, Erik sailed west to Greenland and over wintered there.

In 982, Erik the Red explored the west coast of Greenland. Then he crossed the Davis Strait and explored the Cumberland Peninsula of Baffin Island. In 985, Erik returned to Iceland and led a group of colonists from Iceland to Greenland.

170 LEIF THE LUCKY

Bjarne Herjolfson sailed from Iceland to join the colonists in Greenland, but he was caught in a storm which blew him to a new land. Bjarne sailed up to a place he called Markland and from there sailed to Greenland and became a settler.

Leif Erikson bought Bjarne Herjolfson's ship and sailed out in search of the land Bjarne had found. He came to Markland and made a camp in Trinity Bay.

The camp in Trinity Bay was used as a base camp. Leif made trips south along the coast of the new found land and harvested timber which his men brought back to the base camp. They intended to take the timber to Greenland to sell and make a profit. After several trips gathering timber, Leif took a few days off in the base camp while his men continued to gather timber.

Leif began to worry when his men did not return at the appointed time. A few days later the ship returned. Leif saw that his foster father was not with the men. When Leif questioned the men about it, the leader replied, "Your foster father went into the forest and did not return."

"You left my foster father!" exclaimed Leif.

"We waited a long time and called his name." was the reply.

"We must go back and find him" said Leif.

The leader said, "He is just a thrall. Leave him there."

Leif exclaimed, "He is not just a thrall! He is my foster father! I have known him all my life! We leave to get him first thing in the morning."

The next day, Leif and his crew sailed south and found the shore where Leif's foster father had disappeared. They beached the ship and walked up and down the beech yelling his name. After some time Leif's foster father came walking out of the forest with his hands cupped. He yelled, "Foster son! Look what I have found!"

The men all gathered around Leif's foster father and saw that he held wild grapes and beech nuts. "This is a good land" said the foster father.

Leif said, "It is indeed a good land. I will name this land Vinland."

In 996, Leif Erikson over wintered in Trinity Bay. On the way back to Greenland he rescued some people from a sea wreck. When he arrived back in Greenland he began to be called Leif the Lucky.

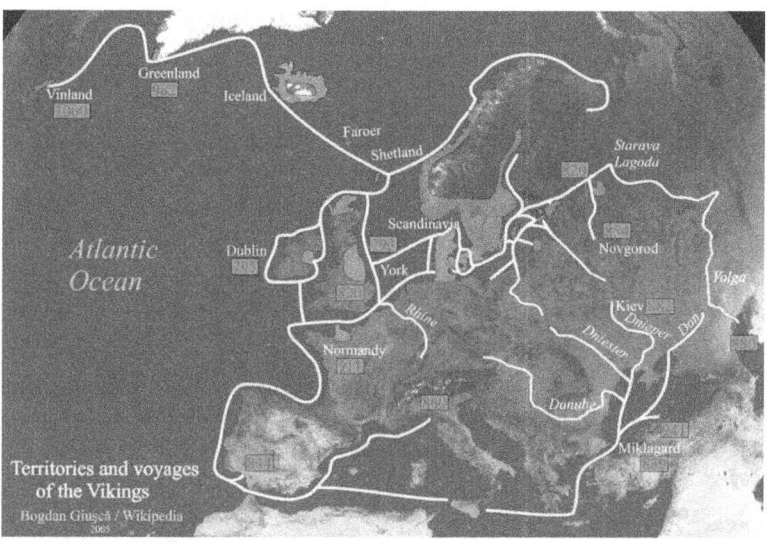

Leif the Lucky sailed to Norway. When Olaf Tryggveson heard that Leif was in Norway, he sent a messenger inviting Leif to his court. Leif accepted Olaf's invitation, went to Olaf's court and was converted to Christianity. Leif over wintered with Olaf Tryggveson. In the summer of 998, Leif the Lucky returned to Greenland with priests and began missionary activities.

171 THORFIN KARLSEFNI
THE VINLAND SAGAS

Thorfin Karlsefni was a descendant of Bjorn Ironsides Lodbrokson. Thorfin lived in north Iceland at Reyniness and was a successful and respected merchant and trader. He took two ships to Erik's Fjord in Greenland and traded with Erik the Red and other inhabitants. Erik invited Thorfin to stay with him over winter in Brattalid and Thorfin accepted.

During the winter of 1004, Thorfin courted Gudrid, the daughter of Thorbjorn, and married her with her father's permission. Thorfin heard much talk of Vinland the Good during the winter and became determined to explore it and build a settlement there. Snorre Thorbrandson decided to go with Thorfin and the two outfitted a ship. Bjarne Grimulfson and Thorhall Gamleson decided to go with Thorfin and also outfitted a ship. Thorfin's fleet reached Bear Island and proceeded south and reached land. They sailed into a fjord and called it Straum Fjord. They drew their ships ashore and established themselves and explored. They over wintered in Straum Fjord.

The winter was hard in Straum Fjord. In the spring Gudrid gave birth to a son, the first European born in the new world. He was called Snorre.

Thorhall wanted to explore north and took nine men and a ship. But Thorhall ran into westerly storms, which drove him to Ireland, where he was attacked by the Irish and killed.

Thorfin spent the summer exploring the land on foot. The land was good and there was plenty of food. They met no people.

In the fall some people showed up at Thorfin's settlement. The Greenlanders called them Skraelings and traded with them. The Greenlanders had cattle and their bull attacked the Skraelings who became terrified and ran. Then a huge number of skraelings entered the settlement and attacked the Greenlanders. The skraelings wielded stone axes, slings and bowand arrow. The Greenlanders wielded iron axes. Some of the skraelings tried to enter the cabin of Karlsefni, but Karlsefni defended the cabin and kept them out. The Skraelings ran to their canoes and paddled away.

In 1006, Thorfin Karlsefni took a ship and sailed south to explore. Thorvald Erikson explored in another direction. Skraelings attacked his party and killed him. Thorfin decided that it was too dangerous to make a settlement here.

In the fall Thorfin Karlsefni and Bjarne Grimulfson launched their ships to sail back to Greenland. The hull of Bjarne's ship had been riddled with holes by beetles and began to sink. Half of Bjarne's crew escaped in lifeboats, but Bjarne went down with his ship. Thorfin made it back to Greenland. Thorfin Karlsefni took his furs and goods from the new world to Norway and sold it.

173 FREYDIS
THE VINLAND SAGAS

Freydis, the daughter of Erik the Red and her husband, Thorvard decided to make the journey to Vinland. With Thorvard went Thorvald Erikson and Thorhall the Hunter. Freydis talked two Icelanders, the brothers Helge and Finbog into coming along with their ships. Three ships glided out of Erik's Fjord in Greenland and set a course west for Vinland. They reached Leif's houses in Markland.

Helge and Finbog started to carry their stuff into Leif's house. Freydis ran up to them and yelled, "What are you doing? This is my brother's house! You cannot stay here! This is where I will be staying."

Helge replied, "Then where will we stay?"

Freydis replied, "I don't care. But you cannot stay in this house. Go build your own house"

The two brothers went into the bush and built a house. The Vikings overwintered in this location.

In the spring a huge fleet of canoes came from the south, landed and attacked the settlement. The Skraelings filled the air with arrows and the Greenlanders fled along the riverbank because they were vastly outnumbered. Freydis came out of her cabin and yelled, "Why are you running from these wretches? I would have thought such gallant men, as you would have slaughtered them like cattle. If I only had a weapon I think I would put up a better fight than any of you!"

Freydis fled after the other Greenlanders but could not keep up because she was pregnant. The Skraelings were gaining on Freydis when she came across Thorbrand, Snorre's son, who lay dead with an arrow through his skull. Freydis stopped, snatched up Thorbrand's naked sword, and turned to face the onrushing Skraelings. She loosened the top of her shift so that it fell down. Then she slapped the sword against her naked breasts. The Skraelings stopped short at the sight of Freydis and became so terrified that they all ran back to their canoes and paddled away.

In 1007, at Straum Fjord, the men began to quarrel over the women and formed into factions. The brothers Helge and Finbog stayed with a group of people in one house while Freydis stayed with the rest of the people in another house. Freydis went to visit Thorvald and Thorhall. When she came back to Leif's house she said, "Helge and Finbog and their men assaulted me and did shameful things to me."

Freydis talked her husband Thorvard into taking action against Helge and Finbog.

At night Thorvard and some men went into the house of Helge and Finbog and took them and their men captive, bound them and took them out one at a time and killed them. Freydis took possession of the belongings of Helge and Finbog. It dawned on Freydis that she could not leave witnesses to accuse her of murder and plundering when they had returned to Greenland. Therefore she wanted Thorvard and his men to kill the 5 women in the house also, but Thorvard refused.

Freydis said, "You are all cowards! I will do it myself. Give me an axe."

They all refused. One by one she looked them in the eyes and snarled, "Give me an axe!"

Finally one of the men handed her a beard axe. Freydis took the axe, entered the house and closed the door behind her. The waiting men heard loud commotions, banging and scream after scream. There were more commotions and loud banging. There were more screams. Finally there was dead silence.

The door opened slowly and there stood Freydis, axe in hand. Her hair was plastered in blood. Her clothes were covered in blood. The blood drops from her blood covered face ran in rivulets down her neck. The axe was dripping with blood, great crimson drops splatting on the ground. "Clean up the mess", she said.

Then Freydis went from man to man and said, "If you say a word of this to anyone, I will come and kill you myself!"

The men all agreed to keep silent on the matter. Then they set fire to the house. After the house was ashes, Thorvard had the ships loaded and all the settlers sailed back to Greenland.

In Greenland the people who were with Freydis kept quiet about what had happened to Helge, Finbog and their crew. There were however too many people involved to keep a secret forever. One day during a drinking bout, one of the men who were with Freydis bragged about the event. The matter then became common knowledge. When Erik the Red heard about it, he would not let his daughter profit from such a betrayal. He seized the goods which had belonged to Helge and Finbog and gave it to their families in Greenland. Freydis never found out who in her party had given away her secret.

173 HARALD GRENSKE

King Harald Grenske of Westfold was married to Asta, a daughter of Gudbrand Kula. Harald sailed a fleet into the Baltic Sea on a raid. He stopped in at Sweden to see his foster sister Sigrid the widow of Erik the Victorious. Sigrid sent men and invited Harald to a feast.

Sigrid received Harald in a very friendly manner. They feasted all evening and everyone got drunk. Harald went to bed and when he was undressed Sigrid came to him with more drinks. They drank together until Harald fell asleep. Then Sigrid went off to her own bed.

When Harald left the next day, Sigrid followed him along the road and saw him off at the ships with many presents. After he came home, Harald was very depressed and missed Sigrid.

In 995, Harald Grenske was depressed all winter and when spring came he got together a band of warriors and rode to the Swedish border to see Sigrid. Harald and Sigrid met at the border and talked together for a long time. Eventually he asked Sigrid to marry him. She refused saying that Harald already had a wife. Harald replied that Asta was a good and clever woman but not high born like Sigrid. But Sigrid pointed out that she would not leave her lands in Sweden and that Asta was pregnant with Harald's child. Sigrid then rode home to Sweden.

After returning home Harald decided to follow Sigrid home. His men advised strongly against it, but Harald went any ways with a fleet of ships. When he arrived at Sigrid's place in Sweden, King Vissavald of Gardarike had just arrived to woo Sigrid. Lodging was given to both Kings in one great house. In the evening much drink was available and every one became drunk.

When both Kings and their men were sound asleep, Sigrid had her warriors surround their house and set it on fire. Any man who tried to leave the house was cut down and both Kings and their men died.

Hrane was watching Harald's ships with some of the warriors. When he heard that Harald had fallen he launched the ships and sailed back to Westfold. There he told Asta all that had happened. Asta was upset that Harald had intended to divorce her. She went home to her father Gudbrand where she gave birth to a son and called him Olaf.

174 KING OLAF TRYGGVESON

Olaf Tryggveson wooed Queen Sigrid of Sweden and they met to make final wedding arrangements. But Sigrid refused to be baptized saying that she respected Christianity but she preferred her ancestor's religion. Olaf became angry and slapped Sigrid's face with a glove saying, "Why should I want to have you, an old faded woman and a heathen jade?"

Sigrid replied, "This may someday be your death".

Then the two departed for their homes.

Olaf continued his journey through Norway and had people baptized. Asta, the widow of Harald Grenske, her husband Sigurd Syr and Asta's son Olaf were baptized and Olaf Tryggveson became Olaf Haraldson's God Father. Sigurd Syr was a king in Ringerige and of Harald Fairhair's lineage.

Thorkel the Tall continued to raid in Wessex.

In the autumn, Olaf built a snekke (long ship), which was bigger than any ship before it. The ship was called the Crane.

Gunhild, Svend Forkbeard's wife became sick and died.

After killing another skald in Iceland, Thangbrand returned to Norway in 999.

Olaf Tryggveson's men kidnapped Eyvind Kinrifa in northern Norway and brought him to the King. The King asked Eyvind to denounce the old gods and accept Christ. Eyvind refused. Olaf threatened Eyvind with torture and still Eyvind refused. Then Olaf had a pan of glowing coal placed on Eyvind's belly. Eyvind's belly burst and he died rejecting Christianity.

Olaf accompanied by Bishop Sigurd took the Crane and a fleet of ships into Godey Fjord. They landed at night on Gylling Island where Raud lived. Raud's ship, the Dragon, was at anchor close to the land.

Olaf and his warriors broke into Raud's house and captured Raud in his sleeping quarters. Raud's servants were bound and some were beaten while others were killed. Olaf had Raud brought to him and offered him baptism. He told Raud that if he accepted Christ, he would be Raud's friend and all would be well. Raud rejected Christ and Olaf became angry and said that Raud would die the worst of deaths.

Raud was bound to a beam of wood with his face turned up. A round piece of wood was set between his teeth to force his mouth open. Olaf ordered an adder to be set into Raud's mouth, but the adder refused to go into the mouth. Olaf put a horn into Raud's mouth and placed the adder in the horn. The adder was forced to go into Raud's mouth by a red hot iron placed at the opening of the horn. The adder went into Raud's mouth and down his throat, and gnawed its way out of Raud's side. Thus Raud died.

Gudrod had become a sea king after fleeing from Norway in 970 A.D. He had spent most of his time raiding in the British Isles. This summer, with a fleet of many ships, he set out from England and set a course for Norway. He landed his fleet in the Vik. He began to plunder and demanded that the people accept him as their King.

The people of the Vik could not hope to go against Gudrod's great army. So they offered to send messengers out to call a Thing to choose Gudrod as King. Gudrod accepted the terms provided that the farmers would feed his warriors so that he could maintain his army. The farmers decided to take turns hosting Gudrod and his army.

When the Thing messenger came to Thorgeir and Hyrning, who were related to Olaf Tryggveson, they gathered ships and warriors and sailed north to the Vik. In the night they came to the farm where Gudrod was a guest and attacked Gudrod. In the battle, Gudrod and most of his warriors fell. Thus died the last of the sons of Erik Bloodaxe.

Svend Forkbeard married Sigrid the Haughty of Sweden.

King Boleslaw was becoming tired of waiting to marry Thyra, Svend Forkbeard's sister. He sent Sigvald Jarl to Svend to demand that the wedding proceed. Boleslaw also sent the message that Thyra was to get all the land and riches, which had belonged to Gunhild. Svend sent Thyra back with Sigvald Jarl to King Boleslaw of the Vends. But Thyra did not want to marry Boleslaw because he was old and a heathen. Thyra wept all the way to Vend land.

In the land of the Vends, Thyra would neither eat nor drink with the heathen. She was married to Boleslaw but ran away after 7 days with her foster father, Ozur Aageson, and a few men and serving maidens. They made their way over land to Denmark where they hid so that Svend would not send Thyra back. After a while they got passage on a ship headed for Norway. Finally they arrived in the court of Olaf Tryggveson in Throndheim.

Olaf was impressed with Thyra and eventually asked her to marry him and they were wed.

Thorkel the Tall brought his fleet of ships into the Thames River and sailed up to Rochester. An army of warriors from Kent went against the Vikings, but were defeated. The Vikings took horses and laid waste the whole of West Kent.

King Aethelred prepared ships and started to collect warriors to go against the Vikings. The English ships were ready, but Aethelred had problems collecting his army. In the battle with the Vikings, the English ships had to retreat and the Vikings over wintered in England.

In the winter of 1000, Olaf Tryggveson had a long ship built which was larger than any other long ship. The new ship was called the Long Serpent.

Queen Thyra wanted Olaf to go to King Boleslaw in Vend land and collect her properties and wealth. Olaf decided to go in the summer. Because he would have to sail through Danish waters, he sent out a war arrow to collect warriors for the expedition. Ragnvald Jarl of Sweden was courting Ingeborg who was the sister of Olaf Tryggveson. Ragnvald was the son of Ulf who was the brother of Queen Sigrid the Haughty of Denmark and he sent a messenger to Sigrid that Olaf Tryggveson was preparing an expedition to Vend land.

Svend sent a message to Sweden inviting Erik Jarl and Olaf Scotking to meet him with an army. He also sent a message to Thorkel the Tall in England telling him to bring the army back to Denmark. Another message was sent to Sigvald Jarl to lead Olaf into an ambush.

When Thorkel the Tall received Svend's message, he took his fleet across the English Channel to Normandy and proceeded north to Denmark. Sigvald Jarl and his wife Astrid sailed to Vend land to visit Astrid's father King Boleslaw and waited for Olaf. Astrid was a friend of Olaf who had been married to her sister Geira.

When summer came, Ragnvald married Ingeborg. After the wedding, Olaf Tryggveson and Thyra left Throndheim with 11 large ships. Olaf's best warriors were with him on the Long Serpent including the 18 year old Einar Tambaskjelve who was already recognized as the best archer in the north. By the time Olaf left Norwegian waters his fleet consisted of 60 war ships. He sailed past Denmark through the Large Belt and on to Vend land.

Olaf met with Boleslaw who gave Olaf the properties and possessions, which had been promised to Thyra. Olaf and Thyra spent the summer with Boleslaw where Olaf visited many of his old friends. Sigvald Jarl and Astrid visited often with Olaf and Thyra.

When they heard that Olaf Tryggveson was in Vend land, King Olaf Scotking and Erik Jarl collected warriors and a large fleet and sailed to meet Svend Forkbeard in Denmark.

Haldor the Unchristian sang of it:

> **"The king-subduer raised a host**
>
> **Of warriors on the Swedish coast.**
>
> **The brave went southwards to the fight,**
>
> **Who love the sword-storm's gleaming light;**
>
> **The brave, who fill the wild wolf's mouth,**
>
> **Followed bold Erik to the south;**
>
> **The brave, who sport in blood -- each one**
>
> **With the bold Jarl to sea is gone."**

When Olaf Tryggveson wanted to sail back home, Sigvald Jarl found reasons for Olaf not to leave. Then one day a messenger came in secrecy to Sigvald from Svend Forkbeard. The message was that the fleets of Svend, Erik and Olaf Scotking were waiting for Olaf Tryggveson at the island of Svold in the Ore Sound.

It had been reported in Vend land that Svend Forkbeard had raised an army to attack Olaf Tryggveson. Sigvald went to Olaf and proposed that he would accompany him with 11 ships saying that the Danes would think twice about attacking Joms Vikings. Olaf thought it a good idea and accepted Sigvald's offer. Olaf and Sigvald left Vend land with 71 ships.

When the fleet approached the Danish islands, Sigvald suggested that the fleet split up. He suggested that Olaf with his large ships follow Sigvald through the Ore Sound while the main fleet sailed back through the Large Belt. Olaf agreed and Sigvald sailed his 11 ships north into Ore Sound. Olaf followed with 11 ships while the rest of the fleet sailed west towards the Large Belt. When Sigvald reached the island of Svold, a rowboat approached and the rower told Sigvald that Svend's fleet was waiting on the other side of the island. Sigvald ordered his sails to be taken down and his ships were rowed behind the island.

When Olaf's eleven ships came opposite Svold, the ships of Svend, Erik, and Olaf Scotking rowed out towards them. Olaf Tryggveson ordered that his ships be lashed together and that the sails be struck. Then war horns sounded and the air was filled with arrows, spears, and stones. Sigvald had his ships drop anchor and stayed out of the fight.

The men on the forecastles of the Norwegian ships threw grappling hooks into the nearest ships of the enemy, drew them close and cleared their decks with arrows and spears. The Danish and Swedish ships approached Olaf's smaller ships, boarded them, cut their cables, and cleared their decks. Olaf Tryggveson's men began to jump from the smaller ships into the large ships. Erik Jarl's ship came next to Olaf Tryggveson's ship and the battle was ferocious. The Long Serpent was taller so that the Norwegians had the advantage of higher ground. As fast as warriors fell in Erik's ship, other Danes and Swedes replaced them.

Einar Tambaskjelve stood by the mast of the Long Serpent and fired arrow after arrow down into Erik's ship. Erik yelled to his archer Fin to shoot the tall archer by the mast of the Long Serpent. Fin shot and the arrow hit Einar's bow just as Einar was drawing it and the bow split in two parts. "What was it that broke with such a noise?" yelled Olaf Tryggveson. Einar replied, "Norway, King, from your hands."

Olaf handed Einar his bow. Einar drew it. Then he threw it away saying, "Too weak a bow from so mighty a King!"

The Saga Kings

Then Einar fastened his shield and drew his sword.

When all the spears, arrows and stones were used up, the ships clustered around the Long Serpent and hand to hand fighting was carried out over the railings. By this time the ships had blown into the Kattegat Strait and the Long Serpent was the only Norwegian ship still fighting.

The Long Serpent began to be boarded by the mast where the warriors had been thinned out. The warriors of the forecastle saw what was happening and rushed back to the mast and forced the boarders off. But warriors then poured into the forecastle and began to clear the deck of the Long Serpent. The Norwegian warriors crowded aft to defend the King.

When the deck of the Long Serpent had been cleared so that there was fighting in only the aft, Olaf's men began to jump overboard. Einar Tambaskjelve jumped overboard and swam under the water for a while. He managed to swim to shore. Olaf Tryggveson jumped overboard on one side and Kolbjorn jumped overboard on the other side. Olaf held his shield over his head and disappeared under the water but Kolbjorn had fastened his shield to his back and it held him up so that he was captured. Thinking that Kolbjorn was Olaf Tryggveson, the warriors brought him to Erik Jarl, who granted him his life. But Olaf Tryggveson did not come to the surface. He was never seen again.

Queen Thyra was found in a room under the Long Serpent's deck. Her sorrow was so great that she refused to eat. She died a few days later.

The bane men of Olaf Tryggveson divided Olaf's Kingdom. Svend Forkbeard took the Vik, which his father used to own. Olaf Scotking got Ranrige, which was the land between the mouth of the Gotaelf River to Swine Sound and some eastern districts. He made Svend Haakonson the Jarl of those districts. Erik Jarl got four districts in Throndheim and the entire west lands Halogaland, Naumudal, the Fjord districts, Sogn, Hordaland, Rogaland, North Agder, Raumarike, and Hedemark.

The Joms Vikings banished Sigvald from their brotherhood because he had fled first at Jorund's Fjord and then again in the battle of Svold. They chose Thorkel the Tall to be their Jarl.

A band of missionaries came to Sweden. Olaf Scotking, Svend Jarl and Erik Jarl became Christians and were baptized. Olaf was the first Christian King in Sweden. Svend Forkbeard remained a heathen but tolerated Christianity.

Erik Jarl took Einar Tambaskjelve back to Norway with him and gave him fiefs in Orkadal so that he became one of the most powerful men in Throndheim. Einar became a great friend of Erik and Svend Haakonson, and married their sister Bergliot.

175 KING AETHELRED

In 1001, Thorkel the Tall raided in Wessex and over wintered in England.

In 1002, King Aethelred met with Thorkel the Tall and paid him 24,000 pounds of silver to leave and Thorkel left. Then Aethelred sailed to Normandy and courted Emma, the sister of Duke Richard the Good. A few weeks later they were married.

In the fall Aethelred ordered that all Danes in England be killed on St. Brice's day. On November 13, 1002 the Danes living in England were attacked. All over England, Danes were killed and many were tortured to death. In Oxford, Gunhild, Svend Forkbeard's sister, fled with her husband Pallig Jarl who was Earldorman of Devonshire. They entered St. Frideswide Church and sought sanctuary. The English surrounded the church and burned it to the ground.

In 1003, Svend Forkbeard arrived in England with a great army seeking revenge for the death of his sister. He sacked Exeter, Wilton, Salisbury, Norwich and Thetford. After the sack of Thetford, Ulfkell Snelling attacked Svend Forkbeard with a large army. Ulfkell's forces were winning and he ordered that the Danish ships be destroyed. While Ulfkell's warriors hesitated, the Danes retreated and managed to escape in their ships. The Danes said that they had never been in a harder battle in Britain than the one Ulfkell gave them.

During the rest of the year and during the year 1004, Svend raided in Wessex and East Anglia. In 1005, the Danish army left England because of a famine.

176 SVEND FORKBEARD IN ENGLAND

The next year, Svend Forkbeard brought his army back to England. He established a safe base at Wight and a strong food cache at Reading. The English boasted that they would slaughter the Danes if they got to Cuckhamsley Knob on Wiltshire downs. When Svend heard about the boast, he took his army to the Cuckhamsley Knob and invited the English to attack. The English attacked but the battle was short and the English fled. Svend gathered food and supplies and his army rode back to their ships.

In England Aethelred approached Svend Forkbeard and paid him 36,000 pounds of silver to leave. He also gave Svend more food and supplies. Svend took his army back to Denmark.

King Aethelred appointed Eadric Streona as Earldorman of Mercia. Then he spent the next two years preparing an army and building a fleet to go against the next invasion.

In 1009, Thorkel the Tall, Jarl of the Joms Vikings, was preparing an expedition to England when Olaf Haraldson who had been a Viking sea king since he was 12 years old brought a small fleet to Joms Castle. Olaf who was fourteen claimed to be eighteen so that he could join the Joms Vikings. Thorkel took a liking to Olaf and took him into his service.

Thorkel, his brother Hemming, and Olaf set a course for England. They ran into a storm and lay in lee of the wind on the beach of Kinlima in Frisia. They landed their ships on the beach. The Frisians attacked them on horseback. Sighvat sang of the battle:

"Under Kinlima's cliff,

This battle is the fifth.

The brave sea rovers stand

All on the glittering sand;

And down the horsemen ride

To the edge of the rippling tide:

But Olaf taught the peasant band

To know the weight of a Viking's hand."

The Joms Vikings retreated to their ships and left Kinlima. Thorkel's fleet joined a fleet of Danish Vikings led by Eilaf Thorgilsson (a brother of Ulf Jarl and grandson of Styrbjorn Staerke). The combined fleets ran into Aethelred's war ships off Sandwich. The Vikings outfought the English. Eighty English ships were put on fire by flaming arrows and 20 defected to the Danes. The rest of Aethelred's fleet took to flight.

Eastern Kent bought peace by paying the Danes 3,000 pounds of silver. Then the Danes attacked London. The city repelled every attack. The Vikings then left and devastated the shires. Oxford was burned and Ipswich was sacked.

In 1010, the Danes laid waste in East Anglia and Cambridge. Then at Ringmere Ulfkell Snelling went against them with Aethelred's army. The battle was fierce and many warriors fell on both sides. Then one of Ulfkell's leaders, Thurcytel, fled with his forces. This left the English lines broken and they had to flee. Because England was now undefended, the Danes laid waste to the shires of Thetford, Oxford, Buckingham, and Bedford.

In 1011, the Danes continued with fire and sword in England and Aethelred made overtures for peace and agreed to pay 48,000 pounds of silver. The Danes took Canterbury and made a prisoner of its Archbishop Aelfeah. It was past Easter in 1012 before the 48,000 pounds of silver could be collected. The Danes wanted a separate ransom for Aelfeah. But Aelfeah would not pay the ransom nor would he permit others to pay it.

One night during a feast, the Danes began throwing bones at Aelfeah. They pelted him with bigger and bigger bones. Thorkel the Tall was appalled and did his best to stop them. He offered everything he owned except his ship. But a big Viking hit the old Aelfeah on the head with his axe and Aelfeah died.

When the 48,000 pounds of silver was paid, the Danes boarded their ships and sailed home except for Thorkel the Tall who transferred his allegiance from Svend to Aethelred. The Joms Vikings with 45 ships went with Thorkel.

In 1013, Svend Forkbeard took a large fleet and sailed for England. He sailed to Sandwich and from there to the Humber. Then he sailed 20 miles up the Trent to Gainsborough deep in Danelaw territory. Uhtred Jarl of all Northumbria submitted himself to Svend. Soon all the Danelaw recognized Svend Forkbeard as their King.

Svend left his ships in Gainsborough under the charge of his son Knud, who was 17 years old, and took his mounted army through Mercia and subdued it. Oxford and Winchester surrendered to Svend. Then Svend attacked London, which was defended by the Joms Vikings and Aethelred's bodyguards commanded by Thorkel the Tall.

Svend left London and conquered the rest of England. Aethelred sent his wife and family to Normandy in Thorkel the Tall's ships. Then he gave hostages to Svend and promised him tribute. But just before Christmas Aethelred, realizing that his position was untenable went to Normandy with Thorkel the Tall leaving Svend Forkbeard as King of all England.

While in Normandy, Olaf Haraldson became a Christian and was baptized.

On February 3, 1014, Svend Forkbeard died suddenly. When the news of Svend Forkbeard's death reached Denmark, the Danes called a Thing and chose Harald, Knud's older brother as King. Svend's warriors swore allegiance to Knud and hailed him as King of England, but the English sent a messenger to Normandy inviting Aethelred back as King.

177 KNUD

In April, Aethelred returned to England with Thorkel the Tall and Olaf Haraldson. English warriors flocked to Aethelred. The fleet sailed up the Thames and assaulted London, which was now a Danish stronghold. A big trading center called Southwark was on one side of the river and on the other side stood a fortified castle. A large wooden bridge, London Bridge, connected the two. On the bridge were parapets and towers from which archers and spearmen could launch their projectiles. Aethelred's forces could not make headway against the fortified bridge.

Aethelred held a council of war. It was determined that the ships be taken under the bridge for an assault. Many ships tried to get under the bridge but were so heavily damaged by boulders thrown down that they had to retreat.

Olaf Haraldson had his men make roofs over his ships from timbers of old houses. When his ships were rowed under London Bridge the boulders cast down bounced off the roofs. When he was under the bridge he fastened cables around the pilings and timbers, which supported the bridge. When his ships were rowed downstream the bridge gave way and collapsed. Many of the warriors on the bridge fell into the water and the rest fled. Then Aethelred's army stormed Southwark and took it. The warriors in the castle could not prevent Aethelred's fleet from going upriver and taking the country so they became afraid, surrendered and took Aethelred as their King. Ottar Svarte sang of the battle:

> **"London Bridge is broken down. --**
>
> **Gold is won, and bright renown.**
>
> **Shields resounding,**
>
> **War-horns sounding,**
>
> **Hild is shouting in the din!**
>
> **Arrows singing,**
>
> **Mail-coats ringing --**
>
> **Odin makes our Olaf win!"**

This song survives today as follows:

"London Bridge is falling down.

Falling down.

Falling down.

London Bridge is falling down.

My fair Lady!"

Sighvat the Bard composed a song about the battle also:

"At London Bridge stout Olaf gave

Odin's law to his war-men brave --

'To win or die!'

And their foemen fly.

Some by the dyke-side refuge gain --

Some in their tents on Southwark plain!

The sixth attack

Brought victory back."

Knud was in Lindsay and much of his army had dispersed. Advisors told him to leave because warriors were flocking to Aethelred and Thorkel the Tall. Knud sailed his fleet down to Sandwich. There he mutilated his father's hostages and set them on shore. While Knud Svendson sailed his fleet home to Denmark, Aethelred with Thorkel and Olaf proceeded into East Anglia where Ulfkell Snelling joined them. Then Aethelred went to Canterbury and attacked the town. Many men fell and the castle was burned. Aethelred then took his army into Lindsay and laid it under him.

All of England hailed Aethelred as King. Aethelred paid Thorkel the Tall 21,000 pounds of silver, and Thorkel took his fleet back to Joms Castle. Olaf Haraldson sailed to Normandy and over wintered on the Seine.

Eadric Streona Earldorman of Mercia had two noblemen, Siferth and Morcar of the Five Boroughs murdered in 1015. Aethelred then arrested Siferth's widow and seized the properties of the two deceased noblemen. Aethelred's son Edmund Ironsides rescued Siferth's widow and married her. Then he took warriors to the Five Boroughs and made himself ruler there. Aethelred was upset with Edmund and a feud was started between Edmund and his brother Eadric.

Knud Svendson received warriors and ships from his brother King Harald. Knud sent a message to Erik Jarl in Norway inviting him to join in an expedition to England. Erik was excited and gathered a fleet. He set his son Haakon in charge in Norway and asked Einar Tambaskjelve to help his son steer his dominions. Then he set sail for England.

Before Knud sailed from Jelling, Thorkel the Tall arrived with a fleet of Joms Vikings and pledged allegiance to Knud. Then Knud and Thorkel took a large fleet to England where they met up with Erik Jarl. Eadric Streona came over to Knud with 40 ships and pledged allegiance to Knud. Thus Knud had half of England.

Aethelred's sons promised Olaf Haraldson Northumberland if he would help conquer England. Olaf brought his fleet to Jungufurda in England. There he and Edmund moved against the castle and took it.

Olaf abandoned Edmund and took his ships to Northumberland. He landed at Valde and attacked the townspeople. He was victorious and looted the town.

Olaf had decided to take advantage of Erik's absence from Norway to make an attempt at the throne. He calculated that if he could kill or drive out Svend Jarl and Erik's son Haakon, Norway would be his. Therefore he took 2 large ships with 220 warriors and set sail for Norway

178 KING OLAF

It was autumn and Olaf ran into storms on his voyage. He arrived from the sea in the middle of Norway and landed on the island of Saela outside Stad. From there he sailed to Ulfa Sound. People told Olaf that Haakon Jarl was in Sogn with a single ship and was expected to come north when the wind was favourable.

Olaf took his two long ships south to Fjalar district and sailed into Saudungs Sound. He laid his two ships on each side of the sound with a cable between them. When Haakon sailed into the sound from the south, he thought that Olaf's ships were 2 merchant vessels and sailed between them. Then Olaf and his men drew the cable up tight with the capstan. The cable caught Haakon's ship in the stern and raised it out of the water so that the bow went under and took on water, causing the ship to flip on its side.

Olaf's warriors threw stones and spears at Haakon's warriors until they were in the water. Then they fished Haakon and his surviving warriors up and made them prisoners. Haakon was brought before Olaf who asked what Haakon would give him if he released him unhurt. Haakon asked what he would take. Olaf replied, "Nothing, except that you shall leave the country, give up your kingdom, and make a solemn vow that you shall never go into battle against me".

Haakon agreed and made the solemn vow. Then Olaf released Haakon and all his men and gave him back his ship.

Sighvat sang of the meeting:

> **"In old Saudungs sound**
>
> **The king Jarl Haakon found,**
>
> **Who little thought that there**
>
> **A foeman was so near.**
>
> **The best and fairest youth**
>
> **Jarl Haakon was in truth,**

That speaks the Danish tongue,

And of the race of great Haakon."

Olaf went east along the land and held Things in an attempt to be declared King. But Svend Jarl had many friends who spoke against him. Then Olaf sailed to the Vik to visit his mother Asta and his stepfather Sigurd Syr. Asta and Sigurd had an infant son whom they called Harald.

Olaf presented his plan to Sigurd who went to a meeting with the Upland Kings. Sigurd spoke to these Kings about the necessity to throw off the yoke of the Danes and the Swedes. Then he presented his stepson's plans to unify Norway under a Norwegian King who was descended from Harald Fairhair. The Kings agreed to enter into a league with Olaf and confirmed it by making solemn vows. Olaf then called a Thing in the Uplands and was declared King. Olaf became known as King Olaf the Stout.

When word of Olaf's progress reached Einar Tambaskjelve, he sent out a war arrow with the message that they were to defend the land against King Olaf. The message went to Orkadal and to Gaurladal. Olaf with 100 men went into Orkadal and advanced in peace until he came to Griotar. There he found 700 armed farmers barring his way. Olaf arrayed his army because he thought the farmers would go against him.

When the farmers saw the warriors of Olaf prepared for battle they tried to get into a formation. But they had no leader and getting a formation went slow and confused. When Olaf saw their confusion he sent Thorer Gudbrandson to them to say that the King did not want to fight them. Thorer told them to select twelve men to go and talk to the King. The farmers were very relieved and agreed to Thorer's proposal.

Olaf explained to the twelve chosen farmers his meeting with Jarl Haakon resulting in Haakon handing over his Kingdom and that the Uplanders had chosen him King at a Thing. He gave them two choices; either proclaim him King or fight him. After much discussion, the 700 farmers swore allegiance to King Olaf. Olaf proceeded to Nidaros.

Svend Jarl was in Throndheim Fjord at Steinker, a merchant town, preparing a Christmas feast, when a messenger came to him from Einar Tambaskjelve. The messenger said that Olaf was on his way to Throndheim. Svend had all his belongings loaded onto his ship and rowed out at night. By daybreak Svend's ship had reached Skarn Sound. Svend laid his ship along the shore where the branches and leaves of a great tree over hung his ship. The weather was calm and Olaf's fleet rowed by Svend's ship without seeing it. When Olaf's fleet was out of sight, Svend's ship rowed to his home at Frosta.

When Olaf reached Steinker, he took all the feast preparations, which Erik had made and loaded it onto his ships. Then he proceeded to Nidaros where he set up the meat and drinks and was ready to celebrate Christmas.

Svend Jarl and Einar Tambaskjelve came overland through Gaurladal with 2000 warriors. When they entered Nidaros, Olaf's mounted look out saw them and galloped to tell the King. Olaf immediately woke his men and they went to their ships and rowed out of the river. Svend's warriors entered the town, took all the Christmas provisions and set fire to the houses.

In 1016, King Olaf over wintered in Hedemark. When spring came he gathered an army. Then he went to the Vik and launched a great fleet. Meanwhile in Throndheim, Svend Jarl gathered a great fleet and sailed to the Vik. The two fleets met in Oslo Fjord near Nesjar.

When Svend saw Olaf's fleet approaching he had his men tie their ships together. Olaf's war horns sounded and the hail of spears and arrows began. Olaf laid his ship next to Svend's. The battle was sharp and many warriors fell. Sighvat the skald sang of it:

> "No urging did the jarl require,
>
> Midst spear and sword -- the battle's fire;
>
> No urging did the brave King need
>
> The ravens in this shield-storm to feed.
>
> Of limb lopping enough was there,
>
> And ghastly wounds of sword and spear.
>
> Never, I think, was rougher play
>
> Than both the armies had that day."

On Svend's ship many warriors fell and Olaf's crew began to board it. Svend called to his forecastle men to cut the cables and let his ship loose. The cables were cut but Olaf's men threw cables around the timberheads (the bow timberhead held the carved dragon head) and held it. Svend yelled for his men to cut the timberheads. The men chopped down the timberheads. Einar Tambaskjelve laid his ship close to Svend's. His men threw the anchor over the bow of Svend's ship and towed it away. Olaf knew Svend's skald Berse Torfason who was standing on the forecastle of Svend's ship. As Svend's ship glided away, Olaf yelled, "Farewell Berse".

"Farewell King", replied Berse.

As the ships of Einar and Svend rowed out of the fjord, Svend's fleet fled. Svend's army dispersed and most of the men went home. Svend with his chosen warriors sailed to Sweden and stayed with Olaf Scotking.

The battle of Nesjar broke all resistance to Olaf in Norway. He sailed to Throndheim and was acclaimed King. Then he went about making friends with the leaders who had supported Svend Jarl.

In 1017, Olaf Scotking's tax collectors arrived in Throndheim to collect the taxes. King Olaf the Stout met with them and ordered them to go home. One of the leaders, Thorgaut returned home with his men, but a second leader, Asgautr, with twelve men went into More and began to collect tax. Olaf the Stout sent men after Asgautr. The men caught the Swedes and hung them all.

After this action against the Swedish King, Olaf the Stout realized that there would be war with Sweden so he took the offensive and sailed south to the Vik and went into Ranrige where Ragnvald Ulfson was Jarl for the King of Sweden. Ragnvald was related to the royal families of both Sweden and Norway so he did not want war. Olaf crossed Ranrige and plundered in West Gotland.

180 OLAF THE STOUT

King Olaf the Stout went about Christianizing the Norwegians. Five of the Upland Kings were very concerned about Olaf's activities and met at Ringsaker in Hedemark to discuss it. One of the Kings related that King Olaf the Stout was killing or mutilating people who would not convert to the right faith. King Hrorik assumed leadership and came up with a plan to end the days of Olaf the Stout.

Ketil of Ringanes was at the meeting with the five Kings. He took forty men and sailed to King Olaf the Stout and told him about the meeting. Olaf the Stout immediately went to Church and had mass given. Then he sailed to Ringsaker with 400 warriors. There he had the warriors surround the houses where the Kings slept. In the morning when the Kings awoke they found themselves outnumbered and had to surrender.

The five Kings were led before King Olaf. Olaf made King Ring and two other Kings outlaws and banished them from Norway. Olaf had King Gudrod's tongue cut out. Then he had King Hrorik's eyes punched out and kept him.

The farmers and Ragnvald Ulfson made petitions to King Olaf the Stout to make peace with Olaf Scotking. Olaf the Stout listened. He sent Bjorn and Sighvat the skald to King Olaf Scotking. At the Thing in Uppsala, Ragnvald Ulfson and a chief of the farmers called Torgny supported Bjorn. There was so much support for peace that Olaf Scotking had no choice but to declare peace. It was decided to seal the peace by the marriage of Olaf the Stout with Olaf Scotking's daughter Ingegerd. The marriage was to be in the fall at Kongshelle.

King Hrorik would ask his serving boy to take him into the woods for a walk. There he beat the boy. Then he would complain to King Olaf the Stout that his serving boy would not serve him. Olaf would then give him a different serving boy. This scenario repeated itself until Olaf appointed Svein as King Hrorik's servant. Svein was from Hrorik's household and was loyal to Hrorik.

Hrorik talked Svein into killing King Olaf. One day the King came out from Vespers and Svein was there wearing a cloak. Under the cloak he had a dagger. But Svein panicked when Olaf came up to him. Olaf seeing Svein's terror said, "What is this Svein? Would you betray me?"

Svein dropped his cloak and dagger, fell at the King's feet and said, "All is in God's hands, and yours King".

Olaf ordered Svein to be seized. Svein was granted his life and he left the country. Olaf had two of his warriors be with Hrorik at all times. Hrorik slept in a house with twelve other men. One night during Easter, Hrorek managed to get all twelve drunk. Then Hrorek walked out of the house. The two warrior guards followed him and were cut down outside by Hrorek's men. The corpses were dragged up the road and Hrorek took to flight.

Sighvat came out that night to use the privy, slipped in the blood of the two warrior guards and fell. When he came back inside, men asked him where he was hurt because he was covered with blood. Then they checked the house of Hrorek and found him gone. King Olaf sent men after Hrorek and caught him before he could board his ship. Olaf had Hrorek transported to Iceland where he died three years later.

In the fall at the appointed time, Olaf the Stout sailed to Kongshelle for his wedding. But the Swedes did not show up and Olaf waited there a long time. The King did not know what to do. He wondered what had become of the Swedes, and whether Ragnvald was to blame.

Olaf the Stout decided to send Sighvat to Ragnvald to discover what the problem was with his betrothal to Ingegerd. After a difficult journey Sighvat arrived at the home of Ragnvald who received him well. Ingegerd's sister Astrid arrived soon after Sighvat to visit and Ragnvald put on a feast for her. Ragnvald told Sighvat that Olaf Scotking hated Olaf the Stout and always called him "Olaf the Fat" or "the Fat Man". Ingegerd had sent letters to Ragnvald which stated that ambassadors had arrived from Russia to King Olaf Scotking asking from King Yaroslav the Wise for Ingegerd's hand in marriage.

Ragnvald asked Sighvat if King Olaf the Stout would marry Olaf Scotking's daughter Astrid instead of Ingegerd. He also said that if he would, they would not ask Olaf Scotking's permission. Astrid told Sighvat that she would like to marry Olaf the Stout and that they should not ask her father's permission. Just before Christmas, Sighvat returned to Olaf the Stout's court and told him what Ragnvald and Astrid had said.

In 1019, Thord Skotakol a nephew of Sighvat went to Ragnvald Jarl with the token of king Olaf the Stout and said that king Olaf would marry

Astrid. Ragnvald selected 120 men and rode with Astrid to Sarpsborg to meet King Olaf the Stout. At Sarpsborg Olaf the Stout and Astrid were married.

In the court of Olaf Scotking, Ingegerd told her father that if she was to marry King Yaroslav, she must have as bride gift the town and Jarldom of Lagoda. She also said that she wanted a man from Sweden to accompany her and that he must receive the same title in Russia as he now had in Sweden. Yaroslav's ambassador agreed to her terms.

Olaf Scotking said, "Who is the man you chose as your attendant?"

Ingegerd replied, "The man I chose is Ragnvald Jarl".

Olaf said, "I have resolved to have Ragnvald hung for giving my daughter to the Fat Man without my permission!"

Ingegerd pleaded long with her father and at last Olaf Scotking agreed to let Ragnvald travel with Ingegerd in peace. Ingegerd sent a message to Ragnvald appointing a meeting place in Gotland. Ragnvald arrived by horseback with a retinue of warriors and Ingegerd met him there. Then Ragnvald bought a ship and they sailed to Russia where Ingegerd married Yaroslav the Wise. Ingegerd gave Ragnvald the town of Lagoda and the Jarldom to go with it.

King Olaf Scotking died in Sweden. His son Jacob Onund became King of all Sweden.

While Olaf the Stout was in the Gaut River, Einar Tambaskjelve approached him with a retinue of men. Einar wanted to make peace with Olaf and Olaf gave Einar some districts in Throndheim.

Erling Skjalgson, who was married to the sister of Olaf Tryggveson, also wanted to make peace with Olaf. Erling's father Skjalg was a great friend of Olaf and met with the King. Olaf the Stout agreed to drop all his complaints against Erling and that Erling be given all the districts he had before.

In 1023, Knud the Great decided that Thorkel the Tall was too dangerous to have as an enemy. He sailed to Denmark to attempt reconciliation. Thorkel met Knud in Denmark where Knud reinstated Thorkel in good standing and made him regent of Denmark. Thorkel and Knud agreed to foster each other's sons. Knud left his and Emma's son Hardeknud with Thorkel and took Thorkel's son back to England.

Einar Tambaskjelve sailed to England and visited his nephew Jarl Haakon Erikson. Then Einar sailed on a pilgrimage to Rome.

In 1024, in Throndheim, Alfhild, the King's slave girl, gave birth to a boy. Olaf the Stout was the father. The priest told Sighvat the skald to wake the King because the boy had to be baptized and he might not survive the night. Sighvat did not want to wake Olaf because he had given strict orders that no one was to wake him. Therefore Sighvat called the boy Magnus and he was baptized.

When Olaf woke and heard what had happened he called Sighvat before him and asked why he was so bold as to have his son baptized without his knowledge. Sighvat replied that he would rather give two men to God than one to the Devil. Olaf asked what he meant and Sighvat said, "The child was near death and would have gone to the devil if he died without baptism, but now it is God's. If you had been so angry that you would kill me, I too would go to God".

Olaf the Stout then asked why he had called him Magnus and Sighvat explained that he had named the boy after Charlemagne (Karl Magnus). At this Olaf was very joyful.

179 KNUD THE GREAT

Knud took his fleet to the Thames River but before he entered the River, Aethelred died. Knud laid siege to London. Edmund Ironsides collected a large army of warriors and attacked the besieging army so hard that Knud's forces were driven back. But Edmund had lost so many warriors in the battle that he had to flee when Knud counter attacked.

Knud suddenly abandoned the siege of London. He took his army to East Anglia and Mercia to gain provisions. Edmund Ironsides came upon them with a large army. The battle went bad for the Danes and they had to flee. Edmund pursued them and killed as many as he could. Eadric Streona changed sides and joined Edmund.

Edmund and Uthred of Northumbria took an army and devastated Staffordshire, Shropshire, and Cheshire. Knud took his army north through Nottingham to York and attacked Uthred. Knud was victorious and Uthred had to surrender. A few days later Uthred was murdered.

Knud regrouped his forces and attacked Edmund Ironsides at Ashingdon. In the fierce battle Erik Jarl met Ulfkell Snelling and Ulfkell fell. Eadric Streona turned and fled with all his warriors. Eadric's flight caused a panic among Edmund's warriors and many fled. Edmund fled to a refuge in Gloucestershire. Knud surrounded the refuge. Both armies were exhausted and negotiations took place. It was agreed that Edmund should have Wessex and Knud the rest of the country. But on November 30, Edmund died and Knud was chosen King of all England.

In England, Knud the Great divided England into four parts. He kept Wessex under his own control. He put Erik Jarl in charge of Northumbria and Thorkel the Tall in charge of East Anglia. Eadric Streona was put in charge of all Mercia. A few months later Knud had Eadric executed. Knud had discovered that Eadric had murdered Edmund Ironsides and that he was not to be trusted.

Knud had a wife whom he had married Viking style. Her name was Aegilfu and he was very devoted to her. Knud also married Emma, Aethelred's widow. This marriage was done Christian style. Knud accepted Christianity and was baptized. He let the English keep their old laws and appointed English people in high places. The Viking raids stopped and Knud rebuilt the churches, which had been laid in ruins by the Vikings. The English loved Knud the Great.

Knud established an army of elite warriors of 3,000 men. The elite warriors were called Thinglid and they had their own laws. Knud was the first to break the law of Thinglid, when he in anger slew one of the Thinglid warriors. The punishment for killing a Thinglid warrior was death. Full of remorse he knelt in front of the warriors and told them to judge him. But the warriors told him that he was King and should judge himself. Knud paid nine times the fine for manslaughter to the dead warrior's family.

Knud passed several laws. Because of the remorse he felt for killing one of his own Thinglid warriors one of the laws he passed made it illegal to be a berserker. He also declared all berserkers outlaws.

When the news of Knud's law regarding berserkers reached Iceland, the Icelanders called an Althing. There they passed laws which made berserkers outlaws and made it illegal to be a berserker.

In the autumn Svend Jarl, who had been plundering in Russia, returned to Sweden where he became sick and died.

In the winter of 1018 A.D., Erik Jarl became sick and died. Knud appointed Haakon Erikson as Jarl of Northumbria.

In the spring Knud paid the Vikings 72,000 pounds of silver to disperse and go home. He also paid them 10,500 pounds to not attack London. The Vikings sailed home except for 40 ships and the Thinglid warriors who stayed with Knud.

King Harald Svendson died. Knud left Thorkel the Tall in charge of England and sailed to Denmark. At the Danish Thing Knud was chosen as King of all Denmark.

Knud the Great spent the next two years establishing his rule in Denmark. Ulf Thorgilsson, whose grandfather was Styrbjorn Staerke, was made Jarl of Jutland. Ulf married Knud's sister Estrid and the English Godwin Jarl married Ulf's sister, Grete.

In 1020, Knud the Great returned to England. Then in 1021, Knud declared Thorkel the Tall an outlaw and Thorkel sailed back to Joms Castle.

In 1022, Knud the Great stationed a large fleet off the Isle of Wight in case Thorkel the Tall decided to make raids in England.

In 1025, Knud sent ambassadors to King Olaf the Stout in Norway. Olaf kept the ambassadors waiting several days. When the ambassadors finally met with the King they gave him the message, "King Knud considers all Norway his property, and insists his forefathers before him have possessed that kingdom. As Knud offers peace to all countries, he also offers peace to all here, if it can be settled, and will not invade Norway with his army if it can be avoided. If King Olaf Haraldson wishes to remain King of Norway, he will go to King Knud, receive his kingdom as a fief from him, become his vassal, and pay the tax which the Jarls before him formerly paid".

King Olaf replied, "It is said that the Dan King Gorm was but a small King of a few people. He ruled over Denmark only. But Kings who succeeded him thought that was too little. Knud rules over Denmark and England and has conquered a great part of Scotland. Now he claims my paternal heritage. Where does his greed end? I will defend Norway with battle axe and sword as long as I live, and will pay tax to no man for my Kingdom".

After the ambassadors sailed home, Olaf sent messengers to King Jacob Onund in Sweden. Olaf's messengers told King Onund the claims that Knud the Great had made on Norway. They added that if Norway fell, Sweden would not be safe. Onund sent the messengers back with the message that King Onund of Sweden wished to ally himself with King Olaf of Norway so that if one were attacked the other would come to his aid. He also called for a meeting of the two Kings.

Aslag and Skjalg, the sons of Erling Skjalgson sailed from Norway to King Knud. They were given fiefs in England.

In the fall, Thorkel the Tall died. King Knud came to Denmark and made Ulf Jarl regent of Denmark. Knud heard that ambassadors had been going back and forth between Norway and Sweden, so he sent messengers to King Onund. The messengers gave Onund great gifts from Knud and told him that peace would prevail between Sweden and Denmark if Sweden would sit out the strife between Olaf and Knud.

In the winter of 1026, King Onund of Sweden rode to West Gotland with 3600 warriors. There he waited to meet King Olaf. The two Kings had decided to meet when they knew what Knud was up to. Knud stayed in Denmark all summer and in the fall sailed back to England. Then Onund and Olaf met at Kongshelle.

Olaf the Stout sent messengers to Iceland demanding that Iceland pay him tax during the next year. He also sent the message that he would invade Iceland the year after if the tax was not paid.

Erling Skjalgson sailed with 5 ships to England.

In 1027, Olaf the Stout raised a levy over all Norway and put together an army. Einar Tambaskjelve did not heed the levy and stayed quietly at home.

Olaf the Stout sailed a large fleet south to Denmark and attacked Zealand. At the same time, King Onund of Sweden attacked Skaane. The Zealanders and Skaanians fled without opposing the invading armies. Olaf and Onund laid waste the land they moved through. The two Kings met and joined their forces on Zealand. Then they announced that they would conquer Denmark.

When Ulf Jarl heard that King Olaf and King Onund were raiding in Denmark, Ulf declared Hardeknud Knudson King of Denmark. Then Ulf and Hardeknud raised a large army in Jutland and assembled a fleet of ships in the Lim Fjord. They thought that they were not strong enough to go against the combined armies of Swedes and Norwegians so they waited for Knud to come.

In England, King Knud heard that Denmark was attacked. He gathered an army and prepared a very large fleet of long ships. Knud had a very large dragon ship with 60 benches of rowers. Haakon Jarl was second in command. His dragon ship had a gilt dragonhead on the bow. Knud made Godwin Jarl regent in England while he was away. Then the fleet sailed towards Denmark.

Sighvat sang of it:

> "Knud is out beneath the sky --
>
> Knud of the clear blue eye!
>
> The king is out on the ocean's breast,
>
> Leading his grand fleet from the West.
>
> On to the East the ship-masts glide,
>
> Glancing and bright each long-ship's side.
>
> The conqueror of great Aethelred,
>
> Knud, is there, his foemen's dread:
>
> His dragon with her sails of blue,
>
> All bright and brilliant to the view,
>
> High hoisted on the yard arms wide,
>
> Carries great Knud o'er the tide.
>
> Brave is the royal progress -- fast
>
> The proud ship's keel obeys the mast,
>
> Dashes through foam, and gains the land,
>
> Raising a surge on Lim Fjord's strand."

When Knud the Great reached Denmark he brought his fleet into the Lim Fjord. Since Ulf had declared Hardeknud King without Knud's permission, he sent a message to Queen Emma and asked if Knud was angry over Hardeknud becoming King. Emma sent a message back to her son Hardeknud which said that if Hardeknud had no say in himself becoming King and had not gone against his father, then things might be all right. The Danish warriors flocked to Knud and showed that they had confidence in Knud and none in Hardeknud. Ulf told Hardeknud that he had only two choices. He could either flee the country with Ulf or they could both go to Knud and throw themselves at his mercy. Hardeknud went to his father, knelt before him and renounced his title as King of Denmark. Ulf sent his son Svend to Knud and begged forgiveness. Knud told Svend to tell Ulf that they had a war to fight.

When Olaf and Onund heard that Knud had a large fleet in the Lim Fjord they crossed over to Skaane and ravaged and burned in the districts. Then they sailed east to the Helga River. Olaf went up River and made a Dam at Helga Lake. Onund kept their fleet of 410 ships at the river mouth.

One evening Onund saw Knud's fleet of 620 ships approaching the Helga River. Onund had the war horns sound, had his ships tied together, pulled them away from the harbour, and sent a messenger to Olaf that Knud had arrived. Olaf broke the dam and traveled down to his ships.

When Olaf pulled the Norwegian and Swedish fleet out of the harbour and sailed east, Knud thought that it was too late in the day to begin a battle so he pulled his fleet into the mouth of the Helga River. In the morning many of Knud's men were ashore when the rush of water from the broken dam burst upon them. The torrent uprooted trees and crushed ships together causing great damage and many men perished. The warriors cut the cables on as many ships as they could and these ships were carried out of the river mouth by the rushing water.

Knud's great dragon ship was carried out among the ships of Onund and Olaf. The Norwegian and Swedish ships pressed against Knud's ship and there was a fierce battle. Knud's ship was larger than the ships of his foes, had a height advantage, and was manned by fierce Thinglid warriors. Gradually the Danish ships came sailing from all sides to assist Knud. But the Swedes and Norwegians were winning. After a short time Ulf Jarl came sailing in with a great fleet of Jutes and Joms Vikings and instantly began battling the Swedes and Norwegians who fled.

Ottar Svarte sang of it:

> "The King, in battle fray,
>
> Drove the Swedish host away:
>
> The wolf did not miss prey,
>
> Nor the raven on that day.
>
> Great Knud might deride
>
> Two kings if he had pride,
>
> For at Helga river's side
>
> They would not his sword abide."

Onund and Olaf set sail and went to Sweden and held a council of war. They had lost over 200 ships in the battle. They decided that Knud could not keep such a large army together for very long and that they should wait in Sweden until it dispersed.

Knud brought his fleet into Ore sound where it stayed until the fall. Knud went to Roskilde where Ulf Jarl prepared a great feast for him. At the feast, Knud played a game of chess with Ulf. Knud made a bad move and Ulf took his knight. Then Knud took his move back and told Ulf to make another move. But Ulf became angry and threw the board and pieces on the floor and left. Knud yelled after him, "Are you fleeing now, you scared wolf (redde ulv)?"

Ulf paused in the doorway, turned and replied, "You would have fled at Helga River if you could. That time you did not call me Scared Wolf, when I came to your aid because the Swedes beat you like dogs".

The next morning Knud commanded his footboy to go and kill Ulf. The footboy went out. When he came back Knud asked him if he had killed Ulf. The footboy replied, "No. I did not kill him because he was at prayer in Saint Lucius' Church".

Then King Knud the Great ordered Ivar the White to go to the church and kill the Jarl.

Ivar walked into the church and thrust his sword through Ulf Jarl who died instantly.

In the autumn Erling Skjalgson and his sons left Knud's army and sailed north to Norway. In Normandy, Duke Richard the Good died and his son Robert the Devil succeeded him.

In the winter of 1028, Olaf the Stout went over land to his home in Norway. Olaf discovered that Thorer, a step son of Kalf Arneson had been in Knud's army and had him seized. Kalf went and pleaded with Olaf for Thorer but Olaf had Thorer executed. Kalf was heartbroken and Thorer had many friends in Throndheim and in the Uplands.

Knud spent the winter gathering warriors and ships. By spring time there were 1200 ships in Ore Sound. Then he sailed the fleet to the Lim Fjord where he collected more ships and warriors. The fleet sailed to Agder where Knud called a Thing where he was proclaimed King. As Knud sailed north along the coast people came and proclaimed him King. Knud brought his fleet into Eger Sound and stayed there a few days. While he was there Erling Skjalgson came with many warriors and joined him. Knud proceeded to Throndheim and landed at Nidaros.

Knud called a Thing and Knud was proclaimed king of all Norway. At the Thing Knud made Haakon Jarl regent of all Norway and he proclaimed Einar Tambaskjelve and Erling Skjalgson as Jarls with large districts. Then he proclaimed his son Hardeknud King of all Denmark. He also passed a law making it illegal to be a berserker in Norway. All berserkers were declared outlaws.

Olaf the Stout waited in the Oslo Fjord until Knud had sailed back to Denmark. It was the beginning of winter and Olaf sailed a fleet of 13 ships north along the coast of Norway. He perceived that Norway had fallen away from him because he could get no one to follow him as he went. When he sailed past Jadar, Erling saw him go by, called his warriors together and launched his ships.

Erling's ships were faster than Olaf's because they had nothing on board except warriors. Olaf saw that Erling's ships greatly outnumbered his. But Erling's ships were of many different types and had different speeds in the wind while Olaf's long ships stayed together. Erling's ship was faster than all the others. Soon Erling's fleet was strung out.

Olaf had his sails gently lowered as he steered into Bokn Fjord where his ships came out of sight. Olaf ordered the sails struck and rowed his fleet behind a rocky point where they waited. Erling sailed his ship into the fjord and saw nothing until he rounded the rocky point. Then suddenly Olaf's ships had surrounded him. Erling's men began to fall right away and his ship was boarded. Erling's warriors died in their place and only Erling was left fighting on the quarterdeck. Olaf yelled to Erling, "You have turned against me today, Erling".

Erling replied, "The eagle turns its claws in defense when torn asunder".

"Will you enter my service?" asked Olaf.

"That I will", replied Erling.

Then Erling took off his helmet and laid down his sword and shield. He went to Olaf on the forecastle deck. King Olaf struck Erling on the chin with the sharp point of his axe and said, "I shall mark you as a traitor to your sovereign".

Then Aslak Fitiaskalle hit Erling on the head with his axe so that it split his skull and Erling fell dead. Olaf said to Aslak, "May bad luck be with you for that stroke. You have just knocked Norway out of my hands".

Sighvat sang of the battle:

> **"Erling has set his ship on sea --**
>
> **Against the king away is he:**
>
> **He who often lets the eagle stain**
>
> **Her yellow feet in blood of slain.**
>
> **His little war-ship side by side**
>
> **With the king's fleet, the fray will bide.**
>
> **Now sword to sword the fight is raging,**
>
> **Which Erling with the king is waging.**

The Saga Kings

The king's men hewed with hasty sword, --

The king urged on the ship to board, --

All o'er the decks the wounded lay:

Right fierce and bloody was that fray.

In Tungur sound, on Jadar shore,

The decks were slippery with red gore;

Warm blood was dropping in the sound,

Where the king's sword was gleaming round.

All Erling's men fell in the fray,

Off Bokn fjord, this hard-fought day.

The brave king boarded, onward cheered,

And north of Tungur the deck was cleared.

Erling alone, the brave, the stout,

Cut off from all, yet still held out;

High on the stern -- a sight to see --

In his lone ship alone stood he.

Skjalg's brave son no mercy craves, --

The battle's fury still he braves;

The spear-storm, through the air sharp singing,

Against his shield was ever ringing.

So Erling stood; but fate had willed

His life off Bokn should be spilled.

No braver man has, since his day,

Past Bokn fjord ta'en his way.

Erling, our best defense of old, --

Erling the brave, the brisk, the bold, --

Stood to his arms, gaily crying,

`Eagles should show their claws, though dying:'

The very words which once before

To Olaf he had said on shore,

At Utstein when they both prepared

To meet the foe, and danger shared.

Thus Erling fell -- and such a gain

To buy with such a loss was vain;

For better man than he ne'er died,

And the king's gain was small beside.

In truth no man I ever knew

Was, in all ways, so firm and true;

Free from servility and pride,

Honoured by all, yet thus he died."

Erling's sons heard of Erling's death and began to collect an army to go against Olaf. Olaf sailed north along the coast until he came north of Stad. Then he learned that Haakon had a great army in Throndheim. Olaf went into Steinavag and stayed there over night but Aslak went to Borgund. In the morning as Aslak was about to board his ship, Vigleig Arneson attacked him to avenge Erling and Aslak fell.

Olaf's men saw a great fleet approach from the north. Olaf had the war horns sound and launched his 12 ships. He sailed south to Valdal where he landed. Olaf traveled over land on foot with his warriors to Sweden. There he left his wife Astrid and his daughter Ulfhild. Then he traveled with his son Magnus to King Yaroslav and Queen Ingegerd in Russia.

In the winter, Einar Tambaskjelve and his followers went to King Olaf Scotking in Sweden and stayed there.

In 1029, Ulf Jarl's widow Estrid married Duke Robert the Devil of Normandy.

Knud the Great loved to be praised. Many of his followers became in the habit of saying, "Knud the rich and mighty rules both the land and the sea".

One day Knud had his chair placed on the beach close to the water. He commanded the waves to not touch him. But the incoming tide brought the waves closer and they ran in over the mighty King's feet. Knud stood up and exclaimed, "This shall all know, that only God the Almighty rules over the waters, but the might of kings is frailty!"

From that day on Knud no longer wore his crown. He placed it on the church altar in front of the image of the Crucified Christ.

In 1030, Einar Tambaskjelve sailed to England and met with King Knud. He asked Knud for the highest title in Norway now that Haakon was gone. But Knud replied that he intended for his son Svend to be the ruler in Norway. Svend was the son of Knud and his mistress Aegilfu.

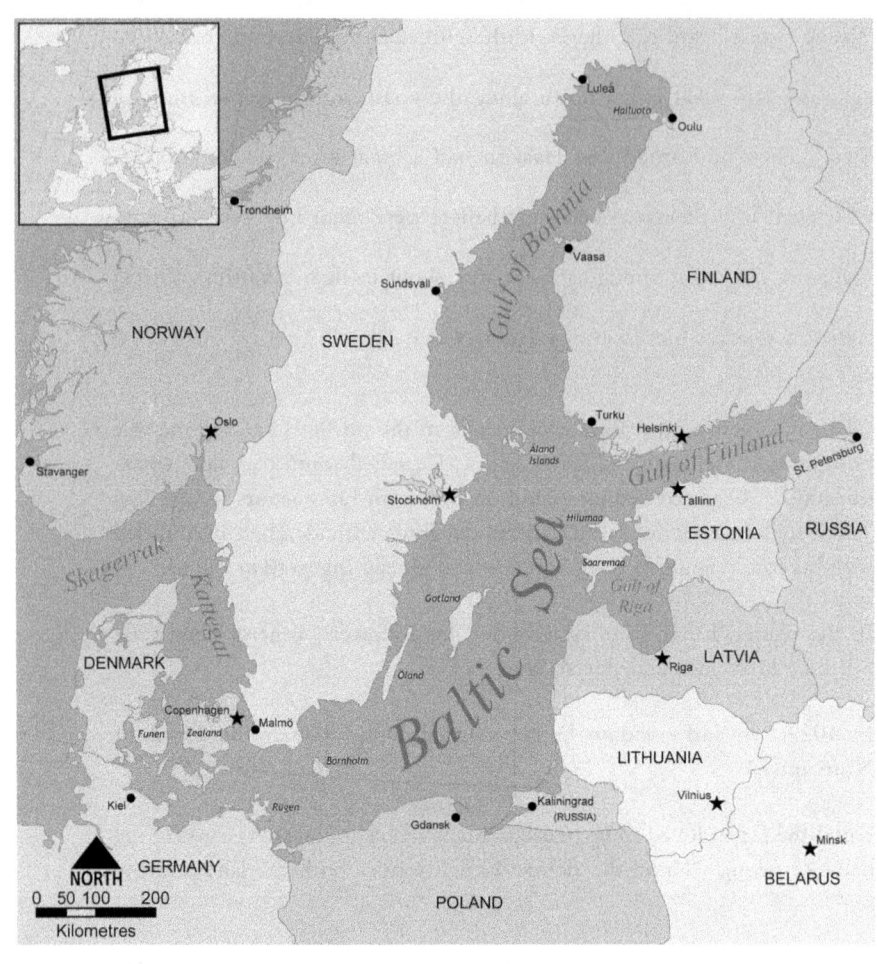

180 THE KINGS OF DUBLIN

Olaf the White's brother, Ivar became involved in many battles, sometimes against the Irish and sometimes the Danes under Halfdan Lodbrokson from York. Finally in 901, the Irish took Dublin. The Norwegians came back and defeated the Irish in the battle of Confey in 916 and again in the battle of Climashogue in 919. These battles secured a large area of Ireland for the Norwegian Vikings. The descendants of Ivar ruled this area for more than half a century. The King of Dublin, Sigtryg married the daughter of Duncan, King of Scotland. Their son was Olaf Kvaran (Olaf Sandal) and he inherited the Kingdom of Dublin after his father. Olaf married Gormflaith, the daughter of King Murchad mac Finn of Leinster. Her first husband was the King of Meath and High King of Ireland, Mael Sechnaill. Olaf and Gormflaith had a son and called him Sigtryg. Eventually Sigtryg became known as Sigtryg Silkenbeard.

The High King of Ireland, Mael Sechnaill gathered an army and went against the Norwegians in Ireland. The Norwegians suffered a great defeat at the battle of Tara in 980. The Irish enjoyed the wealth produced by the great trade centers but had no wish to run the trading towns. Therefore they let the Vikings stay in control of these harbour towns and had them pay tribute to the Irish Kings.

The next year Olaf Kvaran retired and became a monk in the abbey of Iona where he eventually died. When his father retired, Sigtryg Silkenbeard became King of Dublin. At this time there were years of peace in Dublin and Sigtryg's warriors fought in the army of Brian Boru

181 BRIAN BORU

The King of Leinster was overthrown in 998 and replaced by Mael Morda mac Murchada. He raised an army to go against Brian. When Brian discovered what the King of Leinster was doing. He prepared to lay a siege on Dublin which was ruled by Mael Morda's ally Sigtryg Silkenbeard. Mael Morda and Sigtryg decided to meet Brian in battle rather than face a siege.

The battle was fought at Glen Mama in the year 999. The fighting lasted from morning till midnight and many warriors fell. Brian was victorious and sacked Dublin. Then Brian sought reconciliation. Sigtryg was given Brian's daughter Slaine in marriage and was reinstated as King of Dublin. To further the reconciliation, Brian married Mael Morda's sister, Gormflaith, former wife of Mael Sechnaill and also Sigtryg's mother.

In the year 1000, Brian attacked Mael Sechnaill, the High King of Ireland with warriors from Munster, Leinster, and Dublin. The result was that Mael Sechnaill surrendered his title to Brian in 1002.

In 1012, Mael Morda, King of Leinster, rebelled against Brian Boru. Brian divorced Gormflaith and she went to live with her brother, Mael Morda. In 1014, both Mael Morda and Brian collected a huge army to put an end to the strife. Brian's army included Vikings led by Ospak, warriors from Munster, Southern Connacht and the province of Meath whose commander was Mael Sechnaill mac Domnaill. This army arrived at Dublin the week before Palm Sunday. On Palm Sunday, Mael Morda arrived with an army and was joined by Brodir of the Isle of Man and the Jarl of the Orkneys, Sigurd Dige (Sigurd the Stout).

On Good Friday, April 23, Morda arrayed his army and prepared for battle. Brian Boru marched his army out of Dublin and went to meet the opposing army. Sigtryg kept his warriors in reserve in Dublin and watched the events unfold from the ramparts of Dublin's walls. A shield wall was formed around Brian and his army was arrayed in front of it. Brian's forces advanced and the two armies clashed at Clontarf a short distance north of Dublin. The fighting was ferocious. Brodir fought his way through the opposing ranks killing anyone near him until he faced Ulf Hreda. Ulf knocked Brodir down three times. The third time, Brodir fled into the nearby woods.

Kerthjalfad cut down all those in front of him until he reached Sigurd Jarl and cut down Sigurd's standard bearer. When a new standard bearer took up the standard, the fighting broke out again. Kerthjalfad quickly killed the new standard bearer. And all those who were near him. Nobody else dared to pick up the standard so Sigurd picked up the standard himself. A short while later Sigurd died with a spear through his body.

All of Mael Morda's warriors took flight. During the flight Thorstein Hallson stopped and retied the laces of his shoes. Kerthjalfad came up to him and asked him why he was not running. Thorstein replied that he was not running because he could not reach home that night because it was out in Iceland. Kerthjalfad spared his life.

When Brodir saw that the warriors of Mael Morda were fleeing and were being pursued by Brian's warriors, he ran from the woods and charged at the shield wall. After penetrating the shield wall, he killed Brian. Messengers chased the pursuing forces to tell the news. Kerthjalfad and Ulf Hreda turned back and caught Brodir. They slit open his belly and tied his intestines to a tree. Then they forcer him to walk around the tree until all his intestines were out of his body.

Brian Boru was buried in the grounds of St. Patrick's Cathedral in the city of Armagh.

182 SIGTRYG SILKENBEARD

After the battle of Clontarf, Sigtryg was still King of Dublin. Mael Sechnaill became the High King again. In 1015, there was a plague in Dublin and Leinster. Mael Sechnaill attacked and burned the suburbs of Dublin. Sigtryg then made an alliance with Leinster and made an attack on Meath in 1017.

In 1018, Sigtryg plundered Kells. When Sigtryg went south in 1021 for a raid, the King of Leinster, Augaire mac Dunlainge went against him. Sigtryg lost the battle and many of his warriors fell.

Mael Sechnaill died in 1022. The great Irish leaders made war on each other in an attempt to be recognized as High King. They all wanted Dublin because the income from Dublin could finance their wars. In 1025, Sigtryg was forced to give hostages to the King of Cenel Neogain and the Ui Neil. In 1026, he was forced to give hostages again. This time to Donnchad mac Brian.

Sigtryg's son Olaf joined Donnchad of Brega in a raid on Staholmock, County Meath. Sigtryg and Donnchad's army was defeated by the men of Meath under King Roen Ua Mael Sechlainn.

Sigtryg retaliated and at the battle at Lickblaw, Donnchad and Roen were slain.

In 1029, Sigtryg's son Olaf was taken prisoner by the new lord of Brega, Mathghhain Un Riagain. Sigtryg was forced to pay a huge ransom.

In 1030, Sigtryg made an alliance with the King of England, Knud the Great. Knud and Sigtryg raided Wales with their fleets and established a Dublin colony in Gwynedd. In 1032 Sigtryg took his army into the Boyne estuary. There he battled a coalition of three kingdoms at Inbher Boinne and was victorious over the Conaille, the Ui Tortain, and the Ui Meith.

Echmarcach mac Ragnaill, Lord of the Isles, forced Sigtryg to abdicate in 1036. He went to Iona and became a monk. He died there in 1042.

183 SAINT OLAF

In the summer of 1029, Haakon Jarl sailed to England to fetch his English betrothed. He intended to have the wedding in Norway. Haakon left England in the fall. His ship was last seen north of Caithness in a heavy storm. The ship was lost and Haakon was never seen again.

In Russia Olaf the Stout heard that Haakon Jarl was missing at sea. This left Norway without a ruler and Olaf thought he had a good chance of winning back Norway. Leaving his son with King Yaroslav and Ingegerd, he journeyed to Sweden with 200 warriors. When Kalf Arneson heard that Olaf was in Sweden, he sent out a war arrow calling the farmers to defend Norway against Olaf.

King Onund did not dare make another alliance with Olaf but he gave Olaf 500 warriors from his army and permitted him to invite others in Sweden to join him. Olaf collected men from Sweden, outcasts and men on the fringes of society. Dag Ringson Jarl in Vermeland, Sweden came to Olaf with 1400 warriors. Then Harald Sigurdson, Olaf's 15-year-old half-brother arrived with 700 warriors.

Olaf's plan was to strike down all opposition in one battle. This was his only chance to win Norway again because he could not keep this large force together in a prolonged war. He wanted to find the main force of his enemies. He knew that Norway was strongest in Throndheim. Therefore he invaded that district.

Meanwhile, Svend Knudson and his mother Aegilfu sailed from Joms Castle with a large fleet of Joms Vikings and set a course for Norway

On July 29 at Stiklestad, the forces of the Norwegian farmers under Kalf Arneson clashed with Olaf's army very early in the morning. The leaders under Kalf were Thorer Hound and Horek.

Olaf woke early and asked Thormod the bard to sing a song to wake his warriors. Thormod sang the old Bjarkemaal:

Sun is up, topping the forest

Shining all like Gimle's roof

Message it brings, rooster wings,

Rooster crows as day breaks

Wake, wake, Danish heroes!

Jump up and buckle belts!

Day and deed is warrior verse,

Day and deed is warrior verse!

Loud it resounds, flames are calling

Warriors up at morning snap,

Posts creak, flames blaze,

Blazing over green grove.

Wake! Not to the high's speech,

Vine and smile in King's hall!

Hildur's play is now at hand,

Hildur's play is now at hand.

Wake! Plays castles arches

In the red bow shots!

Blaze resounds, Leire falls

Under Skuld's victory song

Hjarvard fire in forest ignites,

Leaves fade, beech trees burn,

Wake must even Dan and Skjold,

Wake must even Dan and Skjold!

The Saga Kings

Up now fight for Rolf Krake

Boldly lifting shield and sword!

For fire he does not dread

But for sight of small works

Ring with luster and sword with edge

Generously he gave with both hands,

Who dares form a ring about him?

Who dares form a ring about him!

In his home, comfortable and peaceful,

Slept so sweet that hero so bold,

Swedish flames he does not flee

With his wide Dane shield.

But ack! Though he stands on embers,

Magic sword and treachery he meets,

Who dares hold shield for him?

Who dares hold shield for him!

The one who called! Hjalte dares,

Zealand's farmer boy dares,

Bjarke dares, into the field

Even if the Fenris wolf itself was lose,

Lust has he with the heart of a lion

To reach Odin himself to slay,

Bodvar Bjarke strikes with his might,

Bodvar Bjarke strikes with his might!

Rolf pales, Bjarke falls,

Hjalte swims in his own blood,

Lejre's arches are in flames

Fallen down at Hjarvard's foot

The field can he not keep,

Before the embers are cold

Slays he the last spark,

Slays he the last spark!

Sun is up, topping the forest

Shining all like Gimle's roof

Message it brings, rooster wings,

Rooster crows as day breaks

Wake, wake, Danish heroes!

Jump up and buckle belts!

Daybreak has gold in mouth,

Daybreak has gold in mouth!

Olaf's warriors rose and many of them went to Thormod and thanked him for his rousing song. Then they went into battle formation. Olaf had some warriors form a shield wall, which was to go in the front of his army. Inside the shield wall he placed himself and his skalds. Kalf attacked with his warriors before Olaf was ready. Dag Ringson had not yet reached his place in Olaf's formation so the right flank was very weak. But Olaf led the battle and went violently forward trying for a quick decisive strike. The Swedes of Olaf's left flank broke rank and fled. Then Olaf's shield wall came to a halt against the mass of Norwegian warriors. Thorer Hound broke through the shield wall. He was dressed in a reindeer pelt, which was stronger than chain mail. Olaf struck Thorer's shoulder with no effect. Bjorn Staller also struck Thorer with no effect. Then Thorer cut down both Bjorn and Olaf.

Just as Olaf fell, Dag Ringson arrived with his warriors and put new vigor into the battle. The Norwegians turned their main force on Dag and he had to flee. As Dag's men fled the Norwegians pursued and Dag fell in flight. Harald Sigurdson was severely wounded but escaped with the help of Ragnvald Bruceson.

Svend and Aegilfu had been sailing north along the coast of Norway during the battle of Stiklestad. They arrived in Throndheim and at a Thing Svend Knudson was proclaimed King of all Norway.

On August 31, there was an eclipse of the sun, which was visible from Stiklestad. The people in Norway who had not fought against Olaf said it was a sign from God that he was displeased over Olaf's death.

The fugitives who survived the battle of Stiklestad went to Sweden. There Harald and Ragnvald spent the winter.

Thorer Hound made a pilgrimage to Jerusalem. He never came back.

Einar Tambaskjelve returned from England and was pleased that he had not been in battle at Stiklestad. Kalf Arneson's brother Fin was angry at Kalf for going against Olaf at Stiklestad where members of the same villages and districts had fought against one another and there were hard feelings. Kalf attempted to be reconciled with his brothers and many messages were sent among Kalf, Fin, Thorberg, and Arne.

After Olaf's death, the Norwegians spread stories of miracles being performed by Olaf. This strengthened Christianity in Norway. In 1031, Archbishop Eystein encouraged by Einar made petitions to the Pope and Olaf the Stout was proclaimed a Saint. Olaf the Stout had become Norway's Patron Saint and was now called "Olaf the Holy" or "Saint Olaf".

Harald and Ragnvald obtained ships and sailed to King Yaroslav in

Novgorod. Yaroslav received them well and made Harald and Ragnvald's son Ellif chiefs in his army. Harald spent several years in Russia fighting border wars for Yaroslav.

In England, Knud the Great went to Glastonbury to pay his respects to Edmund Ironsides who was buried there. He called Edmund, "my brother" and draped the tomb with a magnificent pall embroidered with peacocks.

184 TRYGGVE OLAFSON

In the spring of 1033, King Svend Knudson of Norway heard that Tryggve, the son of Olaf Tryggveson by his English wife Gyda, was assembling a force in the British Isles. He ordered a levy in the north and many men came to him. But Einar Tambaskjelve and Kalf Arneson both stayed at home. Svend sent a message to Kalf to join him. But Kalf sent a message back saying that he no longer wanted to fight his own countrymen. Having sworn allegiance to Svend, Einar and Kalf could not assist Tryggve, but none of the Arneson brothers joined in Svend's army.

Appearing on the ocean from the west, Tryggve's fleet sailed in to Hordaland where he landed. As soon as Svend heard that Tryggve had arrived, he brought his fleet towards him and Tryggve sailed to meet Svend. The two fleets met at Bokn in Soknar Sound close to where Erling fell. The battle was fierce and Tryggve threw spears with both hands. But Tryggve fell with many of his men. Svend gave Tryggve's surviving warriors quarter and their lives.

Sighvat sang of the battle:

> "**From the south towards the battle sailed**
>
> **Trygve forth for honour to seek.**
>
> **Svend from the north against him steered;**
>
> **Battle there was from this meeting.**
>
> **Wild and hastily grew the fighting;**
>
> **Close was I to the battle's din.**
>
> **Warriors had to lose their lives;**
>
> **Sword clang sounded over the waves."**

The Norwegians wanted a Norwegian King. The fall of Tryggve Olafson made a great impression on them. Einar Tambaskjelve and Kalf Arneson held Things in Throndheim and it was determined that Magnus Olafson should be asked to come and be their King.

185 MAGNUS THE GOOD

In 1034, Einar and Kalf journeyed to Novgorod and petitioned King Yaroslav to take the 10 year old Magnus back to Norway with them and train him to be King. It was agreed that Kalf and all the men who had fought against Saint Olaf would be bound by oath to Magnus. It was also agreed that Kalf was to be the foster father of Magnus. An oath was taken by Magnus to not seek revenge for his father's death, to secure full peace, make reconciliation, and be faithful to all the people of Norway.

Robert the Devil, the Duke of Normandy named his seven year old son William as his heir and then made a pilgrimage to Palestine. He died on the way home. William was the son of Robert's mistress, Arletta, and was called William the Bastard.

In the spring of 1035, Einar, Kalf, and Magnus sailed to Sweden. In Sweden, Magnus gathered a great force. Then he went over land through Helsingland and Jamtland and arrived in Throndheim. The Danes and followers of Svend fled to the south to join King Svend in South Hordaland. A Thing was held in Throndheim and Magnus was proclaimed King of all Norway.

When Svend's followers arrived from Throndheim, King Svend called a Thing to organize warriors against Magnus. At the Thing the farmers told Svend that they refused to fight against Magnus and would join him as soon as they got the opportunity. Svend, King of all Norway then went to the Vik and called a Thing. But nobody showed up. Svend, realizing that he had lost Norway sailed to his brother Hardeknud in Denmark and asked for help. Hardeknud gave Svend half his Kingdom.

War raged between Norway and Denmark. Magnus and his army raided the coasts of Denmark. Hardeknud and his army raided the coasts of Norway. But the two armies never met in open confrontation.

In England Knud the Great became sick and died. He was buried at Winchester. The arrangement was that Emma's son Hardeknud was to succeed Knud as King of England, but Hardeknud was too busy with the war against Norway to come to England to be crowned. Harald son of Knud and Aegilfu was made regent in England until Hardeknud could come. Emma kept all the King's treasure.

But Aegilfu wanted her son to be King. She got support for Harald and managed to get the powerful Jarl Godwin on her side. Alfred the Aetheling was a son of King Aethelred. Godwin sent a letter to Alfred in Normandy inviting him to England. When Alfred arrived, Harald had him captured and blinded. He died from infection in his eyes.

Harald Sigurdson left King Yaroslav and went south to Constantinople and became chief of the Emperors bodyguards, the Varangians (Vikings).

In the winter of 1036, Svend Knudson became sick and died.

In the spring, both Hardeknud and Magnus levied men for their armies and arranged to meet at the Gaut River to battle. When the armies met, the advisors of the Kings sent messengers to each other with peace proposals. A truce was called and negotiations proceeded. It was agreed that the two Kings be friends and that Hardeknud should have all of Denmark and Magnus should have all of Norway. It was also agreed that whoever outlived the other would have both Kingdoms if there were no male heirs, and that there would be peace between the two countries as long as both Kings remained alive.

In 1037, Hardeknud's half-brother, Harald Harefoot was recognized as King of England. The English treasure was seized from Emma who fled to Flanders where she stayed with Count Baldwin.

In 1038, Hardeknud took 10 ships and sailed to Flanders to meet with his mother who advised him to be patient because Harald was very sick. Svend, son of Ulf Jarl and Knud's sister Estrid, was left in charge of Denmark as a regent.

Magnus heard more and more about the raising of an army against his father, Saint Olaf by the farmers of Throndheim, and how he died at Stiklestad. He became depressed and bitter.

In 1039, Horek sailed to Nidaros with a petition to King Magnus. When Horek landed and disembarked from his ships, King Magnus and Asmund were standing watching the dock. Asmund recognized Horek and said to King Magnus, "Now I will repay Horek for the murder of my father".

Asmund was holding a small hatchet with a thin blade. Magnus handed Asmund his battle-axe and said, "Your axe is too small. Take mine. There are hard bones in the old man".

Asmund took Magnus's axe, walked down to where Horek was approaching with his retinue, and struck Horek on the head so that the axe penetrated the skull. Horek fell dead. Asmund walked back to the King and returned the axe, which had a turned edge from the blow. Magnus said, "What would your axe have done? Even this one is spoiled".

The farmer, Thorgeir Flek came to the court of King Magnus on business. While Thorgeir made his petition, Magnus pretended that he was not there and made small talk with his courtiers. Then Thorgeir raised his voice in frustration and said so loud that every one could hear (according to Sturlasson):

> "Listen, my lord, to my plain word.
>
> I too was there, and had to bear
>
> A bloody head from Stiklestad:
>
> For I was then with Olaf's men.
>
> Listen to me: well did I see
>
> The men you are trusting the dead corpse thrusting
>
> Out of their way, as dead it lay,
>
> And striking o'er your father's gore."

This caused uproar and some of the courtiers started to evict Thorgeir. But the King called Thorgeir to him and dispatched his business to Thorgeir's satisfaction. Then Magnus promised Thorgeir friendship and favours.

At a feast in Veradal, Einar sat on one side of Magnus and Kalf Arneson sat on the other side. Magnus paid little attention to Kalf. Magnus said to Einar, "Let's ride to Stiklestad. I should like to see the memorials of the events which took place there".

Einar replied, "I can tell you nothing about it. Take your foster father Kalf. He can give you the information about what took place".

Kalf refused to go but Magnus said that he must. Kalf found his servant and gave him instructions to ride home fast and have all his property loaded on his ship before sunset. Then Kalf rode to Stiklestad with Magnus and they dismounted. Magnus asked, "Where is the spot where King Olaf fell?"

Kalf pointed with his spear and said, "There, he lay where he fell".

The King said, "And where were you Kalf?"

Kalf replied, "Here where I now stand".

Magnus exclaimed, "Then your axe could have reached him!"

Kalf said, "My axe did not come near him".

Kalf jumped on his horse and rode straight home. He immediately boarded his ship and cast off He sailed down the Fjord by night and then west. Kalf Arneson spent many years plundering in Ireland, Scotland, and the Hebrides.

Magnus confiscated the property of the farmers who had fallen at Stiklestad. He laid heavy fines on the men who had offered the greatest resistance to Olaf, and drove some of them out of the country. The farmers became upset over the treatment they received from Magnus. In Sogn the farmers gathered an army to go against Magnus if he ever came into the Fjord district.

Magnus was in Hordaland with a large retinue. He decided to go to Sogn. The twelve advisors of the King had a meeting and cast lots to see who would have to tell the King about the farmers. Sighvat lost and went to King Magnus. Sighvat told Magnus about the discontent of the farmers. He also told Magnus that he had broken the oaths he made in Novgorod to not seek revenge for his father's death, to secure full peace, make reconciliation, and be faithful to all the people of Norway. Sighvat exhorted Magnus to observe the laws which his father Olaf the Holy had established.

Sighvat's presentation had a great effect on Magnus. Ever after he sought to rule for the good of the people of Norway. He made new laws and had it recorded in writing. The book was kept in Throndheim and is called "The Grey Goose". The paper it was written on was grey.

The laws established in the Grey Goose were farther advanced in justice than any other set of laws at the time and dealt with subjects which were not in any other code of law in Europe at that time. Subjects dealt with included provisions for the poor, equality of weights and measures, policing of markets and sea ports, provisions for illegitimate children of the poor, inns for travelers, wages for servants, and support for the sick, protection for pregnant women, prevention of cruelty to domestic animals, roads, bridges, vagrants, and beggars. After establishing these laws, Magnus became very popular and became known as King Magnus the Good

On March 17, 1040, Harald Harefoot died of his sickness. Three months later Hardeknud arrived in England with 60 long ships and was proclaimed King. He was reconciled with Jarl Godwin for Godwin's part in the murder of Alfred the Aetheling. Then he had the body of Harald Harefoot dug up and thrown into the Thames River.

In 1042, while King Hardeknud of England was standing and taking a drink, he suddenly fell to the ground with convulsions. He had been poisoned. He did not recover and died on June 8. He was buried at Winchester next to his father. The English held a Thing and chose Edward, a son of Aethelred and Emma, as their King. Edward was a pious man and became known as King Edward the Confessor. Edward married Edith, the daughter of Godwin Jarl.

Hardeknud had no male heir; therefore Magnus was now to be King of Denmark. The only male left of Skjoldung lineage was Svend Ulfson through his mother's side. Magnus sailed to Denmark with a large fleet and held a Thing at Viborg in Jutland where he was proclaimed King of Denmark. When Svend Ulfson heard that Magnus was in Viborg and had been chosen King he sent word to Magnus calling for a meeting. They met at the mouth of the Gaut River. Magnus appointed Svend as Jarl of Jutland and regent and protector of Denmark. Einar Tambaskjelve said to Magnus, "Too great a jarl, too great a jarl foster son!"

The Joms Vikings refused to accept Magnus as their King. Ordulf, son of Duke Bernhard of Saxony was the brother in law of Magnus. He murdered the Jarl of the Joms Vikings, Harald the son of Thorkel the Tall.

When Svend heard of the death of Harald Thorkelsen he went to Viborg where he changed his name from Svend Ulfsen to Svend Estridsen aligning his name with the Danish royal lineage through his mother's name, Estrid, the sister of Knud the Great. Svend was very popular in Denmark. The people recalled the Viborg Thing and chose Svend Estridsen as King of all Denmark.

When Magnus heard that Svend had been acclaimed King of Denmark, he brought his great fleet back to Viborg, but Svend had sailed to Sweden where he took refuge with King Onund. On his father's side Svend was related to the Swedish royal family and had relatives throughout Skaane and Gotland. Svend was the great grandson of Styrbjorn Staerke. Svend went through Skaane and Gotland and was acclaimed King of Denmark in both districts.

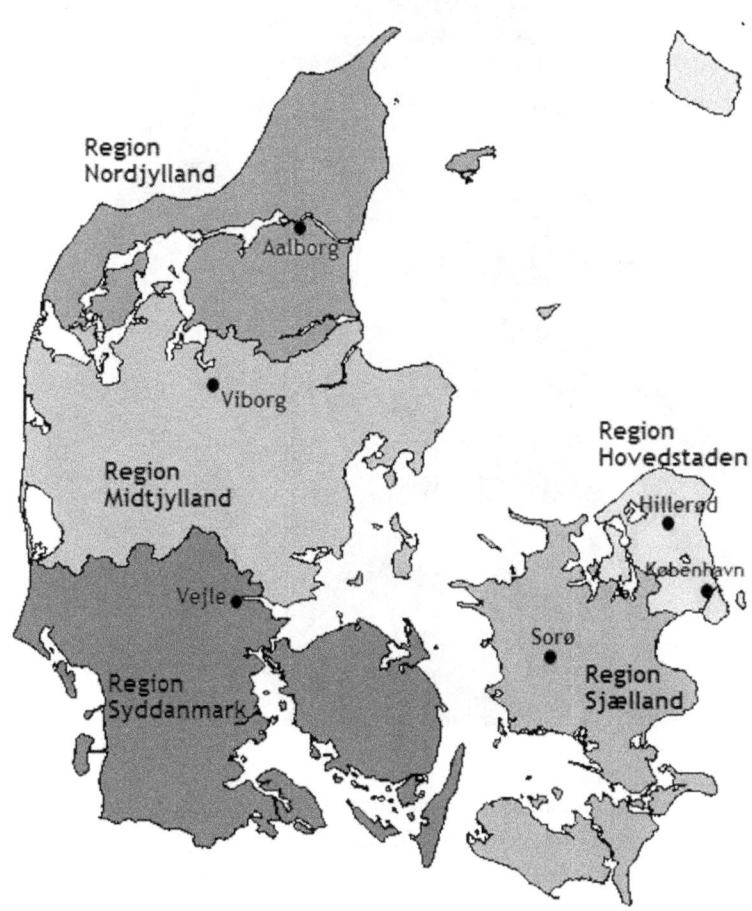

186 SVEND ESTRIDSEN

In 1043, King Magnus gathered a large army in Norway. So large an army had never been seen coming out of Norway before. King Magnus took his army to Vend land and attacked Joms Castle. They entered the Castle and killed most of the Joms Vikings. Joms Castle was burned to the ground. Then Magnus burned the nearby town and devastated the countryside.

Arnor the skald sang of the battle:

> "The robbers, hemmed 'twixt death and fire,
>
> Knew not how to escape your ire;
>
> O'er Joms Castle's highest towers
>
> Thy wrath the whirlwind-fire pours.
>
> The heathen on his false gods calls,
>
> And trembles even in their halls;
>
> And by the light from its own flame
>
> The king this Viking-hold over came."

While Magnus was battling the Vends and the Joms Vikings, Svend Estridsen raised an army in Skaane. After collecting more warriors in Zealand, he went to Fyn and gathered more warriors.

A few days after Magnus had burned Joms castle, the army of the Vends attacked him. Magnus threw off his ring mail coat, and gripped his father's battle axe named Hel. Conspicuous in his red silk shirt, he went into a berserk fury and advanced in the battle. The Norwegian army followed him and dealt death to the Vends who fled east. Magnus pursued them over Hlyskog Heath. Never was there so great a slaughter of men since Christianity came to the northern lands.

After the slaughter on Hlyskog Heath, Magnus turned his army towards Svend. The two armies met at Re near Vestland and battled. Magnus was victorious and Svend fled to Skaane. Magnus sailed his fleet to Jutland where he over wintered in the Lim Fjord.

During the winter of 1044, Svend went to all the Danish islands and collected tax and warriors. In the spring Magnus heard that Svend's fleet was at Aros in Jutland. Magnus sailed his fleet south along the Jutland coast and met Svend's fleet at Aros.

When Svend saw the Norwegian fleet approach, he had his ships bound together and prepared for battle. Each fleet had their ships bound together so that striking and thrusting could be done only at the bows.

Shield walls were erected on the bows and warriors on the forecastle thrust with spears. Behind the spear thrusters were warriors who hurled light spears, and those who were aft of the mast shot with bows.

When the casting spears were exhausted, Magnus shouted, and leaped over the shield wall and rushed forward to the bow. When his men saw Magnus leap, they cheered and rushed forwards. Svend's ship was cleared of all warriors on the forecastle, and Magnus boarded Svend's ship. After Svend's ship was cleared of men, the other Danish ships were also cleared one after the other.

Svend and many of his men fled after many Danes had fallen. After Svend had fled, Magnus gave quarter to the Danes who were left and spared their lives. Svend and the warriors who fled with him sailed to Zealand during the night.

Magnus sailed his fleet to Zealand and landed in the south. Svend fled north over land pursued by Magnus. In northern Zealand, Svend and his men boarded ships and sailed to Fyn. Magnus devastated great areas of Zealand with fire and sword because the Zealanders had joined Svend. When Magnus heard that Svend was in Fyn, he came after him, plundering and burning houses in Fyn. After Magnus had all the Danes submit to him, he appointed some of his own men to govern Denmark and sailed his fleet back to Norway.

When Svend heard that Magnus had sailed back to Norway, he gathered an army in Sweden. Then he rode to Skaane and gathered more warriors. Svend took his army to Zealand and retook it from the Norwegians. After Zealand he retook Fyn and then all the other Danish islands.

When King Magnus heard what Svend had done, he gathered a fleet and sailed to Denmark. He met Svend at Helganes and there was immediate battle. The battle was very fierce and did not stop with nightfall. Spears were thrown throughout the night. Many of Svend's ships were cleared of men and he had to flee.

Svend and his warriors fled to Skaane. But Magnus pursued Svend deep into Skaane. Magnus burned houses and crops as he advanced. When people saw him come they fled. Svend fled to Sweden and stayed there all winter. Magnus went to Falster where he plundered and killed many people. Then he went to Fyn where he devastated large areas of land, and killed many people. Magnus over wintered in Denmark.

187 HARALD HARDRULER

In 1045, Harald Sigurdson arrived in Sweden with an army of Varangians (Vikings). He had been fighting wars for the Emperor in Mikkelgaard (Constantinople). There he had earned the name Hardruler because he was a stern disciplined ruler. He ate only two meals a day and when he was done eating, his men must also stop eating. On his way back from Mikkelgaard, Harald had stopped at Novgorod where he married King Yaroslav's daughter, Elizabeth.

Svend and Harald were both very popular in Sweden where they became friends and made vows to that effect. Harald and Svend made an agreement to first subdue Denmark and then conquer Norway. They outfitted a large army and went into Zealand where they looted and burned houses. Then they went to Fyn and harried.

When Magnus heard about the partnership of Svend and Harold, he sent secret messages to Harold offering him half his Kingdom. Harold sent the messengers back with the message that Harold accepted the offer of Magnus. But Svend found out about the messages and Harald suspected that Svend knew what was happening.

That night Harald laid a log in his bed, covered it with a blanket, and slept somewhere else. During the night, a man crept into Harald's house and struck the log with a big axe. The man ran down to the beach and rowed away in a small rowboat. Harald then woke his men, showed them the axe sticking out of the log and said that Svend was very traitorous. Harald launched his fleet while it was still night and sailed for Norway.

When Harald Hardruler arrived in Throndheim, Magnus the Good invited him to a feast and Harald went with 60 warriors. Magnus gave all the warriors costly gifts and then went to Harald with two sticks and said, "Whish of these two sticks will you have?"

Harald replied. "The one nearest to me".

Magnus said, "With this stick I give you half of the power of Norway, with all the tax and duties. Everywhere you shall be as lawful a King as me. But when we are together, I shall be first in seat, service and salutation. In return for making you King in Norway, you shall strengthen and advance our Kingdom".

Harald stood up and thanked King Magnus the Good for the title of King and dignity. After the feast, Harald returned to his ships.

The next morning Magnus called a Thing and spoke telling everyone what had transpired and that Harald Hardruler was now co-King of Norway. After the Thing was over, Harald had all his treasures brought from his ships and divided it all between himself and Magnus.

In 1046, Harald and Magnus gathered a great fleet and sailed to conquer Denmark. Svend realized that he could not hope to vanquish the combined forces of Harald and Magnus so he fled to Skaane. Harald and Magnus subdued all of Denmark and over wintered in Jutland.

William the Bastard became the Duke of Normandy after the battle of Val-es-Dunes in 1047.

In the summer Harald and Magnus stayed in Jutland. In the fall Magnus became sick. When he knew he was dying he sent Thorer to Svend Estridsen with the message that Magnus had willed the Kingdom of Denmark to Svend Estridsen and that it was only just that Harald Hardruler rule Norway.

After the death of Magnus, Harald held a Thing and announced that he intended to go to the Viborg Thing and have himself declared King of Denmark. He asked that the men follow him to Viborg. Einar Tambaskjelve stood up and said that he would not go to Viborg and that it was his duty to take the corpse of Magnus to Throndheim and bury it beside the grave of Olaf the Saint. Then Einar and all the Thronds boarded their ships and sailed to Throndheim. Harald also returned to Norway.

In the spring of 1048, Harald Hardruler ordered a levy throughout all Norway of half the men and half the ships. Then he sailed south to Jutland where he raided and burned all summer. Harald heard that Thorkel Geysa's daughters had bragged that Harald did not dare to attack Jutland. Therefore he burned the house of Thorkel Geysa and carried off his daughters. Thorkel paid a big ransom for the return of his daughters.

Grane sang of it:

"The gold-adorned girl's eye

Through Hornskeg wood was never dry,

As down towards the sandy shore

The men their lovely prizes bore.

The Norway leader kept at bay

The foe who would contest the way,

And Dotta's father had to bring

Treasure to satisfy the King."

Harald plundered Jutland all summer, but he could not establish a land base. Wherever he came, warriors gathered so that he kept having to return to his ships. In the fall he sailed back to Norway.

In the winter of 1049, Harald married Thora, the daughter of Thorberg Arneson. Then Harald again levied half the men and half the ships to sail against Denmark.

In Denmark, Svend Estridsen also levied half the men and half the ships of Denmark to go against Harald's fleet. Then Svend sent a message to Harald telling him to meet and fight it out at the mouth of the Gaut River.

When he received Svend's message, Harald took his fleet south to the Gaut River and waited for Svend. But Svend did not show up. He was lying with his fleet on the south side of Zealand. When Harald heard where Svend was, he sent his farmers home and kept only his Vikings with him. Then he sailed with 60 ships to Jutland to the south of Vendelskage. He proceeded south to the trading port of Hedeby.

Harald looted Hedeby. Then he burned the town to the ground and sailed north heavily laden with booty. When they reached Vendelskage the wind was against them and they took shelter behind Hlesey Island. In the morning, the wind was gone but a thick fog had come up. As the fog was lifting, Harald's Vikings saw Svend's fleet gliding towards them through the thinning fog.

Harald fled north. All the sailors on the ships were rowing as fast as they could. Svend's ships were smaller and lighter than Harald's and were gaining. Harald ordered all the booty to be thrown overboard. The water was perfectly calm and the floating booty was easily seen floating on the water. Svend ordered his men to ignore the floating treasures and to keep after the Norwegians. Then Harald ordered that all the provisions be thrown overboard. Grain, beer casks, bacon, and bread were hurled into the water, yet still Svend's fleet was gaining on Harald's 60 ships. Then Harald ordered that all the prisoners be thrown overboard. Bound women and children were hurled into the water. Svend ordered his men to rescue the people in the water. While Svend was saving the prisoners, Harald and his fleet rowed away.

King Harald Hardruler was a hard ruler and would sometimes break the law at Things to have his own way. Einar Tambaskjelve would speak out when this happened. He warned Harald that the farmers would not put up with a King who was constantly breaking the law. The farmers warned Einar that there would be troubles for him if he kept opposing the King. Einar then started to keep many warriors with him. When he went to Nidaros, Einar would bring 9 war ships and 500 men.

In 1050, a man accused of being a thief had been caught in Nidaros and he was to be taken before the Thing. Einar knew it would go bad for the accused because he had been in Einar's service. Einar went to the Thing with his men and removed the accused by force of arms. King Harald became angry but men came between them and negotiated. It was agreed that King Harald and Einar meet in the Thing room at the King's house on the Nid River.

Harald entered the Thing house with only a few men. The rest of his warriors stayed in the yard. When Einar came to the Thing house, he told his son Eindride to stay outside with his men because he did not think that there was any danger. When Einar entered the Thing room it was dark because Harald had closed all the shutters. Einar said, "It is dark in here".

Then he was pierced with spears and swords and fell dead. Eindride drew his sword and dashed into the Thing room but was also instantly killed. Then the King's men ran up and placed themselves in front of the door. Einar's men, all farmers, lost courage without their leader. Then Harald Hardraade came out of the Thing room, set up his standard, Land-Waster, and arrayed his warriors. The farmers backed down. Harald and all his men boarded their ships, sailed down the river and out of the fjord.

Einar's wife Bergliot buried Einar and Eindride in the graveyard of Saint Olaf's Church beside Magnus Olafson's resting place. After this event, all the farmers hated King Harald Hardruler.

Fin Arneson and Harald got together and talked about the death of Einar. Fin told Harald that all the farmers were angry with him. All the farmers needed was a leader and they would go to war against the King. Haakon Ivarson of the Uplands was a recognized leader among the farmers. Harald told Fin to ride to Haakon Ivarson and bring about reconciliation between Haakon and Harald. Fin asked, "What shall I offer Haakon as an incentive to agree to reconciliation?"

Harald said, "First listen to what he wants. Then give him anything except the Kingdom".

Haakon Ivarson was the son of Ivar the White, and grandson of Jarl Haakon Erikson who had been a friend of King Knud the Great. When Fin met Haakon, he discovered that Haakon was set on avenging Einar and Eindride. After much discussion, Haakon agreed to be reconciled if he would be given Ragnhild, King Magnus Olafson's daughter as his wife. On behalf of King Harald Hardruler, Fin agreed to the terms.

Haakon Ivarson traveled to Throndheim to meet with King Harald. Harald told Haakon that he would not give him Ragnhild without her consent and that Haakon would have to ask her himself. Haakon went to Ragnhild and asked her to marry him. Ragnhild answered, "I see that you are a handsome man. But if my father King Magnus were alive he would not give me in marriage to any one less than a King. But you are just a farmer. It is not to be expected that I should marry someone who has no dignity nor title".

Haakon went back to Harald and told him what Ragnhild had said. Then he said that to keep his word, Harald must give him a title. He added, "I am of birth and qualifications to be a Jarl".

Harald said that there was to be only one Jarl in the country and that he did not want to take away the title from Orm Jarl. Fin and Haakon became very angry and said that Harald had broken his word.

Haakon outfitted a ship and sailed to Svend Estridsen in Denmark. Svend was married to Gunhild, a daughter of Jarl Svend Haakonson. Svend Estridsen gave Haakon fiefs in Denmark and put him in charge of defending the coasts of Denmark against Vikings.

Asmund was the son of Svend Estridsen's sister. Asmund was raiding in Denmark, killing farmers, and committing atrocities. People complained to King Svend but he told them to see Haakon Ivarson about it. Haakon went with his fleet in search of Asmund. When he found Asmund's ships he immediately attacked. Many men were killed and Haakon finally boarded Asmund's ship. When Asmund's ship was cleared, Haakon fought Asmund man to man and killed him. Then he cut off Asmund's head and took it to king Svend.

When Svend saw the head he became red in the face but said nothing.

Later he sent a message to Haakon telling him to leave his service. The message said that Svend did not mean Haakon any harm, but since Asmund was a relative, he could not keep Haakon any longer.

Haakon traveled back to his home in Norway. Jarl Orm was dead and many men asked King Harald Hardruler to make Haakon the Jarl. Harald reconciled himself with Haakon, made him the Jarl, and gave him Ragnhild as a bride.

Another leader of the farmers was Kalf Arneson who had been raiding in Ireland and Scotland since he departed from Norway. In the winters Kalf stayed with Thorfin Jarl in the Orkneys. Fin Arneson sent a message to Kalf that an agreement had been made with King Harald that Kalf could come home and be safe.

Kalf sailed to Norway with his fleet. Then he and his brother Fin went to King Harald. Kalf swore allegiance to King Harald Hardruler and the King gave Kalf the estates and fiefs, which he had before.

In Sweden, King Onund died and his brother Edmund became King.

In 1051, King Harald Hardruler gathered an army of warriors and sailed a great fleet to Denmark. He brought his fleet to the island of Fyn and arranged his battle formations while his men were still on board their ships. He ordered Kalf to make the first assault and said that he would make a quick landing with the other warriors and come to their assistance.

Kalf landed his warriors and soon a force of Danish warriors came down to defend the beach. Kalf attacked immediately but his army was defeated and he had to flee. The Danes pursued and killed many of the Norwegians. Kalf Arneson fell in flight.

Harald kept his warriors on the ships until Kalf had fallen. Then he landed, defeated the Danish warriors, and went far inland on Fyn. Harald's warriors killed many people, and burned houses and crops.

Arnor sang of the event:

> **"His shining sword with blood he stains,**
> **Upon Fyn's grassy plains;**
>
> **And in the midst of fire and smoke,**
> **The King, Fyn's forces broke."**

Fin Arneson took the death of his brother very hard. The farmers told him that he had been foolish to trust King Harald and hated the King even more. Harald did not care what the farmers said, and seemed very pleased over the death of Kalf. Therefore Fin sailed to King Svend Estridsen in Denmark. Svend made Fin Jarl of Halland. Fin was faithful to King Svend and defended Denmark from Norwegian attacks.

In 1052, Harald Hardruler built a trade town in Oslo Fjord. The town was called Oslo and Harald made it his home. Being much closer to Denmark than Throndheim, it was more convenient for his raids.

In the summer of 1060, Harald Hardruler took a fleet to Denmark and raided in southern Jutland. The Danes collected a force and drove Harald back to his ships. Harald took his fleet north and entered the Lim Fjord where he raided on both shores. But the Danes brought together a large force along the shorelines and Harald retreated back to his ships. Then the news came that Svend Estridsen had brought his fleet to the mouth of the Lim Fjord. The mouth was so narrow that only one ship could pass at a time.

Harald stayed with his ships in the wide part of the Lim Fjord called Lusbred until they ran out of water. He landed on an uninhabited small island and dug down until they found water. Then when it became dark, Harald brought his ships to the extreme west end of the Lim Fjord where only a narrow neck of land separated the Lim Fjord from the North Sea. Harald had the ships unloaded and drawn over the land to the sea. Then the ships were loaded again and sailed back to Oslo.

King Emund the Old died in Sweden. The Swedes held a Thing and chose Stenkil Ragnvaldson as King. Stenkil was married to Emund the Old's daughter.

Harald Hardruler was all winter of 1062 in Nidaros building a ship the same size as the Long Serpent. When it was finished, Harald sent a message to Svend Estridsen to meet him at the Gaut River in the spring to make a decisive battle for both the Kingdoms.

In the spring when the weather became favourable, Harald took his fleet to the Gaut River mouth. The people in the area fled. When he learned that Svend's fleet was lying about Zealand and Fyn he sailed to Halland and laid waste the lands of Halland. He then sailed south along Halland and reached Nis River in Lofu Fjord where he again harried in the land. Then Svend's fleet of 300 long ships was seen gliding towards them.

Harald had his war trumpet sound, and assembled his fleet. Both Harald and Svend had their ships tied together with their own ship in the middle. But the fjord was so narrow that not all the ships could be tied together. Fin Arneson's ship was tied next to Svend's ship. Then the fleets attacked bow against bow.

Svend brought his ship's bow against the bow of Harald's ship. Arrows and casting spears were launched. Haakon Jarl and his warriors had not tied their ships together, but rowed against the Danish ships, which remained loose. The loose Danish ships were defeated or put to flight. Then Haakon's ships rowed outside the battle and rowed in here and there to attack the Danes. In this fashion he caused great losses among the Danes. The battle continued throughout the night.

In the morning, the Danes cut the cables holding their ships together and fled. Harald and his ship's crew boarded Svend's ship, cut down Svend's battle standard, and cleared its deck. Only a few Danes managed to leap overboard. After the battle there were 70 empty Danish vessels and Fin Arneson was captured. Harald's fleet pursued the fleeing Danish ships.

Haakon Jarl did not pursue the Danes because he could not get by the 70 empty Danish long ships. Then a man wearing a wide white hat rowed up to Haakon's ship in a small rowboat and lay in at the bulwarks. He hailed the ship and asked for the Jarl. Haakon came forward and said, "I am the Jarl, and who are you?"

He answered, "I am Vanraad (One in need) and would speak with you".

Haakon leaned over the railing and Vanraad said, "Jarl I will accept my life from you if you will give it".

Haakon straightened up, called two friends to him and said, "Go into the boat, bring Vanraad to land and take him to the farmer Karl. Tell Karl to give Vanraad the horse I gave him yesterday and the saddle and also have his son attend him".

The two men rowed Vanraad to shore and took him to Karl's farm. They told Karl what Haakon had said. Karl understood right away that Vanraad was really King Svend Estridsen. Karl had his wife prepare a meal for the guests.

Karl's wife complained about all the noise, which had kept her awake last night. Karl replied that the Kings were fighting all night. She asked who won. Karl said that the Norwegians did. The wife said that King Svend would have fled. "Nobody knows yet", replied Karl, "whether he has fled or fallen".

The wife replied, "God help us because the King we have is both slow and frightened".

"No", answered Vanraad, "the Dan King is not frightened. He merely does not have luck with him".

Before the meal Vanraad washed his hands and dried them on a towel. The wife snatched the towel from him and said, "You have not been taught well. It is wasteful to dry your hands in the middle of the towel and make the whole towel wet".

Vanraad gently said, "I can come to a place, where I may have permission to dry my hands in the middle of a towel".

After the meal was eaten, Vanraad went out and the horse was saddled. Then Vanraad rode off into the woods accompanied by Karl's son.

Meanwhile King Harald pursued the Danes only for a short time. Then he came back and searched Svend's ship to see if he could find Svend's corpse. His corpse was not found although many believed that he had fallen. Harald had the corpses brought to shore and sent a message to the farmers to come and bury them.

The prisoner Fin Arneson was led to the King on his ship. Harald said, "Fin we meet again. Last time was in Norway. You ran off to Denmark and deserted me. It would be bad business to drag you a blind old man home as a prisoner".

Fin replied, "The North men find it more difficult to conquer now that you are the leader".

Harald said, "Will you accept life and safety, though you have not deserved it?"

Fin said, "Not from you, dog".

Harald said, "Will you accept it from Magnus?"

Magnus, the son of Harald was steering the ship. Fin asked, "Can the whelp rule over life and quarter?"

Harald said, "Will you accept it from your relative, Thora?"

Fin said, "Is she here?"

Harald replied, "She is here".

Harald could see that Fin was unhappy to go back to Norway. Then he said, "I see Fin that you are not happy to be with me and your relatives. Now I will give you leave to go to your friend King Svend".

Fin said, "I accept your offer willingly, and the more grateful the sooner I get away from here".

Then Harald put Fin ashore and proceeded home to Oslo. Fin found some traders going to Halland and caught a ride home.

In 1063, King Harald Hardraade heard that Haakon Ivarson had set Svend Estridsen ashore at the Nis River. He immediately rode towards the Uplands with 900 warriors. He rode all that night and the following day. One of his warriors, Gamal rode to one of the farmers in the Uplands and paid him to ride quickly and tell Haakon that Harald Hardraade was coming for him.

Haakon was enjoying a drink after supper when the farmer arrived. Haakon had all his possessions hid in the forest. Then he took all his people and rode to King Stenkil in Sweden. King Harald arrived at Haakon's house and found it deserted. He stayed there over night and started his journey home in the morning.

When Haakon heard that Harald had gone north, he returned home collected the taxes and stayed there all summer. In the fall he went to Vermeland where King Stenkil gave him fiefs. There he also collected tax.

Harald Hardruler sent men into the Uplands to collect tax. But the Uplanders said that they had already paid the tax to Haakon Jarl. They declared that they would pay tax to Haakon and no one else as long as he was alive and held the fiefs.

It was the year 1064, and the people of both Denmark and Norway were tired of the war. Messengers and ambassadors traveled between Denmark and Norway during the winter looking for ways to make peace. A meeting place was arranged at the Gaut River.

In the spring, King Harald and King Svend assembled many men and traveled to the Gaut River. When the Kings met, their people began talking about the wrongs suffered from raiding and killing so that it nearly came to a battle. But negotiations proceeded and it was agreed that Harald should have Norway and Svend should have Denmark. The boundaries were established and hostages were exchanged. It was agreed that there would be peace as long as Harald Hardraade and Svend Estridsen were Kings.

When he was back in Oslo, Harald sent men into the Uplands to collect the tax. But the Uplanders said they were holding the tax for Haakon Ivarson. In the fall Harald took a fleet of warriors to Kongshelle. At Kongshelle, Harald took his lightest long ships and sailed up the river. The ships were portaged past all the waterfalls and he reached Venner Lake. The ships were rowed east across lake where the warriors disembarked. Leaving some of his warriors to guard the ships, Harald proceeded with his force to make a raid. Harald and some of his warriors were mounted but most were on foot.

Haakon heard that Harald had come to Vermeland and was determined to not let him plunder. With an army of Goth warriors Haakon set out to oppose Harald. When they met in the forest, there was a swamp between them. Harald decided to wait and see what Haakon would do and had his men sit down and rest on a hill. It started to snow and snowdrifts formed. Harald told his warriors that if there was a battle they should wait until the Goths were below the hill.

The chief of the Goths, Thorvid, sat on his horse, which was tied to a stake in the mire. He yelled to his warriors, "We shall let King Stenkil hear that we stood bravely by the Jarl. But if our people give way, let us not retreat farther than that stream. If we give way at the stream, let us not retreat farther than the hill beyond it".

Just then the Harald's Norwegians jumped up, raised a war cry, and with shouts of 'Odin' struck their shields with their weapons. The Goths began to shout and Thorvid's horse shied backwards so that it yanked out the stake, which hit Thorvid on the head. Thinking that he was hit by an arrow, Thorvid fled.

Giving a war cry, Haakon let his banner advance. He was using the banner, which had belonged Magnus the Good. When his warriors reached the bottom of the hill, Harald's warriors rushed upon them. Harald's warriors killed some of the Goths and the rest fled. Harald's warriors pursued for only a short distance. Then they picked up Haakon's war banner and looted the corpses.

King Harald had both war banners carried in front of him and marched his warriors away. The warriors talked among themselves and agreed that Haakon had probably fallen. They could only go in single file along the forest path. Suddenly a man on a horse in full gallop crossed in front of them. He struck a spear through the man carrying Haakon's banner, seized the banner, and carried it with him into the forest on the other side of the path. "The Jarl is alive!" shouted Harald.

In 1065, Harald Hardruler took his warriors into the Upland districts. He started in Raumarige. He accused the farmers of not paying their tax and of helping his enemies. He seized many farmers, killed some, and maimed others. The people who could get away fled. Then Harald plundered Raumarige and laid it waste. He burned whatever he could. When he was done in Raumarige, Harald plundered and burned in Hardeland and Ringerige. King Harald's raids in the Upland districts lasted a year and a half.

188 THE KINGDOM OF ENGLAND

On January 5, 1066, King Edward of England died. The body of Edward was buried in St. Paul's Church and Harald Godwinson was acclaimed King of all England. Harald's brother Toste had been Jarl in Northumbria but was living in exile in Flanders. Toste wanted to be King of England.

Toste Godwinson went to Frisia for help in taking the English Crown, but the Frisians refused to help him. Then Toste sailed to his cousin King Svend Estridsen in Denmark for help. Svend refused to help conquer England. But he invited Toste to stay with him, and offered to make Toste a Jarl and an important man in Denmark. Then Toste replied, "I would go back to England. If I cannot get help from you to make me King, I will help you Svend, if you would take your army to England and win the country as your uncle Knud the Great did".

King Svend replied, "I am so much a smaller man than Knud the Great, that I can with difficulty defend Denmark from the Norwegians. King Knud got Denmark as an inheritance, took England by force of arms, and took Norway without a fight. It suits me better to be guided by my own poor abilities than to try to imitate Knud the Great".

Toste left Svend and sailed to Oslo and met with Harald Hardruler, but Harald had no interest in conquering England. Toste explained to Harald the agreement between Magnus and Hardeknud saying that when Hardeknud died, Magnus should have inherited England as well as Denmark. Harald said, "If he had a right to it, how come he did not get it?"

Toste replied, "Why do you not have Denmark as Magnus inherited it?"

Toste promised that many of the important men in England would come to Harald if he had Toste with him. Therefore, claimed Toste, England would be much easier to conquer than Denmark. Harald sent out the war arrow and began to gather men for an expedition against England. Toste sailed back to Flanders.

When he heard that Harald Godwinson had been acclaimed king of England, William the Bastard, the Duke of Normandy, began to collect an army to go against England. He also sent Archdeacon Gilbert of Lisieux to Rome to obtain the support of the Pope. The Christians in England were more independent than on the continent and their Clergy often paid no attention to papal directives. Therefore Pope Alexander II sent his blessings and a papal banner back to Duke William signifying that the Christian Church had given approval for William to over throw the English King and bring the English Clergy in line.

In May, Toste obtained men from his stepfather, Count Baldwin of Flanders and attacked England with 60 ships. Wherever he landed, he was defeated. Eventually, with his remaining 12 ships, Toste fled to Scotland.

In Throndheim, Harald Hardruler had his son Magnus declared King of all Norway. Then leaving his wife Thora with King Magnus, he sailed towards England with 200 long ships. Harald landed at the Orkney Islands. There he left his wife Elizabeth and his daughters Maria and Ingegerd. While Harald was in the Orkneys, Toste Godwinson and more Vikings joined him.

On September 12, Harald took his fleet of 360 ships south along the coast of Scotland. When he reached England he landed at Klifland and plundered. Then he proceeded south and landed at Scarborough on September 15 and burned the town down. On September 18, Harald's fleet reached the Humber River.

The next day, Harald sailed his fleet up the Humber and then up the Ouse River. He beached his ships about 19 kilometers from York at a town called Riccel and made camp. In the morning, Harald Hardruler and his Vikings advanced on foot against York. At York Morcar Jarl of Northumbria, Walther Jarl of Northampton and Edwin Jarl of Mercia had drawn up battle lines with their troops. Their lines stretched from the Ouse River, across Fulford fields and across a road to a ditch where the terrain was swampy.

King Harald set up his battle standard, Land Waster, and arrayed his warriors. The English advanced and Harald's right flank, along the ditch began to give way. Harald spread his left flank along the center of his array and wheeled his main force to attack the English on his right flank and drove them back towards the ditch where the footing was poor because of the swampy area. Many English men fell along and into the ditch. Soon the English fled to the castle at York.

The people in York decided that they had no chance against Harald

Hardraade and surrendered. It was agreed that the people of York supply food, transportation and 100 hostages. The hostages were to be delivered on September 25 at Stamford Bridge. Harald took his army back to his ships.

While Harald Hardraade battled at Fulford, King Harald Godwinson rode with the Thinglid warriors out of London north towards Yorkshire. On the way north an army from West Mercia and another from East Anglia joined them. On Sunday, September 24, Harald Godwinson reached Tadcaster, 16 kilometers from York where he heard about the battle of Fulford. Godwinson sealed Tadcaster and would let no one in or out to keep his arrival a secret.

On the morning of September 25, Harald Hardraade left one third of his Vikings (5,000 men) with his ships including, his son Olaf, the Orkney Jarls Paul and Erland, and Eystein Orre, a son of Thorberg Arneson. Then he went to Stamford Bridge and waited for the English in York to bring him hostages.

When Harald Godwinson approached Stamford Bridge from the north with his army, Hardruler sent three men back for his remaining Vikings at the ships, and called all his warriors across the bridge from the north to the south side of the Ouse River. Then Godwinson was upon them. Hardraade had a small group of Vikings defend the bridge while he arrayed his army.

The Vikings at the bridge were quickly cut down except for one who backed onto the bridge and defended it with a large battle-axe. Hardraade set up his standard, Land Waster, and arrayed his army into a circle with the warriors close to each other forming a shield wall. The line was not deep but stretched out so that the circle was very large. One of the English warriors took a spear and had two men row him under the bridge. From there he thrust a spear between the bridge planking and into the lone Viking defending the bridge. The Viking fell and Godwinson's men poured across the bridge.

Harald Hardraade and Toste Godwinson watched the English arraying into formations. Twenty Thinglid horsemen rode towards them. They paused some ways from the Viking shield wall. Then the leader approached a little closer and yelled, "Is Toste Jarl in this army?"

Toste replied, "You will find him here".

The leader yelled, "Your brother King Harald sends you greetings with the message that you shall have the whole of Northumbria. He would not have you submit to him. Instead he will give you a third of his Kingdom to rule".

Toste replied, "If I accept this offer, what will he give King Harald Sigurdson for his troubles?"

The horseman replied, "King Harald also spoke of this. He will give Harald Sigurdson seven feet of English ground plus as much as he may be taller than other men".

Toste replied, "Go and tell King Harald to get ready for battle. It shall not be told of me that I left Harald Sigurdson to join his enemies".

The 20 Thinglid men wheeled their horses and returned to the English lines. Hardruler said to Toste, "Who was that man who spoke so well?"

Toste replied, "That was King Harald Godwinson".

The Thinglid warriors attacked. They could not penetrate the Norwegian shield wall because of the Viking spears. Therefore they rode around Hardruler's shield wall in a circle. Because battle was light and there were hardly any casualties, some of the Vikings began to chase the Thinglid warriors. But the pursuit broke the shield wall. The Thinglid warriors then assaulted the Vikings from all sides by riding into the circle throwing spears and firing arrows.

When Harald Sigurdson saw his shield wall broken he went forward where the fight was hardest. He went into a berserk rage, went in front of his warriors and hewed down English warriors with both hands.

Arnor the bard sang of the battle:

"Where battle-storm was ringing,

Where arrow-cloud was singing,

Harald stood there,

Of armour bare,

His deadly sword still swinging.

> The foemen feel its bite;
>
> His Norsemen rush to fight,
>
> Danger to share,
>
> With Harald there,
>
> Where steel on steel was ringing."

Harald was hit in the windpipe by an arrow and fell. The fight stopped. But Toste Godwinson, set up his battle standard, took charge and arrayed the Vikings. Harald Godwinson arrayed his armies once more. Harald Godwinson offered peace and quarter to Toste and all the Norwegians. But the Norwegians yelled out that they would rather all fall than accept quarter from an Englishman. Then the battle was resumed.

Eystein Orre arrived at the battle with the Vikings who had been at the ships. They had run the 19 kilometers in full chainmail armour. Exhaustion made Eystein and his warriors ineffective so they peeled off their armour. But that made them vulnerable and they began to fall. The Vikings were split into small fighting groups and were being cut down. Among the fallen were Toste and Eystein. When it became dark, the Vikings fled.

King Harald Godwinson followed the Vikings to their ships and rounded them all up. The only Viking leader left was Olaf Haraldson. Harald Godwinson gave Olaf quarter and permission to sail back to Norway. Olaf and the remaining Vikings departed in 24 long ships and sailed to the Orkneys to recuperate. A few days later Olaf took his fleet back to Norway.

189 WILLIAM THE CONQUEROR

While Harald and his army were celebrating their victory in York, a messenger came with the news that William the Bastard had landed with a big army near Pevensey in Sussex. The next morning Harald took his army south to London. At London, Harald sent the northern Jarls north to gather more warriors. Then he moved his army to Caldbec Hill near Hastings where he had his men rest.

William brought his army up to the Senlac Ridge of Caldbec Hill. The ridge was flanked on both sides by woods and marshes so that there was only one approach. Senlac Ridge was 1,000 meters long. Harald had the advantage of height and the ridge was so steep that cavalry attacks would be ineffective.

William had archers lay down cover fire while his infantry attacked the hill. When the infantry was about 100 yards from the English, Harald had his archers open fire and many Norman warriors fell. When the Normans reached the English lines, the Thinglid warriors and the Fyrdmen outfought them. After the Normans had retreated, William sent in his cavalry. The steep slope did not allow a galloping attack and the cavalry was trying to use spears to make strikes over the shield wall. But the Thinglid warriors wielded long axes, which brought down both a horse and rider with one blow.

When the cavalry retreated, many English warriors thought that William's army was fleeing and pursued. But the cavalry wheeled about and charged the English who had left the shield wall and cut them down.

There was a lull in the battle. Harald strengthened his shield wall with new warriors who had arrived while William planned his second attack. There were many attacks during the day. In one of the attacks, a Thinglid warrior killed William's horse and the Normans thought he was dead. To keep his army from fleeing, William mounted another horse, took off his helmet and rode along the front ranks of his army to prove he was still alive.

When it was almost dark, William's forces made a last attack. A chance arrow struck Harald in one eye. In the confusion, the shield wall near Harald collapsed and the Normans rushed in and killed him. The Fyrdmen fled down the hill but the Thinglid warriors surrounded the body of their fallen King and protected it to the last man.

The fleeing Fyrdmen lured many of the pursuing Normans into a swamp where their horses got stuck. There the English fired several volleys of arrows at the Normans and killed many. William called a halt to the pursuit and occupied Caldbec Hill.

Edwin and Morcar arrived too late with reinforcements. Walther Jarl managed to flee with some troops. He ran into a division of 100 Normans. When the Normans saw Walther and his warriors they ran into a forest. Walther and his warriors set fire to the forest and burned them all.

The Saga Kings

After the battle of Hastings, William was called William the Conqueror. When he had been crowned King of all England, he sent for Walther Jarl to reconcile with him. When Walther arrived for the meeting with the King, he was seized by the Norman soldiers, led away, and beheaded.

In 1067, at a Thing in Throndheim, Harald Hardruler's two sons Magnus and Olaf were acclaimed joint Kings of Norway. King Svend Estridsen of Denmark declared that since Harald was dead, the peace agreement between Norway and Denmark was no longer in effect and went about collecting warriors. The two Kings Magnus and Olaf also collected warriors and formed an army. But messengers went back and forth between Denmark and Norway, which resulted in the peace coming back into effect and Svend marrying Harald's widow, Elizabeth.

In England, about half of the Anglo-Saxon aristocracy had died in the battle against William. Their wives and daughters fled to monasteries to escape becoming the wives of Norman Lords. William the Conqueror took away all the land from the farmers and gave it to his Lords. The farmers were no longer free. They belonged to the Lords and became known as peasants. The Things in England were abolished and the King and his Lords made all the decisions. The Danelaw passed from a democracy into the Feudal system.

King William the Conqueror had each Lord build a castle of stone on his estate. Inside each castle was built a keep also of stone. The keep was a place of refuge in case an enemy happened to break into the castle.

William declared that all the deer in the land belonged to the King. The deer were for the King's hunting pleasure. It became a law that no bows and arrows were permitted in the forest. The penalty was death.

190 SVEND ESTRIDSEN AND OLAF KYRRE

King Svend Estridsen began to build churches throughout Denmark. His best friend was Bishop Wilhelm in Roskilde. The Archbishop of Bremen came often to Denmark to visit the King. Svend married Harald Hardruler's widow Elizabeth.

In 1069, King Magnus in Norway died of the ringworm disease and Olaf became King of all Norway. Olaf began to build churches throughout Norway and became known as Olaf Kyrre (the peaceful). All the people of Norway loved Olaf Kyrre.

The Saga Kings

Upset over William's treatment of the Danish descendants in northern England, Svend Estridsen gathered an army and with a fleet of 200 ships sailed to England. Svend landed with his army and took York. In 1070, Svend Estridsen was unable to make headway against the stone castles, which had been built in England. Therefore he made peace with William and returned to Denmark.

When King Svend Estridsen died in Denmark in 1076, he had built several hundred churches, and installed three new bishops in Jutland and one in Skaane. Svend was the first to build churches out of stone instead of wood".

"When I am old enough, I will be a Viking", exclaimed Erik.

The story teller looked at Erik and frowned. Then he said," That is impossible my young friend. The Viking age has ended. The Vikings? The Vikings! There are no more in Midgaard. They dwell now only in Valhalla's Halls. The Viking age ended gradually.

The Viking chiefs and Jarls opposed the Christian religion because it destroyed equality. They saw it as being unfair. However Scandinavia did become Christianized. The Christian Kings and Jarls had monks write chronicles and history. They did not keep skalds about them to compose verses of their exploits. In Denmark, the Christian Kings starting with Gorm the Old did not keep skalds. Harald Grey Cloak drove the skalds out of Norway. The only skalds left were Icelanders. Olaf the Stout became so impressed with the Icelandic skald Sighvat that he took him as his main skald and thereafter employed additional skalds. But Olaf the Stout was the only Christian King who kept skalds.

The sagas were stories, which arose from the verses and songs of the skalds. The age of the skalds ended with the close of the age of the Vikings. Therefore the sagas stopped and the Saga Kings were no more".

The story teller drained his beer mug and set it on the table so that it made a loud thump. He stood up and said, "Time for me to leave."

Grete fetched his grey cloak and wide brimmed hat. Khalle shook the story teller's hand and thanked him for the stories. Then the story teller walked to the door adjusted his hat and went outside. The people went outside and stood along the hall watching the old man walk down the lane in the moon light until he was lost from sight in the shadows of the trees.

The people were hoping that the story teller would return. They searched for him throughout the land. But the old man with the grey cloak and the wide brimmed grey hat was never seen again

191 APPENDIX
192 THE VIKINGS IN THE NEW WORLD

The Vikings explored America much further than the modern historians would have us believe. Archaeologist Patricia Sutherland (Curator, Archaeological Survey of Canada, Canadian Museum of Civilization, 2009) found a Viking site on Baffin Island. There was evidence that the Vikings traded peacefully with the Dorset people. The Dorset people easily stock piled items that the Vikings wanted such as fur, walrus tusks and narwhal horns. After Leif Erikson established the base camp at L'Anse aux Meadows, the Vikings kept coming and explored the eastern American continent where they traded peacefully with the native peoples. In Iceland some Icelanders have DNA from native North American Indians.

Eventually the Norse did not need the base camp at L'Ance aux Meadows. But the Vikings still made occasional trips to the new world. Viking artifacts have been found as far inland as Ohio and there is evidence that the Vikings reached and explored Lake Ontario. Frank Joseph (2014) has presented evidence that the Norse also reached as far south as Florida, Andros and Puerto Rico. They also sailed up the Mississippi River (Frank Joseph 2014). Most of the Viking artifacts found in America have been in Ontario and in Minnesota. Some of the artifacts found in America were Norse coins minted by King Olaf Kyrre of Norway.

I will not go through the multitude of evidence that shows the Viking presence in America. But I will present just one more fact because I found it so interesting. The breed of cat known as the 'Maine coon cat' has long perplexed biologists, because they were unable to explain its unique appearance or trace its origins. The animal derived its modern identity from the U. S. state in which it is primarily found, although smaller populations appear in the Atlantic coastal regions of New Brunswick and NovaScotia.

The coon cat is larger than the average house cat. Specimens of over 10 pounds are common. This cat also has unusual hind-quarters, which resemble those of a raccoon. This is what gave it the name "coon cat". Its bushy tail, brown and white striped markings, together with an occasional tendency to wash its food, caused many people to consider that it came from unions between cats and raccoons. But such crossings are biologically impossible, because raccoons are not felines, but belong to the family Procyonidae.

In an attempt to trace the genetic origins of the singular Maine Coon Cat, scientists subjected it to DNA testing. The results were as clear as they were surprising: The Maine Coon Cat is the direct descendant of an unknown, domestic breed that went extinct within the last few centuries and the Norsk Skov Kat, or "Norwegian Forest Cat," brought to the North American continent from Scandinavia 1,000 years ago. As the Website for the Cat Fanciers' Association explains, "These are the cats that explored the world with the Vikings, protecting the grain stores on land and sea, and are believed to have left their progeny on the shores of North America, as a legacy to the future. Is their Norse name accurate? Yes, the skov kat, meaning 'forest cat,' really did come out of the Scandinavian forests in the last 4,000 years."

"Because the large forest cats are determined hunters, they were invariably taken aboard Viking expeditions to keep the long-ships free of vermin. When the Vikings landed on North American coasts, some of these cats deserted by jumping overboard. These new residents mated with that unknown domestic breed that no longer exists. The living descendants of those early days in Viking America are today's Maine Coon Cats. Their majority presence in the state that gave them its name suggests that the Norse did more than briefly establish a settlement at L'Ans aux Meadows; as mainstream scholars insist, but went on to colonize other parts of the Eastern Seaboard. Concentration of the Maine Coon's population in that state implies that the Viking's elusive Vinland was in Maine after all."

193 TRAVEL IN SCANDINAVIA

The following is from Roesdahl, E. 1992.

Sailing from Skaane to Sigtuna took five days. The journey overland took a month.

Going to Trondheim from northern Jutland first took one day to sail to southern Norway. From there sailing along the west coast of Norway would take five days to reach Trondheim.

The route overland to Trondheim from Skaane was very dangerous through the mountains and most people avoided it. That route took two months.

The length of Norway could be covered in one month overland.

In Jutland from Hedeby in the south to Viborg at the Limfjord in the north the journey would take five to seven days overland.

194 VIKING SHIPS

There were two main types of ships; war ships and travel ships.

War Ships

Longships

Longships were low, narrow and long ships with a slender hull, and made of oak. The deck ran the length of the whole ship. Oar ports were evenly distributed along the whole length. They had a high length: width ratio, which gave the hull minimal resistance in water, resulting in high cruising speed. The mast could be easily lowered and raised. This feature was very useful in a variety of circumstances such as military cover activities and moving under bridges. The combination of sailing and rowing ability gave them a unique maneuverability. These ships were capable of carrying a large number of warriors but relatively little cargo. The largest of the known longships were probably more than 50 m long, carrying 200 - 300 warriors..

Busse

The Busse was a class of longships with large cargo capacity and a large crew. They were designed for battle craft to give advantage in war against other ships. They can be regarded as warships. The Long Serpent of King Olav Tryggveson of Norway was a busse. A busse could have as much as 35 pairs of oars and a total length of 50 meters or more.

Skeide

The "Skeide" was also great longships equipped with 20 - 35 pairs of oars. Most likely they had lower gunwales than the Busse class and lower cargo capacity. They were also slimmer and faster. The Skuldelev longship found in Limfjorden in Denmark could be an example of a skeide.

Snekke

The Snekke was a longship used both at war and for travels. The snekke had more the character of being a crew carrier than a pure war ship. They had stems and sterns of more modest height than the more prestigious classes of longships. The Snekke as a term in ship design seem to have been well known both in Scandinavia and in parts of the Baltic Sea.

Dragon-ship

The Dragon-ships were longships with a dragon head placed on the bow. The idea was to frighten the enemy. It became a law during the Viking age that when in port the Dragon head must be removed so that it would not scare the little nisser (the little fairy folk).

Travel Ships

Karv

The karv was substantially smaller than the longships. They were equipped with 13 to 16 pairs of oars. They were very versatile and have been in use both as merchant vessels and at war.

Knar

The knar had a relatively round hull with fewer pairs of oars than the longships. The oars were placed towards each end, leaving the space midships for cargo. The knar was designed for maneuverability, large loading capacity and good sailing abilities offshore.

The Skuldelev-wreck 1 found in the Roskilde fjord in Denmark was a knar. It had a deck fore and aft and the cargo room in the middle. It had a high gunwale, making the ship more seaworthy in rough waters. The ship is regarded as a good example of the kind of knars which were used for trading trips within Scandinavia and further south in Europe. It was a large ship with as much as 35 rooms. Leif the Lucky's ship was a knar. His knar was 80 feet long.

Byrding

The byrding was a smaller vessel used as a domestic freighter along the coast. Their size was a bit smaller than the karv. They were also able to cross great distances offshore, such as between Norway and Iceland. They could be used for carrying supplies to the crew in the larger boats, such as food and water. Reconstructions have shown that these boats were very fast.

Skute

In addition of being fast, these ships also had the advantage of being ready to sail at a short notice. They needed only a small crew with little equipment. These ships could be made ready to sail without attracting attention from the surroundings. They could also be easier hidden than any larger ship. Such ships must have been well suited for transportation of persons, couriers and messenger carriers during wars and conflicts.

Ferry

A ferry was a smaller carrier for crossing shorter distances, like across fjords. It could be rowed back after a mission by one or two men. They were built flat and strong, so that they could carry horses and cattle onboard. The term ferry seems to have spread from Old Norse, and is today part of the English language.

Ships boat

A ships boat was a smaller boat which was towed after a larger ship (due to this they were called the "afterboat") or was stored upside-down onboard a larger merchant ships just behind the mast base and was used for covering cargo. They were also used as landing boats or used for fast transportation between the smaller ships in a fleet. These boats must have had great similarity with the wooden boats in western Norway of today. Three such boats were found inside the Gokstad ship. In construction they are virtually identical with today's Oselvar boat type from Hordaland.

195 STATUS OF WOMEN

When reading about Vikings it is important to understand something about their culture. I find it exasperating to watch Viking programs which misrepresent their culture. They are often represented as if their culture was like the western culture of today.

Pennick (1992) wrote, "In the old pagan era, there was equality of opportunity for men and women, evidenced in documents and artifacts. Rune stones in Sweden tell us that women land owners built roads and bridges. In later times, by contrast, women were not even taught to read or write, as a deliberate policy to keep women from developing their true human potential. The imposition of patriarchal religion and the feudal system transformed women into 'second class citizens'. This state of affairs lasted formally until the twentieth century, and is still not abolished completely".

The Viking women were equal to men in their society. They attended the Thing. Some women took up arms and went a viking. Recently it has been discovered that this was more the case than was originally thought.

A study looked at 14 Viking burials from the era of invasion of the great army in England. The study looked at the Norse grave goods found with them and isotopes found in their bones that reveal their birthplace. The bones were sorted for telltale osteological signs of which gender they belonged to, rather than assuming that burial with a sword or knife denoted a male burial.

It was reported by McLeod that six of the 14 burials were of women, seven were men, and one was indeterminable. Warlike grave goods may have misled earlier researchers about the gender of Viking invaders, the study suggests. Part of the study was a mass burial site called Repton Woods. The study concluded, "Despite the remains of three swords being recovered from the site, all three burials that could be sexed osteologically were thought to be female, including one with a sword and shield. These results, six female Norse migrants and seven male, should caution against assuming that the great majority of Norse migrants were male, despite the other forms of evidence suggesting the contrary. This result of almost a fifty-fifty ratio of Norse female migrants to Norse males is particularly significant when some of the problems with osteological sexing of skeletons are taken into account,"

In contrast when we look at women's status in western Christian society we find:

The Christian religion has downgraded the status of women. This culminated in the witch hunts of the inquisitions.

The establishment of equality of women with men in western society took a long time.

In Canada women had local votes in some provinces, as in Ontario from 1850. It was not until January 1, 1919 that Canadian women were allowed to vote in a Dominion election.

New Zealand's Electoral Act of 19 September 1893 made this country the first in the world to grant women the right to vote in parliamentary elections

Finland was the first western European country to grant women the right to vote in 1906. This was followed soon after by Norway.

In Denmark, women won the right to vote in municipal elections on April 20, 1908. However it was not until June 5, 1915 that they were allowed to vote in federal elections.

The U.S.A. prohibited state or federal sex-based restrictions on voting in 1920

The women of Québec gained full suffrage in 1940

The 21 April 1944 the French provisional government granted suffrage to French women.

Switzerland was the last Western republic to grant women's suffrage; they gained the right to vote in federal elections in 1971

196 GENEOLOGY
197 SKJOLDUNGS (SCYLDINGS)

Odin + Frija (Frigg)
|
Dan + Gefion (daughter of Gylfe of Sweden)
|

Lothar	Humble
	Skjold (Scyld)
	Gram

Guthorm (Gorm)	Hadding
	Peace Frode
	Dan Mikellati (Dan the Peaceful)
	Frode the Vigorous

| Ingjald | Helga | Fridlief | Aasa | Halfdan |

The Saga Kings

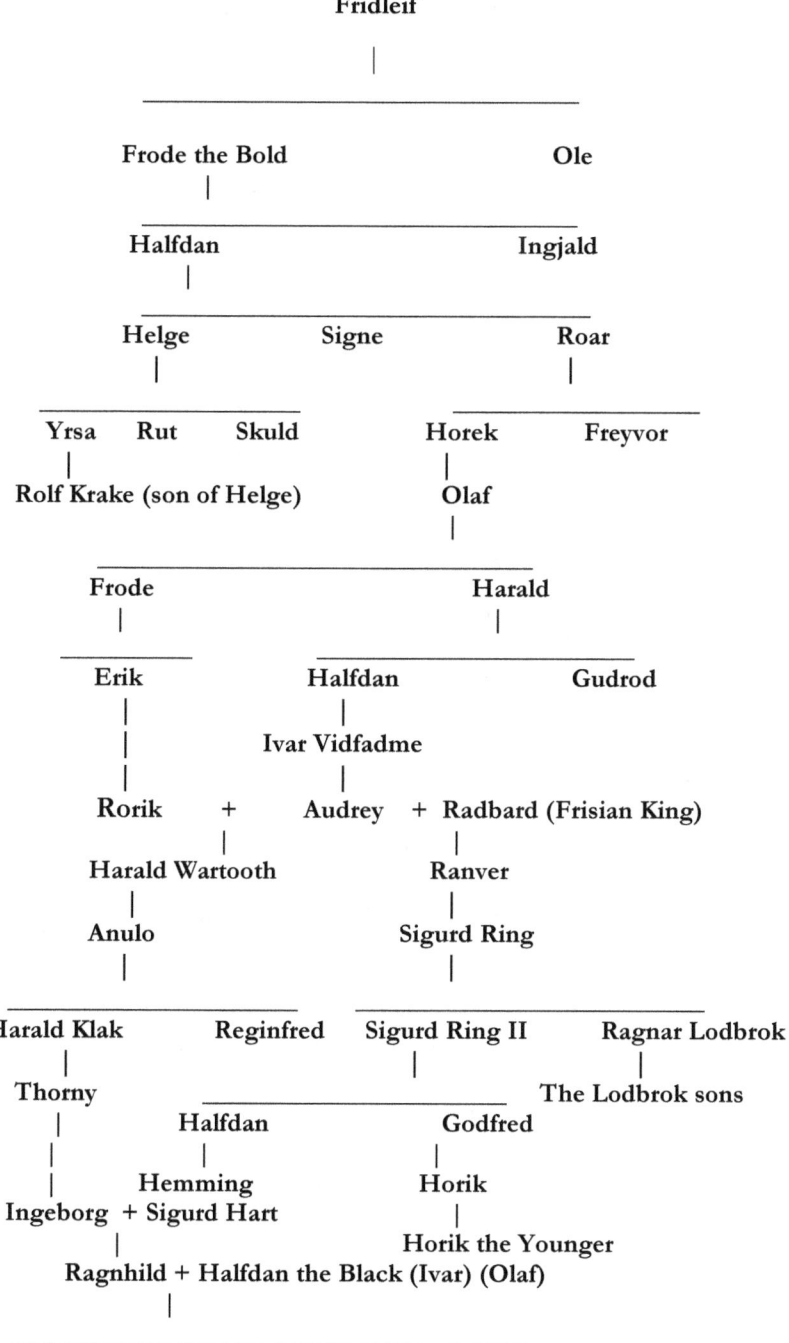

198 ANGLES (MERCIANS)

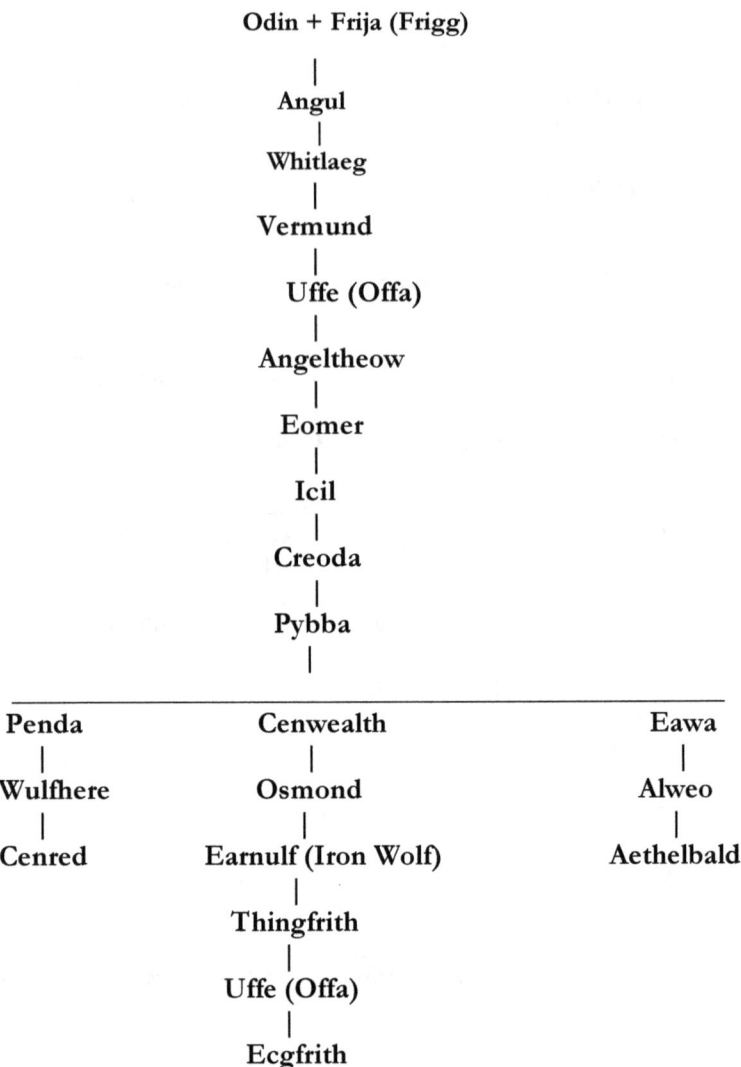

199 RAGNAR LODBROK, SKJOLDUNGS (SCYLDINGS)

Ragnar Lodbrog + Ladgerda
|
Fridleif

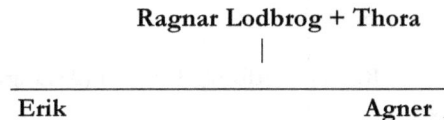

Ragnar Lodbrog + Thora
|

Erik	Agner

Ragnar Lodbrog + Kraka (Aslaug)
|

Ivar	Bjorn	Halfdan	Ubbe	Hastings	Sigurd

The sons of Ragnar Lodbrok:

1. Fridleif
2. Erik
3. Agnar
4. Ivar the Boneless (King of Dublin)
5. Halfdan (Hvidsaerk) (King of York)
6. Bjorn Ironsides (King of Sweden)
7. Ubbe
8. Hastings (Haesten)
9. Sigurd Snake-Eye (King of Denmark)

200 BJORN IRONSIDES (LODBROKSON)

Ivar Vidfadme
|
Audrey + Radbard (King of Frisia)
|
Ranver
|
Sigurd Ring
|
Ragnar Lodbrok + Kraka (Aslaug)
|
Bjorn Ironsides
|

Erik Bjornson		Refil
		Erik Refilson
Bjorn at Hauge	Anund (Edmund)	
	Erik Anundson (Erik Edmundson)	
	Bjorn Erikson	

Erik the Victorious	Olaf Bjornson	
		(Harald Bluetooth's daughter)
Olaf Skotkonge	Styrbjorn Staerke + Thyra	
Astrid	Thorgils Sprakkeleg	
(married St. Olaf)		

Estrid + Ulf	Gyrta (Grete) + Godwin
Svend Estridsen	
	Harald Toste Svend

201 IVAR THE BONELESS (LODBROKSON)

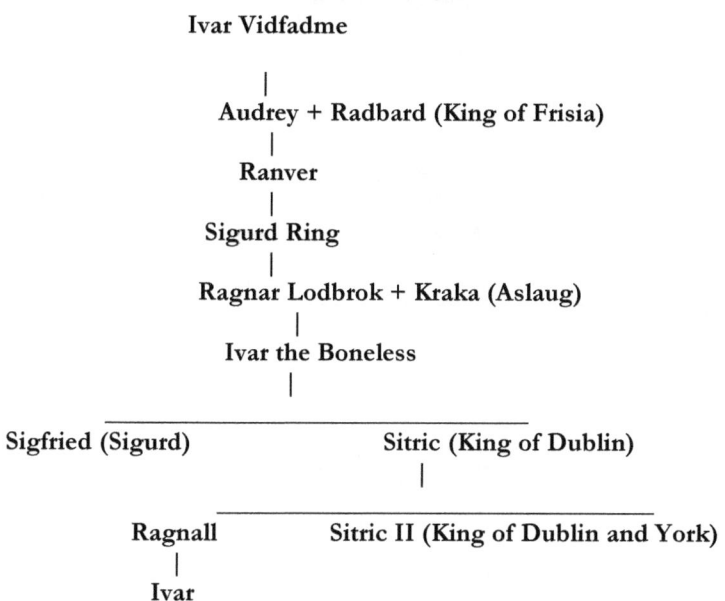

202 SIGURD SNAKE – EYE

```
                    Ragnar Lodbrok + Kraka (Aslaug)
                                   |
      Harald Klak          Sigurd Snake-Eye
           |                       |
        Thorny             Aslaug + Helge The Sharp
           |                       |
       Ingeborg  +  Sigurd Hart
                    |
              Ragnhild  +  Halfdan the Black
                    |
_____
 Harald Fairhair              Eystein Glumra (Eystein Ivarson)
```

The Saga Kings

203 THE JARLS OF LADE

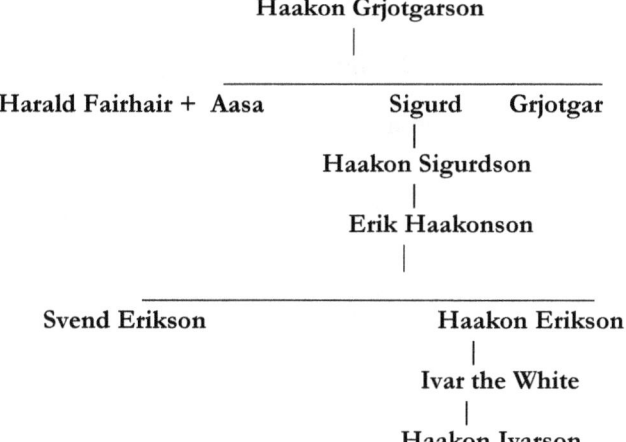

204 THE JUTES (GEATS)

```
                    Odin + Frija (Frigg)
                            |
                      Heimdal (Rig)
                            |
                         Arngrim
                            |
────────────────────────────────────────────────────────────────
Tyrfing Hjorvard Biarbe Hiortar Brod Hiartur Hadding  Hiarrand Brand
Hiarne Tand Angantyr
            |
          Hervor
            |
       ─────────────────────────
    Angantyr              Heidrek
                            |
              ─────────────────────────────────
           Hlod        Angantyr          Hervor
                          |
                       Heidrek
                          |
              ─────────────────────────────
           Hugleik                  Hervor
                                      |
                                   Beowulf
                                      |
                                    Vidar
                                      |
                                   Havelock
                                      |
                                  Hildebrand
                                      |
              ─────────────────────────────────────
    Sigurd Ring + Hild                          Hilde
                |
         ─────────────────────
    Sigurd Ring II      Ragnar Lodbrok
```

205 THE YNGLINGS

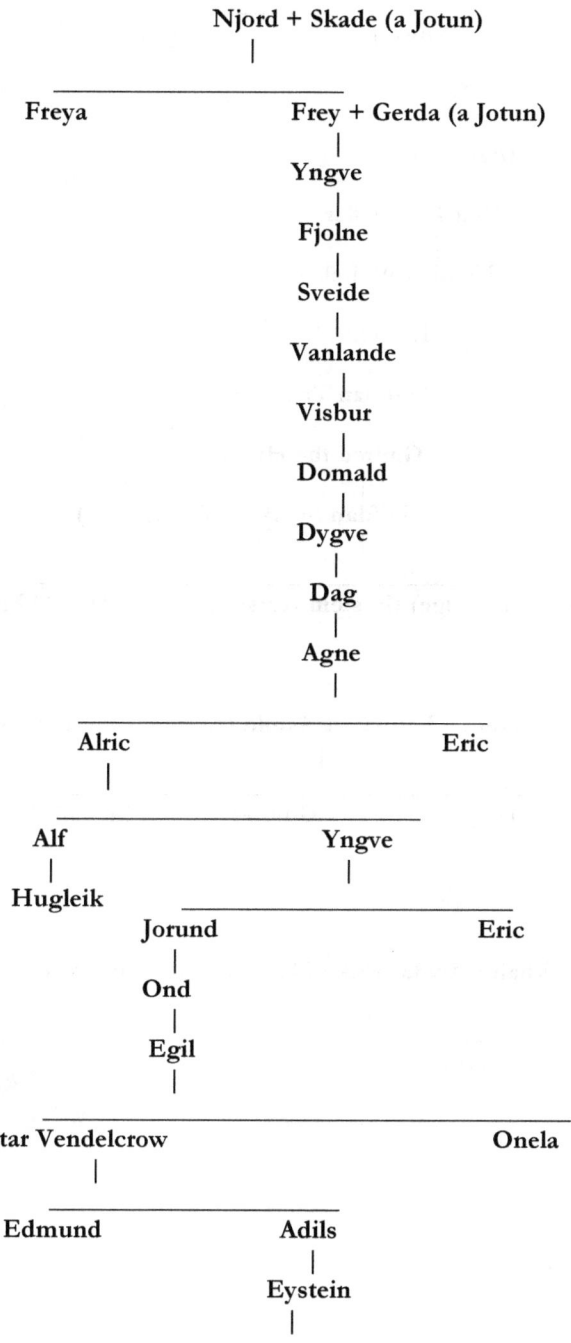

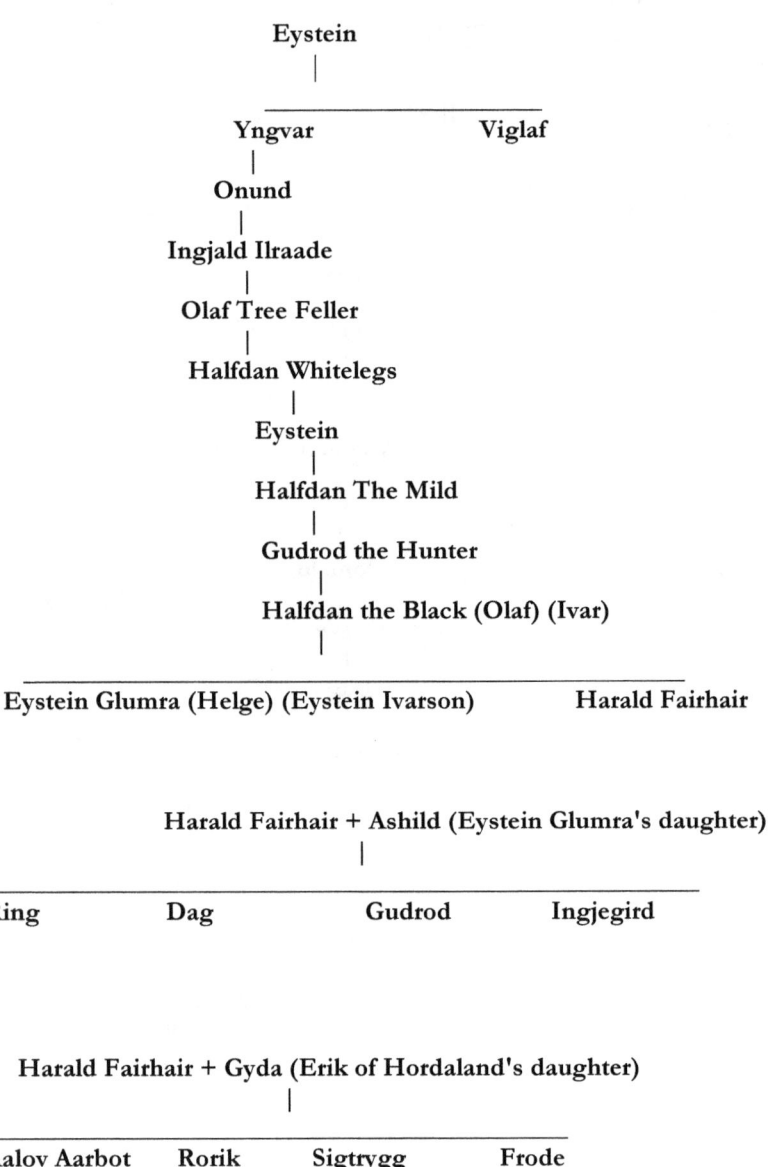

The Saga Kings

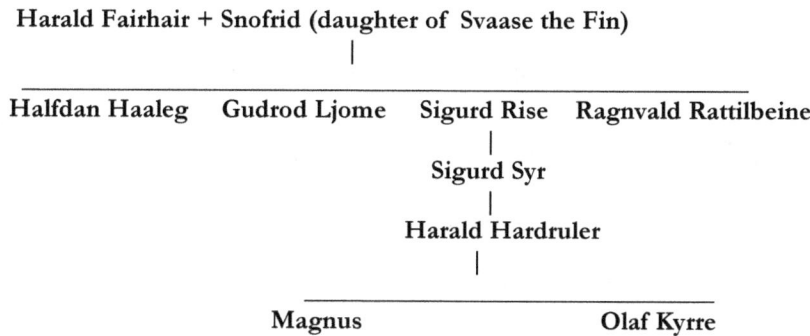

Harald Fairhair + Snofrid (daughter of Svaase the Fin)

Halfdan Haaleg   Gudrod Ljome   Sigurd Rise   Ragnvald Rattilbeine

Sigurd Syr

Harald Hardruler

Magnus   Olaf Kyrre

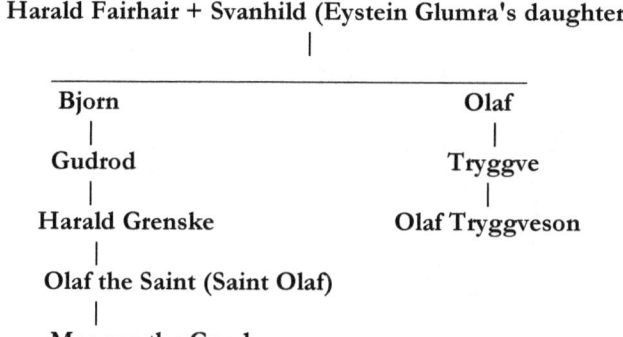

Harald Fairhair + Svanhild (Eystein Glumra's daughter)

Bjorn   Olaf

Gudrod   Tryggve

Harald Grenske   Olaf Tryggveson

Olaf the Saint (Saint Olaf)

Magnus the Good

Harald Fairhair + Tora Masterstrong (Harald Fairhair's maid)

Haakon the Good

Harald Fairhair + Ragnhild (daughter of Erik of Jutland)

Erik Blood Axe + Gunhild (sister of Harald Bluetooth)

The sons of Erik Blood Axe::   Harald Greycloak, Gamle, Guthorm, Ragnfrod, Ragnhild, Erling, Gudrod, Sigurd Sleva, Ragnvald

206 THE KNYTLINGS

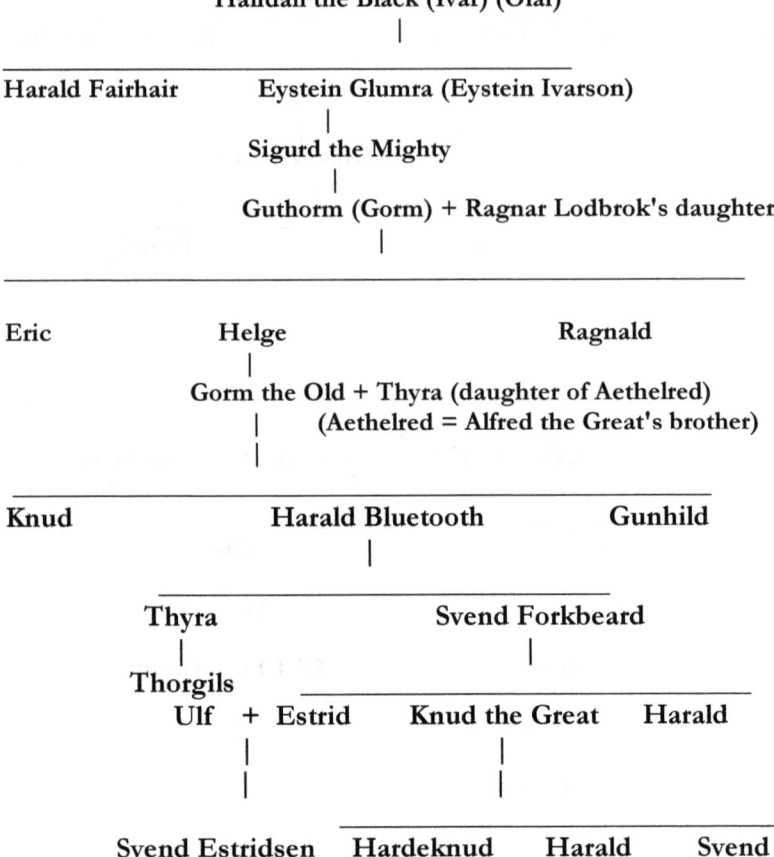

207 THE NORMANS

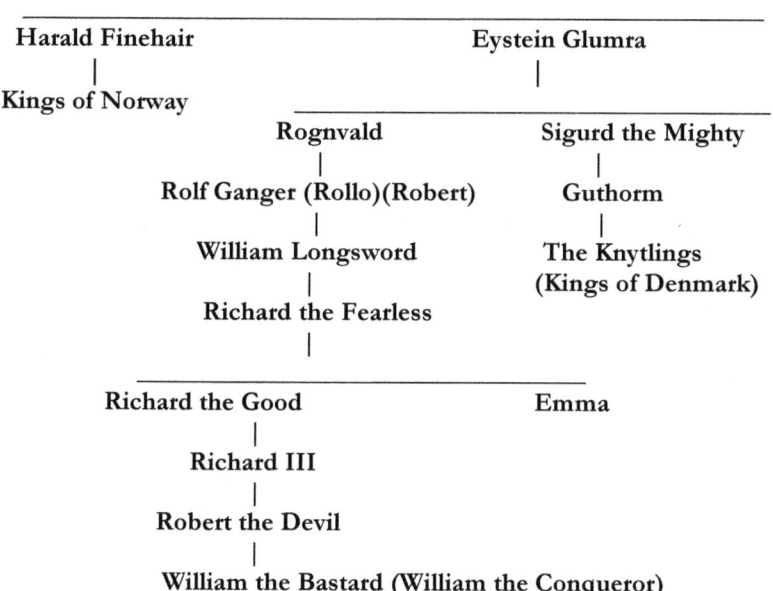

208 THE SIKLINGS

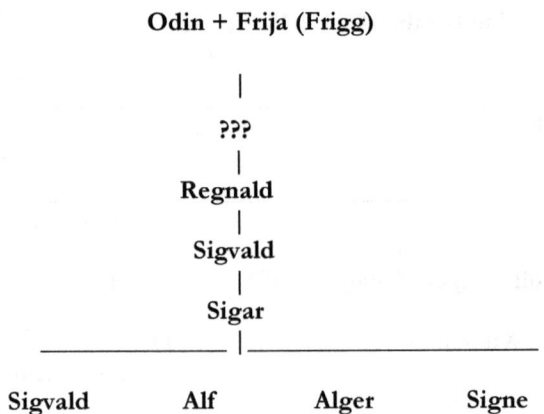

209 THE WEST SAXONS

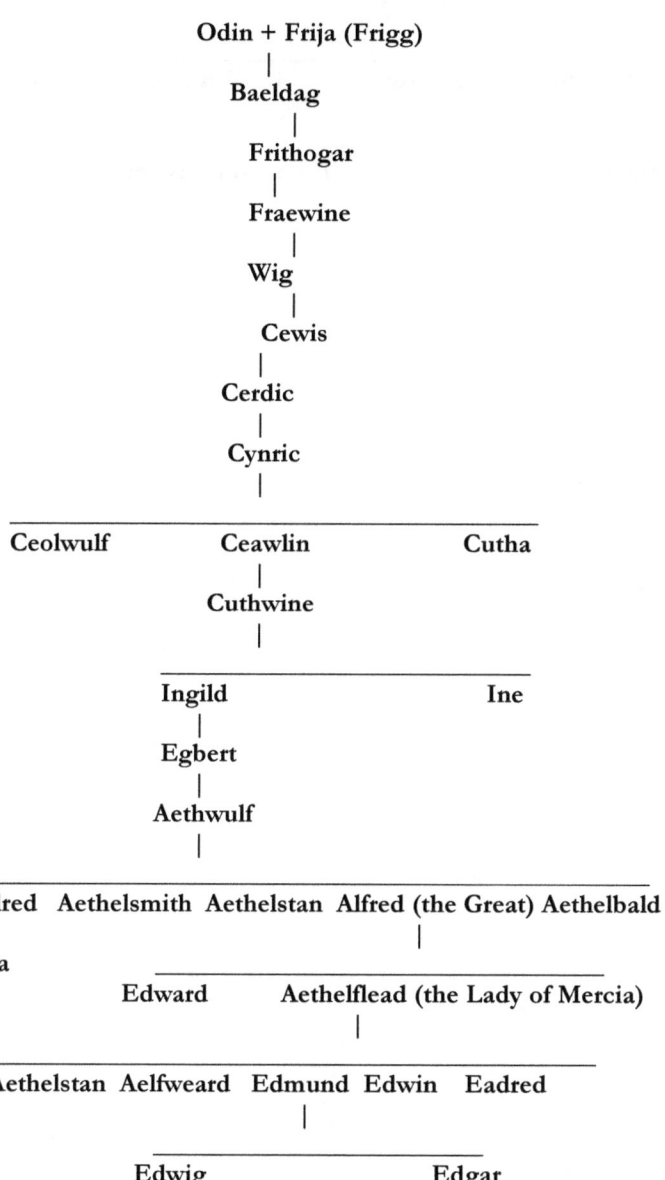

```
                    Edgar
                      |
     ┌────────────────┴────────────────┐
Aethelred the Unready          Edward the Martyr
     |
     ┌────────────────┴────────────────┐
  Alfred                        Edmund Ironsides
```

210 THE CHRONOLOGICAL LINES OF THE KINGS

211 KINGS OF NORWAY

Olaf Treefeller
|
Halfdan Whitelegs
|
Eystein
|
Halfdan the Mild
|
Gudrod the Hunter
|
Halfdan the Black (Olaf) (Ivar)
|
Harald Fairhair
|
Haakon the Good

Harald Greycloak

Harald Bluetooth (King of Denmark and Norway)

Olaf Tryggvesson

Svend Forkbeard (King of Denmark and Norway)

Olaf the Stout (Saint Olaf)

Knud the Great (King of England, Denmark, Norway, and Sweden)

Svend Knudsen

Magnus the Good

Magnus the Good and Harald Hardruler

Harald Hardruler

Magnus Haraldson and Olaf Kyrre

Olaf Kyrre

212 KINGS OF DENMARK

Odin

Dan

Humble

Lothar

Skjold (Scyld)

Gram

Svipdag (Norwegian)

Guthorm

Hadding

Peace Frode

Dan Mikellati (Dan the Peaceful)

Frode the Vigorous

Halfdan

Fridleif

Frode the Bold

Halfdan and Ingjald

Ingjald

Roar and Helge

Roar

Horek

Rolf Krake

Skuld (Queen)

Frode and Harald

Frode

Halfdan

Rorik Fling-bracelet

Ivar Vidfadme (King of Denmark and Sweden)

Harald Wartooth

Sigurd Ring (King of Denmark and Sweden)

Ragnar Lodbrok

Sigurd Ring II (Siegfred)

Godfred

Hemming

Harald Klak and Reginfred

Horik

Horik and Harald Klak

Horik

Horik the Younger

Sigurd Snake-eye

Helge

Gurd and Gnupa (Swedes)

Sigtryg Gnupason

The Saga Kings

Gorm the Old

Harald Bluetooth

Svend Forkbeard

Harald Svendsen

Knud the Great (King of England, Denmark, Norway, and Sweden)

Hardeknud (King of England and Denmark)

Magnus the Good (King of Norway and Denmark)

Svend Estridsen

213 KINGS OF SWEDEN

Gylfe

Odin

Njord
|
Frey
|
Yngve
|
Fjolne
|
Sveide
|
Vanlande
|
Visbur
|
Domald
|
Dygve
|
Dag
|

The Saga Kings

Agne
|
Alrik and Erik
|
Alf and Yngve
|
Hugleik

Hake (Danish sea king)

Yorund
|
Ond

Halfdan (King of Denmark and Sweden)

Ond (again)
|
Egil

Ottar Vendelcrow

Onela

Adils
|
Eystein

Solve (a sea king)

Yngvar
|
Onund
|
Ingjald Illraade

Ivar Vidfadme (King of Sweden and Denmark)

Sigurd Ring (King of Sweden and Denmark)

Eystein

Bjorn Ironsides (son of Ragnar Lodbrok)
|
Erik Bjornson

Refil

Erik Refilson

Bjorn at Hauge

Anund (Edmund)

The Saga Kings

Erik Anundson (Erik Edmundson)

Bjorn Erikson

Olaf Bjornson

Erik the Victorious

Olaf Scotking

Anund Jacob

Knud the Great (King of England, Denmark, Norway, and Sweden)

Edmund the Old

Stenkil

214 SVINFYLKING BATTLE FORMATION

When the Vikings fought a battle on land, they used the formation known as svinfylking, (the boar's head), which was a formation modelled on the shape of a boar's head. It was a wedge shaped squad, led by two champions known as the rani (snout). Behind the champions were three warriors. Behind the three warriors were four warriors. And so on. If the army was large enough there would be several wedges set up.

Svinfolkning Battle Formation

Prepared for battle, the Vikings have set up a svinfylking formation against a straight line set up by their opponents.

Svinfolkning Battle Formation

The running charge, with yells of "Odin!" broke through the opponents lines. The opposing army has been split in two. The effect of having their forces divided was catastrophic for the enemy.

Svinfolkning Battle Formation

At this stage the enemy is at a great disadvantage.

Svinfolkning Battle Formation

Here the opposing army is defeated and the soldiers hope that the Vikings will give them quarter.

215 REFERENCES

Ashe, G. 1957. re issued 1973. King Arthur's Avalon. The Story of Glastonbury. Collins Clear-Type Press London and Glasgow.

Baeksted, A. 1965. Guder og Helte I Norden. Politikens Forlag.

Brondsted, J. 1966. Vikingerne. Gyldendags Ugleboger.

Carson, R. 1965. The Sea Around Us. The New American Library of Canada Limited

Carwin, W. H. 1998. Human Evolution and Abrupt Climate change. The Atlantic Monthly 281(1) 47-64 January 1998

Gronbech, V. 1965. Nordiske Myter og Sagn. Gyldendal Ugleboger.

Gunn, J.D. 2003. Global Climate Change in the First Millennium A.D. Website. Joel D. Gunn, Department of Anthropology, The University of North Carolina at Chapel Hill, Chapel Hill, North Carolina 27514

Joseph, F. 2014. The Lost Colonies of Ancient America. The Career Press Inc. 220 West Parkway, Unit 12 Pompton Plains, NJ 07444 U.S.A.

Jones, G. 1984. re-issued 2001. A History of the Vikings. Cox & Wyman Ltd., Reading Berkshire, Great Britain

Keys D. 2003. Catastrophe. [Secure Microsoft Reader/Palm Reader]

Kinder, H., and W Hilgemann. 1964. Trans. E. A. Menze. 1964. The

Penguin Atlas of World History. Vol. 1. Penguin Books.

Nielsen, N. 1950. Danmarks Historie Fortalt For Born. H.P. Hansens Bogtryggeri. Copenhagen, Denmark

Nytrop, K.A. 2001. Gorm den Gamle. Web page.

Pennick, N. 1992. Rune Magic. The History And Practice Of Ancient Runic Traditions. The Aquarian Press. Harper Collins Pub. Hammersmith London, Great Britain.

Petersen, Sv. Aa. 1946. Vikinger Og Vikingeaand. Sighvat Thordsson og Hans Skjaldskab. Ejnar Munksgaards Forlag. Copenhagen

Pulsiano, Phillip et al., eds. 1993. Medieval Scandinavia: An Encyclopedia. Garland Reference Library of the Humanities 934. New York & London:

Roesdahl, E. 1992. Revised 1998. The Vikings. Penguin Books.

Ramskou, T. 1966. Vikingetiden Skibet, Svaerdet, og Vaegten. Svendborg Avis Bogtrykker.

Saxo. 1158?. The Danish History, Books I – IX. Online Medieval Library.

Sturlasson, S. ca. 1200. Heimskringla Saga.

Sturlasson, S. ca 1200. Prose Edda.

Sturlasson, S. ca 1200. The Orkneyingens Saga

Television Program ……… PBS Program — "SECRETS OF THE DEAD" "Catastrophe! (5–15–2000, 8:00 p.m.)

The Anglo Saxon Chronicles.

Wells, H.G. 1971. The Outline of History Vol. I and II. Doubleday & Company Inc.

Williams, G., P. Pentz, and M. Wemhoff ed. 2014. Vikings life and legend. The British Museum Press. A division of The British Museum Company Ltd.

Wohletz, K. Were The Dark Ages Triggered by Volcano-Related Climate Changes in the 6th Century? THC article Scientists in Their Own Words…

Wohletz, K. 2003. Were The Dark Ages Triggered by Volcano-Related Climate Changes in the 6th Century? the Los Alamos National Laboratory website.

ABOUT THE AUTHOR

Carsten R. Jorgensen was born in Copenhagen, Denmark (1942) where he attended public school to the end of grade two. His love of mythology began in his Danish history class starting with Norse mythology and moving on to the sagas of Denmark.

In 1951, he moved to Canada with his parents and brother. He attended high school in Ontario at Campbellford District High School. After graduating with an Honours Bachelors of Science from Queen's University in Kingston Ontario, he worked for thirty years as a fisheries biologist with the Ministry of Natural Resources.

Now that he has retired, he has enjoyed having the free time these past 8 years to write about the sagas that he enjoyed so much as a child. He is happy to be able to share these stories with you.

www.ingramcontent.com/pod-product-compliance
Lightning Source LLC
Chambersburg PA
CBHW060102170426
43198CB00010B/738